SOCIAL DIFFERENTIATION: PATTERNS AND PROCESSES

Edited by Danielle Juteau

Social Differentiation examines the economic, political, and normatively defined relations that underlie the construction of social categories. Social differentiation, embedded in inequalities of power, status, wealth, and prestige, affects life chances of individuals as well as the allocation of resources and opportunities.

Starting with a theoretical framework that challenges many traditional analyses, the contributors focus on four specific strands of social differentiation: gender, age, race/ethnicity, and locality. They explore the historically specific social practices, policies, and ideologies that produce distinct forms of inequality, in turn revealing and explaining such issues as the formation and maintenance of a gendered order; the privileging of prime-age workers; the penalties incurred by visible minorities in the labour market; the highly disadvantaged position of Aboriginals; and the economic decline of agriculture, resource, and fishing dependent regions. By paying special attention to political processes, norms, and representations, and by indicating how social policies shape economic functioning and relate to normative definitions, this book will interest policy-oriented researchers and decision-makers.

DANIELLE JUTEAU is a professor in the Department of Sociology and holds the Chair of Ethnic Relations at the Université de Montréal.

POLICY RESEARCH: THE TRENDS PROJECT SERIES

The Trends Project Series is a result of the Government of Canada's Policy Research Initiative, an undertaking that seeks to strengthen policy capacity and ensure that policy development benefits from the work of researchers and academics. The Policy Research Initiative, in cooperation with the Social Sciences and Humanities Research Council, undertook a new model for academics and government to collaborate on policy research. Teams of academics examined the forces that are driving change in Canada and identified the potential public-policy implications. This collaboration came to be known as the Trends Project. Under the project, academics, research institutes, and government officials worked in partnership to build a better knowledge base on longer-term issues to support policy development and identify knowledge gaps requiring further research. The Trends Project will result in the following books:

Gordon Smith and Daniel Wolfish, editors,
Who Is Afraid of the State? Canada in a World of Multiple Centres of Power

Edward A. Parson, editor,
Governing the Environment: Persistent Challenges, Uncertain Innovations

Neil Nevitte, editor,
Value Change and Governance in Canada

George Hoberg, editor,
Capacity for Choice: Canada in a New North America

David Cheal, editor,
Aging and Demographic Change in Canadian Context

Danielle Juteau, editor,
Social Differentiation: Patterns and Processes

SOCIAL DIFFERENTIATION

Patterns and Processes

Edited by Danielle Juteau

UNIVERSITY OF TORONTO PRESS
Toronto Buffalo London

© University of Toronto Press Incorporated 2003
Toronto Buffalo London
Printed in Canada

ISBN 0-8020-8404-4

Printed on acid-free paper

National Library of Canada Cataloguing in Publication

Social differentiation : patterns and processes / edited by Danielle Juteau.

(Trends project series)
Includes bibliographical references.
ISBN 0-8020-8404-4

1. Differentiation (Sociology)   I. Juteau, Danielle   II. Series.

HM821.S62 2002   305   C2002-903798-0

University of Toronto Press acknowledges the financial assistance to its
publishing program of the Canada Council for the Arts and the Ontario
Arts Council.

University of Toronto Press acknowledges the financial support for its
publishing activities of the Government of Canada through the Book
Publishing Industry Development Program (BPIDP).

Contents

Preface

Exchanging ideas, perspectives, frameworks, and data between academics and government is, at once, necessary for the development of innovative and effective public policy and difficult to accomplish in times of constant change. The Trends Project, a collaborative effort of the Policy Research Initiative and the Social Sciences and Humanities Research Council of Canada, was conceived as a means of addressing this difficulty by providing a new model by which academics and government might collaborate on policy research and as a means of feeding the policy development process.

Three goals lie at the heart of the Policy Research Initiative and the Trends Project. They are:

- supporting the creation, sharing, and use of policy research knowledge;
- strengthening the policy-research capacity in departments through the recruitment, development, and retention of people; and
- building a policy research community through networks and create vehicles and venues.

The Trends Project provided a unique opportunity for the Policy Research Secretariat and the Social Science and Humanities Research Council of Canada to test a new and innovative model of engaging the academic community in the policy process. In the past, either the government has commissioned research to address government-identified knowledge gaps or the federal granting councils have funded an academic-led research agenda. Under the Trends Project, academics, think tanks, and government officials worked in partnership to identify the knowledge gaps requiring further research. The objective of this governmental and academic collaboration was to identify what we do and do not know, and to understand how we know it. The research undertaken by the Trends Project teams looked ahead to the medium to long term rather than addressing immediate policy concerns.

The make-up of the teams themselves was unique. The project brought together some of Canada's leading academics to head eight teams made up of over fifty researchers from universities across the country. The researchers participating in the project were selected through a call for proposals administered by the Social Sciences and Humanities Research Council of Canada. By creating multidisciplinary teams consisting of participants from across Canada, the Trends Project succeeded in bringing together people who would normally not interact with one another. The result of this multidisciplinary, cross-Canada approach has been that we now have a greater depth and breadth of understanding of the emergent policy areas that Canada is likely to confront in the coming years. The Trends Project research essays have been presented on several occasions across the country at workshops and conferences where Canadian researchers and government officials provided insightful comments and useful feedback. Finally, each of the essays published under the Trends Project has been through the process of anonymous peer review.

The Trends Project was also innovative because it provided a means for academics to have their ideas and research circulated widely throughout government. The overall product was not simply the production of research papers, but also the process of continual collaboration between the governmental and academic communities. The second annual National Policy Research Conference in November 1999 enabled the researchers to showcase their work to over 800 policy developers and experts in the federal and provincial governments.

Commentaries and research excerpts have been featured regularly in *Horizons*, the Policy Research Secretariat's newsletter. *Horizons* targets a broad policy audience throughout the Canadian policy research community, both inside and outside of government, with over 8400 people on its distribution list. By being brought together on an ongoing basis, the governmental and academic communities were exposed to each other's research needs, perspectives, and constraints. The Trends Project is one part of a larger effort to build Canada-wide policy research capacities. It is a model that we would like to build on in the future.

Laura Chapman
Executive Director
Policy Research Initiative

Acknowledgments

Five submissions were chosen for the trend on social differentiation, defined here as a process involving the construction of social categories and group boundaries. Each paper explores, for a specific set of categories, the economic, political, cultural, and normative factors that underlie this process, and examines their linkages and intersections with other strands.

I would like to thank the five authors for their wonderful collaboration; Dr Vasanthi Srinivasan for her unfailing support; Sébastien Arcand and Linda Pietrantonio, my assistants at the Chaire en relations ethniques de l'Université de Montréal, for their highly competent services; the participants who attended the seminar held in Montreal in May 1999 for their useful comments; and Professor William Coleman of Queen's University for his skillful assistance.

Danielle Juteau

Contributors

David Cheal is a professor of sociology at the University of Winnipeg. He has published nationally and internationally on a variety of issues in the social sciences. In recent years he has focused mainly on the study of family relationships and on aspects of economic well-being. His policy-relevant research in the latter area includes analyses of survey data on income poverty and the Employment Insurance Family Supplement.

Danielle Juteau is professor of sociology at the Université de Montréal, where she holds a Chair in Ethnic Relations. She has published on topics related to ethnic and national relations, pluralism and citizenship, and gender. Recent publications include *L'ethnicité et ses frontières* (Presses de l'Université de Montréal, 1999); 'Du dualisme canadien au pluralisme québécois,' in M. McAndrew and F. Gagnon, eds, *Relations ethniques et éducation dans les sociétés divisées* (L'Harmattan, 2000); 'The Challenge of the Pluralist Option,' in Michel Venne, ed., *Vive Québec! New Thinking and New Approaches to the Quebec Nation* (James Lorimer and Co., 2000); 'Ethnicité et nation,' *Dictionnaire critique du féminisme* (Presses universitaires de France, 2000). Juteau was appointed Chair of Canadian Studies at l'Université de Paris III Sorbonne Nouvelle in France, 2001–2). She is currently studying the impact of the city merger in Montreal on ethnic dynamics in Quebec, and is preparing a book on the theorization of ethnicity in the world-system.

Peter S. Li is professor of sociology at the University of Saskatchewan, and Chair of Economic Domain, Prairie Centre of Excellence for

Research on Immigration and Integration. His research areas are race and ethnic studies, immigration, and multiculturalism. He has published nine books and many academic papers. Among his books are *Race and Ethnic Relations in Canada* (Oxford, 1999), *The Chinese in Canada* (Oxford, 1988, 1998), *The Making of Post-War Canada* (Oxford, 1996), *Racial Oppression in Canada* (Garamond, 1988), and *Ethnic Inequality in a Class Society* (Thompson, 1988). Currently, he is conducting research on immigrants' labour-market performance and the Chinese diaspora.

Chris Southcott is associate professor of sociology at Lakehead University. He has published works in the areas of regionalism, resource-dependent communities, and Northern and rural issues. At present he is head of an international research team looking at contemporary social issues in the circumpolar world. He is also part of an international research team looking at regional economic culture. His current research deals with the changes occurring in resource-dependent communities as they adapt to the new world economy.

Leah F. Vosko is Canada Research Chair in Feminist Political Economy, School of Social Sciences (Political Science), Joseph E. Atkinson Faculty of Liberal and Professional Studies, York University. In addition to numerous articles in scholarly journals, Vosko is also the author of *Temporary Work: The Gendered Rise of a Precarious Employment Relationship* (University of Toronto Press, 2000) and co-editor (with Wallace Clement) of *Changing Canada: Political Economy as Transformation* (McGill-Queen's University Press, forthcoming). She is currently the academic director of the Community-University Research Alliance on Contingent Work, conducting research on the legal regulation of contingent work, on organizing and representing contingent workers, on work organization and health among contingent workers, and on new modes of estimating the size and shape of the contingent work force in Canada.

Terry Wotherspoon is head and professor of sociology at the University of Saskatchewan. He has conducted extensive research on social inequality, social policy, and social differentiation related to education systems, Aboriginal people, and racial and ethnic minorities. He has published several scholarly articles, books and book chapters, and discussion papers in these areas. His recent books include *The Legacy of School for Aboriginal People* (with Bernard Schissel, Oxford University

Press, 2000), *First Nations: Race, Class and Gender Relations* (with Vic Satzewich, Canadian Plains Research Center, 2000), and *The Sociology of Education in Canada: Critical Perspectives* (Oxford University Press, 1998). His current research projects are in the areas of teachers' work in Aboriginal communities, and relations among formal and informal learning for Aboriginal people and immigrants.

SOCIAL DIFFERENTIATION:
PATTERNS AND PROCESSES

1. Introducing Social Differentiation

Danielle Juteau

This volume of the Trends series proposes a multidimensional analysis of social differentiation, which is treated here as an economic, political, cultural, and normatively oriented process. This process is viewed as materially based, underlying the construction of gendered, ethnicized, racialized, and age- and spatially related social categories. The specific perspective adopted in this book, providing its unity and coherence, will be compared to other analyses of differentiation. Our use of the term social differentiation will be distinguished from functionalist and neo-functionalist endeavours to examine social change at the societal level and from recent attempts linking social categories solely to processes of signification and identification.

In this introduction, I present the authors' analysis of social differentiation and of its diverse facets: the formation and the maintenance of a gendered order; the privileging of prime-age workers; the penalty incurred by visible minorities in the labour market; the highly disadvantaged position of Aboriginals; and the economic decline of agriculture-, resource-, and fishing-dependent regions. In all cases, social differentiation is linked to social hierarchization: embedded in inequalities of power, status, wealth, and prestige, it affects the allocation of resources and opportunities, including life chances and group monopolies. Finally, I will indicate how these various strands of social differentiation intersect and interact, as gender, ethnicity, 'race,' and age crosscut and reinforce one another, producing heterogeneous social categories and fluid boundaries. The implications of these findings for policy orientations and the development of a more inclusive society will be discussed in the concluding remarks.

1. The Process of Social Differentiation

1.1 Societies and Social Differentiation

As Luhmann points out,[1] for as long as there has been sociological theory, it has been concerned with social differentiation. The concept of social differentiation has many meanings and they have varied over time. It has been used in non-Marxist analyses of social change, first by Spencer and Durkheim, later by Parsons and, more recently, by neo-functionalists such as Luhmann and Alexander.[2] These authors agree that differentiation involves increased structural specialization and growing independence among societal spheres, as economic and political processes detach themselves from religious and familial institutions. They also claim that its relevance for understanding social change in diverse historical formations is limited by the problematic relation between social differentiation and a theory of social change. In Durkheim's and Parsons's attempts[3] to examine social differentiation, there is an internal problem rooted in the absence of a developmental notion of particular phases, which begs for a theorization of social change rather than its mere description.[4] Recent efforts have tended to address the major shortcomings of differentiation theory by widening and diversifying its empirical scope, elaborating its explanatory framework, reconceptualizing the consequences of differentiation, and developing a critical modernism.[5]

Most important for our purposes are the efforts to develop multidimensional and structural models of social change that can account for patterns of uneven and unequal differentiation.[6] Alexander's examination of ethnic relations focuses on the inclusion of outgroups in the United States.[7] Variations in the process, he suggests, depend on an external factor, the structure of society that surrounds the core group – that is, the economic, political, integrative, and religious subsystems – and an internal factor, namely the relationship between the primordial[8] qualities of core group and outgroups. He argues that the possibility of inclusion is greater in more differentiated systems (external factor) and in the presence of primordial complementarity[9] (internal factor) as members of core groups then tend to regard inclusion as desirable. He also contends that the historical core of a society establishes the pre-eminence of some primordial qualities, and uses complementarity to include or exclude outgroups. Thus, Whites would tend to include other Whites and exclude Blacks, Protestants would favour other Protestants and exclude Catholics, Christians would exclude Jews and Muslims, and so on. By emphasizing the subjective perception of differences, Alexander treats differences between individuals and groups as a cause of rejection and lower inclusion: racial differences, between Caucasians and non-Caucasians, have created an initial highly flammable cleavage;[10] religious divides, between Christians and non-Christians for example, as well as cultural divergences also constitute important variables. Thus, Blacks and Asians were excluded from the American societal community[11] because they confronted a less socially differentiated environment and a more intense primordial aversion than white immigrants.

My remarks here will concentrate on the problematic question of primordial ties and complementary primordiality. To argue that the historical core establishes the pre-eminence of some primordial qualities and excludes those who do not fit in is not false, but incomplete. When Alexander affirms that White Anglo-Saxon Protestants ('Wasps') occupied the core of American society and excluded those not sharing their attributes (of 'race,' ethnicity, and religion), he takes as a starting point what must be explained, thus sidestepping fundamental problems. First, the definition of social categories and of social distance, of what is close and what is far away, of what is similar and what is different, is constructed. Second, differences *per se* do not create highly flammable cleavages. Third, social groups, be they core or outgroups, do not exist *sui generis*. So how do they come about? How do categories such as White and Black, Caucasian and non-Caucasian, come into existence and what makes them operative? Why do colour, or language, or religion become relevant and when do they do so? Fourth, how do certain groups come to occupy the core while others are located at the periphery? How did Wasps in the United States and Canada, and not Aboriginals, come to occupy the core? Fifth, what underlies definitions of social closeness and distance? What attributes are chosen as givens? What qualities are construed as divergent? The differences that motivate social actors and orient their behaviour are not givens and are subject to change. Religion, for example, is no longer significant in determining boundaries between French and English Canadians, while language has become central. Furthermore, proximity and desirability fluctuate. A study conducted in the early twentieth century in the United States put French Canadians at the near bottom of a scale of desirability, because they resisted assimilation, not because they were perceived as very different.[12] Sixth, inflammable cleavages can erupt between groups that are close, culturally speaking, such as in the case of Serbs and Croats.[13] Closer to home, one can observe that the most intense ethnic conflict in Canada is between two 'Caucasian' groups that are, relatively speaking, quite close. This is because many Québécois consider that Quebec is a nation not to be contained within the boundaries of another one, not because of a primordial aversion.

It follows, therefore, that the definition of social categories, the differentiated positions of core groups and outgroups, their social closeness and/or distance, and the presence or absence of primordial complementarity cannot be taken for granted and should be explained. This requires that the neo-functionalist analysis of social differentiation be extended so as to include, in addition to the institutional and societal levels, the formation of differentiated social groups and categories. This book focuses precisely on such processes. By linking social differentiation to social hierarchization, it can account for the emergence of socially differentiated, and interrelated, categories, such as Aboriginal and non-Aboriginal, women and men, young and old, Whites and Blacks, rural and urban.

1.2 The Differentiation of Social Categories

In the late seventies, questions arose regarding the construction of social categories and their relation to social class. Traditional social science, which was interested mainly in measuring the impact of attributes such as being an Aboriginal and living in a rural area on income, employment, life expectancy, number of children, values, and so on was strongly criticized. Social categories were not givens and, it was argued, should not be treated as causing differences in employment, income, education levels, and other variables.

Let us take 'race' as a case in point. Racial categories do not exist per se,[14] social scientists began to understand; they are historically specific constructions to which individuals are assigned.[15] Authors focused on racialization, a mechanism through which signification is attributed to certain characteristics. This process leads to the structuring of social relations and the construction of differentiated social collectivities.[16] For Omi and Winant, 'race' constitutes a central axis of social relations. Consequently, the focus should be on 'the process by which social, economic and political forces determine the content and importance of racial categories, and by which they are in turn shaped by racial meanings.'[17]

A similar approach was developed in the area of sex and gender studies and for the analysis of ethnic and age-related categories. Following Simone de Beauvoir, feminists argued that femininity and masculinity are constructed, and are open to changing boundaries and fluctuating meanings. Some constructivist approaches underlined the materiality of this process.

In her pionnering work, Guillaumin[18] argues that racism is an ideology that constructs 'race' as a category based on 'real' biological differences. In other words, race is an ideological construct. However, she does consider that racial categories designate real groups, which are interconnected and unequal. The existence of these groups is grounded in a relation through which the labour power, and bodies, of some humans (slaves) are appropriated by others (slave owners). Markers such as colour of skin are chosen *post factum* to identify the boundaries of these already constituted groups. They do not represent, as is often thought, the basis of social relations.[19] Of course, once established, markers serve as a basis for communalization, for orienting social relations, underlying other forms of exclusion, and bringing about monopolistic closure. This concrete dimension, she adds, cannot be dissociated from a normative one, since these groups are conceived as inferior and treated according to this status.

1.3 Social Differentiation Reinterpreted

The articles included in this volume are located upstream, so to speak, of the work focusing on societal and institutional differentiation, which starts with existing categories. Our analysis of social differentiation explores the social relations and mechanisms that constitute social categories and structure social boundaries, such as colonialism, expropriation, limited access to resources and opportunities, lower rewards, the intended and unintended consequences of social policies, as well as normative dimensions such as being defined as worthless. It examines the economic, political, and normatively defined relations underlying their construction, and subsequently explores how inequality affects the definition of social difference. By taking unequal relations into account, our approach can explain how groups are constituted, how they become dominant or subordinate, and how dominant groups establish themselves as being the core, incarnating the norm; it follows that subordinate groups are viewed as different from the norm.

Schermerhorn's[20] view that the initial sequence of interaction exerts a determining impact on the ensuing ethnic dynamic is important here.

Forms of domination resulting from colonialism and forced migration, such as slavery or indentured labour, are constitutive of unequal social groups and categories such as French and English Canadians, Aboriginals and non-Aboriginals, immigrants and non-immigrants. It follows that relations initially based on slavery will differ in their outcome from those based on colonialism or 'free' migration. Colonized groups often claim political autonomy, while immigrant groups demand cultural accommodation and economic equality; the barriers encountered by descendants of slaves are higher than those faced by immigrants because of their objective position and the racist ideologies used to 'justify' their exclusion. The point here is precisely that Blacks and Chinese did not come as immigrants, but as slaves or indentured labourers. This reality, and not colour of skin, is what underlies the definition of primordial complementarity.[21]

Our perspective must also be differentiated from the constructivist perspective outlined previously. First, the materialism of our constructivist approach should now be evident. We focus on the economic, political, and normative structuration of social categories as well as on processes of signification and identification. Differentiation is linked to social hierarchization, and difference to social inequalities. Our approach, however, should not be confounded with a Marxist one, as we seek to escape what Stuart Hall called horizontal and vertical reductionism.[22] Simply put, this means that economic inequalities are not reduced to social class. It also means that gender and ethnicity are not conceived as located uniquely in the cultural or ideological domain, determined by the material base represented by class. We view social inequalities as rooted in other social relations as well – such as those related to sex and gender, to 'race' and ethnicity, and to age – which are distinct and interdependent.

This standpoint does not preclude class analysis. In choosing to focus on multiple and diverse social relations, on how they operate to structure the labour market, produce monopolistic closure,[23] and create social inequalities, we are broadening and complexifying traditional class analysis. This allows us to account for the presence of differentiated groups within the working class, which is neither sexless nor ethnically and racially neutral. Each chapter thus focuses mainly on the material and normative processes underpinning one strand of social differentiation, for five differentiated pairs – male/female, Aboriginal/non-Aboriginal, visible minorities/non-visible majorities, rural/urban, and youth/non-youth. We are not, however, claiming that gender, age, race, and class relations are independent. As I will indicate in the section on intersectionalities (19ff.), all the authors here pay attention to overlaps between these various strands.

I will now briefly indicate how this perspective on social differentiation also differs from the related notion of social exclusion.

1.4 Social Differentiation and Social Exclusion

In her discussion of social exclusion and social solidarity, Silver notes that the discourse on exclusion first appeared in France in the 1960s, took off in the 1980s, and then spread to the rest of Europe.[24] *Les exclus* were conceived as constituting a social problem, an ever-expanding category of marginalized people including those of social disadvantage as diverse as the mentally and physically handicapped, suicidal people, asocial individuals, single parents, and drug addicts.[25] The category was eventually extended to the point where it lost its usefulness.

Because the expression 'social exclusion' is multi-faceted, no simple criterion could capture the diversity of its meanings. With a view to clarifying matters, Silver suggests that it is rooted in three conflicting social science paradigms and political ideologies.[26] Each paradigm is based on a distinct notion of social integration, and consequently each attributes exclusion to a different cause and offers a particular account of economic disadvantages such as poverty and long-term unemployment.

The solidarity paradigm, which is grounded in French republican political philosophy,[27] defines exclusion as the breakdown of the social bond – primarily cultural and moral – that ties the individual to the society.[28] The specialization paradigm attributes exclusion to social differences, the economic division of labour, and the separation of spheres. Rooted in Anglo-American liberalism, it rests on the assumption that differences between individuals lead to separate social spheres. What becomes important here is ensuring the free movement of individuals across boundaries and preventing discrimination on the basis of social differences. Lastly, the group-monopoly paradigm is tied to a social democratic approach and focuses on power relations. It examines how the interplay between class, status (age, rural-urban, etc.), and political power creates social closure. It argues that social boundaries ensure monopolies over scarce resources, which are used by dominant groups to reproduce inequalities. Institutions and cultural distinctions create boundaries, and are used to perpetuate them.[29]

Our approach to social differentiation differs considerably from the solidarity paradigm in which exclusion is conceived mainly in terms of weak and unstable social bonds.[30] According to the solidarity paradigm, inequality results from class conflicts opposing groups who are seen as integrated since they confront each other face-to-face. Exclusion, by contrast, implies that the social actors contesting the dominant power structures are divorced from the economic and political system. This reasoning is highly problematic. It assumes that inequalities are necessarily linked to social classes, while weak social bonds engender exclusion related, for example, to gender and ethnicity. Class inequalities would constitute economic and political matters, while gender and racial differentiation would remain cultural and symbolic! Such an approach is blind to the existence of the economic and political relations that shape other social boundaries and structure the diversity of inequalities found in contemporary societies. The social-differentiation approach treats this instability as a result of hierarchical power relations and inequalities.

Our approach also differs from the specialization paradigm, since we reject an individualistic perspective that tends to accord disproportionate attention to the attributes of the disadvantaged and often tends to blame the victim. The 'disadvantaged' are not seen as standing outside the society, they are part of it and essential to its functioning. Our approach to social differentiation does share much with the group-monopoly paradigm, since both consider that inequalities and group distinction coincide.[31] But we argue more explicitly that social groups are interrelated, majorities and minorities being socially constituted through hierarchization and unequal life chances. Group distinction is incorporated into the notion of inequality; that is to say, they cannot be disassociated. Silver, by contrast, starts with social differences, which she equates with social differentiation, and contends that not all types of social differences lead to exclusion. My point here is that social differences do not constitute a starting point, and must be treated as something to be explained; social differentiation is a process, and social differences its outcome. Differences are used to define the boundaries of socially constructed categories and to assign individuals to these categories. These boundaries have a structural existence that is repeatedly confirmed through social relations and practices. We also pay greater attention to political processes, norms, and representations, and to social policies, more specifically to how they shape economic functioning and relate to normative definitions. This is what I turn to now.

2. Strands of Social Differentiation

The chapters in this volume look at those mechanisms, such as market forces, structural changes in the demand factor, and mobile labour markets, that link age and spatially related, gendered, and racialized forms of differentiation to the economy. Their scope is macrosociological inasmuch as social differentiation and inequalities are not imputed to intent and individual factors, though the latter are of course present. The authors examine how unequal life chances engender distinct and overlapping social boundaries. They explore how differences are constructed, become salient, and are rendered operative. They study the impact of policies on the distribution and accessibility of societal resources, including material and ideal ones such as prestige. They focus on the relationship between policies and the normative order, and seek to understand how norms are used to institutionalize social differentiation. They reject a single and linear causal analysis.[32]

Before going on to examine each contribution, two other points must be made. First, the authors adopt a genealogical perspective; that is to say, they account for the emergence of specific social categories as well as for their fluctuation. The boundaries of youth, for example, which include persons between fifteen and twenty-four, are currently questioned by the Canadian Youth Foundation, since they do not take into account the prolonged dependency of young adults beyond the latter age. Wotherspoon and Li also indicate how social categories and their boundaries are related to social policies such as affirmative action and multiculturalism. Southcott shows how broad categories such as urban-rural can lose their usefulness, and Vosko indicates how feminization can also affect males. Second, all authors treat the process of differentiation as the principal unit of analysis and each one provides a detailed and integrated understanding of its specificity. The factors accounting for the construction of gender inequalities, for example, are not those that help us understand the relation between Aboriginals and non-Aboriginals. This, of course, is not to deny that multiple forms of differentiation overlap and reinforce one another.

Each chapter's contribution to understanding distinct forms of social differentiation is now presented.[33] Gender and age will be reviewed first, followed by race-ethnicity and, more specifically, aboriginality. Rural-urban differentiation will be examined last, for it is viewed in this context more as a container of social differentiation than as an underlying factor. For the most part, I will emphasize here how these papers collectively develop a dynamic, socially grounded perception of social differentiation as a process involving economic inequalities, normative standards, and policy orientations.

2.1 Gender Differentiation

Leah Vosko's powerful analysis in chapter 2 clearly establishes that gender remains a major organizing principle of differentiation. Gender differentiation in the Canadian labour market, she argues, is rooted in the standard/non-standard employment relationship (SER/NSER) distinction,[34] which has constituted differences between groups or categories of individuals (specifically women and men) as social facts. Vosko examines how legal instruments and policy mechanisms, such as labour law (on collective bargaining, minimum wage, and basic employment standards), unemployment insurance policy, and employment practices in the federal government construct the SER as a masculine norm and the NSER as a feminine norm, thus producing a gendered order that was in place for the most part between the post–Second World War period and the early 1970s. This analysis of the triangular relation between the economic order, normative models, and policies shows how normatively oriented policies foster gender-based social differentiation. For it is the state, employers, and unions who constructed the SER as a (white) male norm associated with the family wage, used this distinction to differentiate between workers, and thereby produced inequalities in the labour market.

A significant aspect of Vosko's contribution resides in her scrutiny of the reconfiguration of gender differentiation in the labour market that occurred between 1970 and 1995. These years were characterized by the extensive growth of NSER employment and an increase in temporary work and self-employment. This change has destabilized the link between sex/gender and non-standard forms of employment, such that the SER/NSER distinction is no longer the primary axis of gender differentiation in the labour market. However, what is intriguing is that gender continues to be a vital organizing feature in the labour market, as indicated by the data presented on the disproportionate percentages of women in NSERs and the increasing polarization within some forms of NSERs. Why is this?

Vosko's detailed examination of policy responses to instability in the SER/NSER employment distinction and the spread of NSERs clearly establishes that gendered notions of standard and non-standard forms of employment are so strongly entrenched that they have become ingrained in the design of labour policies. The structure of labour law, for example, has remained virtually unchanged since the Second World War inasmuch as it has maintained the masculine SER norm even though the norm of full-time, full-year work is fading in practice. Although it is a step in the right direction because it de-couples the SER and collective bargaining, the move towards broader-based bargaining legislation has not been implemented on a large scale in recent decades.[35] Similarly, the new employment insurance program has exacerbated gender differentiation by introducing a family income supplement that assumes an equitable distribution of resources within households and takes women's economic contributions as secondary.

To summarize Vosko's argument, the SER maintains its normative pre-eminence at the policy level; a gendered notion of the SER and the NSER remains despite changes in the labour market itself and the spread of the NSER. Consequently, non-standard workers still have difficulty accessing a comprehensive set of labour and social protections, especially as employment norms deteriorate. Vosko's analysis allows us to understand how gender differentiation is constructed and how social differentiation operates more generally. It clearly establishes that the more porous SER/NSER distinction does not eradicate gender differentiation. It identifies how norms, policies, and economic situations are tightly interwoven. Finally, her redefinition of the feminization of employment and employment norms so as to include the casualization of jobs helps us to rethink the redefinition of social categories and boundaries. Her analysis of this process also sheds light on other strands of social differentiation.

2.2 Age-related Differentiation

David Cheal's incisive analysis of age-related differentiation (chapter 3) begins by focusing on the process of age categorization as he indicates how the social category of youth is not fixed. Factors such as high youth unemployment and the problematic transition from school to work have delayed the integration of young adults into the labour market and the completion of social adulthood. In line with Dagenais,[36] Cheal adds that the definition of age boundaries is also affected by another factor: the age boundaries of 'youth' fluctuate according to the problem under consideration and specific policy interests. The 15–24 youth age bracket, for example, corresponds to programs intended to promote education, whereas intergenerational equity issues shift the boundaries to 16–19. These varying constructions of 'youth' clearly indicate that social categories, even those seemingly grounded in 'nature,' are a product of contextual issues and social policy objectives.

Age-related differentiation is examined in terms of age stratification within the working-age population, a phenomenon Cheal calls the privileging of prime-age workers and which he operationalizes in terms of income inequality. During the 1982–92 period, for example, with the exception of 1987–9, the earnings of entry-level men (aged 20–24) decline both in absolute and relative terms. For women, the contrast is even greater.[37] Many factors, stemming largely from comparative positions in the labour market, account for income inequality and thus for age-related differentiation: the various distributions of (1) unemployment, (2) labour force participation, (3) hours of employment, (4) 'good jobs' and 'bad jobs', and (5) wages. Using existing data, Cheal provides empirical evidence that clearly establishes the differential positions occupied by young and prime-age workers and the presence of internal differentiations within the category of youth. To use Vosko's expression, the employment of youth undergoes a process of feminization, as their participation in part-time employment and other NSERs increases. As Cheal's analysis shows age-related economic differentiation is only the tip of the iceberg – deeper, underlying causes are uncovered. The examination of functional differentiation (market functioning), cohort differentiation (relative cohort size), status differentiation (status in seniority systems), program differentiation (evolution of government programs), and life-course differentiation (position in life course) indicates that all these factors, with the exception of cohort size, merit some recognition.

In addition, it would appear that the recent economic difficulties of Canadian youths are not entirely due to the changing organization of work, but also to the changing organization of rewards from work. Furthermore, age-related distribution is also affected by factors other than market forces, with an important one being agents of the state. This occurs even when it is not a matter of public policy. Employment opportunities in the public service, income transfers, and magnitude of the education debt provide examples. Finally, Cheal strongly advocates that the search for a single explanation for the deteriorated economic circumstances of youth should be abandoned. This problem has been present for about two decades; only its forms and shapes have changed. As such, Cheal proposes a new and more global approach to the question, one that acknowledges the presence of extended social differentiation. Thus, age stratification becomes further differentiated within the market economy into multiple economic divisions: labour force participation, employment and unemployment, hours of employment, wage levels, 'good jobs' and 'bad jobs.' These divisions in employment conditions then affect other sectors of society, namely, families and governments, which are expected to meet unfilled demands. Thus, what stands out is a complex set of interrelated factors operating at many levels.

2.3 Racial and Ethnic Differentiation

Peter Li's insightful paper (chapter 4) analyses social differentiation in terms of the social construction of racial differences. This process, which is defined as the politics of difference, implies that lower market value and social worth are attached to those who are construed as different. It involves the attribution of specific meanings that inform and justify discriminatory practices and policies towards categories designated as different. This brings Li to focus on the construction of ethnic and racial diversity in Canada.

It is a well-known fact that the ethnic and racial composition of Canada has changed over the last century. It is also clear that the rise of ethnic and cultural pluralism was initially European in nature. In 1961, 88 per cent of what is called the third force was of European origin. By 1991, however, largely as a result of changes in 1962 and 1967 to immigration policy, 56 per cent of the third force was European while roughly 25 per cent was Asian and African. Li argues that ethnic diversity has become more noticeable not because of its growth but because of changes in types of diversity. Indeed, his data show that the segment of the population that was non-French, non-British, and non-Canadian in origin (28.5%) in 1996 is comparable to the proportion of non-French and non-British between 1961 and 1991, which remains relatively constant at about 26 to 28 per cent of the Canadian population.

Although demographics are a factor underlying increased racial diversity in Canada, Li argues that this is far from being the only one. For public policy, in this case, the policy of multiculturalism, also constructs social diversity. Embedded in broader social relationships, social policies change, as did the policy on multiculturalism to include an equality dimension. As the author points out, the expression 'visible minorities' received official recognition when Commissioner Rosalie Abella mentioned visible minorities as one of the four designated categories in the 1984 *Royal Commission Report on Equality in Employment.* It was then included in the 1986 Employment Equity Act to designate 'persons who are, because of their race and colour, in a visible minority in Canada.' The concept of visible minorities was operationalized in the 1986 census in terms of ten categories of origin. Census data indicate that the proportion of visible minorities in Canada increased from 6.3 per cent in 1986 to 11.2 per cent of the total population in 1996.[38]

Visible minorities are categories characterized by unequal life chances, since all categories included under visible minorities fall below the national mean and earn less than do whites in Canada. This holds true even after factors such as human capital, labour market experience, and demographic variables have been taken into account. Superficial characteristics of racial minorities became inseparable from the unfavourable social features attributed to them. Consequently, unequal life chances and racially based normative values resulted in lower market value and social worth. Racial diversity thus results mainly from the reproduction of a normative and economic order that reinforces social differentiation based on race and racial origin. Li's analysis brings out the importance of modifying the normative order and of attaching a positive value to diversity.

2.4 Aboriginal/Non-Aboriginal Social Differentiation

Terry Wotherspoon's comprehensive analysis in chapter 5 examines the highly disadvantaged position held by Aboriginals in Canada. He explores how economic and social developments, state policies, and legal definitions interact with social differentiation, and how they unequally affect the identities and life chances of Aboriginals and non-Aboriginals.

The author discards approaches that view groups as distinct and closed cultural entities, as well as micro-level perspectives on discrimination and racism, preferring to emphasize institutional structures, domination, conflict, accommodation, and resistance. This critical perspective accounts for agency while preserving a more global approach that accords a central place to social policies and to their often paradoxical results.

Differentiation with regard to Aboriginals is grounded in the diversity of these populations and the different forms of contact they had with non-Aboriginal groups. These historically constituted differences were codified through government policy and legislation that can deal explicitly with Aboriginals such as the Indian Act, or be 'neutral' in intent. Government policy and legislation concerning Aboriginals, it is shown, is complex and ever-changing, and can often generate contradictory effects. While Bill C-31, for example, abolishes old forms of inequalities and discrimination, it simultaneously creates new forms of divisions.

Another contribution of this chapter lies in its focus on the material and symbolic importance of legal categories. They are material because their definition is intrinsically related to processes of inclusion and exclusion with regard to rights, privileges, and activities. These definitions are symbolic because they regulate subjectivities – they prescribe who belongs to a category and what they should be. In the Canadian context, fundamental aspects of 'Indian' life were not only devalued, but also prohibited. Conditions of enfranchisement reflect the assimilationist bias rooted in cultural dominance.

Wotherspoon then turns to a discussion of Aboriginal/non-Aboriginal differentiation in Canada and to their respective life chances and conditions. This examination takes into account demographic factors, employment and income, education and occupation, and social conditions. For each dimension, Wotherspoon is careful to make appropriate distinctions between and within groups. The data amply demonstrate Aboriginals' highly disadvantaged position in terms of socio-economic indicators and other facets of relative deprivation. While factors such as age, lower education, work patterns, and community location do account for some of the inequalities, much remains 'unexplained.' As in the case of racialized minorities, factors such as racism, discrimination, and personal circumstances must be included as explanatory variables.

Aboriginals present a youth-concentrated age structure and high birth rates at a time when health care needs are thought about in terms of the greying population. The geographical location of this population also differs considerably from the general Canadian population. For example, most of the Canadian population, and more specifically immigrants, are now concentrated in urban centres, whereas roughly 70 per cent of Canada's Aboriginal population lives outside census metropolitan areas. This has considerable impact on demand for and delivery of programs and services.

This analysis of Aboriginal/non-Aboriginal differentiation draws out the complex relationships among the economic, normative, political, and legal orders. It also clearly suggests that policies must take into account the specific situation of distinct collectivities.

2.5 *Region Types and Spatially Based Social Differentiation*

Are we witnessing a 'rural renaissance' or an increased differentiation between urban and rural centres? This question cannot be answered in terms of these categories, Chris Southcott argues in his informative paper (chapter 6). Globalization, technological change, the information revolution, and post-industrialism in general have complex effects that can be assessed only by discarding a binary classification. One of the major problems lies in the very definition of 'rural,' which is conceived in a manner similar to that of minorities such as women, who are defined as the Other in relation to dominant groups who see themselves as universal and incarnating the norm. The Other embodies difference. Furthermore, since rurality was identified with agriculture, the term 'rural' has inadequately dealt with the heterogeneity of non-rural settings and situations. Southcott's point is that measuring the consequences of globalization, post-industrialism, and post-Fordism requires that old categories be replaced by new, more refined ones. This entails examining spatial differentiation, a process that involves unequal access to power and to the resources of power.

Southcott's model of differentiated spatial forms is grounded in the relationship between commodity production, socio-economic production, and socio-historic conditions, all of which engender similarities in socio-economic situation. Region types differ not only because they produce different staples, but also because their foundations were laid during historical periods characterized by different types of industrial relations. This analysis yields a typology of six region types: urban, urban fringe, agriculture-dependent, resource-dependent, fishing-dependent, and northern Native.[39] These areas constitute containers through which various forms of differentiation can be analysed.

A nuanced answer to the initial question concerning increased convergence or divergence can now be provided. Urban and urban-fringe areas are characterized by economic and demographic growth. In urban areas, immigration constitutes an important factor underlying population growth and increasing diversity. This trend is accompanied by greater economic inequality, which may explain the movement to the urban fringe of a well-to-do ex-urban population that lives alongside a less well-off 'native' population. Agricultural, resource-dependent, and fishing regions are all in economic and demographic decline. The northern-Native region offers a slightly different pattern since demographic growth due to high birth rates is not accompanied by economic growth.[40]

Each configuration exhibits a specific pattern of interaction between socio-economic status, gender, and race-ethnicity. The position of women in resource-dependent towns, for example, differs from that of women in agricultural regions, where women's unpaid labour is part of the family economy.

Many factors account for the enduring presence of spatially based differentiation in Canada: the specific combination of competitive capitalism, Fordist industrialism, and post-industrialism; the importance of the tertiary economy (which is resistant to decentralization) in Canada;[41] the greater distance between urban centres and rural areas, which results in rural areas benefiting less from decentralized urban activities; and, finally, the weakness of push factors in urban centres that remain, comparatively speaking, quite problem free.

3. Internal Differentiation and Intersectionalities

Social differentiation is viewed here as a product of inequality and as an instrument of its reproduction. All the authors locate its origins in economic and political relations that create group monopolies and establish social boundaries. They emphasize the complex interplay between the allocation of resources – material and non-material – and group distinction. Each one explores a set of historically specific social practices, policies, and ideologies that produces a distinct form of inequality. Immigration policies and the Indian Act, for example, bring about differentiated categories and boundaries.

The need to go beyond the analysis of static, inert categories and parallelism – that is, beyond the simple tracing of parallels between different forms of hierarchization – is now well established. In her rejection of parallelist arguments, Carby remarks that the simultaneous experience of three types of oppression differs from the addition of three types.[42] The articles here are sensitive to internal differentiation, that is, to the presence of diversity within each dichotomized category, and they provide a deeper understanding of the ways in which different strands of differentiation intersect and interrelate.

Vosko indicates that the SER distinction constructed by the state, employers, and labour as a male norm is also white. She points out that the standard/non-standard distinction was established as a principal axis of gender and racialized differentiation after the Second World War. Cheal notes that the contrast between entry women and prime-age women is even greater than the same contrast observed for men.

Li's discussion attests to the presence of additional obstacles faced by immigrant women as they encounter discrimination in the labour market and other social spheres. His data unequivocally show that Aboriginals are the most disadvantaged of groups in the labour market. Wotherspoon's essay explains this situation by showing how various policies affect income-related factors such as educational achievement and labour market experience. His analyses dovetail with the others presented in this book. For example, the most severe socio-economic conditions are linked to living on reserves, which relates to Southcott's observations about northern-Native regions. As he observes, the age structure of Aboriginals partially accounts for the socio-economic differences between Aboriginals and non-Aboriginals. This finding is not surprising in view of Cheal's conclusions regarding the privileged status enjoyed by prime-age workers. Finally, Southcott's article shows how these diverse forms of differentiation produce specific patterns according to region type. The sexual division of labour in agricultural regions, for example, differs considerably from that observed in fishing communities and urban areas. Clearly, different patterns of social differentiation intersect and often interact.

It is, moreover, possible to move a step further, since the analysis of each strand of social differentiation can contribute to a better understanding of the others. Li argues that a differential market value is attached to people of different racial origins in the Canadian labour market. This important point concerning the link between social value and economic value can be usefully applied to categories such Aboriginals, women, youth, and rurals. It indicates that minority groups – defined here as those with less power – tend to be construed in negative terms and are treated accordingly. Such is often the case for women. Cheal's analyses of the factors underlying income inequality in terms of comparative positions in the labour market are useful for grasping the situation of other social categories. Such an approach could facilitate the development of a gendered, racialized, regionalized, etc. account of economic relations. His concept of extended social differentiation can be used for understanding the situation of other minorities. Wotherspoon's emphasis on policies and internal differentiation provides an effective tool for exploring ethnic, racial, and gendered differentiation. The important and well-publicized example is a gender-differentiated one: Indian women living on reserves lost their status through marriage while men did not. The impact of policies targeting specific groups should thus be examined for untargeted categories. Vosko's examination of the normative distinction underpinning policies offers a tool for examining other social relations. The fact that more jobs now resemble so-called 'women's work' (namely, the often inferior conditions of employment and levels of social protection to which women have been historically subject) sheds light on other forms of social differentiation. For example, between 1976 and 1994, youth (15–24) bore the brunt of the increase in part-time employment, an area of employment that is also highly gendered and racialized. Finally, Southcott's emphasis on the relation between post-Fordism and competitive capitalism can illuminate the structuring of gender and race relations.

Put together, the strands of social differentiation reveal an overall picture indicating that the SER corresponds to a white, urban, prime-age, and non-immigrant male norm. This image sheds light on how society constitutes itself through the creation of economic and normative orders that are closely interrelated and often articulated through policy. These processes and mechanisms will now be examined.

Notes

1 See Niklas Luhmann, 'The Paradox of System Differentiation and the Evolution of Society,' in J.C. Alexander and P. Colomy, eds, *Differentiation Theory and Social Change: Comparative and Historical Perspectives* (New York: Columbia University Press, 1990), 409–11.

2 For a longer discussion, see Alexander and Colomy, *Differentiation Theory and Social Change*.

3 Recall Parsons's sophisticated analysis of the generalized media of symbolic interchange (such as money, power, and influence) circulating from subsystem to subsystem and the cybernetic hierarchy of control, where elements, rich or poor in energy and information, flowed through the system. See Talcott Parsons, *The System of Modern Society* (Englewood Cliffs, NJ: Prentice-Hall, 1971).

4 See Jeffrey C. Alexander, 'Differentiation Theory: Problems and Prospects,' in Alexander and Colomy, *Differentiation Theory and Social Change*, 6.

5 According to Paul Colomy, 'Revisions and Progress in Differentiation Theory,' in ibid., 468.

6 Ibid., 475.

7 See Jeffrey C. Alexander, 'Core Solidarity, Ethnic Out-Groups, and Social Differentiation,' in *Differentiation Theory and Social Change*, 272.

8 He uses 'primordial' as Clifford Geertz does. People connect because of the import accorded to the unaccountable and seemingly natural ties that structure solidarity – race, kinship, religion, territory. Alexander, ibid., 272.

9 By primordial complementarity or complementary primordiality, Alexander means that individuals include those who share similar qualities or attributes, such as religion, ethnicity, or 'race.'

10 Ibid., 277.

11 They were excluded from those upon whom citizenship rights are bestowed.

12 See Stow Persons, *Ethnic Studies at Chicago, 1905-45* (Chicago: University of Illinois Press, 1990).

13 See Max Weber, *Economy and Society* (Berkeley and Los Angeles: University of California Press, 1968 [1921–2]).

14 See the pioneering work of Colette Guillaumin, *L'idéologie raciste: Genèse et langage actuel* (Paris, La Haye: Mouton, 1995 [1972]); and the Centre for Contemporary Cultural Studies (University of Birmingham), *The Empire Strikes Back: Race and Racism in 70's Britain* (London: Hutchinson, 1982).

15 The articles published in *Sociological Theories: Race and Colonialism* under the direction of UNESCO (Paris) in 1980 constitute a good example of this approach.

16 See Robert Miles, who defines racialization as 'those instances where social relations between people have been structured by the signification of human biological characteristics in such a way as to define and construct differentiated social collectivities' In *Racism* (New York: Routledge, 1989), 75.

17 Michael Omi and Howard Winant, *Racial Formation in the United States from the 1960s to the 1980s* (New York: Routledge and Kegan Paul, 1986), 62–3.

18 See Guillaumin, *L'idéologie raciste*.

19 Guillaumin points out that individuals were not enslaved because they were Black, but that they became Black after being enslaved. In other words, it is after the formation of a 'real' social category – slaves – that colour becomes significant as it is used to define social boundaries and explain social position.

20 See Richard A. Schermerhorn, *Comparative Ethnic Relations: A Framework for Theory and Research* (New York: Random House, 1970).

21 Alexander does mention that his theory would have to be specified for different classes of empirical events since inclusion seems to vary in terms of the empirical modes of outgroup contact. My argument here is that the mode of outgroup contact is more than an empirical event and should be included in the process of theorization itself. I consider it to be a factor

influencing definitions of primordial complementarity rather than an external factor related to degrees of societal differentiation. A differentiated and relatively autonomous legal system, for example, can be applied differently, as in the case of the exclusion of Blacks and women from citizenship rights. Alexander in Alexander and Colomy, 277.

22 For a longer discussion on reductionism, see Stuart Hall, 'Race, Articulation and Societies Structured in Dominance,' in *Sociological Theories: Race and Colonialism* (Paris: UNESCO, 1980), 305–45; Stuart Hall, 'Gramsci's Relevance for the Study of Race and Ethnicity,' *Journal of Communication Inquiry* 10.6 (1986): 5–27; and Danielle Juteau, *L'ethnicité et ses frontières* (Montreal: Presses de l'Université de Montréal, 1999), chap. 5.

23 Max Weber indicates how social relations constitutive of socially differentiated groups can be open or closed. In the latter case, differences are used by some groups to exclude others and establish their domination. See Weber, *Economy and Society.*

24 Hilary Silver, 'Social Exclusion and Social Solidarity: Three Paradigms,' *International Labour Review* 133.5–6 (1994): 531–78.

25 Ibid., 2.

26 Ibid., 5.

27 In France, integration, which implies the adoption of an assimilationist perspective, is viewed as countering exclusion. See, e.g., Dominique Schnapper, *La France de l'intégration* (Paris: Gallimard, 1991).

28 M. Xiberras in Silver, 'Social Exclusion.'

29 Ibid.

30 See Michel Wieviorka, *La démocratie à l'épreuve: Nationalisme, populisme, ethnicité* (Paris: La Découverte, 1993).

31 'Our perspective' is used in a broad sense, indicating that all contributors at least implicitly discard the solidarity and specialization paradigms.

32 These points are made very explicitly by Wotherspoon in his analysis of the Aboriginal/non-Aboriginal distinction.

33 As previously noted, the authors' work is based on the main lines of research identified in Canada and provides a critical synthesis of the major issues. See Leah Vosko in this volume, p. 26.

34 The standard employment relationship (SER) differs from the non-standard relationship (NSER) in that the latter forms of employment 'deviated from a full-time, full-year permanent job, and normally carried lower wages, levels of social protection and benefits and limited access to collective bargaining rights.'

35 Only Quebec called for greater parity between SERs and NSERs.

36 Lucie Dagenais, 'La jeunesse,' *Sociologie et sociétés* 28.1 (1996): 89–105.

37 This is because their relative income decline was more pronounced than that of men.

38 It is necessary to deconstruct this concept, but such a task would require an article in itself. Why presuppose that whites are not visible? Why exclude Argentineans and Chileans? Why not acknowledge the diversity between these categories and their internal differentiation? What can be said at this point is that racial categories, though ideologically constructed, operate in the real world and are used to classify and ground differential treatment. The Employment Equity Act thus serves to redress the unequal value accorded to different categories.

39 Cf. Roy Bollman and Brian Biggs, 'Rural and Small Town Canada: An Overview,' in R. Bollman, ed., *Rural and Small Town Canada* (Toronto: Thompson Educational Publishing, 1992). These authors use different criteria, yet come up with similar categories.

40 Terry Wotherspoon's analysis explains this pattern.

41 See William Coffey and Mario Polèse, 'Locational Shifts in Canadian Employment, 1971–1981: Decentralization v. Decongestion,' *Canadian Geographer* 32.3 (1988): 248–56.

42 See Hazel Carby, 'White Woman Listen! Black Feminism and the Boundaries of Sisterhood,' in *The Empire Strikes Back* (see note 14); and Arthur Brittan and Mary Maynard, *Sexism, Racism and Oppression* (New York: Basil Blackwell, 1985).

2. Gender Differentiation and the Standard/Non-Standard Employment Distinction: A Genealogy of Policy Interventions in Canada

Leah F. Vosko

In the early 1970s, the Royal Commission on the Status of Women described gender inequality in the labour market in terms of women's predominance in non-standard forms of employment, low rates of pay, and limited access to training. The Commission linked such disparities to women's disproportionate responsibility for unpaid domestic work and 'traditional and contemporary myths that have tended to keep women dependent and subordinate.'[1] The passage of a third decade is cause for the reappraisal of the post-1970 gender order, which involved greater access to the labour market for women shaped partly by public policy developments. Instead of assessing the successes and failures of equality policy, however, public attention is increasingly fixed on men's deteriorating economic situation, with insufficient concern for other persisting dimensions of labour market inequality – such as the persistent 'revenue gap' between men and women.[2] The popular media is filled with headlines such as 'Where have all the smart men gone?' and 'Young males losing ground in wage stakes' as well as captions characterizing men as 'tomorrow's second sex.'[3]

There is certainly justification for concern about the deteriorating labour market position of specific groups of men; growing income polarization among men as a group, their declining participation in higher education and their relatively high unemployment rates are very troubling indeed.[4] Still, there are dangerously few nuances in the public discourse on gendered labour market trends: the prevailing assumption is that, with falling wages and lower employment rates among men, as well as deindustrialization and the growth of the service sector, women's wages and conditions of employment are improving markedly at the expense of men, particularly young men. The apparent convergence in young women's and men's labour market experience, which obscures new patterns of gendered labour market inequality, is also viewed by some as reducing the need for equality policy.[5]

The notion that gender de-differentiation (and therefore de-segmentation) is occurring in the Canadian labour market is a troubling byproduct of public discourses that oversimplify recent labour market trends, one that gives the impression that sex and gender matter *less* in the contemporary labour market than in the post-1970 period. These perceptions make it necessary to probe prevailing labour force trends more deeply, locating them in a historical context, and to consider, in particular, the place of gender as an organizing feature in a national labour market characterized by the spread of non-standard forms of employment. To this end, this chapter explores the relationship between the standard/non-standard employment distinction and gender differentiation in the Canadian labour market. Comparing the post–Second World War and the post-1970 periods, it probes how this relationship has changed over time, focusing attention on the role of two strands of labour policy – unemployment insurance policy and labour law – as well as employment practices in the federal public service.

In the period immediately following the Second World War, the standard/non-standard employment distinction was the principal axis of gender differentiation in the Canadian labour market. Through labour market policies and employment practices, the state, employers, and, to some extent, organized labour constructed the standard employment relationship as a (white) male norm. In contrast, women and other marginalized groups were largely relegated to non-standard employment relationships, forms of employment that deviated from a full-time, full-year permanent job and normally carried lower wages, lower levels of social protection and benefits, and limited access to collective bargaining rights. Thus, the standard/non-standard employment distinction upheld a racialized and gendered segmentation strategy, one that inhibited women's full participation in the labour market.

With the spread of non-standard employment relationships since the 1970s, the standard/non-standard employment distinction is no longer the primary pivot of gender differentiation in the labour market, although it still holds weight in normative terms. This shift demands careful scrutiny, since the proliferation of non-standard employment relationships fosters the perception that the organization of the labour market is becoming *less* gendered when, in reality, gender differentiation and the feminization of employment remain. Women continue to represent a high proportion of part-time and temporary workers;[6] they also remain concentrated in expanding low-wage sectors, such as sales and services and occupations such as clerical work and child care, which reinforces notions of women as 'dependent' and 'contingent' workers favourably disposed to service work because of their pre-sumed 'natural talents.'[7] In contrast, men still constitute the majority of the high-wage self-employed (both among self-employed employers and the own-account self-employed) and retain a broader occupational spread.[8] In this context, the erosion of minimum standards legislation, the deterioration of collective bargaining, unemployment insurance reforms, and cutbacks in the federal public service are fuelling new patterns of gendered labour market inequality.

In order to explore the relationship between the standard / non-standard employment distinction and gender differentiation, the ensuing discussion is divided into four parts. Part 1 introduces the core concepts used in the chapter and details its leading premises. Part 2 examines the gradual emergence of the standard / non-standard employment distinction as an axis of racialized gender differentation, focusing on policies and practices in the period between the Second World War and approximately 1970. Part 3 continues the policy-centred chronological sketch of gender differentiation in the Canadian labour market into the post-1970 period, illustrating that the standard / non-standard employment distinction became more porous in the mid-1970s and that new patterns of gender differentiation and the feminization of employment accompanied this trend. With this evidence of deteriorating employment norms, part 4 concludes by probing prevailing labour force trends indicative of continued gender differentiation and the feminization of employment norms.

1. Concepts and Definitions

Five related concepts frame this inquiry: the standard employment relationship, non-standard employment relationships, social differentiation, gender differentiation, and feminization.

The *standard employment relationship* (SER) is defined by continuous full-time, full-year employment where the worker has one employer and normally works on the employer's premises under his or her supervision.[9] Its essential elements include an indeterminate employment contract, adequate social benefits that complete the social wage, reasonable hours of work, and employment, frequently, but not necessarily, in a unionized sector. A high level of compensatory social policies, such as pensions, unemployment insurance, and extended medical coverage normally accompanies the SER. Although its origins lie in national and supra-national developments in the interwar years, the SER became the normative model of male employment in Canada in the post–Second World War era.[10]

In contrast to the SER, whose features are easy to discern, *non-standard employment relationships* (NSERs) are best defined by what they are not. In 1990, the Economic Council of Canada first defined them simply as those forms of employment that differ from a full-time job and indicated that they include all forms of employment falling below a thirty-five-hour per week threshold. NSERs range from part-time work, temporary work, self-employment, and contract work to on-call work, home-based work, and multiple job-holding. While these employment relationships are multiple and varied, they usually entail a high degree of insecurity; most non-standard workers have lower levels of social benefits and less extensive statutory entitlements than do standard workers.[11] Social scientists tend to conceptualize the prototypical SER, characterized by security and durability, and NSERs, typically defined by insecurity and a lack of permanence, as constituting a continuum of legal and social norms of employment whereby workers have varying levels of access to employment security, social protections, and benefits.[12] However, as NSERs proliferate and become more standardized and the stability of the SER declines in both normative and real terms, the notion of a continuum loses some of its precision. Still, since this continuum has served as an axis of social differentiation in the Canadian labour market since the Second World War, it is crucial to the ensuing discussion.

Social differentiation is generally defined as the recognition, and the constitution as social facts, of differences between particular groups or categories of individuals. This process is invariably linked to social stratification and, hence, to inequalities of power, status, wealth, and prestige. Based on this understanding of social differentiation, a leading premise of this chapter is that the state, employers, and unions have historically shaped inequalities in the labour market by deploying the standard/non-standard employment distinction, often with conflicting objectives, to differentiate between workers. Thus, the standard/non-standard employment distinction has served as a primary means of social differentiation in the labour market. Consequently, various conventional indicators of social status and wealth, such as skill, wage levels, security, and benefits, follow from the nature of the employment relationship.

Gender differentiation is among the most salient strands of social differentiation produced by distinguishing between standard and non-standard workers in the organization of the Canadian labour market.[13] Men have historically been constructed as standard workers with strong attachments to the labour force and women as non-standard workers with lesser ties to labour force participation due, in part, to separate-spheres ideologies and male-breadwinner norms. Thus, the SER has come to be defined as a male norm associated with the family wage, leaving NSERs to be associated with workers belonging to marginalized groups such as women, immigrants, the elderly, and people presumed to have alternative sources of subsistence to the wage.

In contrast to gender differentiation, the concept *feminization* is used here to label a particular grouping of gendered labour market trends coincident with the spread of NSERs, downward pressure on wages, and growing polarization in the post-1970 period. Also characterized as the creation of 'more *women's work* in the market'[14] and a new set of 'gendered employment relationships,'[15] the feminization of employment entails four core features: the first is rising (or consistently high) formal labour force participation rates among women. The second facet is the casualization of employment or, more precisely, the 'gendering (i.e., feminization) of jobs.'[16] This dimension of feminization means that certain groups of men are experiencing downward pressure on wages and conditions of work, while many women are enduring continued economic pressure. The third feature of feminization is the persistence of sex segregation across occupational groupings within and between industries. The fourth dimension, finally, is income and occupational polarization between women and men, even in the face of growing polarization among women and men themselves, especially by age.[17]

In associating this complex set of developments with the 'feminization' of employment, rather than simply with a 'new set of gendered employment relationships,' I follow Pat Armstrong. Most centrally, for an expanding group of workers, wages, benefits, and other forms of social protection are not sufficient to maintain a man and 'his' family, as Keynes and his counterparts intended in crafting the economic infrastructure integral to the capital-labour accord of the post–Second World War period. Instead, a growing proportion of workers, including many workers engaged in NSERs, earn wages and benefits and endure terms and conditions of employment resembling those historically assigned to women presumed to be dependent upon a male wage. As well, women's continuing role in social reproduction, particularly with declining government supports in health care, elder care, and child care, is critical to the gendered character of prevailing employment trends. For example, persisting occupational segregation (as well as new patterns of differentiation) between men and women reflects the gendered organization of social reproduction: women are often confined to jobs in the market that reflect tasks associated with domestic labour, such as child care and service occupations, and women's presumed status as secondary breadwinners often conditions their location in the labour market and the types of employment contracts to which they are subject.[18]

2. Gender Differentiation and the Standard/Non-Standard Employment Distinction, Post–Second World War to 1970

There is an abundance of scholarship documenting occupational sex segregation in the labour market after the Second World War, rooting it in bars to the employment of married women and other policies and practices designed to limit women's labour force participation.[19] Yet we know surprisingly little about how the standard/non-standard employment distinction materialized and shaped the gender order in the post-war labour market. For this reason, it is instructive to review briefly men's and women's patterns of labour force participation from 1940 to 1970 and to examine the laws and policies shaping the system of labour legislation, unemployment insurance, and patterns of employment in the federal public service. What becomes clear through this type of exploration is that, while the standard/non-standard employment distinction replaced what were formerly explicitly discriminatory employment practices, it reproduced their effects. In a climate of unprecedented, albeit tenuous, compromise between capital and organized labour, idealized notions of 'standard' and 'non-standard' employment were central to the gendered labour market segmentation strategy advanced by employers, endorsed by the state, and supported by many unions.[20]

2.1 Labour Force Trends: The Rise of the SER as a 'Masculine' Norm and NSERs as 'Feminine' Norms

The general patterns of men's and women's labour force participation in the post–Second World War period are well known. Men dominated in auto manufacturing, raw resource, and construction industries as well as other sectors of industrial expansion, where they made considerable security and wage gains aided by Canada's full (male) employment objective and the birth of formal collective-bargaining and freedom-of-association rights.[21] In the decade between 1946 and 1956, rates of unionization in non-agricultural work rose from 15.7 to 23.6 per cent, a development that benefited disproportionately men engaged in blue-collar work.[22] In contrast, following trends in the beginning of the twentieth century, women predominated in occupations such as nursing and domestic work and began to fill the ranks of the rapidly expanding clerical sector; they also increasingly engaged in a narrow range of manufacturing industries, such as clothing and textiles. Moreover, while men's labour force participation rates stabilized at relatively high levels, women's were quite low, varying considerably according to marital status.[23] Although women's participation rate rose by over 8 percentage points from 1939 to 1945, it fell precipitously (almost to pre-war levels) in 1946.[24] Married women's withdrawal from the labour market after the Second World War accounts for much of this decline.

It was in this period that the SER came to be not only a male norm but a white male norm. As many immigrant and migrant male agricultural workers and even industrial workers were denied its benefits, highly racialized divisions of labour arose among men on the basis of the rigid conception of worker-citizenship tied to this relationship.[25] Socially assigned characteristics, such as race and ethnicity, as well as immigration status and class, were also central to shaping women's labour force participation in this era. State actors, employers, and unions used these characteristics to structure women's exclusion from the SER and their integration into specific NSERs; hence, their deployment is central to understanding both how the standard/non-standard employment distinction served as an axis of racialized, gendered labour market segmentation in this period and how NSERs became synonymous with underemployment. When policies and practices designed to spur women's exodus from the labour market were at their height, particular groups of women still engaged in casual and intermittent forms of employment that deviated from the evolving white male employment norm. Domestic work and temporary and part-time clerical work are two notable examples.

Between the mid-1930s and the late 1960s, immigrant women, first from various parts of Europe and then from the Caribbean, dominated the ranks of domestic service in Canada. Canadian-born women, in contrast, rarely pursued this form of non-standard employment because of the low wages, live-in requirements, and the scale of employment abuses associated with it. In the 1930s, Scandinavian women, especially Finnish women, were a preferred source of domestic workers because they were perceived to accept extremely harsh conditions of employment.[26] Subsequently, during the Second World War, when Canada began to experience an acute shortage of domestic workers, the government recruited women refugees from western Europe as the primary source of domestic workers. By the early 1950s, however, with the failure of an assisted passage scheme targeting British and western European women for domestic work, the government began to focus on southern European and Caribbean women, even though there was, until 1967, a clause in its immigration regulations that permitted the government to discriminate on the basis of race.[27] This was in sharp contrast to the situation of the largely white, Canadian-born middle-class married women targeted for part-time and temporary employment in the clerical sector in the 1940s, 1950s, and 1960s. Since immigrant domestic workers were cast as 'foreign' domestic workers, a label that reflected the racialized character of the emerging hierarchy of female-dominated NSERs,[28] many middle-class married women negotiated the dual roles of 'dutiful housewives' and part-time 'office girls.' After the Second World War, the clerical sector grew dramatically, as did women's participation in this domain of employment: between 1941 and 1971, women went from 50.1 per cent of clerical workers to 68.9 per cent.[29] Moreover, women's rising participation in clerical work coincided with the accelerated growth of part-time employment among women. Part-time and temporary work, particularly through temporary help agencies, were sold to women as the ideal way to balance family responsibilities with waged work.[30] Together with the NSERs common among male migrants and immigrants in the agricultural sector, the type of employment relationships common in female-dominated occupations, such as clerical and domestic work, represented the flip-side of the evolution of the SER as a normative model of (white) male employment.

2.2   Institutionalizing the Standard/Non-Standard Employment Distinction through Public Policy

Bars to the employment of married women in certain sectors and occupations and measures designed to ease male veterans back into the labour force contributed to women's subordinate, and men's superior, labour market positions after the Second World War. But, in addition to these explicitly gender-biased practices, the state, employers, and unions also harnessed gender norms to the standard/non-standard employment distinction as a means of labour market segmentation, and institutionalized these norms at the level of public policy.

A.   Labour Law

A highly fragmented system of labour law, regulation, and policy characterized by the rise of collective bargaining rights for workers in core industrial and raw resource sectors, on the one hand, and the extension of minimum standards legislation to workers falling outside this norm on the other hand, evolved in Canada after the Second World War. This bifurcated system of labour regulation, which has been criticized sharply for its bureaucratic structure,[31] demonstrated an inherent bias toward male workers, one that led labour boards to embed discriminatory practices in collective bargaining practices, and, hence, contributed to the feminization of minimum standards legislation.[32]

Collective Bargaining. The centrepiece of the post-war industrial relations system was Order-in-Council PC1003 (1944), which extended legal collective-bargaining and freedom-of-association rights to an unprecedented number of workers. Modelled on the American Wagner Act, this legislative instrument extended key rights to workers by delineating a structure of collective bargaining that entailed union certification by cards and majority vote, exclusive bargaining-agent status defined by bargaining units, protection against unfair practices, and enforceable obligations on employers to bargain in good faith.[33] The features of PC1003 were gradually incorporated into, and elaborated upon, in provincial and federal statutes after the Second World War, cultivating a highly juridified system of collective bargaining and a specific type of 'responsible unionism.'

Through PC1003, legal restrictions on the right to strike were combined with requirements by employers to recognize, and bargain collectively with, unions. This 'marriage' was initially achieved through the certification process, which involved granting exclusive bargaining-agent status to a union that had demonstrated support from over 50 per cent of employees in the bargaining unit.[34] Thereafter, it was governed by the Industrial Relations Dispute Investigation Act (IRDIA, 1948), which set greater restrictions on the use of the strike weapon; under this legislation, unions exchanged certification, protections against unfair labour practices, and third-party arbitration for the agreement not to strike during the term of a collective agreement. Grievance arbitration centralized dispute resolution in the union hierarchy (at the expense of the work group) and contractualism, with its focus on the written agreement as the source of employee rights, was institutionalized.[35] With the introduction of the IRDIA, the collective bargaining system was also set within the context of private law, formally removing the collective bargaining process from direct state intervention. However, since the government intervened in dispute resolution where it perceived that strikes among private sector workers were interfering with the 'public interest,' this distinction was not maintained in practice.

The codification of collective bargaining through the IRDIA gave provincial and federal labour boards the power to make decisions about the definition of bargaining units, further fragmenting the collective bargaining system and also making unions subject to state intervention. As Rosemary Warskett notes, '[T]he determination of the bargaining units' appropriateness – its size, the number of occupational groups to be included – all became the purview of board deliberations and, in this sense, part of the public law system.'[36] However, the role of labour relations boards in further constituting the SER as a gendered norm, a process begun by PC1003 and the IRDIA, is most significant for the present analysis. As they evolved, labour boards developed policies pertaining to 'appropriate bargaining units,' which not only differentiated between standard and non-standard workers but created a host of privileges for the former. Labour boards limited the scope of collective bargaining through two structural features: the presumption that bargaining should take place at the level of the work site and the bargaining-unit determination process.[37] The notion that bargaining should take place on a worksite-by-worksite basis, rather than on an industry-wide or occupational basis, meant that only strong unions could attain anything resembling industry-wide bargaining. Informal enterprise-wide and multi-employer bargaining emerged primarily in the auto, steel, meat-packing, forest, and pulp and paper industries and these structures were always tenuous because they depended on the good-will of all the parties involved as well as stable market conditions.[38] With a few exceptions, such as in the construction industry, this type of bargaining was not legally enforceable. In arriving at a structure for bargaining unit determination, labour boards considered a range of criteria, which varied provincially. Of these criteria, the test used to define the 'community of interest' was most central to institutionalizing the SER as a normative model of male employment and NSERs as feminized employment relationships, since it largely reflected employers' decisions about how to organize production, decisions that often capitalized on dividing workers on the basis of their ascriptive characteristics (e.g., age, sex/gender, race, ethnicity, immigrant status) and their relationship to the sphere of social reproduction.[39]

In the province of Ontario, for example, the 'community of interest' test eventually came to include six narrow components: the nature of work performed; the conditions of employment; the skill of employees; administration; geographic circumstances; and functional coherence and interdependence. Coupled with its base-line assumption that individual work sites were natural bargaining units, the labour board used these criteria to separate women employed in female-dominated workplaces from their male counterparts in similar occupations, adversely affecting women's ability to attain comparable employment relationships and/or contracts, wages, and conditions of work to men in similar occupations. It also became a custom to differentiate between a standard production unit and a standard office unit.[40] Except where office workers were located inside or adjacent to a plant, the board normally separated office and production workers into different units. This practice had the obvious effect of cultivating large and strong bargaining units among men that dominated in manufacturing and resource extraction and creating small and weak units among largely female office workers (where part-time and temporary work were common) and cafeteria and cleaning staff, despite early union efforts to organize the entire shop floor into one bargaining unit.[41] Similar patterns developed in textile and garment manufacturing, where cutters were primarily men and sewers primarily women, a pattern that also has considerable consequences for unionization in the present era of economic restructuring. Most provincial labour boards also developed informal policies of separating part-time and full-time workers into different bargaining units and, in the case of the clothing sector, separating homeworkers and in-house sewers.[42]

The structure and organization of collective bargaining contributed to the emergence of industrial unionism in Canada by mid-century. Alongside increases in union strength came rises in real wages,[43] which were largely attained through a type of profit-sharing pioneered in the male-dominated auto industry and other blue-collar sectors, the extension of fringe benefits such as pensions, paid holidays, shorter work weeks, sick pay and disability insurance, provided through the terms of a collective agreement, and the emergence of seniority as a key factor in distributing job-related benefits. Thus, the legal regime of collective bargaining introduced in PC1003 contributed to the ascendancy of the SER as a specifically male norm. This legislation, and the provincial and federal statutes succeeding it, provided largely male workers with a form of 'industrial citizenship'[44] and it ushered in a variant of responsible unionism much criticized by scholars for its bureaucratization, centralization, and contractualism, but applauded by workers (and their unions) in core sectors of the economy whose narrow economic self-interest was secured. In the context of these developments, the so-called secondary work force, which was composed largely of women, became sufficiently distinct from the so-called primary work force that gendered differences in the terms and conditions of employment and the absence of unionization among the former were viewed as 'natural' and, therefore, unproblematic.

Minimum Wage and Basic Employment Standards Legislation. In addition to collective bargaining, the 'gendered' form of NSERs also evolved through early minimum-wage and basic employment-standards laws that were initially applicable to women only and, therefore, drafted on the assumption that workers typically subject to these laws were entitled neither to a 'family wage' nor to a social wage. Minimum standards legislation has its earliest roots in the Factory Acts of the late 1800s and sex-specific minimum wage legislation. Targeted explicitly to women and young children, the Factory Acts emerged to protect women employed outside the home.[45] They initiated a legal distinction between male labour and female and child labour in the name of protecting women's reproductive capacities and, therefore, virtually ignored women's economic needs. Not surprisingly, these acts failed to cover women working inside homes, prefiguring exclusions in employment standards legislation. Built on a similar philosophy, most early minimum wage legislation was also limited to women.[46] After the Second World War, provinces created administrative boards to set wages for female employees only.[47] In this period, the standard selected was to provide a woman with a wage sufficient to support herself, but no dependants, because the goal was to preserve the health of future mothers in nuclear families.[48] This formula failed to consider the needs of women supporting dependants, who constituted approximately one-quarter of the women in paid employment at that time, or the fact that single women and female lone parents, like their male counterparts, needed to save for sickness and old age.[49] It was designed on the premise that an appearance of '"luxury or extravagance, or even superior comfort" ... would endanger public approval.'[50] Even though many provinces extended minimum wage legislation to men in the late 1930s (although at different levels), gradually abandoned Factory Acts, and introduced fair employment policies (which preceded equal value legislation) by the early 1950s, the character of protective legislation and the low threshold of minimum wage legislation shaped employment standards legislation for decades to come. From its inception, employment standards legislation was designed to extend basic protections to workers falling outside the collective bargaining system. Even in firms in which production units were well organized, office workers were often ignored by unions in the 1940s and 1950s, and organizing drives in the retail sector, as well as the banking sector, confronted considerable barriers to collective bargaining.[51] Covering workers of this sort, employment standards legislation was intended to provide a floor of protections below which wages and benefits could not fall. Provincial legislation and the Canada and Quebec labour codes, the two most comprehensive instruments, initially provided statutory entitlements pertaining to minimum wages, maximum hours of work, overtime rates, termination notice, and statutory holidays.[52] By the 1960s, they also provided for maternity and parental leaves. Still, the limitations of this type of legislation were far-reaching. Employment standards were ill enforced, they provided levels of social protection inferior to those normally extended through collective agreements, and they typically excluded or extended differential protections to highly vulnerable non-standard workers; these limitations reflected the legacy left by the Factory Acts and early minimum wage legislation. Quite ironically, many exclusions also gradually came to be based on a narrow conception of the term 'employee,' one that mimicked the conception in collective bargaining legislation whereby a worker must be economically dependant upon a single employer and must normally perform work on the employers' premises and under his or her control or supervision for an indefinite period. Thus, the system of provincial and federal employment standards legislation that evolved parallel to collective bargaining was subordinate to PC1003, the IRDIA, and accompanying provincial statutes. By extending lower wage levels and labour and social protections to non-standard workers, based on the assumption that workers falling outside the collective bargaining norm were either single or benefited from a 'family wage,' it contributed to constructing NSERs as 'feminized' employment norms. Collective bargaining and minimum standards legislation were simultaneously dichotomized and gendered along the axis of the standard/non-standard employment distinction.

B. Unemployment Insurance Policy

Unemployment insurance was another central part of the package designed to normalize standard work among a sizeable group of male workers. But, unlike the fragmented system of labour legislation, the twin objectives of early unemployment policy were to rescue standard workers from economic crises and to stabilize the larger economic system. As early as the Great Depression, business and labour leaders basically concurred on the need to extend some type of safety net to workers in times of high unemployment because the existing package of minimum wages, workers' compensation, and old age pension were insufficient to cushion workers from the hardships generated by economic depression, recession, and the unevenness of the business cycle.

Unemployment insurance was first introduced in 1935 during the Depression, and the program was formalized in the Unemployment Insurance Act of 1940. Early unemployment insurance policy was designed to protect a narrow category of workers; it was only applicable to jobs in industry and commerce, and it treated married and single women differently. The 1935 legislation introduced a classification system (modelled on the system operating in the United Kingdom at the time) based on age and sex. From 1934 to 1940, it divided women into two categories: female worker and wife/mother, and 'it was, by and large, ideologically anathema for a woman to combine these two categories.'[53] These categorizations meant that single women were 'de-sexed' and, therefore, claimed benefits like their male counterparts. However, to be eligible for unemployment insurance, they had to work in a field of employment covered by the legislation. Hence, women (and men) in occupations such as teaching, nursing, and domestic work were ineligible for coverage.

The fate of the employed married woman was even worse than the single woman's, since she was presumed to be dependent upon a male breadwinner and, therefore, was denied an individual entitlement to benefits, gaining access to benefits through indirect channels only, notably dependants' allowances (except under special circumstances where it could be demonstrated that women had worked 'steadily,' fulfilling the criteria of the 'standard worker'). Hence, by design, unemployment insurance was beyond the reach of women in female-dominated sectors, most married women, and those workers in 'casual' or 'intermittent' employment. As Pierson asserts, it was, rather ironically, 'in their attempt to negotiate the contradiction between the assumed dependency of wives and the "non-realization" of the "family-wage", that women turned to just the sorts of catch-as-catch-can, temporary and impoverished jobs in the informal economy that were deemed uninsurable.'[54] By resorting to NSERs out of economic necessity, women – especially married women – doubly disqualified themselves from unemployment insurance.

While more extensive, the 1940 Unemployment Insurance Act continued pre-existing practices of sex discrimination. The act also only applied to jobs in industry and commerce – workers in agriculture, forestry, fishing, transportation, teaching, government services, domestic service, and the non-profit sector were excluded once again – and part-time workers employed fewer than four hours per day, individuals in casual and seasonal work, the self-employed, and workers employed by a spouse were denied coverage. Simultaneously, however, the act introduced a more comprehensive set of labour protections to those covered. It is perhaps most well known for introducing provisions that made benefits and contributions wage-related, indirectly tying benefits to the type of employment relationship,[55] for making coverage compulsory for all categories of workers included in its scope, and for its introduction of cost-sharing between the federal government, workers, and employers. Following from the standards set out in this act, as well as the 1935 (and 1938) unemployment insurance regulations, amendments to the Unemployment Insurance Act in the 1940s mainly involved fine-tuning coverage, defining which groups of workers constituted 'standard workers.'[56]

Although many changes to unemployment insurance provision in the 1950s and 1960s were tied to the evolving definition of the SER and, therefore, began to be couched in gender-neutral language, there were two notable exceptions to this trend: namely, a rejuvenated married women's regulation and the brief (but symbolic) exclusion of fishermen's wives from coverage. In 1950, the Unemployment Insurance Commission made special regulations pertaining to married women, which included automatically disqualifying them for two years after marriage unless they fulfilled certain conditions that proved their attachment to the labour force. To qualify for unemployment insurance, married women had to work for at least ninety days after marriage if they were not employed at the time of marriage, or ninety days after their first separation from work after marriage if they were working at the time of marriage.[57] According to Ann Porter, these regulations depicted married women as both 'conniving to defraud the system' because they were presumed to benefit from family wages and as 'virtuous protectors' of the private sphere.[58] They even penalized women because of pregnancy – under Regulation 5A of PC5090, married women laid off because of pregnancy were disqualified for a period of two years after the birth. These measures prevailed until 1957, and even in the early 1960s employers called for their reinstatement, particularly those employers relying on temporary and part-time workers.[59]

Paradoxically, just as the married women's regulation was repealed, the government introduced measures discriminating against the wives of fishermen. In the late 1950s, it extended coverage to self-employed fishermen on the loose assumption that they were employees of the merchants and plant owners who bought their fish. To bring them under the scheme, the government began basing qualification on the amount and type of fish caught and processed by a given fisherman and *his family* rather than on weeks of individual earnings.[60] Self-employed women fishers who fished with their husbands or were closely related to the men on fishing crews, however, were disqualified from an individual entitlement to unemployment insurance because they were perceived to be contributing to the number of fish caught and processed by their male counterparts. As a result, as Barbara Neis contends, fishermen's unemployment insurance 'perpetuated the existing discriminatory practice of allocating the wealth and benefits resulting from women's labour to men, and defining women as dependants of men.'[61] Put another way, the case of fishermen's unemployment insurance reveals the malleable character of the standard/non-standard employment distinction and demonstrates just how readily it can be manipulated to cultivate labour market segmentation along gendered lines. The average fisherman did not engage in a prototypical SER, although the government extended unemployment insurance coverage to him and many other seasonal male workers, characterizing them as 'standard workers' for a lengthy period. In contrast, women, especially married women and/or women presumed to be dependant upon a male wage, had to prove their entitlement to unemployment insurance by demonstrating a commitment to waged work through engaging in a form of employment that resembled the SER (narrowly defined), working apart from their male companions, and avoiding female-dominated spheres of employment (e.g., teaching and nursing) that were defined as non-standard even though they frequently entailed full-time, full-year employment with a single employer.

C. Employment Practices in the Federal Public Service

Employment practices in the federal public service offer a third window into how the state used the standard/non-standard employment distinction to facilitate gender differentiation after the Second World War. Moreover, since the state often sets the tone for wider labour market developments, its own employment policies deepen our understanding of how this distinction materialized.

Active discrimination against women in recruitment, job classification, hiring, and placement in the federal public service dates to the early 1900s, when women represented an expanding number of clerks. Beginning in 1908, the federal government introduced an explicitly discriminatory job classification scheme confining women to the third and fourth grades of the civil service – the lowest two tiers of employment – based on the justification that employing women in higher grades would potentially undermine men's authority.[62] Even by 1918, when the government overhauled the Civil Service Act to make room for the First Veterans' Preference Scheme, sex was listed as a limiting factor in employment alongside age, health habits, and moral character that could 'trump merit.'[63] Barriers to women's employment were strengthened in 1921 when new directives permitted the deputy minister to classify the sex of desirable candidates. The classification scheme adopted in these years applied modified principles of scientific management to the organization of employment in the civil service, principles that further eroded the working conditions of female workers.

In addition to these limitations on women's employment, the introduction of the marriage bar, originating in the Report of the Civil

Service Commission of 1908, required women to resign either upon marriage or at the time of first pregnancy. To be exempt from this rule, married women had to prove that they were self-supporting.[64] The marriage bar lasted officially until 1955, making the state both an author and follower of policies denying married women equality of opportunity and substantive equality in the pre– and post–Second World War periods. In practice, however, the marriage bar was never total – it was merely a tool of segmentation since, as early as the 1910s, stenography and typing had been a field so identified with women that few men would accept positions as clerks. In the inter-war years, clerical skills became indispensable to the federal public service and this meant that many unmarried women, and married women who successfully kept their marriages a secret, remained in the service. The crucial proviso was that the government turned what were formerly permanent positions for married women into term and temporary contacts. For example, in the 1920s, married women were obliged to resign; if they wished to stay in the service and were still needed, they were rehired as new appointees in temporary positions and paid the minimum rate in their job class.

These practices did not completely obstruct women's appointment to the civil service during the Second World War – more than 50 per cent of the appointments made during the war were of women – but they did reflect a strategy of containment. Indeed, as Jane Ursel notes: '[W]omen provided a vast reserve of labour [in the war] that was at one and the same time extensively contained within the rhetoric and contracts of temporary placement.'[65] In conjunction with the reinstatement of the Veterans' Preference Clause in 1942 and the decision to 'release' between five and seven thousand women in 1944, early discriminatory measures also permanently shaped women's and men's employment patterns within the civil service. Following the Second World War, the majority of women's jobs saved were low-grade clerical positions: thus, although the service became feminized owing to the high concentration of clerical positions, a male breadwinner model still evolved within it. In the 1950s, limitations on married women's employment were gradually lifted; for example, the restriction against married women in clerk positions was removed in 1951. Still, the bulk of positions attained by women were temporary. In 1954 alone, only 919 women obtained permanent positions, while 10,711 gained temporary ones.[66] The marriage bar was eliminated completely in 1955, and in 1961 'sex' as a qualification for positions was dropped. Still, many civil servants began to see their employment contracts deteriorate in this period: the feminization of employment in the federal public service prefigured the feminization of employment in the broader Canadian labour market.

Inside the civil service, women experienced deteriorating employment conditions earlier than men for two related reasons. First, throughout the 1960s they were still more likely than men to be appointed to temporary positions and/or engaged in NSERs. For example, to remedy a shortage of librarians, statisticians, and economists, the government began to encourage married women professionals to enter into its ranks on a part-time basis through the Public Service Commission Staffing Program begun in 1968.[67] Second, even with the extension of collective bargaining rights through the Public Service Staff Relations Act, a sizeable proportion of women in the service were disqualified from what was a substantial rise in benefits and entitlements because of their status as non-standard workers.[68] If women gained access to collective bargaining rights, the Public Service Staff Relations Board's mandated practice of basing bargaining on occupational lines, which led it to mimic the government's gendered classification system, perpetuated their inferior treatment. The case of employment in the federal public service, therefore, also exhibits how collective bargaining norms designed to serve the interests of largely male blue-collar and white-collar workers were secured through the standard/non-standard employment distinction (and reinforced by occupational divisions) even after explicitly discriminatory employment practices were deemed unacceptable.

Shaped by a legacy of marriage bars and explicitly discriminatory practices directed at women, the extension of formal equality in employment in the civil service did not translate into substantive equality between the sexes. As the federal government granted women access to the service on equal terms with men, it cultivated a segmented workforce based on well-established notions of 'standard' and 'nonstandard' employment. In the larger labour market, this type of strategy, according to Ursel, 'provided the means – through the employment of women in union-resistant sectors [as well as in occupations and employment contracts] characterised by part-time, temporary and seasonal work – for maximum utilisation of their labour while retaining their marginal status.'[69] Labour market segmentation achieved through unemployment insurance policy and labour law as well as more covert mechanisms, such as those discriminatory practices embedded in the job classification system in the federal public service, led to the standard/non-standard employment distinction being fixed along rigidly gendered lines.

3. Reconfiguring Gender Differentiation in the Labour Market, 1970–1995

In the early 1970s, the continuum of legal and social norms dominant since the post–Second World War period, marked by the prototypical SER at one pole and NSERs at the other, started to break down. The growth of NSERs began to outpace the growth of full-time, full-year employment, and polarization intensified in the labour market. Mirroring these trends and women's historic predominance in certain NSERs, women's labour force participation continued to expand (rising from 44.4% in 1975 to 57.5% in 1993) while men's contracted (falling from 78.4% to 73.3% over the same period).[70] Accompanying these developments, real wages began to stagnate in 1980s, so that the real average annual wage of men fell for the first time in seven decades and women's real average annual wages grew less sharply than in the preceding decade.[71] These coincident trends led researchers at Human Resources Development Canada to report that the growth of non-standard employment was so extensive in the 1970s, 1980s, and 1990s that only 33 per cent of Canadians were said to hold 'normal jobs' by 1995.[72] They also led policy-makers to acknowledge that the proliferation of NSERs calls into question the superior package of protections modelled on the SER and the inferior set of measures regulating NSERs.[73]

More critically, the spread of employment relationships conventionally associated with women and other workers perceived to be 'secondary' breadwinners destabilized the link between gender and the standard/non-standard employment distinction in the post-1970 period. This distinction no longer remained the primary axis of gender differentiation in the labour market. Still, gender remained a vital organizing feature in the labour market given the shape of employment trends and developments at the policy level. With the growing legitimacy of equal opportunity policy, it became increasingly unacceptable for the state to use overtly discriminatory principles to formulate labour laws, unemployment insurance policies, and employment practices in the federal public service, but gendered assumptions still underpinned labour market policies.

3.1 Labour Force Trends: The Spread of NSERs and the Feminization of Employment

From the mid-1970s to the late 1990s, Canadians witnessed rapid growth in some forms of NSERs, such as temporary work, self-employment, and home-based work, and more steady growth in others, such as part-time employment. Even with the spread of NSERs, women continued to hold a disproportionate share of these employment relationships relative to men; this persistent pattern of segmentation was compounded by greater gender differentiation within certain NSERs.

From 1976 to 1994, the proportion of workers employed part-time climbed from 11 to 17 per cent, with 15–24 year olds experiencing the brunt of this change.[74] Moreover, in the mid-1990s, part-time work was particularly common among temporary workers and in small workplaces and women continued to dominate in this type of employment; 29 per cent of women versus 19 per cent of men workers worked part-time in 1995.[75] Moreover, recent trends indicate that men's participation in part-time work declines drastically as they rise in age (i.e., until they reach 55), while women see a significant dip when they enter the 25–44 year age group, at which point their participation in part-time work levels off. Parallel to the growth in part-time work, multiple job-holding also increased in Canada, a phenomenon that is particularly prevalent in the service and primary sectors and common among women aged 20–24, 8.8 per cent of whom held more than one job in 1997.[76] The rise in multiple job-holding in this period was indicative of the decline of the relatively high level of remuneration and benefits associated with the SER, since multiple job-holders are subject to lower earnings[77] and fewer job benefits, such as pension, health and dental plans, and union coverage, than workers with a sufficiently remunerable single job. Multiple job-holding is also associated with the decline of the continuous full-time, full-year job with benefits; for example, only 83 per cent of multiple job-holders, versus 89 per cent of single job-holders, held a permanent job in 1997.

A revival in self-employment also occurred in the 1980s and 1990s. Historically men have dominated the self-employed work force. However, women's share of self-employment grew substantially in the 1980s and 1990s: in 1981, women constituted 26 per cent of the independently self-employed and 17 per cent of self-employed employers. By 1991, these proportions increased to 34 and 24 per cent respectively.[78]

Notably, from 1980 to 1989, the percentage of women self-employed employers grew sharply, but this trend reversed itself between 1989 and 1996, so that own account self-employment expanded more rapidly among women in the late 1990s.[79] As well, 11 per cent of immigrant workers versus 8 per cent of Canadian-born workers were self-employed in 1991, and both immigrant men and women were more likely to be self-employed than their Canadian-born counterparts.[80] In contrast to part-time work and multiple job-holding, however, self-employment continued to be the preserve of older workers in the 1990s.[81]

Unlike self-employment, temporary employment, which grew in the late 1980s and early 1990s, was especially common among young people, who represented 32 per cent of all temporary workers in 1995.[82] Employment through temporary help agencies grew especially rapidly in the 1980s as the temporary-help industry expanded into sectors and occupations ranging from health care to public sector work and trucking.[83] The rise and spread of the temporary employment relationship (a triangular relationship involving a worker, an agency, and a client firm) in the 1980s and 1990s attests to the spread of precarious NSERs, since this employment relationship contravenes all the core features of the SER and, therefore, escapes regulation under Canada's fragmented system of labour legislation.[84] Still, despite the high level of insecurity associated with temporary-help work and the absence of a continuous employment relationship in this type of non-standard employment, temporary-help workers had surprisingly high average job tenures in the 1990s, a trend that reflects the changing employment practices of firms and the standardization of non-standard employment.[85] The spread of this form of non-standard employment signalled the erosion of benefits and entitlements among workers, as well as the growing ineffectiveness of minimum standards legislation, rather than a decline in the duration or continuity of employment.

Combined with developments like the growth of triangular employment relationships, growing polarization (both between standard and non-standard workers and among non-standard workers) is also suggestive of a relationship between NSERs and precarious employment. In the 1980s and 1990s, there were signs of growing polarization in earnings among Canadians. Young male workers were most affected by this trend, as evidenced by the widening gap between the highest- and the lowest-earning men. As René Morrissette notes: 'Between 1981 and 1988, the real hourly wages of men in the bottom earnings quintile remain virtually the same, while those of men in the top quintile increased by almost 4%. At the same time, the average number of hours worked by men in the bottom quintile fell by almost 2 hours per week (to 30.9 hours) while those in the top quintile rose almost 2.5 hours (to 45.0 hours).'[86] This development marked a growing relationship between polarization in wages and trends in overtime in the 1980s and 1990s, where full-time and professional workers worked more overtime (though largely unpaid) than their low-wage counterparts in part-time or other NSERs, who were more likely to moonlight than work overtime in their main job.

The declining earnings of young men are frequently interpreted as promoting greater access to better jobs for women, particularly younger women who have benefited from greater access to education and training and equality policies more broadly. However, recent studies on the earnings of women suggest a more complex conclusion: they signal growing income polarization between women on the basis of age and persisting income polarization between men and women in all age categories. For example, a study by Katherine Scott and Clarence Lochhead recently found women's wage gains in the 1980s and 1990s to be restricted largely to members of the baby-boom generation or those 40 to 54 years of age. For example, 11.3 per cent fewer women in this age category earned under $24,000 in 1994 than in 1984, but only 0.5 per cent fewer women aged 18 to 24 and 0.6 per cent fewer women aged 25 to 39 earned under $24,000 in 1994 than in 1984.[87] These figures indicate a convergence of earnings between men and women under age 25, attributable largely to declining wages among young men rather than rising wages among young women. In scrutinizing the declining wage gap between young men and women, however, it is important not to lose sight of the fact that the wages of older men in higher income deciles stabilized in the 1980s and the 1990s and that gender differences in earnings persisted in all age groups.[88] Whether the declining wage gap between the young women and men of the 1980s and 1990s will continue when they join successive age groups, where they may have to accommodate workplace arrangements around children, is still an open question.

Despite the apparent downward pressure on young men's wages, evidence of gender asymmetries in earnings, consistently high percentages of women in NSERs, and increasing polarization within certain forms of non-standard employment suggests that gender differentiation persisted with the decline of the SER as a normative model of male

employment. Even with more men engaging in NSERs, women continued to hold a disproportionate share of these employment relationships
in the 1980s and 1990s. In 1989, 1994 and 1998 respectively, approximately 35%, 40%, and 42% of women engaged in one or more NSER. In
contrast, approximately 22%, 27%, and 29% of men held NSERs in the
same years.[89] This type of gender differentiation, which reflects the
dominant pattern of the post–Second World War period, was compounded by heightened gender differentiation within the most rapidly
expanding NSERs. Self-employment is a case in point. Consistent with
the view of scholars who argue that a sizeable percentage of the
contemporary self-employed are involuntarily self-employed,[90] the
growth of self-employment among women in the 1990s was largely
confined to the category of independent (or own-account) self-employment and to relatively low-wage occupations such as child care and
sales.[91] In 1991, male self-employed employers earned $51,300 per year
on average while female self-employed employers earned just $29,100
on average, and male independent self-employed workers earned
$32,000 on average while female independent self-employed workers
earned $19,300 on average.[92] Thus, the sharp wage differences between
self-employed employers and the own-account self-employed were
compounded by gender-based distinctions within each category. The
latter trend is clearly related to persisting sex segregation by industry
and occupation since the 1970s. These complex developments are
important to highlight – they reveal that the proliferation of NSERs
meant casualization or the 'gendering of jobs,' such that there was more
'women's work' in the market in the post-1970 period, on the one hand,
but continuing income and occupational polarization by sex (as well as
gender differentiation by employment relationship), on the other.

3.2 Public Policy Responses to the Spread of NSERs

Labour market trends illustrate that NSERs spread rapidly and that
segmentation among non-standard workers on the basis of gender, as
well as other characteristics such as age and immigration status, grew
in the post-1970 period. Thus, the increasingly porous character of the
standard/non-standard employment distinction did not result in gender de-differentiation in the labour market. Rather, instability in the
standard/non-standard employment distinction led to new patterns of
gender differentiation (i.e., sex segmentation along multiple axes). It
also contributed to elevating the role of gender as an organizing fea-

ture in the labour market, since gendered notions of 'standard' and 'non-standard' employment proved to be well entrenched at a normative level and, thus, ingrained in the design of labour policies. These patterns are evident in the responses to the spread of NSERs in the three policy areas under study.

A. Labour Law

As noted above, by the end of the post–Second World War period, Canada's fragmented system of labour law rested on a highly gendered standard/non-standard employment distinction. In the post-1970 period, structures of labour law remained virtually unchanged. With respect to collective bargaining legislation, federal and provincial governments still adopted the 'masculinized' SER as a model, even though it was a fading norm; efforts to advance broader-based bargaining in the late 1980s and 1990s at the provincial level were the only indications of a declining commitment to the SER on the part of policy-makers. Unions, too, fell into a holding pattern (especially where innovative organizing policies were concerned) after the early 1970s, when they first benefited from the extension of collective bargaining in the public sector. Not surprisingly, minimum standards legislation also continued to extend a relatively low threshold of benefits and entitlements to non-standard workers and non-unionized standard workers after 1970. Consequently, by the end of the late 1980s and the early 1990s, as NSERs proliferated, statutory mechanisms originally designed to regulate 'feminized' employment relationships extended to a wider segment of the labour force.

Collective Bargaining. By the early 1970s, the fragmented structure of labour law stabilized, amounting to considerable gains for certain groups of workers, especially public sector workers benefiting from the extension of collective bargaining rights. The benefits of this extension had a particularly strong impact on unionization among women, whose union density rose from 15.9 per cent in 1967 to a high of 29.8 per cent in 1992.[93] Women's greater access to collective bargaining rights, however, were primarily the product of the women's movement's efforts, especially its attempts to pressure the government to establish a Royal Commission on the Status of Women, rather than of the structure of collective bargaining itself. The Commission's report demonstrated pervasive sex discrimination in the labour market and in government legislation,[94] leading the government to dismantle discriminatory laws and develop programs to compensate for systemic gender biases embedded in various public institutions.

Despite the positive developments in the realm of formal equality policy, unionization rates began to stagnate in the mid-1990s due to the proliferation of small firms and NSERs, the contraction of public sector employment, and the two distinct paths followed in the public and private sectors in the organization of collective bargaining.[95] In the 1990s, there was a movement toward centralization in bargaining structures in the public sector; as employers, federal and provincial governments pursued centralization as a means of limiting expenditures.[96] In contrast, the tendency toward decentralization in bargaining structures accelerated in the private sector early in this decade. Although some large industries, such as the automobile, steel, pulp and paper, and meat-packing, resisted the decentralized bargaining structures advocated by labour boards in the post–Second World War period and established informal bargaining structures to limit fragmentation, through the provision of master agreements and pattern bargaining, industrial restructuring undermined compromise strategies such as pattern bargaining. For a lengthy period, the legal bargaining structure established by the bargaining-unit determination process did not determine the form in which bargaining took place in these industries.[97] However, the experience of these sectors in the 1980s and 1990s underscores the extent to which the decline of the (always tenuous) post–Second World War capital-labour accord undermined informal bargaining structures that required the voluntary agreement of all parties.

Together, these developments demonstrate that a collective bargaining regime prioritizing the interests of standard workers is less viable in a climate of deteriorating employment norms. In the post-1970 period, various provincial governments as well as leading unions began to openly recognize the limits of the collective bargaining regime forged under PC1003 for the first time since the Second World War. In their search for alternatives, some even explored the viability of broader-based bargaining structures, although their efforts led to few substantive outcomes.[98]

Building on the tradition of broader-based bargaining in Canada, largely the models used in construction and the Quebec decree system, a few provincial governments formulated proposals to encourage this type of bargaining structure for a brief period in the late 1980s and 1990s, several of which were quite comprehensive. Chief among these proposals was the Baigent-Ready report (1992), which proposed to initiate broader-based bargaining certification and collective bargaining in British Columbia. This report stressed the limits of the industrial model of unionism, criticized its fixation on the SER as a norm, and called for a form of sectoral certification. It recommended that unions at small firms, in sectors that have been historically underrepresented by trade unions, be allowed to amalgamate their bargaining units for the purpose of bargaining jointly with their employers. Thus, it encouraged sectors composed of low-waged, precariously employed workers to bargain together through the introduction of sectoral designation whereby one bargaining unit certification would cover all workers in a given sector or geographic region. It also proposed to permit the extension of sectoral agreements to new workplaces midway through a collective agreement, 'if the union could demonstrate sufficient support of additional locations within the sector,' a feature of the proposal that was highly controversial.[99]

Beyond its obvious merits,[100] the prime significance of Baigent-Ready was its capacity to de-link collective bargaining and the SER, arguably both male norms, and hence potentially upset gender differentiation forged through the rigid standard/non-standard employment distinction embedded in labour law. In this way, although its recommendations never came to fruition, this proposal, as well as complementary developments in other jurisdictions like Ontario, which briefly extended freedom of association rights to domestic workers in the early 1990s, signalled a slight shift in emphasis among legislators and policy-makers to take account of the rise of NSERs. But, given that broader-based bargaining legislation was not implemented on a large scale in the post-1970 period, collective bargaining legislation still remained bound by gendered notions of 'standard' and 'non-standard' employment.

Employment Standards Legislation. Even with some attempts on the part of provincial governments to decouple the SER and collective bargaining legislation, a strong relationship persisted in the 1970s and 1980s, and it continued to exist in the 1990s. The flip side of this trend was an enduring linkage between non-standard workers and basic employment standards legislation, labour laws that a greater number of workers were forced to resort to in the face of the spread of NSERs.

Following from the elimination of sex-specific minimum wages, the women's movement and organized labour successfully advocated for employment standards applicable to all workers regardless of their sex.[101] Consequently, minimum wages of general application, hours-of-work regulation, public holidays, paid vacations, and notice of termination became the norm in most provincial jurisdictions across Canada around 1970.[102] Women also began to benefit from the enactment of employment protections for pregnant women required to take temporary leave from employment: by 1973, protections for pregnant women were provided in the federal jurisdiction as well as in six provinces and, by the late 1980s, statutory parental leave and benefits were provided across Canada.[103] Still, this expansive set of minimum standards remained inferior to collective bargaining legislation given the exclusions permitted and the level of social and labour protections provided for those workers covered.[104] The province of Ontario is a case in point.

Continuing on the path followed in the post–Second World War era, the Employment Standards Act of Ontario still excluded agricultural workers, domestic workers, and many temporary workers from a range of standard protections after 1970; these exclusions were rooted in the nature of the work performed, such as piecework, the location of the workplace, and the minimum service requirements tied to some protections. In addition to these exclusions, the act replicated power differentials in the labour market in other crucial respects, by enforcing poor standards of compliance and linking protections to the existence of a single, continuous employment relationship. Four specific problems, common to this act and comparable legislation in other jurisdictions, are particularly worthy of emphasis here: namely, the failure to provide a living wage, a fact long criticized by the union movement, which advocates pegging the minimum wage at 70 per cent of the average industrial wage; the inattention to income and job security in a climate where employers resort to so-called flexibility-enhancing strategies designed to adjust the size of their workforces with limited penalties;[105] the absence of effective enforcement mechanisms to ensure that workers benefit from the protections to which they are entitled, a shortcoming that has especially severe consequences for homeworkers and domestic workers, whose conditions of employment often require special monitoring because of the location of the workplace;[106] and the routine exploitation of non-standard workers through, for example, the failure to mandate equivalent pay for all part-time and full-time workers in the same job or job class.[107]

Of these four shortcomings, the absence of provisions promoting parity between standard and non-standard workers in the act and its inattention to job security underscored its continued subordination to collective bargaining legislation. In both these cases, the act failed to be sensitive to the issue of equity. It is well established that part-time, temporary, and self-employed workers receive lower levels of social and labour protections than do standard workers and that, with the drive for greater 'flexibility' among employers, many of these workers engage in NSERs 'involuntarily.'[108] Moreover, in the 1980s and early 1990s, several prominent government commissions of inquiry made viable proposals to mandate prorated benefits and benefit schemes for non-standard workers, such as part-time workers, normally denied such coverage.[109] According to Judy Fudge, these proposals revealed that 'the lower wages of non-standard workers is not the only reason for the increasing rise of (non-standard) work. The extra cost of fringe benefits is central to understanding the shift to non-standard forms of work.'[110] The Royal Commission on the Economic Union and Development Prospects for Canada (1985), the *Report of the Commission of Inquiry into Part-Time Work* (1983), and the Economic Council of Canada's report *Good Jobs, Bad Jobs* (1990) all suggested that non-standard workers with a clear attachment to the labour force should be entitled to prorated benefits, offering statutory remedies to facilitate the extension of benefits to these workers and introducing the notion of portable benefit schemes or payment in lieu of benefits.[111]

Quebec was the only province to act on calls for greater parity between standard and non-standard workers. In 1990, it amended its Labour Code to make it illegal for an employer to pay an employee at a lower rate than that granted to other employees performing the same tasks in the same establishment for 'the sole reason that the employee usually works less hours each week' (s. 41.1). The intended effects of these changes were twofold: on a practical level, they were designed to ensure that part-time and full-time workers were treated equally with respect to vacation leaves and, more generally, to discourage employers from resorting to part-time work with the exclusive aim of lowering labour costs.[112] Despite important forward-looking changes in the Quebec Labour Code, most other provinces maintained a vague definition of 'the employee' in their employment standards legislation in the 1980s and 1990s, preventing the introduction of extension mechanisms. Most also failed to introduce prorated benefit schemes.[113] As a consequence, in Ontario and elsewhere, it was relatively easy for employers to manipulate the provisions in this type of legislation to avoid employment-related responsibilities even where workers were clearly economically dependent, as is common among the own-account self-employed.[114]

In addition to revealing the subordinate character of minimum standards legislation in comparison to collective bargaining legislation in the post-1970 period, the preceding illustrations highlight that the standard/non-standard employment distinction was also crucial to defining the terms of employment standards legislation in practically every province in Canada after 1970: non-standard workers were treated even less favourably than were standard workers under minimum standards legislation, and their inferior treatment rested partly on a vague (but exclusive) definition of the term 'employee'[115] reminiscent of the definition common under collective bargaining legislation. In most respects, increasing awareness of the rise of NSERs and their growing multiplicity was not matched by changes in employment standards legislation designed to better protect non-standard workers. In this way, the path followed in this arena of labour legislation parallels that of collective bargaining legislation, where some provinces entertained the prospect of embracing broader-based bargaining but a lack of intervention was the dominant pattern.

In the realm of policy design, legislators and policy-makers did little to displace the standard/non-standard employment distinction after 1970 and, in the face of this inaction, NSERs flourished. Moreover, minimum standards legislation remained 'feminized' in character – perpetuating the false presumption that the growing number of workers subject to it were 'secondary' or 'contingent' – and collective bargaining legislation continued to model itself on a fading 'masculine' norm. As a result, gender remained a pivotal organizing principle in labour law even though, at the level of the labour market, the relationship between gender differentiation and the standard/non-standard employment distinction grew more complicated.

B. From Unemployment Insurance to Employment Insurance

In the post-1970 period, patterns in unemployment insurance policy design and delivery were highly contradictory. On the one hand, policy-makers continued to demonstrate a bias toward the SER as a normative model of employment, basing the system on the standard/non-standard employment distinction. On the other hand, by the late 1990s they began to extend unemployment insurance coverage to new groups of non-standard workers, such as multiple job-holders and part-time workers working fewer than fifteen hours per week, and shifted to an 'hours system' rather than tying eligibility and benefits to the number of hours worked per week over a given period. The result was the emergence of a two-tiered unemployment insurance system that gestured at stemming casualization by providing previously ineligible workers with coverage, but still gave standard workers priority status and, in so doing, permitted the feminization of employment norms.

In 1970, unemployment insurance coverage extended to approximately 67 per cent of the workforce and policies that were explicitly discriminatory to women became virtually non-existent.[116] Marked by the introduction of a new Unemployment Insurance Act (1971), this decade represented a growth period for the program based on the government's recognition that traditional, stable jobs could not be assumed and, therefore, that workers required a stronger insurance system, especially in times of high unemployment. The 1971 act increased coverage to all paid workers except the self-employed, the elderly (70 years and over), and individuals earning less than one-fifth of the maximum insurable earnings. As well, eligibility requirements became less onerous under the act, benefit rates and maximum weekly benefits were increased, and sickness benefits were introduced. Maternity provisions were also introduced for the first time, although they imposed the most stringent requirements of any benefits under the Unemployment Insurance Act, thereby retaining the notion that pregnancy was a 'voluntary state of affairs' left over from the 1950s.[117] These stringent requirements were eventually relaxed despite the infamous *Bliss v. Attorney General of Canada* decision, which ruled them to be acceptable under the Bill of Rights. To account for increasing regional disparities, the unemployment insurance program also provided an extra six to eighteen weeks of benefits to workers in geographic areas where unemployment rates exceeded the national average.[118] As well, the 1971 reforms introduced some funding from general revenue in addition to payroll taxes to support extended benefits in high unemployment areas and special insurance for self-employed fishers and their crews.[119] The only two minor drawbacks were an increase in the waiting period before receiving benefits and the taxation of unemployment insurance benefits. Indeed, unemployment insurance policy was at its height in the early 1970s and this translated into an expanded, though still 'masculine,' conception of the standard worker but, at the same time, a recognition that women workers required certain 'special' provisions such as benefits during maternity and pregnancy leaves. The 'golden age' of unemployment insurance lasted only briefly, as changes in 1976 initiated a new emphasis in this policy domain. These changes entailed an increase in the maximum disqualification period for 'voluntary leavers' from three to six weeks, disentitlements for persons over 65 years of age, and the elimination of special benefit rates for low-income persons with dependants or the chronically unemployed in favour of one uniform benefit rate (67%) for all claimants.[120] They were succeeded by an increase in the number of weeks of insurable earnings needed to qualify for unemployment insurance from eight to ten weeks to ten to fourteen weeks (1978), lowered benefit rates of 60 per cent (1977–9), and the introduction of tougher qualifying requirements for 'marginal workers' deemed to have a weak attachment to the labour force in the next three years. In the late 1970s, the definition of marginal workers included part-time workers with fewer than twenty hours per week, new labour force entrants, re-entrants, and 'repeat users' of unemployment insurance. As Jane Pulkingham incisively notes: 'Unlike the amendments pursued in the 1950s, these changes do not appear overtly to be designed to target and exclude women. Nevertheless, they were of particular significance for women, and arguably, the underlying rationale was to disqualify a significant proportion of the burgeoning ranks of women (especially married women) entering or re-entering the paid labour force during this period.'[121] The dramatic rise in women's labour force participation from 1975 onward supports Pulkingham's assertion, but her observation points to an ever more important development. In the arena of unemployment insurance policy in the late 1970s, gender differentiation was maintained by granting standard workers privileged access to this program. Even as the government expanded the definition of the SER to include largely male seasonal workers and self-employed fishers (unquestionably 'non-standard' workers), various groups of non-standard workers remained excluded from coverage. In lieu of evoking explicitly discriminatory provisions, the government effectively used its discretionary powers to feminize certain forms of dependency.[122]

In the period between 1979 and 1989, there were few notable changes in the design and delivery of unemployment insurance. In the 1980s, the program rested on the standard/non-standard employment distinction and achieved gender differentiation along this axis, and it did not depart from its aims as an unemployment insurance program. Although the mid- to late-1970s marked the end of the 'golden age' of unemployment insurance provision, for the next decade, the focus was on fine-tuning the program rather than refashioning it completely.[123]

Changes to unemployment insurance after the early 1990s contrast sharply with those of the 1970s and 1980s. Beginning in 1989/90, the Canadian government restructured dramatically the unemployment insurance program, changing its financing from the tripartite arrangement to one that was financed by workers and employers only, a development that coincided with the introduction of its deficit reduction program. Still, the government retained its administrative role, introducing some of the most drastic cutbacks ever introduced to the program. Following policy prescriptions at the international level, forged by institutions like the OECD in the early 1990s, benefit rates were lowered from 60 to 57 per cent of employment income (except for low-income beneficiaries with dependants), stricter reporting requirements were imposed for claimants, and 'voluntary quits' were disqualified from unemployment.[124] More restrictions to the duration of claims were also imposed and entrance requirements rose from twelve to twenty weeks.[125] The ratio of unemployment insurance claimants to the unemployed dropped considerably in the 1990s as a consequence of these changes. As the Canadian Labour Congress notes, '[In] 1990, before the government began slashing benefits, 87% of the unemployed were U.I. beneficiaries and at the end of 1994, 58% were receiving U.I.'[126] Still, the federal government proceeded with changes to unemployment insurance in its 1995 budget, cutting the program by 10 per cent and announcing a national social security review. A discussion paper produced by Human Resources Development Canada, entitled 'Agenda: Jobs and Growth' (1994), and a report of the Standing Committee on Human Resources Development, entitled 'Security, Opportunity and Fairness: Canadians Renewing Their Social Programs' (1995), were the products of this review and they laid the groundwork for future changes.

These discussion papers led to a new 'employment insurance' program, phased in between 1996 and 1997, which initiated a switch to an hours system as opposed to a system based on calendar weeks; the extension of coverage to all part-time workers; the introduction of an 'intensity rule'; and the introduction of a family income supplement for claimants with dependant children in low-income families. These changes are exacerbating gender differentiation in the labour market in the late 1990s.[127] The new family income supplement has been criticized for its introduction of family income testing – that is, using the family, rather than individual, income to determine need.[128] Although an early gender impact study commissioned by Human Resources Development Canada claimed that women will be the main beneficiaries of the supplement because they are more likely to be low-income claimants – it suggested that lone-parent families headed by women will see their benefits increase by an average of 11% – other reports indicate that women will be disproportionately excluded from the supplement because they are 'secondary' earners.[129] The larger symbolic consequences of this change, however, are more far-reaching than its immediate practical outcomes. Using 'the family' as a unit of analysis for determining benefits assumes that there is an equitable distribution of income and resources in households: it is a circuitous route toward denying women an important individual source of income and is, thus, reminiscent of the early post–Second World War period when married women were excluded from coverage altogether. In contrast to the family income supplement, the extension of coverage to part-time workers appears to be a progressive measure, at least on the surface, in that it has the potential to reduce the centrality of the notions of 'standard' and 'non-standard' employment in determining coverage. However, teamed with the introduction of an hours system, this development is resulting in contradictory outcomes. While the new employment insurance program formally extends coverage to part-time workers and multiple job-holders, their likelihood of accessing coverage is minimal. Owing to the increased number of hours of work required to qualify for employment insurance (and the 35-hour per week conversion), the number of hours required to qualify has increased dramatically. Under unemployment insurance, the standard claimant was required to work the equivalent of 180 to 300 hours in the 52 weeks preceding the claim (adjusted to regional unemployment levels); under employment insurance, however, s/he is required to work 420 to 700 hours; the equivalent figures for 'new entrants' are 300 hours and 910 hours. Thus, while many part-time workers will be insured for the first time, the nature of the qualifying requirements will render many benefits out of their reach[130] unless they increase their hours or become multiple job-holders. Women are more likely to be affected adversely by these requirements because they are both the majority of part-time workers and, based on 1993 figures, they account for over three-quarters of all workers working between fifteen and thirty-five hours per week.[131] In contrast, full-timers working thirty-five hours or more, the majority of whom are men, are virtually unaffected by the new legislation, except by the reduction in the maximum number of weeks (45 weeks beginning in 1997) of benefits. Essentially, this example illustrates that, in the late 1990s, the government extended unemployment insurance coverage to non-standard workers (specifically part-time workers and multiple job-holders) with one hand and limited their access to unemploy-ment insurance benefits with the other. On the surface, the standard/non-standard employ-ment distinction became less central to the design of employment insurance. However, at a deeper level, it still held sway as a source of gender differentiation.

C. Employment Practices in the Federal Public Service
The post-1970 period was an era of both continuity and change for civil servants in Canada. Building on the Public Service Employment Act and the Public Service Staff Relations Act, which provided the framework for collective bargaining for federal government employees and helped bring women into the union movement, equality was the mantra of the period. Women workers were no longer formally barred from permanent positions and jobs in the highest grades of the civil service, and the movement to attain equal pay for work of equal value gained force. Despite these gains, however, employment norms remained gendered in the federal public service. Here, the rate of growth of women's employment (68.3%) doubled men's (32.4%) between 1970 and 1976; yet in 1977 three-quarters of women still performed clerical work, in contrast to 12.5 per cent of men.[132] Women were also largely relegated to jobs labelled 'administrative support' (58.5%), a category composed mainly of clerical sub-categories.[133] These parallel, but in many ways conflicting, developments led the standard/non-standard employment distinction to serve as a central axis of gender differentiation in the public service into the 1980s. However, just as women gained entry into SERs, especially in management and various professional posts as a consequence of the royal commission,[134] terms and conditions of employment in the service began to deteriorate, a development overlooked by the organized women's movement's owing to its emphasis on lobbying for equality policies. Women's continuing second-class status as employees of the federal government was even reproduced inside the Public Service Alliance of Canada (PSAC), which had the largest number of women members of any union in the country by the mid-1970s. In this period, male dominance in PSAC was largely the product of two variables. First, conservatism in union politics meant

that men were over-represented in the top leadership positions.[135] Second, the fact that women were disproportionately represented in temporary and term appointments made them less able to attain membership in the union (even if they were routinely fired and rehired) due to the legislated practice of excluding temporary workers with short-term contracts from collective agreements. To complicate matters further, section 7 of the Public Service Staff Relations Act excluded the classification system (which effectively relegated women to the lowest tiers of the service) from the scope of collective bargaining, making formal bargaining structures less useful in facilitating women's equality gains in the service.[136] Unionization cultivated a productive adversarial relationship between the state (as an employer) and civil servants, but for a lengthy period in the 1970s PSAC and other public-sector unions encountered formidable obstacles to redressing gender inequalities based on a classification system underpinned by notions of SERs as male and NSERs as female.

Given the limited scope of collective bargaining in the federal public service, and the continuing pattern of sex-segmentation in its ranks, women's groups and unions channelled their efforts to eliminate gender inequality through reform-oriented political means. For example, wielding the report of the Royal Commission on the Status of Women, the National Action Committee on the Status of Women (NAC) and, eventually, PSAC argued that women's low status in the public service was intricately connected to their low job classification. Notably, however, the royal commission's finding that women were concentrated in clerical jobs in the lowest tiers of the service did not immediately result in statutory intervention aimed at altering the classification scheme.[137] Nor did it lead to the extension of the scope of the Public Service Staff Relations Act or even allow civil servants unions' to intervene on this issue. Instead, it led social movement groups to focus on attaining equal value legislation. Although attempts at equal pay for work of equal value legislation were not very fruitful in the 1980s, the strength of the equality discourse was underscored by the introduction of equal value provisions in the complaint-based Canada Human Rights Act.[138]

The success of the equality campaign should not be underplayed, as it galvanized the women's movement and forged links between the union movement and the women's movement. Still, it contributed little to decentring the standard/non-standard employment distinction and the type of gender differentiation that it generated. Alongside the apparent success of the equality strategy at a political level, several sets of developments in the late 1970s pre-empted the positive economic gains that it could have delivered for women. Public service expansion ceased in the late 1970s, dropping by 4.4 per cent alone between 1978 and 1979. Notably, at the same time as employment declined in the federal public service, women's concentration grew within it. Men's employment in the service dropped by 6.2 per cent between 1975 and 1980 and women's grew by 7.1 per cent.[139] Second, non-standard forms of employment, especially temporary employment through temporary help agencies, contract work, and part-time employment became more common in the service; a range of financial incentives, discouraging managers from increasing their operating costs through the provision of fringe benefits to permanent employees and encouraging them to increase indirect employment costs by hiring casual employees, contributed to this trend.[140]

These developments were exaggerated by the climate of restraint in the federal public service in the 1980s. In this decade, parallel to the introduction of a sex equality guarantee in the Constitution of 1982 and the endorsement by all three political parties of equal pay for work of equal value, the federal government introduced wage controls that targeted its own employees and suspended their collective bargaining rights.[141] The Public Sector Compensation Restraint Act (Bill C-124) rolled back the wages of public-sector workers in signed agreements with increases above 5 per cent and 6 per cent, and it temporarily removed their right to strike and bargain collectively by arbitrarily extending existing collective agreements for two years. Although most of its measures were phased out by 1985, the act symbolized a growing willingness on the part of the federal government to limit the free collective bargaining rights of civil servants. It also corresponded with the increasing resort to ad hoc back-to-work legislation on the parts of federal and provincial governments, so that there were forty-three cases between 1980 and 1987, undermining the benefits and entitlements that made up the SER package extended to civil servants in the late 1960s. Moreover, when PSAC challenged the limits placed on its members' collective bargaining rights, the Supreme Court of Canada first merely confirmed the Treasury Boards' prior classification of civil servants as 'essential' (and thereby legitimized the conservative approach taken by the Public Service Staff Relations Board in designating 'essential' workers), and subsequently upheld '6 and 5' on the basis that neither collective bargaining rights nor the freedom to strike were protected by the clause on freedom of association in the Canadian Charter of Rights.[142] At the same time as women civil servants made legal equality gains,[143] civil servants as a whole endured rollbacks in their wages, their employment contracts,[144] and their rights as workers. These developments were by-products of the tendency toward centralization in the structure of public-sector collective bargaining and of the government's embrace of monetarist economic policies in the 1980s.

Of course, restraints and cutbacks in public administration did not thwart PSAC's or NAC's work entirely in the 1980s. But their successes were limited both within the broader union movement, where it was especially difficult to implement equal pay for work of equal value policies in less prosperous economic times,[145] and within the federal bureaucracy.[146]

By the mid-1990s, even government researchers established that privatization, deregulation, limits on collective bargaining rights, and, more specifically, the rise of NSERs in the public service were cause for concern – the Civil Service Commission went as far as suggesting that formal equality gains may have come at the expense of employment security.[147] Still, the Liberal government, elected in 1993, reduced the public sector by an equivalent of 15,000 full-time positions during their first sixteen months in power and eliminated 45,000 more jobs between 1995 and 1998.[148] Elsewhere, I have argued that the accelerated rise in women's labour force participation rates in the late 1970s and 1980s was accompanied by the feminization of employment and employment norms more broadly – that is, the spread of NSERs characterized by low pay, poor benefits, and a high level of insecurity that have been historically associated with women. Nowhere is this conclusion more clear than in the federal public service, where the 1980s and 1990s were marked by the rise of NSERs and deteriorating conditions of employment against a backdrop of a well-articulated, legally focused equality agenda.

4. Conclusion: The Feminization of Employment Norms

This chapter began with the observation that not only is men's deteriorating economic situation an increasing source of public concern but, with the passage of over thirty years of equality policy, there is a growing tendency among social commentators to view men's recent misfortunes as the flip side of women's gains in the labour market since the

1970s. Taking this observation as its point of departure, this chapter used the standard/non-standard employment distinction as a lens into the differences between the post–Second World War and the post–1970 gender orders in the Canadian labour market.

The standard/non-standard employment distinction first became a principal axis of gender differentiation in the labour market in the period immediately following the Second World War. In the aftermath of the Great Depression, when women were explicitly excluded from various segments of the labour market through marriage bars and other statutory limitations to their employment, and again after the Second World War, when women were temporarily integrated into the labour market more fully, the state, unions, and employers used this distinction to establish labour market segmentation along gendered lines. Consequently, women came to predominate in certain NSERs and in certain sectors and occupations, while SERs became the preserve of men.

With the sharp rise of NSERs after 1970, patterns of gender differentiation in the labour market shifted, upsetting the relatively consistent gendered logic of the standard/non-standard employment distinction. Beginning in the late 1970s, men increasingly engaged in NSERs so that, by the late 1980s, gendered divisions became more apparent *among* non-standard workers. Still, the normative pre-eminence of the SER continued at the level of labour policy, where, for example, non-standard workers still had difficulties accessing collective bargaining rights and standard workers remained the chief beneficiaries of the transformed employment insurance system. Changes in one important sphere of employment for women – the federal public service – confounded these new patterns of gender differentiation. The equality strategy advanced by both organized labour and the women's movement certainly contributed to numerous gains for women – for example, the federal government facilitated the promotion of women to managerial ranks and restructured the discriminatory classification system. But formal legal equality proved ineffective in curbing the spread of NSERs and atypical employment contracts in the 1980s and 1990s as well as the inferior conditions of employment that routinely come in their trail.

The sum of contemporary trends is a complex mixture of new patterns of gender differentiation in the labour market and deteriorating (but still gendered) employment norms. Divisions between men and women engaged in specific forms of non-standard employment, such as self-employment, multiple job-holding, and temporary work, and in different sorts of NSERs are growing in the late 1990s. Furthermore, labour laws, employment insurance policies and employment policies, and practices in the federal public service are either facilitating deteriorating conditions of employment or failing to stem casualization. Magnifying 'new' patterns of gender differentiation in the labour market and developments at the policy level that sustain them, perhaps the most significant development in the 1990s is the feminization of employment norms. This trend entails more than simply women's mass entry into the labour market; it amounts to the spread of *feminized* employment relationships, a development rooted in the enduring relationship between the abstract notion of 'non-standard' employment and so-called women's work and the lack of fit between labour policies central to the occupational welfare state and NSERs. Granted, not all NSERs are either precarious or 'feminized' and there is growing (often gendered) polarization in the wages and conditions of employment of non-standard workers. Still, employment contracts associated with NSERs are generally inferior to the standard employment contract. Equally important, these contracts, as well as the terms and conditions of employment that they dictate, reflect long-standing assumptions of how best to regulate employment relationships associated with women perceived to be 'secondary' breadwinners and/or workers presumed to have alternative sources of subsistence beyond the wage. In this sense, they are 'feminized.' In this way, gender remains a vital organizing feature in the contemporary Canadian labour market, even though certain NSERs are no longer primarily limited to one sex (i.e., women). The task of illustrating that the standard/non-standard employment distinction underpinned a gendered segmentation strategy endorsed by employers, the state, and organized labour in the post–Second World War period is relatively straightforward. It is far more difficult to reveal the persistently gendered character of 'standard' and 'non-standard' employment relationships in a labour market where this distinction is both becoming more porous and is no longer the primary axis of gender differentiation. Still, the persistence of these gendered categories of employment and their centrality to labour policies pose numerous challenges in the late 1990s precisely because of the proliferation of NSERs – particularly the challenge to improve the subordinate and feminized labour and social protections tied to NSERs, to which a growing number of workers (female and male) are subject.

Notes

I am grateful to Caroline Andrew, David Cheal, Judy Fudge, Danielle Juteau, Gerald Kernerman, Peter Li, Chris Southcott, Vasanthi Srinivasan, Terry Wotherspoon, Nancy Zukewich, and Participants in the Institute for Research on Women (Rutgers University) seminar on the public sphere for their comments on earlier drafts of this paper. I also thank the Social Sciences and Humanities Research Council of Canada and the Policy Research Secretariat for funding this project.

1 See F. Bird et al., *Report of the Royal Commission on the Status of Women* (Ottawa: Ministry of Supply and Services, 1970), 2, 105.
2 Despite the declining wage gap between men and women, especially those in full-time, full-year employment relationships, there is considerable evidence of the persistent revenue gap between women and men in the workforce as a whole – even after taking into account factors such as educational attainment, field of specialization, years of work experience, and hours worked. For recent studies documenting the revenue gap between men and women, see, Statistics Canada, 'Earnings of Men and Women, 1997,' Catalogue 13-217-XIB (Ottawa: Statistics Canada, Income Statistics Division, 1998); David Coish, 'The Wage Gap between Men and Women: An Update,' Catalogue 750002MPE95014 (Ottawa: Statistics Canada, Income Research Paper Series, 1995); and Marie Drolet, 'The Persistent Gap: New Evidence on the Canadian Gender Wage Gap,' Catalogue 75F0002MIE99008 (Ottawa: Statistics Canada, Income Research Paper Series, 1999).
3 See 'Tomorrow's Second Sex,' *The Economist*, November 1998, A23; 'Where Have All the Smart Men Gone?' *Globe and Mail*, 28 Dec. 1998, A18; and Barbara Turnbull, 'Young Males Losing Ground in Wage Stakes,' *Toronto Star*, 28 July 1998, A2.
4 For a discussion of the deteriorating situation of young men, see David Cheal in this volume.
5 For example, according to a recent editorial in The Globe and Mail, which juxtaposes women's economic gains since the 1970s to young men's deteriorating labour market position: 'The female inequities of 30 years have blinded us to the male inequities of today. There is still far more worry about the under-representation of women in fields such as engineering and hard sciences than widespread notice of the female-dominated numbers everywhere else. There is more concern about a glass ceiling in a woman's workplace than the unseen concrete ceiling that under-aged men are constructing for themselves.' ('Where Have All The Smart Men Gone?').

6 See Anne Duffy and Norene Pupo, *The Part-time Paradox* (Toronto: McClelland and Stewart, 1992); Monica Townson, *Non-Standard Work: The Implications for Pension Policy and Retirement Readiness*, (Ottawa: Women's Bureau, Human Resources Development Canada, July 1997); and Leah F. Vosko, *Temporary Work: The Gendered Rise of a Precarious Employment Relationship* (Toronto: University of Toronto Press, 2000).

7 See Jane Jenson, 'The Talents of Women, the Skills of Men,' in S. Wood, ed., *The Transformation of Work?* (London: Unwin Hyman, 1989), 141; and J. Rubery, 'Women in the Labour Market: A Gender Equality Perspective' (Paris: OECD, October 1998).

8 See Patricia Armstrong and Hugh Armstrong, *The Double Ghetto*, 3rd ed. (Toronto: McClelland and Steward, 1994); and René Morissette, 'Declining Earnings of Young Men,' *Canadian Social Trends* (Autumn 1997): 8.

9 See Ulrich Mückenberger, 'Non-Standard Forms of Employment in the Federal Republic of Germany: The Role and Effectiveness of the State,' in G. Rogers and J. Rogers, eds, *Precarious Employment in Labour Market Regulation: The Growth of Atypical Employment in Western Europe* (Belgium: International Institute for Labour Studies, 1989), 267; and Grant Schellenberg and Christopher Clark, *Temporary Employment in Canada: Profiles, Patterns and Policy Considerations* (Ottawa: Canadian Council on Social Development, 1996).

10 I characterize the SER as a 'normative' model of employment for two reasons. First, by labelling this employment relationship a norm, I aim to avoid over-generalizing about the character of employment in the two consecutive time periods under study. Second, I use the term as an interpretative device, helpful in examining the nature and form of employment trends and the social forces related to them. I take norms to be conventions of behaviour and standards of value that have the capacity to exercise a coercive influence and have descriptive and prescriptive dimensions. In this way, the SER is not taken to represent a singular material employment relationship even though references to 'standard work' were common in the wake of the post–Second World War capital-labour entente. Rather, it is considered an ideal-typical model upon which policies and practices pertaining to employment were based after the war.

11 See Brenda Lipsett and Marc Reesor, *Flexible Work Arrangements: Evidence from the 1991 and 1995 Survey of Work Arrangements* (Ottawa: Human Resources and Development Canada, 1997); and Leah F. Vosko, 'The Rise of the Temporary Help Industry in Canada and Its Relationship to the Decline of the Standard Employment Relationship as a Normative Model of Employment,' background paper prepared for Collective Reflection on a Changing Workplace (Ottawa: The Labour Program, HRDC, 1997).

12 To be clear, the conceptual distinction made between SERs and NSERs in this paper is not analogous to the distinction that dual labour market theorists make between jobs in the 'primary' and 'secondary' sectors. Not only do workers engage in SERs and NSERs in all segments of the labour market, but notions of 'primary' and 'secondary' are overly rigid. Moreover, dual labour market theory is ahistorical and its neglect of characteristics such as sex, ethnicity, and race in shaping the labour supply is well documented by third-generation segmented labour market theorists. For this reason, this inquiry is preoccupied with employment *relationships* that cut across the labour market and with racialized gender-based labour market differentiation. See J. Rubery and F. Wilkinson, *Employer Strategy and the Labour Market* (Oxford: Oxford University Press, 1994); and J. Peck, *Work Place: The Social Regulation of Labor Markets* (New York: Guildford Press, 1996).

13 Throughout this chapter, I take the social category 'gender' to encompass the entire system of relationships that may include sex but are not necessarily determined by sex. And I define 'gendering' as the social production of gender that generates differential experiences, meanings, and results for women and men. See Joan Scott, *Gender and the Politics of History* (New York: Columbia University Press, 1988); Joan Acker, 'Class, Gender and the Relations of Distribution,' *Signs* 13.3 (1988): 473; and Gillian Creese, 'Gendering Collective Bargaining: From Men's Rights to Women's Issues,' *Canadian Review of Sociology and Anthropology* 33.4 (1996): 437.

14 See Patricia Armstrong, 'The Feminization of the Labour Force: Harmonizing Down in a Global Economy,' in I. Bakker, ed., *Rethinking Restructuring: Gender and Change in Canada* (Toronto: University of Toronto Press, 1996), 30.

15 See Jane Jenson, 'Part-time Employment and Women: A Range of Strategies,' in Bakker, *Rethinking Restructuring*, 92; and Rubery, 'Women in the Labour Market,' 5.

16 See Vosko, *Temporary Work*, chap. 1.

17 Polarization between women by age is an increasing source of discussion among feminist scholars. For example, in referring to patterns of employment in the United Kingdom, Sylvia Walby notes: 'To a large extent, women are polarising between those, typically younger, educated and employed, who engage in new patterns of gender relations somewhat convergent with men, and those, particularly disadvantaged women, typically older and less educated, who built their trajectories around patterns of private patriarchy. These new patterns are intertwined with diversities and inequalities generated by social divisions including class, ethnicity and

region' (*Gender Transformations* [London: Routledge, 1997], 145). While employment patterns in Canada conform with Walby's observations for the United Kingdom in some respects, a more finely grained description is necessary in the Canadian context. As part 3 below demonstrates, women of the baby boom generation (i.e., those 40–54 years of age) are fairing better in the Canadian labour market than those aged 55 and over, but many young educated women (like their male counterparts) are confronting increasing economic hardships. And gender differences in earnings still persist in all age groups.

18 While I opt to use the term *feminization* of employment to characterize the restructuring that is taking place in the labour market, I am cognizant of some of the potential drawbacks to this choice of phraseology. In particular, I am aware of (and concerned about) the problem of associating women with what are largely a negative set of labour market trends; this problem was widely discussed, for example, in debates over the most appropriate way to label a phenomenon that has come to be known as the 'feminization of poverty' in the late 1980s. Still, I deliberately use the term 'feminization' as the most suitable available option for keeping both sex and gender central to our understanding of contemporary labour market trends and, at the same time, in tension with one another.

19 See Graham Lowe, *Women in the Administrative Revolution: The Feminization of Clerical Work* (Toronto: University of Toronto Press, 1987); Nicole Morgan, *The Equality Game: Women in the Federal Public Service, 1908–1987* (Ottawa: Canadian Advisory Council on the Status of Women, 1988); and Ruth Pierson and Beth Light, *No Easy Road: Women in Canada 1920s to 1960s* (Toronto: New Hogtown Press, 1990).

20 Although this chapter deals primarily with state policies designed to secure the SER, it is important to note that various branches of organized labour supported discriminatory policies that were consistent with 'securing a male breadwinner norm' in the post–Second World War period. See Alvin Finkel, *Business and Social Reform in the Thirties* (Toronto: Lorimer, 1979); and Julie Guard, 'Womanly Innocence and Manly Self-Respect: Gendered Challenges to Labour's Postwar Compromise,' in C. Gonick et al., eds, *Labour Gains, Labour Pains: 50 Years of PC 1003* (Winnipeg, Society for Socialist Studies / Fernwood Publishing, 1995), 119.

Organized labour's support for the male breadwinner norm in the 1940s was intricately tied to the evolution of the 'sheltered proletariat' that grew out of the post-war compromise (i.e., the sizeable group of primarily male blue-collar workers employed in large firms and benefiting from the collective bargaining rights prescribed under PC 1003). Unions made considerable gains in this era, since blue-collar workers earned the right to 'lay claim to a respectability that had previously only been associated with skilled craftworkers' (see Guard, 'Womanly Innocence,' 120). However, these gains led many of organized labour's more radical segments to abandon a wider political platform that involved seeking social justice for all working people and wealth redistribution among various segments of the working class as well as between women and men. More specifically, the gains led groups like the Canadian Congress of Labour (CCL), which had called for maternity benefits and day nurseries for working mothers during the war, to abandon such issues in exchange for the notion of the 'family wage,' and the Trades and Labour Congress (TLC), which was always conservative when it came to women's issues, to remain divided over the issue of whether married women should be eligible for unemployment insurance. See Finkel, *Business and Social Reform*; and Guard, ibid.

21 See R. Campbell, *The Full-Employment Objective in Canada, 1945–1985: Historical, Conceptual, and Comparative Perspectives* (Ottawa: Economic Council of Canada, 1991).

22 See Bob Russell, *Back to Work? Labour, State, and Industrial Relations in Canada* (Scarborough, ON: Nelson, 1990).

23 See Julie White, *Women and Unions* (Ottawa: Canadian Advisory Council on the Status of Women, 1980), 38.

24 See Armstrong and Armstrong, *The Double Ghetto*, 17–18.

25 See Donald Avery, *Reluctant Host* (Toronto: McClelland and Stewart, 1995).

26 See Varpu Lindstrom-Best, '"I Won't Be a Slave": Finnish Domestics in Canada, 1911–1930,' in *Looking into My Sister's Eyes: An Exploration in Women's History* (Toronto: Multiculturalism Historical Society of Ontario, 1986), 32.

27 See Agnes Calliste, 'Race, Gender and Canadian Immigration Policy: Blacks from the Caribbean, 1900–1932,' *Journal of Canadian Studies* 28.4 (1993): 131; Franca Iacovetta, '"Primitive Villagers and Uneducated Girls": Canada Recruits Domestics for Italy, 1951–52,' *Canadian Women's Studies* 7.4 (1986): 14; and Makeda Silvera, *Silenced* (Toronto: Sister Vision Press, 1983).

28 See Sedef Arat-Kroc, '"Importing Housewives": Non-Citizen Domestic Workers and the Crisis of the Domestic Sphere in Canada,' in M. Luxton, H. Rosenberg, and S. Arat-Kroc, eds, *Through the Kitchen Window* (Toronto: Garamond, 1990), 81.

29 See Lowe, *Women in the Administrative Revolution*, 49.

30 For example, as I have argued elsewhere, beginning in the 1950s, the temporary-help industry positioned the temporary-help agency as a 'halfway house for housewives,' a labour market intermediary involved in interviewing, testing, and placing women clerical workers in temporary posi-

tions to serve employers' needs in a context where full-time, permanent
work for married women was prohibited in various segments of the public
and private sectors. See Vosko, *Temporary Work*, chap. 3.

31 See Greg Albo, 'The "New Realism" and Canadian Workers,' in *Canadian
Politics: An Introduction* (Toronto: Broadview Press, 1990), 471; and Leo Panitch and Donald Swartz, *The Assault on Trade Union Freedoms: From Consent
to Coercion* (Toronto: Garamond Press, 1993).

32 See Creese, 'Gendering Collective Bargaining' Ann Forrest, 'Securing the
Male Breadwinner: A Feminist Interpretation of PC 1003,' in C.Gonick et
al., eds, *Labour Gains, Labour Pains: 50 Years of PC 1003* (Winnipeg: Society
for Socialist Studies / Fernwood Publishing, 1995), 139; and Judy Fudge,
'The Gendered Dimension of Labour Law: Why Women Need Inclusive
Unionism and Broader-based Bargaining,' in L. Briskin and P. McDermott,
eds, *Women Challenging Unions: Feminism, Militancy and Democracy* (Toronto: University of Toronto Press, 1993), 231.

33 See J. O'Grady, 'Beyond the Wagner Act, What Then?' in D. Drache, ed.,
Getting on Track (Montreal and Kingston: McGill-Queen's University Press,
1991), 153.

34 See Rosemary Warskett, 'The Politics of Difference and the Inclusiveness
within the Canadian Labour Market,' *Economic and Industrial Democracy* 17
(1996): 587.

35 See Judy Fudge and Leah Vosko, 'Gender, Segmentation and the Standard
Employment Relationship in Canadian Labour Law and Policy,' *Economic
and Industrial Democracy* (forthcoming).

36 See Warskett, 'The Politics of Difference,' 595.

37 See Fudge, 'The Gendered Dimension of Labour Law,' 231.

38 See Ann Forrest, 'Bargaining Units and Bargaining Power,' *Relations Industrielles / Indutrial Relations* 41.4 (1986): 840.

39 Other criteria included the practices and history of collective bargaining;
the desirability of separating white- and blue-collar employees; the aversion to 'fragmentation' within bargaining units; agreement between parties; the desires of employees; the organized structure of employees;
geography; and traditional methods of unionization.

40 See Creese, 'Gendering Collective Bargaining,' 437.

41 See Craig Heron and Robert Storey, 'Work and Struggle in the Canadian
Steel Industry, 1900–1950,' in C. Heron and R. Storey, eds, *On the Job: Con-
fronting the Labour Process in Canada* (Kingston and Montreal: McGill-
Queen's University Press, 1986).

42 Citing case law in Ontario in the 1960s and 1970s, Ann Forrest highlights
the gender-biased assumptions of the labour board, whose long-time doc-

trine implied that most part-time workers not only chose to engage in this form of employment but were secondary breadwinners: '[The practice of creating] separate units for part-time workers ... reflects the view that these workers do not share a community of interest with full-time employees. The former are "primarily concerned with maintaining a convenient work schedule which permits them to accommodate the other important aspects of their lives with their work and with obtaining short-term immediate improvements in remuneration, rather than with obtaining life insurance, pension, disability, and other benefit plans; extensive seniority clauses; and other long-term benefits." Accordingly, part-time workers will be segregated at the request of either party.' (see Forrest, 'Bargaining Units,' 846).

43 See Abdul Rashid, 'Seven Decades of Wage Changes,' *Perspectives on Labour and Income*, Summer 1993: 9.

44 See H. Arthurs, 'Developing Industrial Citizenship: A Challenge for Canada's Second Century,' *Canadian Bar Review* 45 (1995): 787.

45 See Constance Backhouse, *Petticoats and Prejudice: Women and the Law in Nineteenth-Century Canada* (Toronto: Women's Press, 1991); Veronica Strong-Boag, 'The Girl of the New Day: Canadian Working Women in the 1920s,' *Labour / Le Travail* 4 (1979), 31–64.

46 Minimum wages for women were accepted by unions, by early maternalist women's organizations and, eventually, by employers for distinct reasons. In the case of unions, they were perceived to protect male wages from downward pressures. In contrast, in the wake of the First World War, maternalist women's groups like the National Council of Women of Canada (NCWC) viewed state intervention in the area of minimum wages for women to be necessary for two reasons. First, The loss of young male soldiers was predicted to limit women's chances of marriage. Second, the NCWC saw minimum wages as an essential part of a package of protections that would decrease infant mortality. As McCallum notes: 'Once NCWC accepted the link between low wages and poor mothering, it added the minimum wage to its list of demands for pure milk and water, government-inspected abattoirs, well-baby clinics, school nurses, public parks, and a federal department of health ... [Its maternalist approach] helped discredit the argument that because poverty was a matter of individual depravity, the state should not intervene even to enforce a subsistence wage.' (See Margaret McCallum, 'Keeping Women in Their Place: The Minimum Wage in Canada,' *Labour / Le Travail* 17 [1986]: 30.) Ironically, when employers' organizations, such as the Canadian Manufacturers' Association, began to support a minimum wage for women, they used the arguments of the NCWC. In this case, however, their support for a minimum

wage for women was rooted in the failed efforts of a National Industrial Conference (in 1919) to introduce compulsory collective bargaining, the 8-hour day, and a living wage for all adults. On the surface, employers advocated minimum wages for women to demonstrate a 'conciliatory spirit.' At a deeper level, however, their support for minimum wages for women came at a time when they were attacking proposals for fair wages for all adults. In this context, a minimum wage for women was critical to maintaining labour market segmentation given the growing militancy among workers as a whole. (See Bob Russell, 'A Fair or Minimum Wage? Women Workers, the State, and the Origins of Wage Regulation in western Canada,' *Labour / Le Travail* 28 [1991]: 59–88.)

47 See McCallum, 'Keeping Women in Their Place'; Jane Ursel, *Private Lives, Public Policy: 100 Years of State Intervention in the Family (Toronto: Women's Press, 1992).*

48 See L. Kealey, 'Women and Labour during World War II: Women Workers and the Minimum Wage in Manitoba,' in M. Kinnear, ed., *First Days, Fighting Days: Women in Manitoba History* (Regina: Canadian Plains Research Centre, 1987); McCallum, 'Keeping Women in Their Place,' 29–56.

49 See Gillian Creese, 'Sexual Equality and the Minimum Wage in B.C.,' *Journal of Canadian Studies* 26 (1991): 120–40; Russell, 'A Fair or Minimum Wage?'

50 See McCallum, 'Keeping Women in Their Place,' 57.

51 See R. Meyerwitz, 'Organizing the United Automobile Workers: Women Workers at the Ternstedt General Motors Parts Plant,' in P.R. Milkman, ed., *Women, Work and Protest* (London: Routledge and Kegan Paul, 1985); E. Sufrin, *The Eaton's Drive: The Campaign to Organize Canada's Largest Department Store 1948 to 1952* (Toronto: Fitzhenry and Whiteside, 1982); Warskett, 'The Politics of Difference,' 587.

52 See Paul Malles, *Canadian Labour Standards in Law, Agreement and Practice* (Ottawa: Economic Council of Canada, 1976); Elisabeth Prügl, 'Biases in Labor Law: A Critique From the Standpoint of Home-Based Workers,' in E. Boris and E. Prügl, eds, *Homeworkers in Perspective: Invisible No More* (New York: Routledge, 1996), 203.

53 See Ruth Pierson, 'Gender and the Unemployment Insurance Debates in Canda, 1934–1940,' *Labour / Le Travail* 25 (Spring 1990): 77.

54 Ibid., 97.

55 Still, although high-income claimants received benefits equal to or greater than their counterparts' in dollars, they received a lower proportion of their incomes in unemployment insurance, giving the system a redistributive cast.

56 To this end, changes in 1946 involved extending unemployment insurance to seasonal workers during their on-season and changes in 1950 led to the provision of supplementary benefits for these workers (in the off-season) and other workers unable to qualify for regular benefits. These measures took into account Canada's dependence upon raw resource extraction for economic growth and the considerable percentage of male workers engaged in related industries. (See Barbara Neis, 'From "Shipped Girls" to "Brides of the State": The Transition from Familial to Science Patriarchy in the Newfoundland Fishery Industry,' *Canada Journal of Regional Service* 17.2 [Summer 1993]: 185; and Jane Pulkingham, 'Remaking the Social Divisions of Welfare: Gender, Dependency and UI Reform,' *Studies in Political Economy* 7 (Summer 1998): 18.)

57 Married women were only exempt from these regulations (i.e., the regulation period was reduced to 60 days) if their separation from work was due to a shortage of work or a marriage bar, if their husband had died or become incapacitated, or if they were permanently separated.

58 See Ann Porter, 'Women and Income Security in the Post-War Period: The Case of Unemployment Insurance, 1945–1962,' *Labour / Le Travail* 31 (Spring 1993): 118, 125.

59 See Vosko, *Temporary Work*, chaps. 2 and 3.

60 See Neis, 'From "Shipped Girls"'; B.J. McCay, 'Fish Guts, Hair Nets, and Unemployment Stamps: Women and Working Cooperative Fish Plants,' in P.R. Sinclair, ed., *A Question of Survival: The Fisheries and Newfoundland Society* (St John's, Nfld.: Institute of Social and Economic Research, 1988).

61 See Neis, 'From "Shipped Girls,"' 199.

62 Subsequently, the government made additional restrictions aimed at preventing a female monopoly in the third tier of the civil service. In 1909, it instituted new rules requiring women to take a test designed for the second division in order to acquire a position in the third division. See Kathleen Archibald, *Sex and the Public Service* (Ottawa: Ministry of Supply and Services, 1970), 16; and Morgan, *The Equality Game*.

63 See Judy Fudge, 'Exclusion, Discrimination, Equality and Privatization: Law, the Canadian State, and Women Public Servants, 1908–1998,' unpublished paper (Toronto: Feminist Legal Institute of Osgoode Hall Law, 1998).

64 See Archibald, *Sex and the Public Service*; Morgan, *The Equality Game*, 16; and J.E. Hodgetts et al., *The Biography of an Institution: The Civil Service Commission of Canada, 1908–1967* (Montreal and Kingston: McGill-Queen's University Press, 1972).

65 See Ursel, *Private Lives, Public Policy*, 185.

66 See Morgan, *The Equality Game*, 10.

67 See Archibald, *Sex and the Public Service*, 111–12.

68 To be covered under a collective agreement, temporary civil servants had to be appointed for more than six months and they had to be certified by the Public Service Commission, leading to the covert practice of firing and rehiring temporary workers every six months. See Archibald, ibid., 18.

69 See Ursel, *Private Lives, Public Policy*, 204.

70 See Statistics Canada, Cat. 75-507E, 1994.

71 See Rashid, 'Seven Decades of Wage Changes,' 9.

72 See Lipsett and Reesor, *Flexible Work Arrangements*.

73 See Government of Canada, *Collective Reflection on the Changing Workplace: Report of the Advisory Committee on the Changing Workplace* (Ottawa: Public Works and Government Services Canada, 1997); and Joan Wallace, *Part-Time Work in Canada: Report of the Commission of Inquiry into Part-Time Work* (Ottawa: Labour Canada, 1983).

74 See Harvey Krahn, 'Non-standard Work on the Rise,' *Perspectives on Labour and Income*, Winter 1995: 35.

75 See Townson, *Non-Standard Work*, 21.

76 Ibid., 26.

77 As Deborah Sussman recently found: '[L]ower hourly wages are associated with higher moonlighting [multiple job-holding] rates. Specifically, workers who earned less than $10.00 per hour in their main job had the highest moonlighting rate [6%] in 1997, while those who earned $20.00 or more per hour had the lowest [4%].' Deborah Sussman, 'Moonlighting: A Growing Way of Life,' *Perspectives on Labour and Income*, Summer 1998: 28.

78 See A. Gardner, 'Their Own Boss,' *Canadian Social Trends*, Summer 1995: 27.

79 See Statistics Canada, Cat. 71-005-XPB, 1997.

80 See Gardner, 'Their Own Boss,' 28.

81 See Suzan Crompton, 'The Renaissance of Self-Employment,' *Perspectives on Labour and Income*, Summer 1993: 22; Krahn, 'Non-standard Work in the Rise,' 35.

82 See Statistics Canada, Cat. 7100MGPE.

83 See Daood Hamdani, 'The Temporary Help Service Industry: Its Role, Structure and Growth,' in *Service Indicators, 2nd Quarter*, Cat. 63-016XPB: 73 (Ottawa: Statistics Canada, 1996).

84 See Vosko, *Temporary Work*.

85 See Statistics Canada, Cat. 7100MGPE.

86 See Morissette, 'Declining Earnings of Young Men,' 9.

87 See Katherine Scott and Clarence Lochhead, 'Are Women Catching up in the Earning Race?' (Ottawa: Canadian Council on Social Development, 1997), Paper no. 3, 1997.

88 For another comprehensive study that demonstrates the persistence of the revenue gap between men and women, see also Drolet, 'The Persistent Gap.'

89 See Statistics Canada, *General Social Survey, 1989* (1991); Statistics Canada, 'Labour Force Survey, December 1998.' *Statistics Canada Daily,* http://www.statcan.ca/Daily/English/990108/d9 (1999).

90 See Marc Linder, *Farewell to the Self-Employed: Deconstructing a Socioeconomic and Legal Solipsism* (New York: Greenwood Press, 1992).

91 See Statistics Canada, Census of Canada, 1991; Statistics Canada, *Catalogue 71-005-XPB.*

92 See Statistics Canada, Census of Canada, 1991.

93 See E.B. Akyeampong, 'A Statistical Portrait of the Trade Union Movement,' *Perspectives on Labour and Income,* Winter 1997: 45.

94 See Bird et al., *Report on the Status of Women;* Creese, 'Sexual Equality.'

95 See Akyeampong, 'A Statistical Portrait.'

96 See Fudge and Vosko, 'Gender, Segmentation, and the Standard Employment Relationship.'

97 See Forrest, 'Bargaining Units.'

98 Broader-based bargaining is shorthand for a range of mechanisms designed to protect workers who are unable to organize under existing collective bargaining legislation. (See Chris Schenk, 'Fifty Years after PC 1003: The Need for New Directions,' in C. Gonick et al., eds, *Labour Gains, Labour Pains: 50 Years of PC 1003* [Winnipeg: Society for Socialist Studies / Fernwood Publishing, 1995], 193.) Such an approach is not completely foreign in the Canadian context, where several alternative models have coexisted with the post–Second World War model of industrial unionism. For example, province-wide bargaining in the construction industry is an established practice in Canada. Similarly, the Status of the Artist Act (1992), which extends collective bargaining rights to actors, visual artists, and musicians, is a piece of legislation with considerable legitimacy. Quebec's Collective Agreement Decrees Act (1934) is perhaps the best-known example of legislation designed to encourage broader-based bargaining in Canada. A product of the Great Depression, this act enables a provincial government to extend judicially some provisions of a collective agreement to both workers and employers in a particular location or sector who were not parties to the original agreement. It was designed originally to reduce unfair competition between different employers in the same region or in a specific sector by raising labour standards. Under this system, either employers or workers may apply to the minister of labour for the extension of key provisions of a collective agreement – including those related to wages, hours of work, and

apprenticeships – to non-unionized firms in the same sector. In such circumstances, extension is conditional upon these provisions being 'voluntarily accepted' by a substantial percentage of the industrial sector (a rather imprecise measure). Once extension occurs, a committee of an equal number of employers and employees is responsible for enforcing the decree. (See Barbara Cameron, 'From Segmentation to Solidarity: A New Framework for Labour Market Regulation,' in D. Drache and A. Ranikin, eds, *Warm Heart, Cold Country: Fiscal and Social Policy Reform in Canada* [Ottawa: Caledon Institute of Social Policy / Robarts Centre for Canadian Studies, 1995], 193; and Schenk, 'Fifty Years after PC 1003.')

The model of collective bargaining that the decree system is premised upon is particularly relevant to raising standards in small workplaces, since it requires no formal certification before negotiations take place. Consequently, a large number of economic sectors covered by decrees are composed of highly competitive small- and medium-sized workplaces, making them a valuable mechanism for reaching unorganized workers in a given sector. (See Gilles Trudeau, 'Temporary Employees Hired through a Personnel Agency: Who Is the Real Employer?' *Canadian Labour and Employment Law Journal* 5 [1998]: 375.) However, aside from the fact that decrees only cover about 6% of Quebec's workers, the most significant weakness of the legislation is its undemocratic nature, the discretionary power that it gives to the Ministry of Labour over both the introduction and enforcement of decrees. (See Schenk, 'Fifty Years after PC 1003,' 203.)

99 The Baigent-Ready proposal had two shortcomings: first, it focused exclusively on sectors, rather than on groups of workers, that were historically underrepresented by unions, setting clear limits on the number of workers that would actually benefit from the legislation. Second, it stipulated that each workplace in a given sector could not employ more than 50 employees (or their equivalent) and, therefore, set unnecessarily strict criteria for certification.

100 I am referring here to its capacity to offer a modicum of security to workers without access to collective bargaining rights under the prevailing collective bargaining regime.

101 See Creese, 'Sexual Equality'; and Malles, *Canadian Labour Standards*, 12.

102 See Malles, *Canadian Labour Standards*, 12–13; and Ursel, *Private Lives, Public Policy*, 246.

103 See Nitya Iyer, 'Some Mothers Are Better than Others: A Re-examination of Maternity Benefits,' in S. Boyd, ed., *Challenging the Public/Private Divide:*

Feminism, Law, and Public Policy (Toronto: University of Toronto Press, 1997), 168; and Malles, *Canadian Labour Standards*, 12–13.

104 See David Broad, 'The Casualization of Labour Force,' in A. Duff et al., eds, *Good Jobs, Bad Jobs, No Jobs: The Transformation of Work in the 21st Century* (Toronto: Harcourt Brace, 1997), 53; and Judy Fudge, *Labour Law's Little Sister: The Employment Standard Act and the Feminization of Labour* (Ottawa: Canadian Centre for Policy Alternatives, 1991).

105 See Jenson, 'The Talents of Women.'

106 See Prügl, 'Biases in Labor Law.'

107 See David Broad and Della McNeill, 'A Matter of Control: Saskatchewan Labour Standards and Part-Time Work,' Occasional paper (Regina: University of Regina, Social Administration Research Unit, 1995); Fudge, *Labour's Little Sister.*

108 See Economic Council of Canada, *Good Jobs, Bad Jobs: Employment in the Service Economy* (Ottawa: Ministry of Supply and Services, 1990), 11; Krahn, 'Non-standard Work'; and Wallace, *Part-time Work in Canada.*

109 See Government of Canada, *Royal Commission on the Economic Union and Development Prospects for Canada* (Ottawa: Ministry of Supply and Services, 1985); and Wallace, *Part-time Work in Canada*, 171.

110 See Fudge, *Labour's Little Sister*, 36.

111 Although its recommendations were directed explicitly to the federal jurisdiction, the Report of the Commission of Inquiry into Part-Time Work (1983), chaired by Joan Wallace, advanced the earliest and clearest set of proposals. It recommended that the federal government amend the Canada Labour Code (Part III) to introduce a new labour standard that would ensure that part-time workers are included in all fringe-benefit and pension plans (on a prorated basis) where an employer provides these benefits for full-time workers doing similar work.

112 In the mid-1990s, Quebec also considered facilitating sectoral negotiations for the employees of temporary help agencies through the Collective Agreement Decree Act (1934) to provide a means for employees in the same sector to attain the same levels of protection, wages, and union representation regardless of whether they are engaged in a bilateral or a triangular employment relationship. Such changes have not yet come to pass. (See Vosko, *Temporary Work*, chap. 6.) Still, there are voices within the bureaucracy and the Quebec academy advocating their introduction since, as Gilles Trudeau has noted, sectoral designations and the agreements flowing from them 'provide an interesting way of protecting employees in fragmented and competitive sectors with low union den-

sity,' sectors where NSERs are particularly common. (See Trudeau, 'Temporary Employees,' 375.)

113 Saskatchewan did introduce prorated benefits for part-time workers under its labour standards legislation in the 1990s, but this represented primarily a symbolic move because the resulting legislation only mandated the extension of benefits to workers working 15 hours or more per week, thus encouraging employers to employ workers for even fewer hours. (See Broad, 'The Casualization of Labour Force,' 65, 67; and Broad and McNeil, 'A Matter of Control,' 11.)

114 See Fudge, *Labour's Little Sister*; Linder, *Farewell to the Self-employed*; and Leah F. Vosko, 'Legitimizing the Triangular Employment Relationship: Emerging International Labour Standards in Comparative Perspective,' *Comparative Labour Law and Policy Journal*, Fall 1997: 43–77.

115 In the 1980s and 1990s, a consensus that 'employee' and 'employer' are ambiguous concepts within the common law began to emerge among labour law practitioners and theorists. It is now widely agreed that the variety of tests, relating primarily to economic dependence, control, and ownership of tools, used to define both terms lead to a range of inconsistent results. Consequently, some scholars argue that the distinction between 'employees' and other workers, such as the self-employed and independent contractors, should be eliminated and that the notion of the standard employment contract should be abandoned in favour of 'contracts for the performance of work.' Still, despite these long-standing criticisms, 'employees' continue to be defined narrowly in employment standards legislation. See A. Brooks, 'Myth and Muddle – An Examination of Contracts for the Performance of Work,' *University of New South Wales Law Journal* 11.2 (1988): 48; and R. Hunter, 'The Regulation of Independent Contractors: A Feminist Perspective,' *Corporate and Business Law Journal* 5 (1992): 165.)

116 See Paul Green and Craig Riddell, 'The Economic Effects of Unemployment Insurance in Canada: An Empirical Analysis of UI Disentitlement,' *Journal of Labour Economics* 11.1–2 (1993): 596; Ursel, *Private Lives, Public Policy.*

117 See Iyer, *Some Mothers Are Better*; and Porter, 'Women and Income Security.'

118 See Green and Riddell, 'The Economic Effects of Unemployment Insurance.'

119 See Martha MacDonald, 'Gender and Recent Social Security Reform in Canada,' prepared for Radcliffe Public Policy Institute, Boston (1997), 6.

120 Ibid.

121 See Pulkingham, 'Remaking the Social Dimensions of Welfare,' 18.

122 See Leah F. Vosko, 'Recreating Dependency: Women and UI Reform,' in D. Drache and A. Ranikin, eds, *Warm Heart, Cold Country* (Toronto: Caledon Press, 1995), 213.

123 See MacDonald, 'Gender and Recent Social Security Reform'; and Vosko, 'Recreating Dependency.'

124 See Vosko, 'Recreating Dependency'; and Leah F. Vosko, 'Irregular Workers, New Involuntary Social Exiles: Women and UI Reform,' in J. Pulkingham and G. Ternowetsky, eds, *Remaking Canadian Social Policy: Social Security in the Late 1990s* (Toronto: Fernwood Press, 1996), 265.

125 See Vosko, 'Irregular Workers,' 261.

126 Canadian Labour Congress, 'Federal Budget 1995: Canadian Labour Congress Analysis,' unpublished brief, 27 February 1995.

127 Since before these changes were formally introduced, organized labour and the women's movement voiced their vehement opposition to them, threatening and subsequently launching court challenges to reveal the largely gender-based inequities that they perpetuate. Consequently, under pressure from these groups, the government may be beginning to rethink its changes in several areas. The information presented in this chapter is accurate to 1 July 1999, at which point it was submitted for publication.

128 See Vosko, 'Recreating Dependency'; and MacDonald, 'Gender and Recent Social Security Reform.'

129 Canadian Council on Social Development, 'Executive Summary: CCSD Response to Bill C-12, An Act Respecting Employment Insurance in Canada' (submitted to the Standing Committee on Human Resource Development), 1996.

130 For example, under the old unemployment insurance system, a woman had to work for 20 weeks to access pregnancy or parental benefits; this qualifying requirement equalled 300 hours (i.e., 20 weeks with a 15-hour weekly minimum). Under employment insurance, at 15 hour per week, she must work for 47 weeks to qualify for benefits.

131 Canadian Council on Social Development, 'Executive Summary,' 7–8.

132 See Morgan, *The Equality Game*, 25.

133 As well, men and women's pay rates were also highly polarized in the service. In 1975, for example, 70% of women earned less than $10,000 per year and 73% of men earned more than $10,000 per year. And in 1976, well after married women gained full access to the service, women constituted 48% of temporary workers and less than one-third of permanent ones. (See Vosko, *Temporary Work*, chap. 3.)

134 For example, the Public Service Employment Act added 'sex' to its list of prohibited grounds of discrimination, recognizing that married women had returned (if they ever left) to paid employment for good, and the

Royal Commission on the Status of Women made 14 recommendations to improve the status of women in the service. See F. Bird et al., *Report on the Status of Women*.

135 See White, *Women and Unions*, 66.

136 See Gene Swimmer, 'Collective Bargaining in the Federal Public Service of Canada: The Last Twenty Years,' in G. Swimmer and M. Thompson, eds, *Public Sector Collective Bargaining in Canada* (Kingston: Industrial Relations Centre, Queen's University, 1995), 371.

137 See F. Bird et al., *Report on the Status of Women*, 18.

138 See Rosemary Warskett, 'Political Power, Technical Disputes, and Unequal Pay: A Federal Case,' in J. Fudge and P. McDermott, eds, *Just Wages: A Feminist Assessment of Pay Equity* (Toronto: University of Toronto Press, 1991), 172.

139 See Morgan, *The Equality Game*, 39.

140 See Swimmer, 'Collective Bargaining in the Federal Public Service,' 397.

141 See Government of Canada, *Royal Commission on the Economic Union*, 308–9; Swimmer, 'Collective Bargaining,' 382.

142 See Panitch and Swartz, *The Assault on Trade Union Freedoms*; Swimmer, 'Collective Bargaining,' 377.

143 For example, the federal government announced that a formal affirmative action policy would govern the service in 1983.

144 For example, between 1983 and 1988 alone, term (i.e., temporary) employment increased from 11 to 14.3% and the percentage of women in these positions rose dramatically. See Government of Canada, *Beneath the Veneer: The Report of the Task Force on Barriers to Women in the Public Service* (Ottawa: Ministry of Supply and Services, 1990), 85–6.

145 See Rosemary Warskett, 'Can a Disappearing Pie Be Shared Equally? Unions, Women, and Wage "Fairness,"' in L. Briskin and P. McDermott, eds, *Women Challenging Unions: Feminism, Democracy, and Militancy* (Toronto: University of Toronto Press, 1993).

146 This was particularly true beginning in the mid-1980s, when the Conservative government was elected on a platform to shrink the federal public service and, subsequently, cut the number of federal employees by 15,000 over five years. At this juncture, the federal government retained its strong commitment to employment equity, but this commitment did not prevent it from limiting wage increases through wage controls and initiating back-to-work legislation in response to strike action.

147 See Government of Canada, *Beneath the Veneer*, 85–6.

148 See Swimmer, 'Collective Bargaining,' 397; Townson, *Non-Standard Work*, 10.

3. Finding a Niche: Age-related Differentiations within the Working-age Population

David Cheal

1. Introduction: The Economics of Youth as a Contemporary Social Problem

The principal feature of changing age differentiation within the working-age population is the way in which economic production, and its payoffs in wages and benefits, has tended to accumulate among middle-aged people. This trend will be referred to here as the privileging of prime-age workers. The most prominent aspect of the privileging of prime-age workers is the way in which full-time employment has tended to become concentrated in the 30–55 age group. As we shall see, that is only one part of the picture of relative advantage and relative disadvantage between the middle aged and the young.

In recent years, some of the greatest challenges facing young people have arisen from changes in labour markets.[1] Young people joining the labour force have often found it difficult to obtain full-time jobs at good wages. This situation has been described as producing a pauperization of youth.[2] Real incomes of Canadian families with young heads have fallen since the early 1980s, as the earning power of young workers has declined.[3]

Difficulty in obtaining employment at decent wages has had ripple effects. For example, it has delayed exit from the educational system into the full-time labour force for some young people.[4] The transition from school to work is becoming more prolonged, and its outcomes are less certain.[5] Persistently high youth unemployment rates suggest that there is a basic problem of transition from school to work today. That transition is especially difficult during economic downturns; for example, employment rates of youths and young adults fell more than those of older workers during the recessions of the early 1980s and the early 1990s.[6] Employment and unemployment levels in Canada have been more volatile among young people than among other age groups since the early 1970s.[7]

Not surprisingly, there is much concern about delayed or incomplete social adulthood of young people aged 15–24, especially in the province of Quebec.[8] Employment problems of the young are not confined to one province, or to one part of Canada, however. In Ontario, too, a survey of social assistance recipients found strong evidence that the transition from school to work has become increasingly problematic.[9]

Many young people who do not turn to social assistance for support delay the transition from familial dependence to adult independence. During the 1980s there was an increased tendency for young adults who were not forming couples to live in their parents' homes.[10] Most of this increase occurred in the first half of the 1980s, in a period that included an economic recession and increased time spent in further education. Co-residence with parents by young adults is related to their being unemployed or not in the labour force, and to having a low income.[11] Living at home under such conditions has the long-term effect of prolonging financial dependence upon parents well into adulthood. However, the alternative is a disturbingly high rate of poverty among unattached young adults.[12] Families have therefore played an important role in dampening the effects of the declining economic status for youths.[13]

Although the relative disadvantages of young people are generally recognized today, there is less agreement about the factors that have contributed to them. In this chapter, we will examine several different approaches to this issue, and we will consider some of the evidence for and against each one. Before doing so, however, it is necessary to begin by commenting on the nature of youth as an age category. The reason is that 'youth' is a socially constructed population type. The same forces that affect young people as a group also reflexively influence how 'youth' as a social category is publicly defined.

1.1 Age Stratification

For statistical purposes, Statistics Canada considers youth (or 'young people') to be a category consisting of persons aged 15 to 24. Since the present report relies heavily upon official statistics, the usual conventions will be followed here, in most respects. However, it should be noted at the outset that not everyone agrees with this point: some observers believe that the category of youth is currently in need of redefinition.

The Canadian Youth Foundation has argued that the definition of youth as ages 15 to 24 is unrealistic, and out-of-date. The Foundation claims that the economic difficulties of youth now extend until age 29. Furthermore, according to Armine Yalnizyan, the age segmentation of the labour market now devalues the work of all people under age 35 by comparison with those over that age.[14] It is claimed that failure to acknowledge the recent extension of youth means that government policies often miss the mark. Of course, it is not possible to assess the accuracy of this definitional claim using data compiled according to the customary age classifications. In the Canadian Youth Foundation's opinion, this situation results in the difficulties of Canadians aged 25 to 29 being largely hidden from view. The first recommendation to be made here, therefore, is that new research into statistical classifications is needed to determine what upper boundary is currently the most relevant for differentiating the economic characteristics of youth from those of other age groups. The Government of Quebec, for example, publishes statistics for the age group 15 to 29.[15]

There is also a deeper point to be made about age categorization, concerning the social construction of the category of youth within discourses of social policy. Lucie France Dagenais has shown that the upper age limits for conceptualizations of youth fluctuated during the decades of the 1970s and 1980s, depending on the particular problem that was the main focus of attention at each moment.[16]

The definition of youth as ages 15 to 24 was introduced in the early 1970s, as a consequence of government programs intended to promote further education for young people. Seen from that perspective, youth is defined as the period in life when people are preparing themselves for adult employment. However, it soon became apparent in the early 1980s that the policy of further education had not succeeded for everyone. In reaction, there was a tendency to extend the upper limit of youth to age 30. The immediate context for this was increased concern about rising unemployment among graduates, who had completed their formal education but could not find work related to their field of study. Seen from this later point of view, youth is the period of preparation for employment *and* of transition from school to work.

In the late 1980s, Dagenais suggests, the policy discourse shifted again, to address questions about intergenerational equity between the elderly and the young. For that purpose, young people were defined as being persons 16 to 19 years of age. The context for that approach was increased recognition of the growing differences between the age groups at the beginning and the end of the life cycle. Concern was expressed about the comparative amounts of public support given to young people and the elderly, conceptualized as groups who exist largely, or entirely, outside the labour force.

Finally, in a postscript to Dagenais's account, it should be added that in the late 1990s the interests of policy-makers have tended to focus once more mainly upon the 15 to 24 age group. The context now is a revised view of the welfare state, in which the main goal of the state is to promote improved economic performance by investing in human capital.[17] In this context, youth is once again identified primarily as the period in life of preparation for work.

In summation, the discourse on social policy in Canada has contained a variety of perspectives on youth, each reflecting a different policy interest and each involving a different construction of youth as a social category. Selected points of view will be discussed further in section 2 of this chapter. Before returning to that issue, however, it is necessary to survey the evidence about the main dimensions of economic differentiation, as identified in the main lines of research conducted in Canada.

1.2 Economic Differentiation: The Privileging of Prime-age Workers

Overall, the most significant aspect of the privileging of prime-age workers has been the continued strength of their earnings, in a period when the earnings of the young have been volatile and have tended to decline. Earnings trends can be illustrated from a study, by Ross Finnie, of men's and women's earnings during the period 1982–92, excluding students.[18] The age group that Finnie characterizes as 'Entry Men' (aged 20–24) saw its earnings fall in absolute and relative terms for most of the period, with the sole exceptions of the boom years 1987–9. For this group of young men, the early 1980s recession effectively trailed right through to 1986; their recovery was far from complete in the following growth years, and then the early 1990s recession hit them harder than any other group. Overall, the mean earnings of the 'Entry Men' group fell by 23.7 per cent from 1982 to 1992. In contrast, the prime-age group of 'Prime Men' (aged 35–54) did rather better. For this group of workers, mean earnings dropped slightly during the 1982–3 recession, then grew steadily throughout the rest of the 1980s, and dropped somewhat in the early 1990s. In 1992 they were no worse off than they had been a decade before.

Among women, the contrast in the fortunes of young workers and prime-age workers is even greater. The mean earnings of 'Entry Women' changed in a similar fashion to those of 'Entry Men,' culminating in an overall decline that was almost as great at 19.7 per cent.[19] 'Prime Women', on the other hand, had a unique income trajectory in the decade 1982–92. Their mean earnings rose in every year except one, and they finished with an overall earnings gain of close to 20 per cent.

Earnings growth has been especially strong among full-time, full-year prime aged women, relative to other age groups of men and women.[20] The relative income decline of young women has therefore been more pronounced than that of young men. Whereas historically the earnings differentials between younger and older women were much smaller than the corresponding differentials for men, over the past two decades the differentials among women have risen sharply.[21]

To turn now to a decomposition of underlying factors, analyses of income inequality within the working-age population locate its origins mainly in comparative positions in the labour market. The principal factors of inequality are (1) the distribution of unemployment; (2) the distribution of labour force participation; (3) the distribution of hours of employment; (4) the distribution of 'good jobs' and 'bad jobs'; and (5) the distribution of wages. Here, young people have encountered multiple disadvantages in recent years.[22]

1.2.1 The Age-related Distribution of Unemployment

Unemployment has been a topic of special interest in policy discussions about problems of the young, partly owing to concerns about psychological depression and other long-term effects of having no work.[23] A large survey of the health of young people aged 15 to 24 living in the province of Quebec in 1987 found that those who had attempted suicide were greatly over-represented among youths who were not employed and not in school, and under-represented among employed youths.[24] Concern about such problems has grown, as the employment difficulties of young people have become more apparent.[25]

The unemployment gap between youths and all adults doubled over the past thirty years, from an average of three percentage points in the mid-1960s to six percentage points or more by the mid-1990s. Not unreasonably, it was predicted in the mid-1990s that, as the business cycle in Canada turned up, the youth-adult unemployment rate differential should decline gradually toward the 4 to 5 percentage point range.[26] The unemployment rate differential did finally start to decline in 1998, but it is still a long way from being even a 5 per cent gap.[27] The best year for employment growth in Canada since the start of the decade was 1998. For youths, it was the best in twenty years, with substantial gains in both full-time and part-time employment.[28] Nevertheless, the unemployment rate for youths ended the year at 14.4 per cent, 6.4 percentage points above the national unemployment rate at 8 per cent, and 7.6 percentage points above the rate of 6.8 per cent for adults aged 25 and over. By the summer of 1999, the youth unemployment rate had fallen slightly to 14.1 per cent, but it remained stubbornly at 6.4 percentage points more than the national rate, 7.7 per cent. A year later, in the summer of 2000, the youth unemployment rate had responded to robust economic growth by falling much further, to 12.6 per cent. This drop was large enough to push the gap between the youth rate and the national unemployment rate down to 5.8 percentage points. However, the unemployment rate differential between young people and adults was still high by comparison with economic predictions based on past experience. In July 2000, the youth unemployment rate of 12.6 per cent was 6.9 percentage points higher than the unemployment rate for adult women (5.7%), and a full 7.1 percentage points higher than the unemployment rate for adult men (5.5%). It seems that a large unemployment rate differential between young people and adults is a problem that will not go away.

One reason why young workers experience higher unemployment is that they are more likely than older workers to experience a job separation, whether voluntary or involuntary.[29] This does not mean that older workers are not affected by unemployment. On the contrary, although fewer workers over age 45 lose their jobs at the onset of a recession, older workers who are thrown out of work as the recession deepens are less likely to be re-employed when the recession ends. The primary employment difficulty for workers above age 45 is that of replacing a job when it is lost.[30] Older workers are therefore more vulnerable to long-term unemployment, which can lead to premature retirement from the labour force.[31] Retirement is not an option for young people, financially, socially, or psychologically. Nevertheless, unemployment among the young is sometimes followed by withdrawal from the labour force, often to return to some kind of further education or job training. In this respect, the situation of young labour-force leavers may be more similar to that of other leavers than is sometimes imagined. It would not be surprising if awareness of long-term unemployment has had a broad impact on decisions to stay in school, or return to school, across a broad spectrum of youth, just as it has affected the early-retirement decisions of older men.

1.2.2 The Age-related Distribution of Labour Force Participation

The labour force participation rate of youths in Canada peaked at the end of the 1980s, and it fell sharply after that.[32] It finally picked up again in 1998, rising from 60.8 per cent in December 1997 to 63.5 per cent in December 1998.[33] However, it remains well below the level it had reached at the end of 1989, when it was 70 per cent.

Declining labour force participation among the young is associated with rising educational participation.[34] Recent estimates suggest that for every 100 young persons who leave the labour force in an economic downturn, between 50 and 65 go back to school. Young people have increased their involvement in formal education, sometimes as a passive response to poor employment opportunities, but also in an active attempt to improve their career prospects in an era of technological and organizational change. The upward trend in the proportion of youths enrolled in full-time studies was one of the most important factors contributing to the decline in youth participation in the labour force between 1989 and 1997, especially among older youths 20–24 years of age.[35]

Although deferred entry into the labour force by some older youths is a well-known phenomenon, more attention needs to be paid to the volatile labour force participation of teenagers, who have traditionally used casual and part-time jobs as a first stepping stone into the labour market.[36] Today, fewer young people aged 15 to 19 have work experience of any kind.[37] This may subsequently impede their transition into full-time employment, and slow their rate of upward occupational mobility.

1.2.3 The Age-related Distribution of Hours of Employment

Although the number of young people employed in Canada has dropped overall in recent years, there is one type of employment where the participation of many young people has increased. More young Canadians are now working part-time than ever before.[38] That is especially true for young women, who make up the majority of young, part-time employees.[39] As discussed by Leah Vosko in the present volume (chapter 2), young women continue to be heavily involved in non-standard employment relationships.

Half of all young male and female workers in Canada would like to work more hours for pay, compared with less than one in five of workers aged 45 and over.[40] Almost one-quarter (23%) of all youths working part-time in 1998 would have preferred to work full-time.[41] More young women experience involuntary part-time employment than young men.[42] Of course, educational participation diminishes the demand for work by students. Even so, half of all young secondary students with a job say they would prefer more hours of work; and one in three young full-time post-secondary students with part-time work state a preference for more hours of paid employment.[43] Clearly, increased part-time work has not filled all of the employment needs of young people, and it is not unreasonable to characterize this section of the population as underemployed. Together with falling wage levels, fewer hours of employment help to account for lower earnings among young people today.[44]

Although overall youth participation in part-time employment has been increasing, that is not the case for all young people. The Canadian Council on Social Development reports that fewer 15 to 19 year olds held part-time jobs in 1997 than in 1988.[45] It may well be that this development is a knock-on effect of the employment difficulties among people at ages 20 to 24 that is creating a new pattern of age stratification within youth. Many Canadians in their early twenties, who would have had full-time jobs in the past, are now taking the part-time jobs that teenagers previously held. The end result is fewer hours of employment for 'older young people,' and less labour-force participation of any kind among 'younger young people.'

1.2.4 The Age-related Distribution of Good Jobs and Bad Jobs
Some of the most influential discussions on age differentiation in Canada during the 1980s and the early 1990s revolved around ideas about the changing nature of work in a post-industrial economy. These discussions were stimulated by an unflattering description of new forms of service employment by the Economic Council of Canada, which suggested that the labour market was becoming segmented into two categories – 'good jobs' and 'bad jobs.'[46] The Economic Council's demographic concern was mainly with the effects of the new economy

upon older workers, especially those aged 55 to 64. Older workers who lost a 'good job' during the business restructuring of the 1980s were often unable to replace it with another 'good job'; and they were slower than young workers to obtain employment in a changed labour market.[47] This could have negative implications for older workers' access to private pension plans offered by some employers. One recent study of registered pension plan coverage suggests that on average any losses experienced by older workers have not been as great as the losses experienced by younger workers. Between the mid-1980s and the mid-1990s, pension coverage dropped significantly for younger men, remained fairly constant or declined slightly for older men and younger women, and increased considerably for older women.[48] The drop in young men's pension coverage was associated with a decline in union affiliation, employment shifts from high coverage industries to low coverage industries, and a drop in real wages. Conversely, most of the growth in pension coverage among older women seems to have been due to their entry into well-paid jobs with a high probability of pension plan membership.

A more significant problem for younger workers is that 'bad jobs' are often their point of entry into the labour force, with negative consequences for economic insecurity.[49] Young white men with little formal education were more likely to lose their jobs in Canada than in the United States during the mid-1980s, in part because more Canadians were in temporary or seasonal employment.

Early awareness of the impact of 'bad jobs' upon the young coincided with the economic restructuring of the 1980s. At that time, it was often thought that negative developments in labour markets must be due to an international reorganization of the division of labour, between occupations and industries, including a shift from manufacturing to services. However, it subsequently became clear that a restructured division of labour was not the only, or even the primary, factor explaining the relative economic decline of young Canadians.[50] Recent shifts in the distribution of earnings appear to be mainly due to changes within occupations and industries. It is therefore changes in the terms and conditions of employment that account for most of the relative economic decline of young people. Furthermore, these changes seem to be independent of the falling rate of unionization among young workers.

1.2.5 The Age-related Distribution of Wage Levels
The manner in which wages and incomes are distributed in Canada

has been a major field of research activity over the past half-decade. A lot of this activity was stimulated by the discovery, by John Myles, Garnett Picot, and Ted Wannell, that in the first half of the 1980s hourly wage rates of jobs held by young workers declined, while the hourly wage rates of jobs held by workers over age 35 increased. This finding was upheld by other researchers, and the pattern has also been confirmed as holding through the late 1980s and into the 1990s.[51] Overall, the decline in annual earnings of the young appears to have more to do with changes in relative wages than in working time. It is consistent with all of these findings that in the mid-1990s, over 40 per cent of youths aged 22–24 were dissatisfied with their financial situation.[52]

The downward shift in the wage levels of young workers has occurred independently of other changes in employment relationships. For example, it might be thought that the fall in wage levels among young workers was due to growing employment in part-time jobs, which usually pay lower wages. However, Myles, Picot, and Wannell concluded that very little of the growth in low-paying jobs among young workers could be attributed to an increase in part-time employment. Morissette, Myles, and Picot also concluded, from a study of the thirteen-year period 1969–91, that changes in the earnings distribution observed in the 1980s were not due solely to the 1981–3 recession. For men under age 25, the downward trend in wages began earlier, in 1977. It accelerated during the recession beginning in 1981, but showed little recovery for the remainder of the decade.

There is an important conclusion to be drawn here about the source of employment difficulty among young Canadians. It does not seem to be due to an institutionalized inflexibility in wages. One explanation that is sometimes advanced for relatively great difficulties in finding employment is that the average wage levels in a group may exceed the value of its work to employers, but the group is either unable, or unwilling, to reduce the price of its labour under changed market conditions. The recent labour market experiences of youths in Canada do not fit this pattern. The relative wage levels of Canadian youths began adjusting downwards in the late 1970s, but without producing any obvious employment benefits for them.

1.2.6 *Multiple Labour Market Divisions*

The studies reviewed above demonstrate that increased income differences between younger Canadians and older Canadians are due to a number of disadvantages that different segments of young people have experienced. It is therefore suggested that the young, particularly young men, are now part of a 'contingent workforce' that is either unemployed, employed involuntarily part-time, or holding non-permanent employment.[53]

Young people are not all disadvantaged in the same way. The 'younger young' (15–19) have experienced a greater decline in labour force participation than the 'older young' (20–24) since the start of the early 1990s recession. The gap in labour force participation rates between the 15–19 and 20–24 age groups widened during the 1990s.[54] Unlike the situation for 'older youths,' most of the drop in labour force participation among 'younger youths' was not associated with increased school enrolment, but was due to falling labour force participation among students. Many older youths were able to maintain something close to an adult role in society by combining education and part-time employment. For younger youths, however, the passage to social adulthood through part-time employment has become more restricted. Staying in school is no solution for these young people, because they are already in school.

2. Differentiation Processes

It is clear that large numbers of young people in Canada have experienced difficult labour market conditions throughout the 1980s and the 1990s. It is also clear that many middle-aged workers have enjoyed more favourable conditions, even though economic uncertainty grew for most sectors of the labour force in this period and the real earnings of the average Canadian stagnated. It is therefore necessary to look into the underlying causes of economic differentiation that produce age-related inequalities in a country like Canada. Any analysis of underlying causes is derived from some theoretical model, or theoretical approach, that links disparate events into a general explanation. In the following sections of this chapter we will review and compare five main approaches to the economic problems of youth. They are theories of (1) functional differentiation; (2) cohort differentiation; (3) status differentiation; (4) program differentiation; and (5) life course differentiation. Each of these five approaches will be outlined, and its strengths and weaknesses will be evaluated.

2.1 Functional Differentiation

In labour markets, some people with different skills seek to do work of particular kinds (i.e., they supply labour) and other people require work of particular kinds to be done (i.e., they demand labour). The relationship between these groups gives rise to a division of labour, consisting of specialized functions with different productivities, which receive different, and unequal, rewards. The result is a functional differentiation of earning power.

Work, and its rewards, have been reorganized and redistributed by employers in Canada over the past two decades.[55] Employers have done this in order to improve the competitiveness and profitability of their businesses in a changing marketplace. One result of this restructuring has been a changing mix of occupations. For example, there are now fewer jobs in manufacturing and more jobs in consumer services. Since the latter types of jobs often pay less than the former, it is possible that changes in occupational opportunities might account for declining wage levels in young workers. However, according to Myles, Picot, and Wannell, this is not the case. Most of the downward shift in the wage distribution of young workers occurred within industries and occupational categories, rather than between them, and the decline in youth wage levels is therefore broad-based. As a result of this important finding, alternative explanations for the economic difficulties of the young have been sought in other aspects of labour market functioning.

2.1.1 Education, Employment, and Wages

One explanation for the economic problems of young people is that they may be inadequately prepared for work by their educational experiences. This answer assumes that a labour market operates as a functional system, which allocates different types of labour to different types of tasks. Within such a system, any distinctive employment difficulties of young people would be due mainly to a 'mismatch' between the skills that young workers have to offer and the skills for which employers have the greatest demand. This point of view has attracted a great deal of attention in recent years.[56]

Mismatching would seem to be most likely to occur in times of rapid technological and economic change. At such times, old ways of working (and old jobs) are being discarded and new ways of working are being introduced, for which there has been little opportunity to prepare. Under these circumstances of skills-biased technological change, mental flexibility, positive attitudes toward new technology, and readiness and ability to learn are presumably real advantages. If anybody possesses these advantages, it should be the well-educated young.

In fact, the labour market position of post-secondary graduates deteriorated significantly during the 1980s.[57] They suffered from increases in unemployment (especially males), as well as in part-time employment (especially females). No group of graduates was entirely immune to the difficult labour market conditions. Consistent with the functionalist thesis, those with the least occupationally relevant training generally fared the worst. This was reflected not only in the difficulties in finding work by graduates of generalist programs, but also in the falling incomes of humanities graduates compared with graduates from professional programs. How much of this decline was actually due to skill-biased technological change, and how much of it was due to falling demand in sectors like the public service that have traditionally employed generalist graduates, is hard to say.

Job mismatch is a difficult concept to measure, partly because it requires detailed information about relevant skills and how they should be defined. Also, job skill requirements are not determined only by the nature of the task or the technology used, but also by the way in which beliefs about productivity and ability are socially constructed within powerful groups. Furthermore, some of the observed job mismatch may simply be due to a depressed labour market. Individuals who have prepared for higher-level occupations, but who are unable to enter them, may end up taking lower-level jobs in clerical, sales, and service occupations, for which they are overqualified.

Evidence about education-job matching among young people in Canada is ambiguous. On the one hand, there is clear evidence that university graduates from programs that provide practical training and career development, like the health professions, education, and engineering, are more likely to be employed in fields related to their skills, and they are least likely to feel overqualified.[58] On the other hand, it is also the case that graduates in certain applied fields, such as business and management, often complain that their skills are underutilized in their jobs.[59] This raises questions about allegations of skill shortages, as well as about the capacity of some employers to make optimum use of the skills available in the youth workforce.

Interestingly, the rate of education-job mismatch appears to fall as young workers gain more experience in the labour market.[60] This suggests that initial employment difficulties may be due as much to job search problems as to unwanted skills. Also, it should be noted that having a high level of occupationally relevant technological training does not protect young people when the aggregate demand for labour declines. Engineering and data processing graduates both fared poorly in the recession of the early 1980s, and the usually close relationship between education and occupation in the health sciences field has fallen whenever major cutbacks at hospitals reduced employment for nurses.[61] Most young Canadians have acquired the general skills of literacy and numeracy that are necessary to learn new tasks in a post-industrial society.[62] In this regard, older workers are clearly at a greater disadvantage.[63] If young people have distinctive employment difficulties that are due to major deficiencies in skill levels, it would seem that the skills in question would have to be ones that are job-specific and are therefore gained mainly through experience on the job. It is therefore interesting to note that between 1988 and 1991 there was an increase in the percentage of post-secondary graduates whose jobs required previous work experience.[64]

2.1.2 Age and Experience Wage Premia

Influential analyses of labour markets have tended to view the privileging of prime age workers as due to some comparative productivity advantage they possess, such as greater work experience.[65] However, the presumed advantages of work experience are not so easy to identify as an independent factor, partly because age and experience are closely related in most cases. There is some indirect evidence to suggest that work experience can substitute for education in the acquisition of occupationally relevant skills. In general, lack of education is associated with higher unemployment, but that relationship is not as close in older workers (55–64) as it is among workers in other age groups.[66]

The key question here is whether the comparative productivity advantage that older workers possess as a result of their accumulated work experience has in fact increased in recent years. In an intriguing analysis, Paul Beaudry and David Green suggest that it has not.[67] They postulate that, if the financial returns to work experience had increased in recent years, then it should follow that more recent (i.e., younger) cohorts of workers would experience greater wage growth as they age than that experienced by older cohorts. However, their data do not demonstrate this pattern. On the contrary, they found that among men, cohort-specific age-earning profiles in general have been getting flatter in recent years. They therefore conclude that recent earnings changes for men have arisen from worsening outcomes in more recent cohorts rather than from increasing returns to experience.

2.2 Cohort Differentiation

Differences in cohort outcomes are sometimes explained by processes of demographic change. Here, the main problem facing young people could be that they are among the most recent entrants into a saturated labour market, which cannot absorb everyone who wants paid employment. In the 1970s, the employment problems of young people were often attributed to the size of the baby-boom cohorts who were entering the labour market at that time. This demographic effect was sometimes referred to as 'generational crowding.' Whatever impact generational crowding may have had during the 1970s, it should have disappeared a long time ago. The proportion of youths in the labour force peaked in the 1970s, and it fell steadily through most of the 1980s and 1990s.[68] In the mid-1980s, Canadians aged 20 to 24 still constituted a relatively large proportion of the Canadian population, but their relative size shrank through the 1990s.[69]

It is unlikely that the economic difficulties of young people, which have lasted right through to the end of the 1990s, could be explained solely as a delayed effect of the baby boomers crowding the following generation out of the labour market. Perhaps surprisingly, given the popularity of ideas about demographics, Doug Hostland has concluded emphatically that '[d]emographic shifts clearly cannot account for differences in unemployment rates between demographic groups.'[70] Research in the United States has concluded that aggregate, time-series effects of relative cohort size can be observed for the period 1945–80, but after 1980 they are either very weak or non-existent.[71]

It is important to note that the economic position of young people should actually have improved in the late 1980s and 1990s as their numbers shrank. Young persons should have had fewer competitors for entry-level jobs; and employers should have bid the wages of youths up as they competed for employees to replace older workers, many of whom began taking early retirement during this period. The curious fact that improvement for young workers did not happen when it should have raises thought-provoking questions about why the labour market suddenly became a much more difficult place for young people, and about what can be expected in the future.

As noted earlier, the economic problems of youth have not been confined to problems in finding employment. Young people have also experienced falling average wage levels relative to older age groups. There is a sense in which the latter trend is yet another surprising outcome, because more young Canadians now have some post-secondary education than ever before. Higher educational qualifications should have paid off for the current generation of young people in higher average wage levels. Individually, higher education does indeed pay off (eventually) in better jobs and higher average wages, because it provides a relative advantage in a competitive labour market. However, more education for young people has not always protected them as a group from falling relative wage levels. The downward shift in wages in jobs held by young workers during the 1980s and 1990s occurred irrespective of educational qualifications.[72]

The earnings gap between more educated and less educated workers seems to have increased somewhat in recent years, but this was mainly because of a greater fall in the relative wage levels of young workers with the least education.[73] Real wages for male university graduates declined, while those of female university graduates rose only slightly.[74] After accounting for inflation, there was little change in the relative earnings of trade/vocational, college, and university graduates, who graduated in 1982, 1986, and 1990 and who were employed full-time at two years and five years after graduation.[75] Paradoxically, higher educational qualifications seem to have had the greatest positive benefit in increasing wages for older workers.[76]

Part of the explanation for the fact that nothing seems to have had a very positive impact on the incomes of the young may lie in a comment made in a report for the Conference Board of Canada that the swelling pool of educated young people 'is an opportunity for many firms to choose extremely well-trained young employees at modest salaries.'[77] Unlike the situation in the United States, post-secondary enrolments grew strongly in Canada in the 1980s, which possibly had a depressing effect on the relative earnings of well-educated young Canadians.[78] However, that development might not have mattered very much if many Canadian employers had not felt free to pay younger workers less than others.

2.3 Status Differentiation

It is possible that part of the reason why older workers have derived greater returns from education in recent years is that they benefited more from the internal structures of organizations, in which they are more firmly established. Considered as social systems, all organizations are status hierarchies in which rewards and privileges are distributed according to collective judgments about social value. Such judgments typically include achieved criteria of skill and productivity, as well as ascribed criteria based on fixed personal characteristics. It is not necessarily the case that achieved criteria will always take precedence over such ascribed criteria as seniority.

Seniority systems consist of formal or informal rules that allocate economic benefits to employees within an organization based upon an employee's accumulated years of service therein.[79] Related to seniority is a lesser system of benefits based on date of origination. Here, benefits are determined by the point at which a certain status, such as membership in the organization, commenced.

A particular type of origination system that gave rise to some concerns in Canada in the 1980s is that of tiered compensation systems.[80] In tiered compensation systems, employees who joined a firm before a certain date have different benefits from those who joined the firm later. Wage levels and other benefits of early joiners are inevitably higher than those of later joiners. The effect of such a system is to implement a wages and benefits cut, but without actually cutting the wages or benefits of existing employees because the impact of the cuts falls upon later hires.

Systems of seniority and origination could help to explain some of the relative disadvantages of youths in the past two decades. However, the significance of these factors is hard to gauge. Tiered compensation systems have been particularly important in certain service industries, but overall they do not seem to have been incorporated into much more than about 5 per cent of collective agreements.[81] By contrast, seniority clauses in collective agreements have been more prevalent. Louise Dulude estimates that up to three- quarters of unionized workers in the early 1990s had collective agreements that included seniority clauses concerning layoffs.[82] Nevertheless, it is important to note that many workers in Canada today do not belong to unions, and so the overall effect of seniority clauses may not be that great. According to Dulude's estimates, no more than a quarter of all workers in Canada in the early 1990s would have been affected by a seniority provision on layoff. That number is large enough to have an influence upon the employment relationships of young people, but not large enough to be a determining factor.

The really important question here is whether the unionized sector of the labour force in fact operates under a completely different set of rules from the rest of the labour force, or if a similar range of labour practices are found throughout the economy, being more formal in union workplaces and more informal elsewhere. There is no conclusive evidence on this point. Informal employment relationships are the norm in Canada, but it seems that very little is known about them.

2.4 Program Differentiation

More needs to be known about several factors, including the relationships between young people and the state. Since the modern welfare state emerged mainly to compensate for relative disadvantages created by markets, it might be expected that the young would benefit more than others from government income supports. That is not the case. Young adults aged 18 to 24 are, in certain respects, a marginalized group.[83] Income transfers do not go as far in relieving the poverty experienced by youth as they do for the population as a whole.[84] In the Canadian welfare state, public income support for unattached young people tends to be low.[85] Also, it is often contingent upon approved conduct; and much of it takes the form of loans that are expected to be repaid. Conduct-contingent repayable loans for young people have grown in popularity as a way of enabling, and encouraging, them to continue their education.

The major public benefit provided to youths by governments is the (implicit) transfer of part of their education costs.[86] However, this benefit has proven to be a double edged sword. More young people have been pursuing their education for longer periods of time, as noted earlier in this report. As a result, the financial relationships between students and educational institutions are having a bigger impact upon young people's lives. The recent history of that relationship has not, on the whole, been favourable to students.

In the 1980s, many young people turned toward higher education. University enrolments grew strongly, but government grants to universities failed to keep pace.[87] In an attempt to cope, many universities suppressed their costs during the 1980s, but their cost structure rebounded in the first half of the 1990s. The result was a period of large increases in university fees in the early 1990s.[88] Major fee increases occurred at the very same time as difficult labour markets made it harder for both students and their parents to pay for the larger fees. The proportion of family income needed to pay for a student's fees rose from its low point in 1981, and it jumped in the first half of the 1990s.

As we have seen, many young people took up part-time employment to help pay their way through college. However, they often ended up working fewer hours than they wanted, in 'bad' jobs that paid low wages. One obvious solution to the problem of financing higher education under these circumstances was to borrow money. Inevitably, more graduates have borrowed to finance their education, and they have borrowed more.

Total student borrowing has been rising since the early 1980s, and college and bachelor's degree students who graduated in 1995 borrowed more from student loan programs than any group of graduates in the previous fifteen years.[89] The burden of student borrowing, measured as the amount owed to student loan programs as a proportion of annual income earned after graduation, has gone up. Graduates with higher debt burdens tend to pay back their loans at a slower rate, and recent graduates are therefore taking longer than earlier cohorts of graduates to repay their loans. Recent graduates have also found it more difficult to make their loan repayments. According to the latest study of Canada Student Loans by Statistics Canada, one in three students who left school in 1995/96 had repayment difficulties in the first year, compared with one in five students in 1990/91. The one-year rate of repayment default increased during this period, from 17.6 per cent to 21.8 per cent.

Low earnings after graduation are a significant factor in lower loan repayments. This appears to be the main reason why female bachelor's graduates report having more difficulty than male bachelor's graduates in repaying their student loans. Repayment difficulties are especially widespread for those who work part-time, who are unemployed, or who are not in the labour force. Variations in amount of employment, and therefore in income, are likely to reflect family-related decisions to some extent, especially among recent female graduates. Becoming a full social adult means, for many women, not only graduating and getting a good job, but also starting a family.

2.5 Life Course Differentiation

The growth of student debt in Canada, and the difficulties that a minority of students have in repaying their educational loans, may result in long-term problems of indebtedness lasting well beyond youth itself. That potential problem brings to our attention the fact that youth is just one stage in life, which must be understood in relation to what comes after. It is therefore necessary to consider the interconnections between youth and other stages in the life course.

Economic events that occur when people are young could affect later stages of their lives, positively or negatively. Or those effects might be superseded by later events. In an optimistic scenario, any negative effects of low incomes during the period of youth could be washed out by higher incomes in later life due to upward mobility. The latter outcome is presupposed in an interesting argument about the economic life cycle, reported by Gøsta Esping-Andersen.[90]

Esping-Andersen thinks it may be inevitable, in the current economic environment, that an acceptable level of employment can be maintained only by a low-wage 'bad job' strategy, which is adopted by employers and acquiesced in by governments. Nevertheless, a low-wage employment strategy could still be reconciled with demands for intergenerational equity, as long as there is a high rate of upward occupational mobility accompanied by substantial financial improvement. In that case, social policy would be directed toward ensuring that most young entrants into 'bad jobs' do not become trapped in them as chronic losers.

Esping-Andersen's argument raises a number of interesting questions. In the first place, we know relatively little about vertical mobility over the life course (i.e., intragenerational mobility), especially as it affects income levels. A second potential problem, which we have already touched upon in the previous section, is that even if rates of upward mobility are high, intergenerational equity is not likely to be achieved when the private costs of education are so great as to leave the current generation of students with large debts. Finally, a major issue to be considered is that the individual life course does not consist only of the economic life cycle. Dynamics of the family life cycle must also be considered, which occur alongside and interact with the dynamics of the economic life cycle. The different stages of the economic life cycle, of youth, middle age, and old age, can be considered as welfare substitutes in theory. In practice, they have different characteristics that may produce different welfare outcomes.

2.5.1 Vertical Mobility

As young people get older they usually get better jobs, and their earnings tend to move up.[91] In the period 1971 to 1986, rather high correlations were to be found between mean ages of men and socio-economic rankings of occupations.[92] This suggests that male career sequences from lower to higher occupations existed in that period. It is questionable whether upward mobility will have a similarly large impact on the current generation of young people. That is because the forces of restructuring that degraded the job market for young people have also affected traditional paths of upward occupational mobility. Case studies of workplaces in Nova Scotia show that factors of technological change (accompanied by de-skilling of middle-level occupations), organizational downsizing (accompanied by compression of managerial hierarchies) and outsourcing of work (accompanied by disconnection of central from peripheral employees), have all combined to erode career paths by which many people in the past moved up from entry-level jobs into secure, well-paying positions.[93] A 'crowding out' of younger employees from professional/managerial occupations has occurred, as the share of professional/managerial positions among younger male and female employees declined, while that of older employees increased, over the period 1981–94.[94] A particularly disturbing fact is that the number of youths who have never held a job has increased sharply. The proportion of all youths with no job experience jumped from 9.8 per cent in December 1989 to 24.6 per cent in December 1997.[95] Having no job experience may have a 'scarring' effect on some youths, who find themselves in a cycle of 'no experience, no job / no job, no experience.' The limited data on vertical mobility of youths is ambiguous. Young men with low earnings were slightly less likely to rise into a higher earnings group after the mid-1980s than before.[96] On the bright side, the mobility prospects of youths with higher education appear to be reasonably good. Workers with a university education continue to be more likely to move up out of low-earning jobs than workers whose highest level of educational attainment is high school or less.[97]

More young Canadians are gaining a university education now than ever before, and this bodes well for their future chances of upward mobility. However, if management hierarchies have been flattened and hollowed out in many organizations, in both the public and private sectors, then more highly educated young people could mean intensified competition for a limited number of well-paying jobs. The likely result in that case would be an increased emphasis on formal qualifications as a hiring criterion, and escalating educational requirements for jobs with the same, or lower, rates of pay. Under this scenario, the role of educational credentials in the labour market would be mainly as a form of exclusion.[98]

2.5.2 Children in Life Course Differentiation
It remains to be seen whether or not the financial difficulties of many of today's cohort of young people will be overcome, or compensated for, in later life. Even if they are, there would still be cause for concern, if the special characteristics of youth are not taken into account in public policy.

It is important to remember that a significant number of young adults have children to support. Increased poverty among young adults inevitably means increased poverty among some children. Sharif and Phipps have concluded that young age of household head is a key factor influencing the probability of child poverty.[99] Additional analysis of the sources of low income led them to conclude that creating 'good jobs' for young Canadians is particularly important if child poverty is to be alleviated.

Tolerating a low-wage, 'bad job' labour market strategy for youth, in the expectation of life course equity, would be a dangerous social policy in a country like Canada. It would put the well-being of a significant number of young children at risk, and it contradicts publicly stated goals of lowering the number of children who live in poverty. For the same reason, educational policies which assume that post-secondary students can take on a larger share of the costs of their education, in the expectation of higher earnings in the future, should be treated with caution. Unless childbearing is deferred even further, the peak period in the life course for repaying student loans will coincide with the time for having young children. That could possibly have negative effects on child poverty.

2.6 Extended Social Differentiation

Several accounts of age-related differentiations within the working-age population have been reviewed here, dealing with market functioning, relative cohort size, status in seniority systems, the evolution of government programs, and position in the life course. Among these factors, only relative cohort size is of no apparent importance today.[100] All the other factors deserve some recognition. Unfortunately, both the quantity and the quality of available research on these factors is uneven, which makes it difficult to draw comparative conclusions. Nevertheless, there are three general themes that can be identified as bases for debate because they cut across several factors.

First, it is very clear that the recent economic difficulties of Canadian youths are not entirely due to the changing organization of work. They are also due to the changing organization of rewards from work. What remains unclear is exactly why the financial rewards from work should have changed in the way that they did. On the one hand, it appears that new technologies have created new advantages for highly skilled individuals who possess the right combinations of education and work experience, whereas people who lack such employable skills have been overlooked. Young people, who are relatively lacking in work experience, and whose education is provided by institutions that often struggle to keep up with the rapid pace of change, are at a disadvantage from this point of view. On the other hand, it appears that the benefits of more education have a less favourable impact upon labour market outcomes for young people than do demands for labour from employers. Seen from this point of view, the main effect of education is to provide some young people with a competitive advantage in qualifying to be considered for employment, which may be partially offset by such limitations to competition as seniority provisions and established social ties within work organizations, which favour older workers.

The second general theme is that the age-related distribution of economic life chances is affected not only by market forces, but also by agents of the state, even when that is not a matter of public policy, and even if it is not acknowledged by governments. Government agencies offer or withhold employment opportunities for the young (e.g., in the public service and in the health sector); they offer or deny income transfers (such as social assistance and employment insurance); and as well they influence the timing and costs of the transition from school to work (including the magnitude of education debts). Research and policy studies that examine, or simply take for granted, market forces of globalization and economic restructuring need to be balanced by equally detailed analyses of the effects of the public sector upon young people in Canada.

The third, and final, point to understand about the various accounts of age-related differentiations within the working-age population is that the most important issue is not which account has the right explanation for the deteriorated economic circumstances of youth. The most important single statistic about the current economic strains of youth is that they have lasted for approximately two decades. During that time, the nature of the problem has changed continuously, and it has taken on subtly different shapes and forms. The main conclusion to be drawn about what has been happening is that we have been witnesses to a process of extended social differentiation. In such a process, some form of differentiation that emerges in one sector of social life has an impact upon another sector of social life, so that the latter too becomes more differentiated, and so on in a chain of linked differentiations.

Lines of differentiation that began in the age stratification of the human life course first became further differentiated within the market economy (and the shadow economy of collective bargaining) into multiple economic divisions. These are the divisions of labour force participation, of employment and unemployment, of hours of employment, of wage levels, and of 'good jobs' and 'bad jobs'. The adverse effects upon some groups of these divisions in employment conditions then flowed into other sectors of society, which were held responsible for meeting unfilled demands for life chances. Families and governments were the first to feel the effects of this socializing of unfilled economic demands: the former in their traditional role as providers of last resort, the latter in their erstwhile role as providers of social policy. Neither group has been comfortable with taking on a higher level of responsibility, under conditions that were not of their own choosing.

Much of the unfilled demand for better life chances by youth has therefore devolved upon post-secondary educational institutions, seen as the gatekeepers to a brighter future. Within the post-secondary sector, a portion of youths' current low economic life chances is being transformed into future financial obligations, in the form of increased indebtedness. Part of the demand for current income by youth is being met by drawing on future (projected) income, in the form of educational debt.

Here the life course re-enters the picture, as a temporal structure of life chances. The latest stage of social differentiation is one in which successive cohorts of youths are being differentiated not only in terms of their amount of income, but also in the amount of debt that they carry forward into their adult years. This is unlikely to be the end of the story. Indebted youths, when they reach full adulthood, will need good, well-paying jobs in order to pay off their student loans.

3. Policy Issues

Greater efforts are needed to bring about the full economic inclusion of young people.[101] The argument has been made elsewhere that emphasis upon more training, and improving the education-job mismatch, is an inadequate substitute for a well-thought-out strategy for economic growth, the distribution of work, and employment relationships.[102]

A collective strategy to improve conditions for the young should be directed not only at private employers, but also at the public sector, where there has been a significant decline in younger employees, especially in younger male employees.[103] Apparently, the shift in the age distribution of employment away from the public sector accounted for a small part of the fall in relative wage levels observed in this period. It seems that the life chances of young people have to some extent been made worse by the actions of governments, at the same time as governments have wanted to improve their situation.

There is also a case to be made for changing existing government legislation, with a view to more positive inclusion of young people. If young people today constitute a chronically disadvantaged section of the population, then perhaps they should be included as a designated group under the Employment Equity Act (alongside women, Aboriginals, persons with disabilities, and members of visible minorities). In any event, the Employment Equity Act should be reviewed. At present, the act explicitly endorses seniority rights, which are deemed not to be employment barriers within the meaning of the act.[104]

Over the period 1978–93, the average annual layoff rate was 8.3 per cent among workers aged 15–24, falling to 7.6 per cent among those 25–34, 6.4 per cent among those 35–44, and around 6.2 per cent among those over age 45.[105] It is consistent with this pattern of age-related job losses that in 1988–90 the youngest workers (16–24), who represented about one-fifth of the workforce, accounted for a disproportionately high 35.4 per cent of permanent layoffs.[106] It is possible that the observed age distribution of layoffs is entirely due to optimal human resource decisions by employers. However, the widespread existence of legally enforceable employee seniority rights with respect to layoffs would seem to suggest otherwise.

4. Research Directions: Opening Windows

Few of the issues raised in this report can be regarded as completely settled, if only because events themselves are constantly changing. It is possible that the economic position of young people might improve in the future, if the expected decline in the number of young workers in fact gives them greater bargaining power in the labour market. However, that outcome is not inevitable, since position in the labour market is influenced by a number of factors in addition to relative age- group size.

Age-related differentiations within the working-age population do seem to be worthy of continued research attention. However, existing research programs should be supplemented with new information. Extensive survey data is now available in Canada for factors that are relevant to individuals as the unit of analysis (e.g., education). Excellent investigations have been conducted using these data, from which much has been learned. Nevertheless, it became apparent during the course of the present study that much less is known about factors relevant to organizations as the unit of analysis. These factors include the nature of compensation practices, as well as seniority and origination systems. It is desirable to open more windows into Canadian organizations, in order to throw greater light on such factors.

One of the key facts that should be recognized in any consideration of youthful marginalization in Canada is that it cannot be due solely to the particular relationship of youth with employers (e.g., as new entrants into the labour force). The sharp drop in economic opportunities for young people is just the young end of a general age-related redistribution of life chances, in which the relative positions of all age groups have been shifting. This conclusion arises especially from recent research on wage rates, which has emerged as critical to understanding contemporary youth issues.[107] There has been a systematic re-differentiation of age groups in the labour market, which has disadvantaged the youngest age groups the most.[108] The reasons why this has happened are not entirely clear.

The possibility exists that some of the comparative economic disadvantages faced by young people in Canada may have arisen, not only from the functioning of national and provincial labour markets, but also from the operation of stratification systems within organizations. The extent of any impact of the latter factor is currently very hard to evaluate. We need to know much more about differential treatment given to different categories of workers within places of employment. Increased publication of research into age-related features of collective agreements would be helpful. However, the major area where information is lacking concerns informal rights and privileges affecting the terms and conditions of employment for non-unionized workers.

The most troubling research problem of all is the precise nature of the relationship between youth, education, and income. Here, there is an odd contradiction of arguments to be observed in the economic literature. On the one hand, it is argued that increased education of young people has failed to raise their wages significantly, because employers can benefit from the increased supply of educated young workers by reducing their wage costs. On the other hand, it is argued that increased education of older workers has helped to raise their wages significantly, because education has made them more productive and thus more valuable to their employers. An outside observer might think that both of these arguments can not be true simultaneously; unless it is assumed that education somehow produces opposite effects on people of different ages.

Kapsalis, Morissette, and Picot have suggested that a substantial part of the increase in the wage gap between younger and older workers is due to growth in the relative educational attainment of the latter.[109] In the past, younger workers had higher levels of education than older workers. However, the aging of the cohort that dramatically increased its education in the 1960s means that workers aged 45 to 54 are now much better educated than they were in the past. It is therefore possible that many older workers today continue to benefit from greater job experience, while no longer having a comparative disadvantage in educational attainment. Following this line of argument, Crompton and Vickers have concluded: 'In the 1990s, the human capital of older workers outstripped that of younger workers.'[110]

A few words of caution should be added here concerning the above analysis and the conclusions that may be drawn from it. In the first place, it should be noted that Kapsalis, Morissette, and Picot did not include workers under the age of 25 in their study, for technical reasons. Any extension of their thesis about changing relative educational attainment to the age group under discussion here is therefore plausible, but not definitive. Second, the authors concluded from their research that the growth in the relative educational attainment of older workers explains about one-quarter of the increase in the age-wage gap that occurred between 1981 and 1988, and between one-half and three-quarters of the increase in the gap between 1989 and 1995. Since the relative earnings of young workers were in decline from the late 1970s through the 1990s, changing relative educational attainment cannot be the sole factor, or even a major factor, in the cumulative comparative disadvantages of young people over this entire period. The changing composition of the labour force accounted for at most 30 per cent of the growth in the age-wage gap during the 1980s. As Kapsalis, Morissette, and Picot note: 'The remaining 70% is due to changes in the relative returns to characteristics.'

The financial returns to education seem to have fallen in Canada during the 1980s and 1990s, especially for young men. Kapsalis, Morissette, and Picot report that between 1989 and 1995, young male university graduates experienced a dramatic drop in their real weekly earnings of up to 19 per cent. The question of whether, or the extent to which, young Canadians can actually expect to benefit financially from further education would seem to be crucial to federal government policy concerning youth and the labour market.[111] Special attention should be paid to the distinction between an individual's relative advantages in a labour market, and a cohort's relative rewards in a structure of intergenerational inequality.

To see why this is such a challenging problem, consider the following contrasting findings. On the one hand, it is very clear that the more education people have, the less likely they are to be unemployed, and the higher their average incomes will be. On the other hand, the financial returns to education for recent graduates declined in both relative and absolute terms during the 1980s and 1990s. Labour market outcomes at ages 25 to 29, for successive cohorts of high school and university graduates between 1979 and 1993, show that real incomes and employment rates have declined for all groups except female university graduates.[112]

An important question for policy research concerns the relationship between public investment in education and the total effect of education. If the total effect of investing in education is that some individuals who acquire more education gain a relative advantage over others in their cohort, within a shrinking income pool for each successive cohort, is that a productive investment, or not? What criteria do we use to make that kind of decision, and do we have the appropriate analytical tools for setting priorities in policy making?

5. Conclusion: Opening Doors

Full utilization of Canada's human resources is a long-standing policy objective of governments, and the position of youth in the labour market has therefore been a matter of varying concern over the years. Today, policy-makers are concerned because employment difficulties for the young, which became visible in the early 1980s, have persisted for most of the past two decades. It is possible that future improvements in the Canadian labour market may restore young workers to a more equitable position in society. However, this optimistic outcome cannot be taken for granted, and past disappointments justify caution about the economic prospects for youth.

In the absence of immediate and dramatic improvements in conditions for young workers, some additional thought needs to be given to the sources of their difficulties. It is important to note that most young Canadians are not work-shy, nor do they easily give up hope of productive employment. Only a negligible proportion of youths without jobs in the mid-1990s said that they were not looking for work because they 'believed no work was available' or because they were simply 'not interested in finding work.'[113] As long as such positive attitudes remain intact, economic change is unlikely to threaten the social cohesion of Canada. It is very important that such positive attitudes should be reinforced. The most reliable way to reinforce them is to reward them by opening more doors to opportunity.

Notes

1 See Miles Corak, 'Introduction,' In Miles Corak, ed., *Labour Markets, Social Institutions, and the Future of Canada's Children* (Ottawa: Statistics Canada, 1998), 1–9; and Richard Marquardt, *Enter at Your Own Risk* (Toronto: Between the Lines, 1998).

2 See Marc-André Deniger, 'Une jeunesse paupérisée,' *Apprentissage et Socialisation* 14.1 (1991): 11–17.

3 See Ted Wannell, 'Losing Ground,' in C. McKie and K. Thompson, eds, *Canadian Social Trends* (Toronto: Thompson Educational Publishing, 1990), 221–3; David Ross and Clarence Lochhead, 'Changes in Family Incomes and Labour Market Participation in Post-War Canada,' *Transition* 23.1 (1993): 5–7; and Garnett Picot and John Myles, 'Social Transfers, Changing Family Structure and Low Income among Children,' *Canadian Public Policy* 22.3 (1996): 244–59.

4 See Deborah Sunter, 'Youths – Waiting It Out,' *Perspectives on Labour and Income* 6.1 (1994): 31–6.

5 See Harvey Krahn, 'The School to Work Transition in Canada,' in W. Heinz, ed., *The Life Course and Social Change* (Weinheim: Deutscher Studien Verlag, 1991), 43–69; Statistics Canada, *Labour Force Update* (Ottawa: Statistics Canada, 1997); and Gordon Betcherman and René Morissette, *Recent Youth Labour Market Experiences in Canada* (Ottawa: Statistics Canada, 1994).

6 See Statistics Canada, 'Working Teens,' *Canadian Social Trends* 35 (1994): 18–22.

7 See Claude Lavoie, 'Youth Employment, Some Explanations and Future Prospects,' *Applied Research Bulletin* 2.2 (1996): 3–5.

8 See Simon Langlois, 'Les rigidités sociales et l'insertion des jeunes dans la société québécoise,' in F. Dumont, ed., *Une société des jeunes?* (Quebec: Institut québécois de recherche sur la culture, 1986), 301–23; Madeleine Gauthier, 'La jeunesse au carrefour de la pauvreté,' *Apprentissage et Socialisation* 14.1 (1991): 51–61; Jacques Hamel, 'Brèves notes sur une opposition entre générations,' *Sociologie et sociétés* 26.2 (1994): 165–76; Conseil permanent de la jeunesse, *Actes du colloque 'Jeunes adultes et précarité'* (Quebec: Gouvernement du Québec, 1995); and Marc-André Deniger, 'Crise de la jeunesse et transformations des politiques sociales en contexte de mutation structurale,' *Sociologie et sociétés* 28.1 (1996): 73–88.

9 See Michael Ornstein, *A Profile of Social Assistance Recipients in Ontario* (North York: Institute for Social Research, 1995).

10 See Dominique Meunier, Paul Bernard, and Johanne Boisjoly, 'Eternal Youth?' in M. Corak, ed., *Labour Markets, Social Institutions, and the Future of Canada's Children* (Ottawa: Statistics Canada, 1998), 157–69; Don Kerr, Daniel Larrivée, and Patricia Greenhalgh, *Children and Youth: An Overview* (Ottawa: Statistics Canada, 1994).

11 See Monica Boyd and Edward Pryor, 'Young Adults Living in Their Parents' Homes,' *Canadian Social Trends* 13 (1989): 17–20.

12 Madeleine Gauthier, 'Les jeunes sans emploi sont-ils pauvres?' in M. Gauthier, ed., *Les nouveaux visages de la pauvreté* (Quebec: Institut québécois de recherche sur la culture, 1987), 45–65; Madeleine Gauthier and Lucie Mercier, *La pauvreté chez les jeunes* (Quebec: Institut québécois de recherche sur la culture, 1994); National Council of Welfare, *Poverty Profile 1996* (Ottawa: National Council of Welfare, 1998).

13 See David Card and Thomas Lemieux, *Adapting to Circumstances* (Cambridge: National Bureau of Economic Research, 1997).

14 See Canadian Youth Foundation, *Youth Unemployment* (Ottawa: Canadian Youth Foundation, 1995); and Armine Yalnizyan, *The Growing Gap* (Toronto: Centre for Social Justice, 1998).

15 See Secrétariat à la Jeunesse, *Indicateurs jeunesse* (Quebec: Gouvernement du Québec, 1996).

16 See Lucie Dagenais, 'La jeunesse,' *Sociologie et sociétés* 28.1 (1996): 89–105.

17 See Keith Banting, Charles Beach, and Gordon Betcherman, 'Polarization and Social Policy Reform,' in K. Banting and C. Beach, eds, *Labour Market Polarization and Social Policy Reform* (Kingston: Queen's University School of Policy Studies, 1995), 1–19; and T.J. Alexander, 'Human Capital Investment,' *Policy Options* 18.6 (1997): 5–8.

18 See Ross Finnie, *Earnings Dynamics in Canada: The Distribution of Earnings* (Ottawa: Human Resources Development Canada, 1997).

19 See Ross Finnie, *Earnings Dynamics in Canada: Earnings Patterns by Age and Sex* (Ottawa: Human Resources Development Canada, 1997).

20 See Kelly Morrison, *Canada's Older Workers* (Ottawa: Human Resources Development Canada, 1996).

21 See Card and Lemieux, *Adapting to Circumstances*.

22 See David Blanchflower and Richard Freeman, 'Why Youth Unemployment Will Be Hard to Reduce,' *Policy Options* 19.3 (1998): 3–7.

23 See Susan Empson-Warner and Harvey Krahn, 'Unemployment and Occupational Aspirations,' *Canadian Review of Sociology and Anthropology* 29.1 (1992): 38–54; Antoon Leenaars and David Lester, 'The Changing Suicide Pattern in Canadian Adolescents and Youth,' *Adolescence* 30.119 (1995): 539–47; and Julian Tanner, Harvey Krahn, and Timothy Hartnagel, *Fractured Transitions from School to Work* (Toronto: Oxford University Press, 1995).

24 See Lise Côté, Christine Ross, Jocelyne Pronovost, and Richard Boyer, *Les comportements suicidaires chez les jeunes québécois de 15 à 24 ans* (Montreal: Santé Québec, 1992).

25 See Canadian Youth Foundation, *Youth Unemployment*; and Nadene Rehnby and Stephen McBride, *Help Wanted* (Ottawa: Canadian Centre for Policy Alternatives, 1997).

26 See Doug Hostland, *Structural Unemployment in Canada* (Ottawa: Human Resources Development Canada, 1995).

27 See Statistics Canada, *Labour Force Update* (Ottawa: Statistics Canada, 1999).

28 See Statistics Canada, 'Labour Force Survey, December 1998,' *Statistics Canada Daily*, 8 Jan. 1999; 'Labour Force Survey, July 1999,' *Statistics Canada Daily*, 6 Aug. 1999; and 'Labour Force Survey, July 2000,' *Statistics Canada Daily*, 4 Aug. 2000.

29 See Garnett Picot and Zhengxi Lin, *Are Canadians More Likely to Lose Their Jobs in the 1990s?* (Ottawa: Statistics Canada, 1997); and Kelly Morrison, *Job Loss and Adjustment Experiences of Older Workers* (Ottawa: Human Resources Development Canada, 1995).

30 See Miles Corak, 'Unemployment Comes of Age,' in S. Gera, ed., *Canadian Unemployment* (Ottawa: Supply and Services Canada, 1991), 89–97.

31 See Syed Rahman and Surendra Gera, 'Long-Term Unemployment in Canada,' in S. Gera, *Canadian Unemployment*, 99–115; Morrison, *Canada's Older Workers*; and David Cheal and Karen Kampen, 'Poor and Dependent Seniors in Canada,' *Ageing and Society* 18.2 (1998): 147–66.

32 See Statistics Canada, *Labour Force Update* (Ottawa: Statistics Canada, 1998).

33 See Statistics Canada, *Labour Force Update* (1999).

34 See Philip Jennings, *School Enrolment and the Declining Youth Participation Rate* (Ottawa: Human Resources Development Canada, 1998); and Richard

Archambault and Louis Grignon, *Decline in the Youth Participation Rate since 1990: Structural or Cyclical?* (Ottawa: Human Resources Development Canada, 1999).

35 See Statistics Canada, *Labour Force Update* (1998).

36 See Statistics Canada, 'Working Teens.'

37 See Jean Kunz and Grant Schellenberg, *Youth at Work in Canada* (Ottawa: Canadian Council on Social Development, 1999).

38 See Statistics Canada, *Labour Force Update* (1998).

39 See Richard Marquardt, 'Quality of Youth Employment,' in *High School May Not Be Enough*, ed. Statistics Canada (Ottawa: Statistics Canada, 1998), 43–50.

40 See Marie Drolet and René Morissette, *Working More? Working Less?* (Ottawa: Statistics Canada, 1997).

41 See Statistics Canada, *Labour Force Update* (1999).

42 Marquardt, 'Quality of Youth Employment.'

43 See Lee Grenon, 'Juggling Work and School,' in *Work Arrangements in the 1990s*, ed. Statistics Canada (Ottawa: Statistics Canada, 1998), 85–102.

44 See René Morissette, 'Declining Earnings of Young Men,' *Canadian Social Trends* 46 (1997): 8–12; and Statistics Canada, *Labour Force Update* (1997).

45 See Kunz and Schellenberg, *Youth at Work in Canada.*

46 See Economic Council of Canada, *Good Jobs, Bad Jobs* (Ottawa: Supply and Services Canada, 1990).

47 See Rahman and Gera, 'Long-term Unemployment.'

48 See René Morissette and Marie Drolet, *The Evolution of Pension Coverage of Young and Prime-Aged Workers in Canada* (Ottawa: Statistics Canada, Analytical Studies Branch, Research Paper Series no. 138, 1999).

49 See Gordon Betcherman and Norman Leckie, *Age Structure of Employment in Industries and Occupations* (Ottawa: Human Resources Development Canada, 1995); and Human Resources Development Canada, 'Unemployment among Young People,' *Applied Research Bulletin* 4.1 (1998).

50 See John Myles, Garnett Picot, and Ted Wannell, *Wages and Jobs in the 1980s* (Ottawa: Statistics Canada, 1988) and 'Does Post-industrialism Matter?' in G. Esping-Andersen, ed., *Changing Classes* (London: Sage, 1993), 171–94; and René Morissette, 'The Declining Labour Market Status of Young Men,' in M. Corak, ed., *Labour Markets, Social Institutions, and the Future of Children* (Ottawa: Statistics Canada, 1998), 31–50.

51 See René Morissette, John Myles, and Garnett Picot, 'Earnings Polarization in Canada,' in K. Banting and C. Beach, eds, *Labour Market Polarization and Social Policy Reform* (Kingston: Queen's University School of Policy Studies, 1995), 23–50; W. Craig Riddell, 'Human Capital Formation in Canada,' in Banting and Beach, *Labour Market Polarization*, 125–72; Surendra Gera and Philippe Massé, *Employment Performance in the Knowledge-based Economy*

(Ottawa: Industry Canada, 1996); Constantine Kapsalis, *An Explanation of the Increasing Age Premium* (Ottawa: Statistics Canada, 1998); and Garnett Picot, *What Is Happening to Earnings Inequality and Youth Wages?* (Ottawa: Statistics Canada, 1998).

52 See Marquardt, 'Quality of Youth Employment.'
53 See Corak, 1998, and Morissette, 'Declining Labour Market Status of Young Men.'
54 See Jennings, *School Enrolment*; and Claude Lavoie and Ali Béjaoui, *La situation de l'emploi des jeunes au Canada* (Ottawa: Human Resources Development Canada, 1998).
55 See Advisory Committee on the Changing Workplace, *Collective Reflection on the Changing Workplace* (Ottawa: Human Resources Development Canada, 1997).
56 See Government of Canada news release, 'Youth Employment and Learning Strategy to Lay Groundwork for Modernizing School to Work Measures (April 1994).
57 See Scott Davies, Clayton Mosher, and Bill O'Grady, 'Trends in Labour Market Outcomes of Canadian Post-secondary Graduates,' in L. Erwin and D. MacLennan, eds, *Sociology of Education in Canada* (Toronto: Copp Clark Longman, 1994), 352–69.
58 See Association of Universities and Colleges of Canada, 'Making the Transition,' *Research File* 2.4 (1998): 1–11.
59 See Lindsay Redpath, 'Education-Job Mismatch among Canadian University Graduates,' *Canadian Journal of Higher Education* 24.2 (1994): 89–114; and Karen Kelly, Linda Howatson-Leo, and Warren Clark, 'I Feel Overqualified for My Job,' *Canadian Social Trends* 47 (1997): 11–16.
60 See Geoff Bowlby, 'Relationship between Postsecondary Graduates' Education and Employment,' *Education Quarterly Review* 3.2 (1996): 35–44.
61 See Garnett Picot, Ted Wannell, and Doug Lynd, *The Changing Labour Market for Postsecondary Graduates* (Ottawa: Statistics Canada, 1987).
62 See Statistics Canada, *Adult Literacy in Canada* (Ottawa: Statistics Canada, 1991).
63 See Douglas Willms, *International Adult Literacy Survey* (Ottawa: Statistics Canada, 1997).
64 See Lynn Barr-Telford, Geoff Bowlby, and Warren Clark, *The Class of 86 Revisited* (Ottawa: Statistics Canada, 1996).
65 See Riddell, 'Human Capital Formation in Canada'; and Gera and Massé, *Employment Performance.*
66 See Morrison, *Canada's Older Workers.*
67 See Paul Beaudry and David Green, *Cohort Patterns in Canadian Earnings* (Toronto: Canadian Institute for Advanced Research, 1997).

68 See Doug Hostland, *What Factors Determine Structural Unemployment in Canada?* (Ottawa: Human Resources Development Canada, 1995).

69 See Don Kerr and Bali Ram, *Population Dynamics in Canada* (Ottawa: Statistics Canada, 1994).

70 Hostland, *What Factors Determine*, 27.

71 See Fred Pampel and H. Elizabeth Peters, 'The Easterlin Effect,' in J. Hagan and K. Cook, eds, *Annual Review of Sociology* 21 (Palo Alto, CA: Annual Reviews Inc., 1995).

72 See Myles, Picot, and Wannell, *Wages and Jobs in the 1980s*; and Garnett Picot and Andrew Heisz, *The Performance of the 1990s Canadian Labour Market* (Ottawa: Statistics Canada, Analytical Studies Branch, Research Paper Series no. 148, 2000).

73 See Riddell, 'Human Capital Formation in Canada.'

74 See Neil Guppy and Scott Davies, *Education in Canada* (Ottawa: Statistics Canada, 1998).

75 See Don Little, 'Earnings and Labour Force Status of 1990 Graduates,' *Education Quarterly Review* 2.3 (1995): 10–20; and Michael Paju, *The Class of '90 Revisited* (Ottawa: Human Resources Development Canada, 1997).

76 See Myles, Picot, and Wannell, *Wages and Jobs in the 1980s*; Kapsalis, *The Increasing Age Premium*; and Guppy and Davies, *Education in Canada*.

77 See Nicholas Chamie, *Why the Jobless Recovery* (Ottawa: Conference Board of Canada, 1995), 2.

78 See Richard Freeman and Karen Needels, 'Skill Differentials in Canada in an Era of Rising Labor Market Inequality,' in D. Card and R. Freeman, eds, *Small Differences That Matter* (Chicago: University of Chicago Press, 1993); and Riddell, 'Human Capital Formation.'

79 See Kathryn MacLeod, *The Seniority Principle* (Kingston: Industrial Relations Centre, 1987).

80 See Julian Walker, *Two-Tier Wage Systems* (Kingston: Industrial Relations Centre, 1987); and Johanne Pes and Anne-Marie Blanchet, 'La rémunération à double ou à multiples paliers dans les conventions collectives en vigueur au Québec,' *Le Marché du travail* 9.3 (1988): 79–89.

81 See Yves Turcot, 'La rémunération à double palier dans les conventions collectives au Québec,' *Le Marché du travail* 13.11 (1992): 9–10, 78–94; Québec, Ministère du Travail, *Vers une équité intergénérationelle* (Quebec: Gouvernement du Québec, 1998).

82 See Louise Dulude, *Seniority and Employment Equity for Women* (Kingston: Industrial Relations Centre, 1995).

83 See David Cheal, *New Poverty* (Westport, CT: Greenwood, 1996).

84 See Shelley Phipps, 'Poverty and Labour Market Change,' in K. Banting

and C. Beach, eds, *Labour Market Polarization and Social Policy Reform* (Kingston: Queen's University School of Policy Studies, 1995), 59–88.

85 See Colin Lindsay, Mary Sue Devereaux, and Michael Bergob, *Youth in Canada* (Ottawa: Statistics Canada, 1994).

86 See Chantal Hicks, 'The Age Distribution of the Tax/Transfer System in Canada,' in M. Corak, ed., *Government Finances and Generational Equity*, (Ottawa: Statistics Canada, 1998), 39–56.

87 See Don Little, 'Financing Universities,' *Education Quarterly Review* 4.2 (1997): 10–26.

88 See Don Little and Louise Lapierre, *The Class of 90* (Ottawa: Statistics Canada, 1996); and Ross Finnie and Saul Schwartz, *Student Loans in Canada* (Toronto: C.D. Howe Institute, 1996).

89 See Ross Finnie and Gaétan Garneau, 'Student Borrowing for Postsecondary Education,' *Education Quarterly Review* 3.2 (1996): 10–34; Finnie and Garneau, 'An Analysis of Student Borrowing for Postsecondary Education,' *Canadian Business Economics* 4, no. 2 (1996): 51–64; Statistics Canada, 'Paying Off Student Loans,' *Statistics Canada Daily*, 8 Dec. 1998; and Statistics Canada, 'Student Debt,' *Statistics Canada Daily*. 30 July 1999.

90 See Gøsta Esping-Andersen, *Welfare States in Transition* (London: Sage, 1996).

91 See Ross Finnie, *Earnings Dynamics in Canada: The Earnings Mobility of Canadians* (Ottawa: Human Resources Development Canada, 1997); and Richard Marquardt, 'Labour Market Participation, Employment and Unemployment,' in *High School May Not Be Enough* (Ottawa: Human Resources Development Canada, 1998), 29–42.

92 See Frank Denton, Peter Pineo, and Byron Spencer, *The Demographics of Employment* (Ottawa: Institute for Research on Public Policy, 1991).

93 See Lars Osberg, Fred Wien, and Jan Grude, *Vanishing Jobs* (Toronto: Lorimer, 1995).

94 See Kapsalis, *The Increasing Age Premium*.

95 See Statistics Canada, *Labour Force Update* (1998).

96 See Morissette, 'The Declining Labour Market Status of Young Men'; and René Morissette and Charles Bérubé, *Longitudinal Aspects of Earnings Inequality in Canada* (Ottawa: Statistics Canada, 1996).

97 See Marie Drolet and René Morissette, *The Upward Mobility of Low Paid Canadians* (Ottawa: Statistics Canada, 1998).

98 See Raymond Murphy, 'A Weberian Approach to Credentials,' in L. Erwin and D. MacLennan, eds, *Sociology of Education in Canada* (Toronto: Copp Clark Longman, 1994), 102–19.

99 See Najma Sharif and Shelley Phipps, 'The Challenge of Child Poverty,' *Canadian Business Economics* 2.3 (1994): 17–30.

100 Relative cohort size is a potentially significant factor in Canada's Aborigi-
      nal population. The proportion of young people aged 15–24 is greater in
      the Aboriginal population (18%) than in the general population (13%),
      and large increases will occur in the Aboriginal youth population over the
      next decade. Aboriginal youth employment is emerging as an important
      policy issue, especially in the western provinces. See Statistics Canada,
      '1996 Census: Aboriginal Data,' *Statistics Canada Daily,* 13 Jan. 1998.

101 See David Cheal, 'Repenser les transferts intergénérationnels,' in C.
      Attias-Donfut, ed., *Les solidarités entre générations* (Paris: Nathan, 1995),
      259–68.

102 See Advisory Group on Working Time and the Distribution of Work,
      Report (Ottawa: Human Resources Development Canada, 1994); Thomas
      Dunk, Stephen McBride, and Randle Nelsen, *The Training Trap* (Halifax:
      Fernwood, 1996); Gordon Betcherman and Graham Lowe, *The Future of
      Work in Canada* (Ottawa: Renouf, 1997); and David Foot and Rosemary
      Venne, 'The Time Is Right,' *Canadian Studies in Population* 25.2 (1998): 91–
      114.

103 See Kapsalis, *The Increasing Age Premium*; Joseph Peters, *An Era of Change*
      (Ottawa: Renouf, 1999).

104 See Government of Canada, Employment Equity Act, 8.1 and 8.2 (1995).

105 See Picot and Lin, *Are Canadians More Likely to Lose Their Jobs?*

106 See Morrison, *Job Loss.*

107 See Morissette, Myles, and Picot, 'Earnings Polarization.'

108 See Riddell, 'Human Capital Formation.'

109 See Constantine Kapsalis, René Morissette, and Garnett Picot, *The Returns
      to Education, and the Increasing Wage Gap between Younger and Older Workers*
      (Ottawa: Statistics Canada, Analytical Studies Branch, Research Paper
      Series no. 131, 1999).

110 See Suzan Crompton and Michael Vickers, 'One Hundred Years of Labour
      Force,' *Canadian Social Trends* 57 (2000): 2–13.

111 Compare Ministerial Task Force on Youth, *Take on the Future* (Ottawa:
      Government of Canada, 1996); and see Jerry Paquette, 'Scolarité et rev-
      enu,' *Policy Options* 18.6 (1997): 57–61.

112 See Guppy and Davies, *Education in Canada.*

113 See Marquardt, 'Labour Market Participation.'

4. Visible Minorities in Canadian Society: Challenges of Racial Diversity

Peter S. Li

As with many other modern societies, Canada's demographic composition is ethnically heterogeneous, in the sense that its citizens have come from many countries of origin and cultural backgrounds. However, since the late 1970s and early 1980s, there has been a growing perception that Canadian society has become more diverse as a result of an influx of immigrants from non-traditional source regions, mainly Asia and Africa. The perception of Asia and Africa as non-traditional immigrant-sending sources and of Asians and Africans as newcomers to Canada is not without grounds, since historically immigrants from these regions were not welcome in Canada, and since it was the changes in immigration regulations in 1967 that enabled Canada to adopt a universal system to screen immigrants without resorting to the category of racial or national origin. Still, the notion that Canada has been homogeneous ethnically and culturally prior to the arrival of recent immigrants from Asia and Africa is not supported by historical facts. The purpose of this chapter is to show how cultural diversity and racial differentiation are constructed in Canada society. There is no doubt that the history of a country and its subsequent demographic formations play a part in shaping the nature of diversity in that society. However, immigration and demographic forces represent only one aspect that contributes to the construction of diversity, since 'diversity,' in terms of differences between social groups, is also produced and reproduced in the way social groups are given or denied opportunities, and in the way normative values are used to asses their social worth. In other words, superficial features such as skin colour are insufficient in themselves to produce racial differentiations. However, they can be used as social markers by which social groups can be deemed to be fundamentally different, and by which opportunities of rewards and privileges are regulated. Thus, a distinction should be made between superficial differences of 'races' and the social construction of racial diversity based on phenotypical differences.

1. The Social Construction of Racial Difference

It has long been recognized that no scientific basis exists to justify using superficial features such as skin colour to categorize people as though the resulting groupings are logical genetic classifications.[1] However, the term 'race' is routinely used both as a meaningful folk notion and a legitimate scientific concept. As a result, there is confusion between the phenotypic traits used to justify the construction of race, on the one hand, and the social attributes given to racial groupings, on the other. Some authors prefer to use the term 'social race' to highlight the fact that selected phenotypic attributes are important only in the social construction of racial categories but otherwise trivial in genetic classifications.[2] In other words, physical and cultural traits of people being racialized take on specific meanings such that 'race' becomes what Banton calls a 'role sign,'[3] and that superficial physical variations serve as markers of racial roles.

'Racialization' is a term typically used to refer to the process by which society attributes social significance to groups on superficial physical grounds; people so marked may be referred to as racialized minorities in terms of their relation to a dominant group.[4] Over time, racialization systematically pairs superficial features of people with often undesirable social characteristics to give the false impression that the social import of race comes from a primordial origin, and not society's attribution.

In short, while superficial physical features of people do not provide the scientific grounds for classifying them into logical genetic groups, phenotypic features are used in the social construction of race. Over time, as it becomes socially acceptable to consider people on 'racial' grounds, physical and cultural characteristics that are originally trivial become socially significant, since they represent convenient markers by which people and groups, and their implied characteristics, can be distinguished.

To the extent that it is socially meaningful to regard people on racial grounds, it implies that society has attributed normative values and expectations to people of certain identifiable features that are primordial in origin. Such a normative scheme provides people with a rationale and a guide for evaluating race and racial origin. Over time, as certain ideas of race take root in the minds and hearts of people, and as social actions continue to reflect the meaning of race, the normative order associated with race becomes a part of the culture that people internalize in their way of life and perpetuate through social actions.

The racially based normative order is manifested in many aspects of life; for example, as racism in the ideological realm and as social practice embedded in institutions. In short, racialization makes it socially meaningful to regard people on racial grounds, and it attributes social value to people according to racial origin. In this sense, 'race' can be considered as having a social base in that it affects the life chances of people, as well as having a normative manifestation that places unequal values on the social groups being racialized. It should be noted that social value does not derive from the essential nature of race, but from society's placing relative social worth on superficial physical and cultural characteristics of people. In this way, the normative value and social consequence of race tend reinforce each other as racial ideas and social practice.

The above analysis of race and racial differentiation provides a useful framework for understanding how racial diversity is constructed in a society. In the sections to follow, we first examine how cultural diversity in Canada was officially constructed in the recent past in reaction to the politics of biculturalism. Such a construction provided a coherent perspective for interpreting cultural diversity in Canadian society in light of Canada's commitment to bilingualism. However, as changes in immigration altered the racial composition of recent arrivals, there was a sense that the conventional cultural balance was upset by an increase in racial diversity in Canadian society. The politics of national unity and multiculturalism as well as the reality of racial inequality gave new meanings to cultural diversity, which became increasingly associated with racial differences. In the final analysis, the challenge of cultural diversity for Canada is how to deal with the question of race normatively and socially, especially in light of the expected growth of the visible minority and in light of Canada's increasing engagement in a global context.

2. Ethnic Diversity in Canada

When, in 1965, the Royal Commission on Bilingualism and Bicultural-ism wrote about the 'Third Force' of Canada, it was clearly referring to those Canadians not of British and French origin, who collectively made up another force distinct from the two charter groups.[5] The rec-ognition of this third elememt was essentially how the royal commis-sion chose to recognize cultural diversity in Canada. In the end, the royal commission decided to include in its final report recommenda-tions about Canadians outside the two charter groups to stress the point that Canada was a mosaic, or a multicultural society, made up of three basic elements: the British, the French, and other Canadians.

The royal commission used a relatively simple trichotomy to describe Canada's diversity, one that clearly stressed the charter status of the British and the French, while acknowledging the contributions of other non-charter groups, mainly Europeans. This framework has been essen-tially adopted as the proper way to discuss the nature and composition of Canada's population diversity.

Historically, the numeric predominance of those of British and French origin was unquestionable. Before the great wave of European migration to Canada from 1896 until the beginning of the First World War in 1914, Canada's population was indeed made up mainly of those of British and French origin. For example, the 1871 Census of Canada shows that 61 per cent of Canada's 3.5 million people were of British origin, and 31 per cent French origin; Europeans not of British or French origin accounted for only 7 per cent of Canada's population in 1871 as well as in 1881.[6] This demographic composition basically persisted until the turn of the century.

The wave of immigration to Canada before the First World War began to increase the stock of Europeans not of British or French ori-gin. Between 1896 and 1914, Canada was eager to have immigrants for agricultural settlement. Under Canada's immigration policy, British and American immigrants were considered the most desirable, fol-lowed by North Europeans; other Europeans were tolerated and non-whites were not welcome.[7] When the supply of emigrants from England and western Europe was dwindling, Canada began recruiting people from eastern and southern Europe, such as Poles, Ukrainians, Hutterites, and Doukhobors. Over three million immigrants came to Canada between 1896 and 1914. In the period from 1915 to 1945, another two million immigrants came to Canada. These waves of immigration, together with a relatively high birth rate, contributed to the population increase; by 1941, Canada's population stood at 11.5 million people.[8]

The census data of Canada indicate that Canadians of European origin other than British and French increased from 8.5 per cent of the total population in 1901 to 14.2 per cent in 1921, and to 17.8 per cent in 1941.[9] In contrast, Canadians of British origin declined in relative terms from 57 per cent of the total population in 1901 to 50 per cent in 1941; but those of French origin remained at around 30 per cent of the total population in 1901 and in 1941. In short, if the composition of Canadians of European origin other than British and French is used as an indication of ethnic plurality, then there was an increase in diversity between 1901 and 1941. Much of the increase is accounted for by the relative decline of Canadians of British origin, which dropped 7 per cent during this period; in contrast, Europeans not of British or French origin gained 9 per cent for the same period.

Between 1941 and 1961, the proportion of Canadians of European origin other than British and French increased further. In 1941, they made up 17.8 per cent of Canada's total population; by 1961, they rose to 22.6 per cent (table 4.1). In contrast, those of British origin declined in relative terms from 49.7 per cent in 1941 to 43.8 per cent in 1961 (table 4.1). Thus, the expansion in ethnic diversity between 1941 to 1961 was in the direction of increasing the proportion of Canadians of European origin other than British and French, and decreasing the proportion of Canadians of British origin. However, Canada's population in 1941, as in 1871, was made up of people mainly of European origin, which accounted for 98 per cent of the total population in 1941 and in 1871, despite the fact that the population had increased from 3.5 million people in 1871 to 11.5 million in 1941. The ethnic composition of the Canadian population continued overwhelmingly to feature those of European origin, which remained at 97 per cent of the total population in 1961 and 96 per cent in 1971 (table 4.1). Thus, when the Royal Commission on Bilingualism and Biculturalism wrote about the 'Third Force' and about its place in the Canadian mosaic, it was writing from the vantage point that multicultural Canadian society was made up mostly of those of British, French, and other European origin. This framework of cultural diversity created a balance of sorts that upheld the charter status of the British and French, while acknowledging that other Canadians, mostly of European origin, had also contributed economically and culturally to the building of the nation.

TABLE 4.1
Population by ethnic origin, Canada, 1921–1971 (%)

Ethnic origin	1921	1931	1941	1951	1961	1971
British	55.4	51.9	49.7	47.9	43.8	44.6
French	27.9	28.2	30.3	30.8	30.4	28.7
Other European	14.2	17.6	17.8	18.2	22.6	23.0
Asian	0.8	0.8	0.6	0.5	0.7	1.3
Aboriginal	1.3	1.2	1.1	1.2	1.2	1.5
Black	0.2	0.2	0.2	0.1	0.2	0.2
Other	0.2	0.1	0.4	1.2	1.2	0.8
Total %	100.0	100.0	100.0	100.0	100.0	100.0
Total number	8,787,949	10,376,786	11,506,655	14,009,429	18,238,247	21,568,310

Source: Compiled from Census of Canada, 1971, Population: Ethnic Groups, Cat. 92-723, vol. 1, pt, 3, Bulletin 1.3, table 1.

3. Changes in Post-war Canadian Immigration Policy

Historically, Canada had relied upon western Europe, in particular Great Britain, as the major supplier of immigrants to Canada. In the two decades after the end of the Second World War, Canada maintained its policy of favouring immigrants from the United States, the United Kingdom, and other European countries. However, in the 1960s, there were major changes in the Canadian immigration policy that placed more emphasis on educational and occupational skills as criteria for selecting immigrants, although sponsored immigrants under family unification remained an important component in immigration.

Until the immigration regulations of 1962 were adopted, the postwar immigration policy of Canada was guided by the statement of Prime Minister Mackenzie King, on 1 May 1947, in the House of Commons:

> The policy of the government is to foster the growth of the population of Canada by the encouragement of immigration. The government will seek by legislation, regulation, and vigorous administration, to ensure the careful selection and permanent settlement of such numbers of immigrants as can advantageously be absorbed in our national economy ...
>
> There will, I am sure, be general agreement with the view that the people of Canada do not wish, as a result of mass immigration, to make a fundamental alteration in the character of our population. Large-scale immigration from the orient would change the fundamental composition of the Canadian population. Any considerable oriental immigration would, moreover, be certain to give rise to social and economic problems of a character that might lead to serious difficulties in the field of international relations. The government, therefore, has no thought of making any change in immigration regulations that would have consequences of the kind.[10]

King explicitly indicated that the government did not wish to alter the fundamental composition of the Canadian population as a result of immigration, especially Oriental immigration. He further stated that the government was not prepared to change 'the existing regulations respecting Asiatic immigration' except to revoke the 1923 Chinese Immigration Act and the 1931 order-in-council regarding naturalization.[11] In essence, it was a policy in favour of expanding the intake of immigrants from the traditional sources of Europe and the United

States and of maintaining a tight control of immigration from Asian countries. The statement reflected the conventional stand of the government and a widely accepted value of Canadian society to accept cultural diversity only as defined by European ethnic cultures, but not racial differences.

In 1952, the Government of Canada passed the Immigration Act, which laid down the framework for managing Canada's immigration policy and gave sweeping power to specially designated immigration officers to determine what kinds of people were admissible.[12] But a decision in the Supreme Court of Canada compelled the government to refine the categories of admissible people that were listed in an order-in-council, which excluded Asian countries as among those whence immigration to Canada was permitted.[13] By the 1960s, it had become clear that although Europe was still the main source of immigration to Canada, there were indications that the quality of immigrants, in terms of occupational and educational qualifications, had been diluted by the increased number of unskilled immigrants from southern Europe, and a corresponding decrease in the proportion of skilled immigrants in professional and managerial occupations. The 1962 immigration regulations revoked the special provisions of admission that applied to British, French, and American citizens and replaced it with a policy in favour of immigrants with educational, professional, and technical qualifications. Of the four categories of immigrant admission, the first two were given to independent immigrants with educational and professional skills, and the remaining two were for sponsored immigrants. However, sponsorship of immigrants outside of Europe and America was restricted only to close relatives.[14]

Further changes in the immigration regulations in 1967 finally resulted in a universal point system of assessment that was to be applied to all prospective immigrants, irrespective of country of origin or racial background.[15] Under the point system, an immigrant seeking entry under the independent class could apply either independently or as a nominated relative sponsored by a Canadian citizen or permanent resident. In either case, the immigrant would be assessed as well on the basis of his or her education, occupational demand, and age. The point system was further modified in 1978.[16] The new regulations reaffirmed the importance of educational and occupational qualifications in the selection of independent immigrants; for example, of the maximal 100 points used in the assessment, 60 points were given to educational level, vocational training, work experience, and occupational demand.

The 1978 immigration regulations also permitted the immigration of entrepreneurs, that is, immigrants who had the ability to establish a business and to create employment opportunities for Canadians. The 'business immigrant program' was further expanded in 1985 and in 1990.[17] There is evidence to indicate that the changes in immigration regulations in 1962 were prompted, in part at least, by the influx of unskilled immigrants from southern Europe, who were able to immigrate as relatives of Canadian citizens and permanent residents. At the same time, there were also concerns over the potential of an influx of unskilled non-white immigrants once national origin was not being considered in assessing prospective immigrants. Such worries were well summarized by Dr Davidson, deputy minister of Immigration, in an internal memorandum in 1962:

> Our prime objective in the proposed revision is to eliminate all discrimination based on colour, race or creed. This means that, if we continue to allow Greeks, Poles, Italians, Portuguese and other Europeans to bring in the wide range of relatives presently admissible, we will have to do the same for Japanese, Chinese, Indians, Pakistanis, Africans, persons from the Arab world, the West Indies and so forth. The only possible result of this would be a substantially larger number of unskilled close relatives from these parts of the world to add to the influx of unskilled close relatives from Europe.[18]

The subsequent amendments in 1962 reflected these concerns. On the one hand, the 1962 immigration regulations allowed individuals with educational qualifications and technical skills to immigrate to Canada; on the other hand, they restricted the range of immigrant sponsorship for those from outside of Europe and America.

There is further evidence to show that the changes in Canadian immigration policy in the 1960s were prompted by the rising demand for skilled labour and the competition for such labour from the United States.[19] In the two decades before 1967, Canada had been losing many professional and technical workers to the United States, as the post-war industrial boom there also demanded a large volume of skilled labour. Between 1953 and 1963, there was a net outflow of 41,263 professionals and 38,363 skilled workers from Canada to the United States.[20] However, Canada was able to benefit from a net gain of 125,242 professionals and skilled workers for the same period only because of a large volume of incoming immigrants from around the world. Between 1950 and 1963 Canada was experiencing an average annual outflow of 5476 professionals to the United States and the United Kingdom. Despite an average volume of 7790 professionals immigrating to Canada annually from around the world, the average net gain per year was only 2314 professionals.[21] These structural conditions compelled Canada to change its policy in 1962 to facilitate the immigration of skilled workers.

In 1965, the United States passed a new immigration act to replace the McCarran-Walter Act of 1952. The 1965 act abolished immigrant selection based on national origin quotas and used a preferential system to facilitate the entry of immigrants with professional and technical qualifications as well as those with skills in demand. The changes in the U.S. immigration policy made it even more urgent for Canada to broaden its capacity to admit skilled immigrants. The amendments in the 1967 immigration regulations reflected Canada's attempt to compete for skilled labour around the world.

The impact of the changes in the 1967 immigration regulations can be seen from immigration statistics. Between 1954 and 1967, 423,638 people emigrated from Canada to the United States, and 173,873 people immigrated to Canada from the United States; thus, Canada experienced a net loss of 249,755 people.[22] For the period after 1967, between 1968 and 1986, Canada had a moderate gain of 55,393 people from immigration to and from the United States. Before the 1967 changes in immigration regulations, the exodus of skilled labour from Canada to the United States reached a climax. In total, for the thirteen years between 1954 and 1967, Canada lost 60,230 people in professional, technical, managerial, and entrepreneurial occupations to the United States. In return, Canada received 33,119 immigrants in these occupations from the United States. Thus, the net loss of skilled labour for Canada for this period was 27,111 people. No doubt this exodus was related to the economic boom and the corresponding employment opportunities in the United States during the fifties and sixties, as well as the relative ease with which immigrants from Canada were accepted by the United States. One of the consequences of the changes in the 1967 immigration regulations was a reversal of this trend, as Canada placed more emphasis on human capital as the basis of immigration. For the eighteen-year period between 1968 and 1986, Canada experienced a net gain of 16,349 immigrants in professional, technical, managerial, and entrepreneurial occupations from the United States.

In other words, Canada's immigration policy in the 1960s was under pressure in having to deal with the problem of brain drain to the United States, and the problem of not being able to replace the net loss of labour power with new immigrants from conventional source countries.

4. Post-war European Immigration to Canada

Although Europeans constituted the majority of immigrants to Canada in the post-war period, their importance, in terms of the proportion of the total immigrants admitted, declined after 1967. In the 1940s and 1950s, immigration to Canada was made up almost exclusively of immigrants from Europe. For example, in the post-war years from 1946 to 1953, Canada admitted slightly fewer than one million immigrants to Canada, about 96 per cent of whom came from Europe; British immigrants alone accounted for 35 per cent of this stream of immigration.[23] Between 1954 and 1988, Canada admitted 4.8 million immigrants, 56 per cent of whom came from Europe, and 20 per cent came from the United Kingdom alone.[24] However, this relatively high percentage of post-war European immigration was largely a result of the almost exclusive reliance on European immigration before 1967. Between 1954 and 1967, 1.6 million immigrants, or 83 per cent of all immigrants to Canada, came from Europe. But between 1968 and 1988, European immigrants to Canada declined to 1.1 million, or 38 per cent of the total immigration to Canada. The percentage decline for British immigrants to Canada was from 28 per cent for 1954–67 to 14 per cent for 1968–88.

There is little doubt that the changes in the Canadian immigration regulations in 1967 had facilitated the entry of immigrants in managerial, professional, and technical occupations. In the few years before 1967, between 1961 and 1967, new immigrants in professional, technical, managerial, and entrepreneurial occupations made up 22 to 27 per cent of all immigrants entering Canada and destined to the labour force every year. Between 1968 and 1972, this type of skilled immigrant increased to 30 to 34 per cent of the annual number of immigrants coming to Canada and entering the labour force. Although the number of immigrants in managerial and professional occupations fluctuated from year to year in the post-war decades, the percentage from Europe declined from about 80 per cent in the 1950s to less than 50 per cent after 1967. In contrast, from 1968 to the 1990s, the proportion of immigrants in professional and technical occupations from non-European countries exceeded 50 per cent of the annual total immigrants in these occupations; and for some years, as for example between 1987 and 1992, professionals and technical workers from non-European countries accounted for over 70 per cent of all immigrants in professional and technical occupations entering Canada every year.[25]

The foregoing statistics clearly indicate that the volume and proportion of European immigrants to Canada had declined since their peak in the 1950s. The changes in the immigration regulations in the 1960s enabled Canada to abandon national origin as a selection criterion, and to select immigrants from all over the world, especially those in managerial, professional, and technical occupations. In the first two decades after the Second World War, Canada had relied upon European countries, particularly the United Kingdom, as the main sources for immigrants with managerial and professional skills. After 1967, the supply of these sources of skilled labour was broadened to include non-European countries, as European countries declined in their supply of immigrants to Canada, especially those with managerial and technical skills.

In a sense, the shift in immigration policy in the 1960s to facilitate those from outside of Europe to immigrate to Canada was a necessary measure to address the problem of a skilled labour shortage created by the brain drain to the United States and the drying up of prospective qualified immigrants from traditional source countries. These conditions prompted the changes in the immigration policy, which in turn, hastened the growth of the visible minority population in Canada.

5. Emergence of the 'Visible Minority' in Canada

In Canada, the emergence of the visible minority to constitute a sizeable segment of the population is a rather recent phenomenon that has resulted mainly from the changes in immigration regulations in 1967, although historically Canada had relied upon waves of Oriental labour in the development of major industries and megaprojects in western Canada.[26] The term 'visible minority' received official recognition in 1984 when Commissioner Rosalie S. Abella identified this 'group' as constituting one of the four designated categories in the royal commission report on equality in employment, in accordance with the terms of reference of the commission.[27] The subsequent Employment Equity Act of 1986 also specifically included 'persons who are, because of their race or colour, in a visible minority in Canada' as one of the designated groups whose employment opportunities employers on federal works or federal crown corporations had to take special measures to improve.[28] In the 1986 census, Statistics Canada operationalized membership in a visible minority to include respondents who chose any one of the ten origins in the 'ethnic origin' question: Black, Indo-Pakistani, Chinese, Korean, Japanese, South East Asian, Filipino, Other Pacific Islanders, West Asian and Arab, and Latin American, excluding Argentinean and Chilean.[29]

In 1986, members of visible minorities made up 6.3 per cent of Canada's population; by 1991, they climbed to 9.4 per cent; and by 1996, to 11.2 per cent.[30] Among the 3.2 million people who identified themselves as members of a visible minority in 1996, Chinese origin accounted for 27 per cent, South Asian origin 21 per cent, and Black 18 per cent.[31]

No doubt, the single most important factor contributing to the growth of the visible minority in Canada has been immigration since the 1970s. The changes in immigration regulations in 1962 and then in 1967 removed national origin as a consideration in selecting immigrants. Since 1967, immigrants have been able to enter Canada on the basis of educational and occupational qualifications and of family ties with citizens and permanent residents of Canada. Prospective immigrants from Asia, Africa, and other non-traditional sources that historically were restricted to enter Canada have been evaluated for admission under the same immigration regulations as applicants from Europe and the United States. The removal of racial or national barriers in immigrant selection has facilitated the immigration from Third World countries.

Immigration statistics for the period after 1967 show that there has been an increase in the proportion of immigrants from Asia and Africa, and a corresponding decrease in the proportion of immigrants from Europe (table 4.2). In the five years after 1967, 1968–72, Canada admitted 737,124 immigrants, of whom slightly over half came from Europe, 15.5 per cent from the United States, and 15 per cent from Asian countries. Thereafter, the proportion of immigrants from Europe continued to decline: from 38 per cent for 1973–7 to 22.6 per cent for 1988–92. In contrast, immigrants from Asia increased from 25.4 per cent for the period between 1973 and 1977 to 40 per cent for 1978–82, and then further to 51.8 per cent between 1988 and 1992. Similarly, immigrants from Africa, which made up only 5 per cent of immigrants between 1973 and 1977, rose to 6.7 per cent between 1988 and 1992.

In total, for the period of 28 years from 1968 to 1995, Canada admitted 4.4 million immigrants, of whom 39.5 per cent came from Asia, 5.1

TABLE 4.2
Immigrant arrivals by countries of last permanent residence, 1967–1995

Period	Europe	United States	Central/South America	Caribbean	Asia	Africa	Australasia	Oceania	Not stated	Total
1968–72	387,670 (52.6)	114,615 (15.5)	24,863 (3.4)	53,100 (7.2)	112,584 (15.3)	22,014 (3.0)	18,656 (2.5)	0 (0)	3,622 (0.5)	737,124 (100)
1973–77	324,131 (37.9)	102,141 (11.9)	63,598 (7.4)	86,627 (10.1)	216,837 (25.4)	42,748 (5.0)	10,870 (1.3)	7,937 (0.9)	0 (0)	854,889 (100)
1978–82	196,546 (33.2)	49,407 (8.4)	36,262 (6.1)	39,362 (6.7)	236,596 (40.0)	21,946 (3.7)	6,438 (1.1)	4,502 (0.8)	232 (0.0)	591,291 (100)
1983–87	124,344 (24.2)	36,214 (7.1)	56,442 (11.0)	39,079 (7.6)	226,326 (44.1)	24,027 (4.7)	2,774 (0.5)	3,771 (0.7)	38 (0.0)	513,015 (100)
1988–92	237,666 (22.6)	33,686 (3.2)	91,061 (8.7)	59,911 (5.7)	545,410 (51.9)	70,744 (6.7)	4,771 (0.5)	8,534 (0.8)	0 (0)	1,051,783 (100)
1993–95	126,509 (18.3)	19,433 (2.8)	39,119 (5.7)	36,599 (5.3)	418,016 (60.4)	45,255 (6.5)	3,476 (0.5)	3,791 (0.5)	0 (0)	692,198 (100)
Totals, 1968–95	1,396,866 (31.5)	355,496 (8.0)	311,345 (7.0)	314,678 (7.1)	1,755,769 (39.5)	226,734 (5.1)	46,985 (1.1)	28,535 (0.6)	3,892 (0.1)	4,440,300 (100)

Source: Compiled from Immigration Statistics, Employment and Immigration Canada, 1973–1991, annual edition; Immigration Statistics, Citizenship and Immigration Canada, 1995.
Note: Figures in parentheses are percentages of the total.

per cent from Africa, and 7.1 from the Caribbean. If immigrants from these regions were considered as members of visible minorities in Canadian society, then about 51.7 per cent of the 4.4 million immigrants coming to Canada between 1968 and 1995 would have been members of visible minorities. In addition, if some of the immigrants from Central and South America were also counted as members of racial minorities, then the proportion of visible minorities among immigrants to Canada between 1968 and 1995 would have been 58.7 per cent. For the same period, European immigrants made up 31.5 per cent of all immigrants entering Canada, and immigrants from the United States accounted for 8 per cent (table 4.2).

The foregoing immigration statistics suggest that about 2.3 to 2.6 million members of visible minorities were added to the Canadian population between 1968 and 1995. In view of the fact that the total number of members of visible minorities was 1.6 million individuals in the 1986 census, 2.6 million individuals in the 1991 census, and 3.2 million individuals in the 1996 census,[32] then it is clear that immigration between the 1970s and 1990s alone would largely account for the growth of the visible minority population. The immigration pattern also means that most visible-minority members are first-generation immigrants born outside of Canada, in contrast to most European-Canadians who, because of a historical immigration policy in favour of their admission, tend to be native-born in Canada.

6. Changes in Ethnic and Racial Diversity

When the Royal Commission on Bilingualism and Biculturalism referred to the three elements that made up the mosaic of Canada, that mosaic was, without any doubt, one that was overwhelmingly European in origin. Even the 'Third Force,' after the British and the French, was composed of mostly those of European origin. The 1961 census of Canada, taken just two years before the 1963 royal commission, clearly shows that about 88 per cent of those not of British or French origin, or what the royal commission would call the 'Third Force,' were of European origin (table 4.3). This Canadian mosaic of Europeans has a history that dated back as early as the late nineteenth century, and it persisted for much of the twentieth century. Changes in the mosaic before the 1970s were mainly in the direction of having more European diversities in the Canadian population other than British and French. For example, in 1961, out of a total population of 18.2 million people in

TABLE 4.3
Composition of non-British and non-French ethnic origins in Canada, 1961–1991

	1961		1971		1981		1991	
	N	%	N	%	N	%	N	%
Non-British and non-French, single ethnic origin:								
European (non-British & non-French)	4,116,849	87.6	4,959,680	86.0	4,648,675	75.8	4,146,065	55.7
Aboriginal	220,121	4.7	312,760	5.4	413,380	6.7	470,615	6.3
Asian	121,753	2.6	285,540	5.0	694,830	11.3	1,607,230	21.6
African*	32,127	0.7	34,445	0.6	55,760	0.9	251,050	3.4
Latin, Central & South American**					117,550	1.9	179,930	2.4
Pacific Islanders					80,340	1.3	7,215	0.1
Other single origin	210,382	4.5	171,645	3.0	120,990	2.0	780,035	10.5
Total number of people of non-British and non-French single origin	4,701,232	100	5,764,070	100	6,131,525	100	7,442,140	100
Non-British and Non-French single origins as % of total population		25.8		26.7		25.5		27.6
Total population	18, 238,247		21,568,310		24,083,495		26,994,045	

*Includes 'Negro' for 1961 and 1971, 'North African Arab' for 1981, and 'Black origins' for 1991.
**Includes 'North American origins' (excluding 'Native peoples') for 1981 and 'Caribbean origins' for 1991.

Source: Compiled from Dominion Bureau of Statistics, 1961 Census of Canada, Population: Ethnic Origins, vol. 1, Cat. 92-911 (Ottawa: Minister of Trade and Commerce, 1962); Statistics Canada, 1971 Census of Canada, Population: Ethnic Groups, vol. 1, pt. 3, Bulletin 1.3, table 1 (Ottawa: Minister of Industry, Trade and Commerce, 1973); Statistics Canada, 1981 Census of Canada, Population: Ethnic Origin, vol. 1, Cat. 92-911, table 1 (Ottawa: Minister of Supply and Services Canada, 1984); Statistics Canada, 1991 Census of Canada, Ethnic Origin: The Nation, Cat. 93-315, table 1A, (Ottawa: Minister of Industry, Science and Technology, 1993).

Canada, 97 per cent were of European origin. However, the British-origin portion had declined in proportion from over 50 per cent in the 1920s and 1930s to about 44 per cent in 1961; at the same time, Canadians of European origin other than British and French had grown from 14 to 17 per cent in the 1920s and 1930s to about 23 per cent in 1961 (table 4.1). Thus, the rise of ethnic or cultural pluralism in this period was synonymous with the growth of European pluralities in the ethnic origin of Canadians, since those not of European origin made up only 3.2 per cent of the total population in 1961 (table 4.1).

By 1971, Canadians of European origin continued to account for 96 per cent of the 21.5 million people in the total population. Those of European origin other than British and French remained the dominant element within the 'Third Force.' Table 4.3 clearly shows that European Canadians other than British and French accounted for 86 per cent of the 5.8 million people who declared a non-British and non-French ethnic origin in the 1971 census. However, by 1981, this group had declined to 75.8 per cent of those not of British or French origin. By 1991, despite the growth of the non-British- and non-French- origin component to 7.4 million people, the European component of the 'Third Force' had further declined to 55.7 per cent.

Hence, between 1971 and 1991, despite the fact that those not of British or French origin remained at around 26 to 28 per cent of the total Canadian population,[33] there were changes in the ethnic and racial differentiation in the 'Third Force' to include a growing segment made up of non-European origin. For example, in 1971, those of Asian origin accounted for only 5 per cent of those not of British or French origin; by 1981, they had grown to 11.3 per cent, and by 1991, they had further increased to 21.6 per cent. Similarly, those of African origin rose from less than 1 per cent of those not of British or French origin in 1971 to 3.4 per cent in 1991.

By the time the 1991 census was taken, 55 per cent of the 'Third Force' was still made up of Europeans, but about one-quarter of it was accounted for by Asians and Africans. Those originating from Pacific Islands and Latin America accounted for another 2.5 per cent of those not of British or French origin. Hence, it is not so much the increase in the proportion of the 'Third Force' in the total population as the growth of racial minorities within the 'Third Force' that makes ethnic diversity more noticeable in Canada in the 1980s. This point is also evident in the 1996 census, despite a substantial number of Canadians choosing the 'multiple origins' and 'Canadian origins.'[34] On the sur-

TABLE 4.4
Composition of ethnic origins in Canada, 1996

	Number		%	
British single origin	3,267,520		11.5	
French single origin	2,683,840		9.4	
British/French multiple origins	8,547,145		30.0	
Non-British & non-French single and multiple origins	14,029,610		49.2	
Other European		3,742,890		13.1
Canadian origins (single and multiple)		5,906,045		20.7
Aboriginal		477,630		1.7
Asian		1,968,465		6.9
Arab origins		188,435		0.7
African		137,315		0.5
Latin, Central, & South American		423,930		1.5
Pacific Islanders		5,765		0.0
Other (single and multiple origins)		1,179,135		4.1
Total non-British & non-French		14,029,610		49.2
Total population	28,528,115		100	

Source: Statistics Canada, 1996 Census of Canada, 'Total Population by Ethnic Categories (36) and Sex (3), for Canada, Provinces, Territories and Census Metropolitan Areas, 1996' (Census 20% Sample Data) (93f0026XDB96002) (Ottawa: Statistics, 1998).

face, it would appear that the non-British and non-French segment of Canada's population had grown to 49 per cent in 1996 (table 4.4). In reality, about 20.7 per cent of the total population chose 'Canadian origins.' Thus, the segment of the population that was of non-British, non-French, and non-Canadian origin made up 28.5 per cent in 1996, which is comparable to the proportion of non-British and non-French reported in the 1961 to 1991 censuses (table 4.3). Even within the more broadly defined category of non-British and non-French origins, 'other European origins' and 'Canadian origins' accounted for about two-thirds of this group.

The growth of visible minorities within the 'Third Force' creates the impression that there has been a proliferation of cultural diversity in the Canadian population, even though the Canadian population continues to consist overwhelmingly of those from British, French, or other European origins. Undoubtedly, the increased immigration from Third World countries since the 1970s has contributed to the growth of Asian, African, and other visible minorities in Canada. The tendency of recent immigrants to settle in metropolitan areas also reinforces the sense that there has been a dramatic intensification in diversity. For example, even though nationally visible minorities made up 11.2 per cent of Canada's population in 1996, they accounted for 32 per cent of the population of the Toronto CMA (Census Metropolitan Area) and 31 per cent of the Vancouver CMA.[35] Thus, the more conspicuous presence of visible minorities in Canadian society, especially in major urban centres, has given a new demographic and political reality to multiculturalism in Canada.

This new reality has upset what is widely perceived by many as the normative tradition of Canada, one that is premised upon the cultural balance between the British and the French, and one that is characteristically European in flavour. Breton has suggested that one way to interpret the tensions related to changing linguistic and ethnocultural diversity in Canada is that it is often perceived by members of the dominant group as a contestation to restructure the symbolic and cultural order of Canada.[36]

7. Racial Diversity and the Politics of Multiculturalism

One factor that has contributed to the social construction of cultural diversity is Canada's official policy of multiculturalism. The policy and its evolution can be seen as the state's attempt to regulate diversity in providing a symbolic framework to incorporate and to interpret cultural differences. Over time, the politics of multiculturalism intensify, as competing interest groups attempt to redefine multiculturalism and attribute merits and woes to the policy to suit their political agenda.[37]

When the federal multiculturalism policy was first announced in 1971, it was described as an enlightened policy to allow individuals to pursue a cultural life of their free choice.[38] The policy was designed as complementary to the policy of bilingualism in that although, linguistically, only English and French would remain official languages of Canada, culturally everyone would be equal. The multiculturalism policy was launched, in part, to counteract Quebec nationalism and, in part, to appease the 'Third Force' that was made up of mostly 'other Europeans' in the 1960s. Thus, throughout the 1970s, the Multicultural-ism Directorate promoted many programs aimed at helping ethnic groups to preserve their traditions, customs, dances, and languages to reinforce the multicultural tradition and image of Canadian society.

By the 1980s, as the composition of the 'Third Force' became more racially diverse, the idea of the multiculturalism policy as a vehicle for cultural preservation became less appealing to many members of visi-ble minorities who were more concerned with jobs and other opportu-nities as they faced racism and discrimination in Canadian society. During the hearings of the House of Commons Special Committee on Participation of Visible Minorities in Canadian Society in 1983, many witnesses representing national organizations of racial minorities testi-fied about the prevalence of racial discrimination in Canadian society and the need of the government to make institutional and legislative changes, including strengthening the multiculturalism policy, in order to combat racism.[39] Gary McCauley, a Liberal party Member of Parlia-ment and the vice-chairman of the Special Committee, commented that many groups were organized in the past two to three years 'because they are concerned about racism and not about multicultural festi-vals.'[40] In its report to the House of Commons, the committee noted the urgency of making policy changes to include visible minorities in key public institutions. As the committee put it. '[M]any submissions made to the Committee stressed the fact that visible minorities are perceived to be underrepresented or even excluded from many of these key bod-ies. As a result the Committee believes that the federal government must now quickly take action to ensure the presence of visible minori-ties in these very important public institutions, in order to adequately reflect the multicultural and multiracial nature of Canadian society.'[41] The committee was obviously responding to the population growth of the visible minority in Canada and to the concerns of members of visi-ble minorities when it characterized Canadian society as 'multicultural and multiracial.' Among the committee's many recommendations was its support for strengthening initiatives of the Multiculturalism Direc-torate towards a greater emphasis on race relations, notwithstanding reservations from some ethnic groups that were more concerned with cultural preservation. In its report, the committee wrote:

In fiscal 1983–84 the entire budget for the Directorate was projected to be

$20 million, with approximately $1.7 million earmarked for initiatives in the field of race relations. These figures appear to belie the concern expressed by some non-visible minority ethnic groups that a dramatic shift in emphasis has occurred in federal multicultural policy generally, and within the Directorate specifically. On the contrary, a review of the evidence received and its own investigation have led the Committee to conclude that a greater emphasis on race relations and the concerns of visible minorities should be given a high priority in federal multicultural policy in the near future, regardless of what approach is taken to structural revisions.[42]

It would appear that the expansion of the demographic base of visible minorities had intensified the concerns expressed over the federal multiculturalism policy as being too much oriented towards cultural preservation, and not enough towards promoting social equality. The 1987 House of Commons Standing Committee on Multiculturalism had suggested that it was not always accurate to assume that the cultural orientation of the multiculturalism policy was enunciated by 'established' ethnocultural communities, mostly of European origin.[43] Yet the committee's description of the differences between the cultural orientation and equality orientation suggests that European ethnocultural groups had different expectations from the multiculturalism policy than did visible minorities. As the visible minority population increased, and along with it a greater concern was voiced over the question of racism and discrimination, the apparent contention between the cultural orientation and equality orientation of the multiculturalism policy was sharpened.

Increased racial diversity in Canadian society in the 1980s had created a new demographic and political reality that demanded some changes in the multiculturalism policy. Judging from the changes in the multiculturalism program and the statements made by the minister of state for multiculturalism in the 1980s, it is clear that a greater emphasis was placed on the multiculturalism policy as a vehicle to promote racial equality and racial harmony in Canadian society.

It would be incorrect to assume that the demographic basis of racial diversity alone was sufficient to promote an emphasis of the multiculturalism policy towards greater social equality. It must be remembered that the federal government in the early 1980s was much concerned with the patriation of the constitution from the United Kingdom, and in the process was trying to seek an agreement from provinces and lobbying groups to enshrine a charter of rights and freedoms in the constitution. The success of constitutional patriation needed, among other things, a public awareness and support of social values pertaining to equality, justice and freedom. Thus, the policy emphasis of the federal government of the 1980s on greater social equality was consistent with the political priority of constitutional patriation. Undoubtedly, public discussions of the Charter of Rights and Freedoms and its eventual entrenchment in the Constitution also instilled a greater awareness of social equality among the Canadian public. However, the failure of the Meech Lake Accord in 1990 and the subsequent rejection of the Charlottetown Accord had shaken the public's confidence in the government and, along with it, weakened public support for the multiculturalism policy.[44] The political concerns of the constitutional patriation, together with the emergence of visible minorities as a demographic reality, would account for the greater emphasis of the multiculturalism policy towards promoting equality and eradicating racism in the 1980s. Subsequent political developments of constitutional amendments and waning public support of the government would provide a rationale as to why there was an apparent retrenchment of the multiculturalism policy in the 1990s.[45]

The greater racial diversity in Canadian society also introduced another element to the politics of multiculturalism. The increased presence of immigrants of visible minorities in Canada throughout the 1970s and 1980s created a new ethnic constituency for both politicians and community leaders. Throughout the 1980s, many minority groups organized national associations to promote their collective welfare and interests in Canadian society. These groups spoke out on many occasions to urge the government to address problems of racism and racial discrimination, and to strengthen multiculturalism policy to defend the interests and rights of visible minorities. Leaders from these groups often claimed to represent and to speak for a broadly-based minority community. During the hearings of the House of Commons Special Committee on Participation of Visible Minorities in Canadian Society in 1983, many leaders of national ethnic organizations appeared before the committee on the basis that they represented the members of their respective ethnic community. For example, the past president of the Federation of Sikh Societies of Canada, formed in 1981, claimed to present to the committee what he called 'the views, the ideas and concerns of over 200,000 Sikhs of Canada.'[46] Other ethnic community leaders who appeared before the Special Committee came from many national minority associations, including the Canadian Federation of Vietnamese Associations, the National Black Coalition, the Canadian Arab Federation, the National Federation of Pakistani Canadians, the National Congress of Black Women, the Chinese Canadian National Council, the Jamaican Canadian Association, the National Association of Japanese Canadians, and the United Council of Philippino Associations. As well, many regional or local ethnic associations also sent representatives to speak before the committee.[47] The formation of many of these national associations since the 1980s means that new political opportunities have been created for community leaders of ethnic communities, for they serve as a political bridge between the government and the community they seek to represent.

It is often difficult to determine the extent to which these national and local visible-minority associations reflect the divergent views of community members they claim to represent. Still, the proliferation of national associations for visible minorities throughout the 1980s and, along with it, the creation of a political elite from ethnic communities have produced a new political force that politicians have to reckon with. In turn, the state's recognition of community leaders to speak on behalf of the somewhat arbitrary ethnic constituency they claim to represent, and the state's occasional adoption of recommendations from community leaders, give further legitimacy to the ethnic elite. Thereby, the state also shapes the political format under which the government would deal with the demands and aspirations of racial minorities.

There are many reasons to explain why politicians are often interested into dealing with leaders of national organizations as a means to address the concerns of visible minorities. It is often easier to communicate with a smaller number of individuals and to garner their political support than to seek out divergent interests and viewpoints from a broad ethnic community. The government's acceptance of the views of the ethnic elite would create the impression of a democratic participation in the formulation of public policies, while the rejection of recommendations from community leaders would not have the same implication as rejecting opinions from the populace. Furthermore, national associations often can be qualified to receive grants from the federal government, as for example through the multiculturalism program. The ability of the government to provide financial support to these community-based associations also means that it is able to exert an influence over them with regard to the type of programs and activities to be promoted or discouraged. It would be incorrect to imply that community leaders of racial minorities are necessarily exaggerating their representation as a means to secure personal political gains. Many community leaders are no doubt dedicated individuals who are committed to noble causes. The point is simply that the expansion of the demographic base of visible minorities has created a new political arena, as individuals make use of community-based organizations to promote what they construe as the collective interests of racial minorities. This is also a venue for politicians to relate to the demands and aspirations of visible minorities, and for the government to manage the politics of racial and cultural diversities in conjunction with other political priorities.[48]

8. Racial Inequality and the Politics of Difference

Despite such demographic changes, racial differences in Canadian society are also reproduced by unequal life chances and by racially- based normative values that result in lower market value and social worth being accorded to those of non-white origin. Thus, the politics of difference are reinforced economically and normatively by unequal experiences that members of visible minorities encounter in Canadian society.

Substantial evidence is now available to indicate that the Canadian labour market provides lower economic returns to visible minorities' participation.[49] Visible minority women, in particular, suffer substantial market disadvantage. For example, data from the 1986 census indicate that visible minority women earned about 49 per cent of what white men made in the labour market, while visible minority men earned about 80 per cent.[50] Data from the 1991 census further show that visible minorities earned substantially less than white Canadians even after differences in human capital and other factors have been taken into account.[51] Data from the 1996 census also indicate that when nativity and gender are controlled and after adjusting for variations in human capital and urban features, visible minority status depresses the earnings of men relative to men of majority origin.[52]

Many other studies have produced similar evidence to indicate that visible minorities such as Asians and blacks have lower economic returns in the Canadian labour market than white Canadians and that life chances for various minorities are not the same as that of the majority.[53] Several factors have been identified as creating barriers of employment and social mobility for non-white Canadians, especially those who are immigrants. These factors include the difficulty faced by many non-white immigrants in having their credentials fully recognized in Canada,[54] and employment discrimination against racial minorities with identifiable linguistic characteristics and racial features.[55]

Besides direct job discrimination, Canadians of non-white origin often face other obstacles in the labour market. It has been suggested that non-native speakers of the dominant language encounter discrimination in employment and in access to services because of their language characteristics, and that their lack of fluency, their accent of speech, and their deviations from the language standard of the dominant group can be used as bases of unfavourable treatment, and as surrogates for racial discrimination.[56] Ethnographic accounts by immigrant women also indicate that their accent and colour set them apart from mainstream society, despite their ability to speak English.[57] These studies offer some explanations as to how those of non-white origins are associated with a lower market value; in essence, it has much to do with racial minorities being disadvantaged in the labour market as a result of racial discrimination, or differential treatment based on superficial differences.

In addition to unequal life chances, racial differences are also reproduced as normative values in Canadian society. Canada has a long history of maintaining discriminatory policies and practices towards Canadians deemed to be racially different based on skin colour and other superficial features. Over time, differential treatments and unfavourable policies targeted towards racial minorities became in themselves identifiable characteristics of these groups. In this way, superficial characteristics of racial minorities are inseparable from unfavourable social features attributed to them.

There is substantial evidence to indicate that, to this day, Canadian society continues to attribute unequal social value to people of different origins. Many studies have shown that Canadians regard non-white minorities as socially less desirable and less favourable than people of European origin,[58] and that the notion of 'race' remains meaningful to many people as a means to make sense of their everyday experiences.[59]

The politics of difference were well articulated in public discourse in the early 1990s, when the debate over the constitutional and sovereignty claims of Quebec divided Canada and prompted a retrenchment of the multiculturalism policy, one that was seen by some as divisive.[60] Several opinion polls indicate that there has been a persistent degree of unwillingness on the part of some Canadians to accept those of 'non-White' origins as worthy Canadians. For example, a 1991 national attitudinal survey commissioned by Multiculturalism and Citizenship Canada found that Canadians consider the notion of 'race' meaningful in two major ways.[61] First, as many as 45 per cent of the respondents agreed that discrimination against non-whites is a problem in Canada, and 36 per cent agreed that it is more difficult for non-whites to be successful in Canadian society than whites. In other words, a substantial segment of the general population thought that 'race' is a barrier for non-whites in Canadian society. Second, respondents themselves displayed differential degrees of comfort level towards individuals of various ethnic groups. Ethnic groups of European origin have higher social rankings than those of non-white origin, mostly Asians and blacks, in terms of having a larger percentage of respondents reporting the highest comfort levels in being with them.[62] The same survey also indicates that Canadians showed contradictory tendencies with respect to the principle of equality and support of minority rights. For example, 85 per cent of the respondents indicated they support a multiculturalism policy that promotes equality among all Canadians, regardless of racial or ethnic origin.[63] At the same time, 28 per cent of the people being surveyed said 'people who come to Canada should change to be more like us.'[64]

Another public opinion poll conducted in 1993 also indicated the unpopularity of the multiculturalism policy at the time: as many as 72 per cent of the respondents believed that 'the long standing image of Canada as a nation of communities, each ethnic and racial group preserving its own identity with the help of government policy, must give way to the U.S. style of cultural absorption.'[65] Another survey, conducted by Ekos Research Associates in 1994, found that most respondents agreed there are too many immigrants, especially from visible minority groups, and that 60 per cent of respondents agreed that 'too many immigrants feel no obligation to adapt to Canadians' values and way of life.'[66] These results indicate that a segment of the Canadian public persistently sees visible minorities as being the major problem of immigration, and believes that their alleged unwillingness to adapt to Canadian values and lifestyle is undermining Canada's 'social cohesion.'

Despite the absence of evidence that non-white immigrants are weakening the unity and cohesion of Canada, it is often suggested that too much racial and cultural diversity will lead to the fragmentation of Canadian society.[67] An example of such a position widely circulated in immigration consultation circles is the following: 'Many people ... are also worried that their country is becoming fragmented, that it is becoming a loose collection of parts each pursuing its own agenda, rather than a cohesive entity striving for the collective good of Canada. Many Canadians are concerned that immigration and citizenship policies attend too much to the concerns of special interest groups, rather than to those of average Canadians.'[68] Often, concerns over racial differences are couched in a discussion of the problems of high cost and the country's limited capacity to integrate immigrants of diverse cultural backgrounds.[69] The corollary of this argument is that unless the cost and capacity of absorbing differences in Canadian society are increased, social stresses and tensions would be created in trying to incorporate people of diverse cultural origins, and that it is justifiable and necessary to control the rate of immigration that contributes to racial and cultural diversity, which in turn contributes to social disruption. Over time, a vicious circle emerges in the public discourse of racial differences: racial diversity and the multiculturalism policy are seen as divisive, and public opinions about racial diversity become evidence of how cultural differences result in clashes in values and lifestyles; in turn, public policies have to take cognizance of the need to manage diversity to prevent further fragmentation and disharmony. In this way, managing diversity becomes synonymous with promoting social cohesion.

The salience of these political debates suggests that despite the multiculturalism policy and the legal entrenchment of human rights in the post-war decades, Canadian society continues to consider it meaningful to use 'race' as a basis to evaluate the social standing, competence, and desirability of others. As well, these debates show that non-white racial minorities in Canada are often regarded as less desirable as compared to people of European origin. In this way, racial difference in Canadian society is perpetuated through the incorporation of race in the normative order, by which the social worth of people of colour is evaluated. It should be recognized that the social value and market value attached to racial origin are related.[70] It can be seen that economic disadvantages associated with certain racial origins reinforce their low social standing, since people so marked carry a lower market worth. In the long run, economic disparities according to racial origins help to maintain the social reality of race by giving a discounted market value to certain racial groups. In turn, the low social value given to certain racial origins creates obstacles that further limit market outcomes for people being racialized.

9. Conclusion

Many forces have helped to produce cultural and racial diversity in Canadian society. Notwithstanding the consequences of immigration and demographic changes, diversity is socially constructed in the way society attributes collective meanings to phenotypical differences, as well as in the way racial differences result in unequal life chances. As well, racial difference is influenced by state policy towards diversity, and by the politics that surround the contestation over different frameworks to articulate the symbolic and cultural order.

The statistics on Canada's ethnic diversity show that, since the turn of the century until the 1960s, there had been an increase in the proportion of those not of British and French origin. Yet such an increase was largely accounted for by more European diversities, other than British and French, entering the Canadian population. Throughout much of the twentieth century and until 1971, over 96 per cent of the Canadian population was made up of people of European origin. Since 1971, there have been only nominal changes in the ethnic diversity of Canada in terms of increases in the proportion of Canadians not of British or French origin. Canada remains a country that is made up overwhelmingly of people of European origin, despite changes in the national origin of immigrants coming to Canada since the 1970s. However, within the 'Third Force,' that is, the group made up of non-British and non-French, there have been changes in the direction of a larger proportion being made up of members of visible minorities. These changes were largely brought about as a result of more immigrants from Asian, Africa, and other non-European regions being admitted into Canada after national origin was removed from the selection criteria for immigrants in the 1960s. By 1991, visible minorities accounted for 9.4 per cent of the total population in Canada, and by 1996, 11.2 per cent.[71] Thus, recent immigration from Asia and Africa does not necessarily increase the cultural diversity of Canada relative to the two charter groups, but the racial characteristics of these recent immigrants have transformed the meaning of diversity to emphasize racial differences.

The growth of the visible minority in Canada in the 1980s created a new demographic and political reality and, along with it, growing concerns about the plight of racial minorities in Canadian society, as they experienced unequal life chances in Canada. The demand for greater social equality and for equal participation in Canadian society was voiced by the leaders of visible minority communities and some politicians. The government changed the emphasis of multiculturalism policy in the 1980s to pay more attention to issues of racial equality and racial harmony. It would appear that while the emergence of visible minorities in Canada created the political constituency to lobby for more racial equality, the political agenda of constitutional patriation had also produced a political climate for the state to support public awareness of racial equality and social justice.

Among other things, the reality of racial diversity in Canada has also created a new minority constituency that provides new political opportunities for ethnic leaders. Spokespersons from visible minority communities gain recognition on the basis that they are able to convey the viewpoints and recommendations of the group they claim to represent to the government; in turn, the government's willingness to accept them as community leaders gives them further legitimacy. In short, the emergence of a greater degree of racial diversity in Canadian society has added a new dimension to the politics of multiculturalism. In turn, the politics also provided further meaning to racial differences in Canadian society.

The politics of difference are also articulated in Canadian society as unequal life chances that disadvantage visible minorities, as well as normative values that attribute a lower social worth to those of non-white origin. Substantial evidence is available to indicate that visible minority origins carry an earning penalty in the Canadian labour market, even after differences in other factors have been taken into account. Foreign-born visible minorities and non-white women in particular encounter added obstacles in the labour market due to various forms of discrimination.

Substantial survey data are available to indicate that Canadians have incorporated racial differences in their normative orientation, in the sense that race has provided a meaningful concept for making sense of people and relations. From this reference point, Canadians have expressed in many polls their view of a racial hierarchy in Canadian society, in which some groups are deemed more desirable than others.

One other example in the politics of difference involves the debate over the social cost of racial diversity. Racial diversities are often assumed in public discourse to be divisive and costly in Canadian society, a view that, in turn, justifies public policies to control the rate of that component of immigration which contributes to the disorderly expansion of 'cultural diversity' beyond Canada's means and capacity to absorb differences. In short, 'cultural diversity' and 'cultural differences' become codified concepts to signify the fundamental distinctions of 'races' and the injurious consequences such distinctions bring to what otherwise would be a socially and culturally cohesive Canada. Despite the absence of scientific evidence showing how Canada's 'cohesiveness' has become more fragmented as a result of the growth of the visible minority population, unfavourable opinions expressed in public polls towards various aspects of the visible minority, immigration, and integration are often used as self-evident indicators of 'social fragmentation' and 'racial tension.'

Thus, the challenge of cultural or racial diversity has less to do with the threat of visible minorities to Canada's 'social cohesion' than with Canada's unwillingness to see itself as other than a conventionally European society, and with an unease to position itself as a global nation of many cultures and people. In short, racial diversity is created less by demographic changes than by the reproduction of a normative and economic order that reinforces social differentiation based on race and racial origin.

There is no doubt that the growth of visible minorities in Canada has created a new demographic and political challenge for the future of Canada, despite the fact that numerically they only accounted for 11.2 per cent of Canada's 1996 population. Projections into the twenty-first century indicate that the visible minority population in Canada will continue to grow faster than the total population, albeit at a declining rate.[72] Using various scenarios of population growth, it is estimated that the visible minority will constitute from 19.4 to 20.6 per cent of Canada's population by 2016. The prospect that one-fifth of Canadians would be non-white should be alarming to those who already feel that the European tradition and social fabric of Canada have been undermined by the current non-white population, and who defend a social and nominal order that accentuates 'racial' differences.

It would appear that Canada has the policy option of following the alarmists' narrow vision of cultural dominance based on race and the superficial features of people, and continuing to frame polices that implicitly recognize the social significance of race. Alternatively, Canada may abandon its cultural parochialism and treat racial and linguistic diversity in Canadian society as potential resources through which multilateral trade, international diplomacy and other global exchanges can be further advanced. In short, in recognizing the value of cultural differences and racial diversity, Canada is also better positioning itself in a world that is becoming increasingly globalized in its economy and culture. Canada committed itself to such a future when it entrenched the principles of equality and non-discrimination in its Charter of Rights and Freedoms. The question for Canada's future is how to bridge the gap between what it commits to de jure and what it does de facto.

Notes

1 See John Rex, *Race Relations in Sociological Theory* (London: Routledge, 1983), 1–5; and Robert Miles, *Racism* (London: Routledge, 1989), 41–50.
2 See Michael Banton, 'Analytical and Folk Concepts of Race and Ethnicity,' *Ethnic and Racial Studies* 2 (1979): 127–38.
3 See ibid., 129.
4 See Peter S. Li, 'The Market Value and Social Value of Race,' in V. Satzewich, ed., *Racism and Social Inequality in Canada* (Toronto: Thompson, 1998), 113–30; Miles, *Racism*; and Vic Satzewich, 'Race, Racism and Racialization: Contested Concepts,' in Satzewich, *Racism and Social Inequality*, 113–30.
5 In response to rising political discontent in Quebec, the federal government appointed a ten-person royal commission to examine bilingualism and biculturalism in Canada in the summer of 1963. The order-in-council striking the commission stated that the commissioners were to 'inquire into and report upon the existing state of bilingualism and biculturalism in Canada and to recommend what steps should be taken to develop the Canadian Confederation on the basis of an equal partnership between the two founding races, taking into account the contribution made by other ethnic groups to the cultural enrichment of Canada and the measures that should be taken to safeguard that contribution' (P.C. 1963–1106, cited in *Report of the Royal Commission on Bilingualism and Biculturalism*, vol. 1, Ottawa, 1967). The royal commission wrote a five-volume report; the first was published in 1967, the last in 1970. Throughout the reports of the commission, the framework used was a trichotomy composed of the British, the French, and other Canadians, which paid little attention to the First Nations as people with distinct Aboriginal rights and entitlements. See *Preliminary Report of the Royal Commission on Bilingualism and Biculturalism* (Ottawa, 1965) and *Report of the Royal Commission on Bilingualism and Biculturalism, vol. 4 – The Cultural Contribution of Other Ethnic Groups* (Ottawa, 1969).
6 See Madeline A. Kalbach and Warren E. Kalbach, 'Demographic Overview of Ethnic Groups in Canada,' in P.S. Li, ed., *Race and Ethnic Relations in Canada*, 2nd ed. (Toronto: Oxford University Press, 1999), 27.

7 See Department of Manpower and Immigration, *The Immigration Program* (Ottawa: Information Canada, 1974); and Peter S. Li and B. Singh Bolaria, 'Canadian Immigration Policy and Assimilation Theories,' in J.A. Fry, ed., *Economy, Class and Social Reality* (Toronto: Butterworths, 1979), 411–22.

8 See Statistics Canada, *Historical Statistics of Canada*, 2nd ed. (Ottawa: Minister of Supply and Services Canada, 1983), tables A125–63.

9 See Kalbach and Kalbach, 'Demographic Overview,' 27–30.

10 House of Commons, Debates, 1 May 1947, 2644–6.

11 See House of Commons, *Debates*, 1 May 1947, 2646. See also Statutes of Canada, An Act respecting Chinese Immigration, chap. 38, 1923, and Privy Council 1931-1378, 17 June 1931.

12 See Freda Hawkins, *Canada and Immigration: Public Policy and Public Concern* (Montreal: McGill-Queen's University Press, 1988), 101–7.

13 See Privy Council 1956-785, *Canada Gazette*, part II, vol. 90, no. 11 (24 May 1956), 545–8.

14 See Privy Council 1962-86, *Canada Gazette*, part II, vol. 96, no. 3 (18 Jan. 1962), 126–44.

15 See Privy Council 1967-1616, *Canada Gazette*, part II, vol. 101, no. 17 (16 Aug. 1967), 1350–62.

16 See Privy Council 1978-486, *Canada Gazette*, part II, vol. 112, no. 5 (23 Feb. 1978), 757–88.

17 See Privy Council 1985-3246, *Canada Gazette*, part II, vol. 119, no. 23 (31 Oct. 1985), 4582–6; and Privy Council 1990-2317, *Canada Gazette*, part II, vol. 124, no. 23 (25 Oct. 1990), 4888–93.

18 Quoted in Freda Hawkins, Canada and Immigration: Public Policy and Public Concern (Montreal: McGill-Queen's University Press, 1988), 130.

19 See Peter S. Li, 'The Economics of Brain Drain: Recruitment of Skilled Labour to Canada, 1954–86,' in V. Satzewich, ed., *Deconstructing a Nation: Immigration, Multiculturalism and Racism in '90s Canada* (Halifax: Fernwood Publishing, 1992), 145–62.

20 See L. Parai, *Immigration and Emigration of Professional and Skilled Manpower during the Post-war Period* (Ottawa: Economic Council of Canada, 1965), 47–57.

21 Ibid., 33.

22 See Li, 'The Economics of Brain Drain.'

23 Statistics Canada, *Historical Statistics of Canada* (Toronto: Macmillan of Canada, 1965), series A316–36.

24 Statistics on immigration are compiled from Immigration Statistics and Annual Reports of the Department of Citizenship and Immigration (1956–65); Immigration Statistics and Annual Reports of the Department of Man-

power and Immigration (1966–76); Immigration Statistics and Annual
Reports of the Department of Employment and Immigration (1977–91); and
Immigration Statistics and Annual Reports of the Department of Citizen-
ship and Immigration (1992).

25 Data are compiled from Immigration Statistics, Department of Manpower
and Immigration (1966–76) and Immigration Statistics, Department of
Employment and Immigration (1977–88).

26 See Peter S. Li, *The Chinese in Canada*, 2nd ed. (Toronto: Oxford University
Press, 1998).

27 *Royal Commission on Equality in Employment, Report of the Commission on
Equality in Employment* (Ottawa: Minister of Supply and Services Canada,
1984).

28 The 1986 Employment Equity Act defines the four designated groups as
'women, aboriginal peoples, persons with disabilities and persons who are,
because of their race or colour, in a visible minority in Canada.' See Statutes
of Canada, Employment Equity Act, 1986, c. 31, s. 3.

29 Statistics Canada, *1986 Census Public Use Microdata File on Individuals*: *Documentation and User's Guide*, 1990, 71–72.

30 See Statistics Canada, *The Daily,* 17 Feb. 1998, 1. In the 1996 census, a new
question (no. 19) was included to ask respondents to specify which of the
following groups they belonged to: White, Chinese, South Asian, Black,
Arab/West Asian, Filipino, South East Asian, Latin American, Japanese,
and Korean. Membership in 'visible minorities' includes those who did not
chose 'white.' Since the variable 'visible minority' in the 1996 census was
based on direct answers and previous censuses constructed this variable
based on inferences from the 'ethnic origin' question, Statistics Canada suggests using caution in comparing visible minority data between the 1996
census and previous censuses. See Statistics Canada, *1996 Census Questions*
and *1996 Census Public Use Microdata File on Individuals*, Documentation.

31 See Statistics Canada, *The Daily,* 17 Feb. 1998, 5.

32 See Statistics Canada, *1991 Census of Canada, Age, Sex and Marital Status*: *The
Nation*, Cat. 93-310 (Ottawa: Minister of Industry, Science and Technology,
1992) and Statistics Canada, *The Daily,* 17 Feb. 1998.

33 Calculations on ethnic origins of the Canadian population are complicated
by changes in the questions used in various censuses. Since 1981, respondents to Canadian censuses were allowed to choose 'multiple origins' as an
answer to the ethnic origin question. As a result, 1,838,615 individuals, or
7.6 per cent of the total population in 1981, chose 'multiple origins' as an
answer to the 'ethnic origin' question. In the 1991 census, 7,794,250 individuals, or 28.9 per cent of the total population, chose 'multiple origins.' Fur-

thermore, 88.5 per cent of those who chose multiple origins in 1991 made a selection that involved either British or French and other combinations. See Statistics Canada, 1981 Census of Canada, Population: Ethnic Origin, vol. 1, Cat. 92-911 (Ottawa: Minister of Supply and Services Canada, 1984) and Statistics Canada, 1991 Census of Canada, *Ethnic Origin: The Nation*, Cat. 93-315 (Ottawa: Minister of Industry, Science and Technology, 1993).

34 In the 1996 census, 10.2 million persons, or 36% of the total population, reported more than one ethnic origin, and about 5.9 million persons, or 20% of Canada's population, indicated having 'Canadian origins.' See table 3.4 and Statistics Canada, *The Daily*, 11 Feb. 1998.

35 See Statistics Canada, *The Daily*, 11 Feb. 1998.

36 See Raymond Breton, 'The Production and Allocation of Symbolic Resources: An Analysis of the Linguistic and Ethnocultural Fields in Canada,' *Canadian Review of Sociology and Anthropology* 21.2 (1984): 123–44; and R. Breton, 'Intergroup Competition in the Symbolic Construction of Canadian Society,' in Li, *Race and Ethnic Relations in Canada*, 291–310.

37 See Yasmeen Abu-Laban and Daiva Stasiulus, 'Ethnic Pluralism under Siege: Popular and Partisan Opposition to Multiculturalism,' *Canadian Public Policy* 18.4 (1992): 365–86; and Rhoda E. Howard-Hassmann, '"Canadian" as an Ethnic Category: Implications for Multiculturalism and National Unity,' *Canadian Public Policy* 25.4 (1999): 523–37.

38 See Peter, S. Li, 'The Multiculturalism Debate,' in Li, *Race and Ethnic Relations in Canada*, 147–76.

39 House of Commons, *Minutes of Proceedings and Evidence of the Special Committee on Participation of Visible Minorities in Canadian Society*, 1983.

40 Ibid., no. 20, p. 22.

41 House of Commons, *Equality Now*, Report of the Special Committee on Visible Minorities in Canadian Society (1984), 50.

42 Ibid., 55.

43 House of Commons, *Multiculturalism: Building the Canadian Mosaic*, Report of the Standing Committee on Multiculturalism (1987), 22–4.

44 The Meech Lake Accord was the 1987 agreement of the first ministers of Canada on constitutional changes after the Constitution of Canada was patriated from England to Canada in 1982 with nine of the ten province, except Quebec, approving the patriation. In 1985, the Liberal party won the provincial election in Quebec, and shortly after Quebec presented five conditions for rejoining the 'constitutional family.' The conditions were recognition of Quebec as a distinct society; a greater provincial role in immigration; a provincial role in appointing three judges to the Supreme Court of Canada; limitations on federal spending; and a veto for Quebec on

constitutional amendments. On 30 April 1987, the first ministers signed the Meech Lake Accord; the final accord was concluded on 3 June 1987. The accord had to be ratified by the 11 legislatures in compliance with the amending procedure of the Constitution Act of 1982. The legislatures of Manitoba and Newfoundland and Labrador failed to approve Meech Lake before its final ratification deadline on 23 June 1990, and the accord was rendered null and void. This failure led to another attempt by the federal government to have the first ministers agree to constitutional reform. The ministers met in Charlottetown, Prince Edward Island, on 27 and 28 August 1992 and concluded a constitutional agreement that came to be known as the Charlottetown Accord. On 26 October 1992, a referendum was put to all Canadians to seek their opinion on the following question: 'Do you agree that the Constitution of Canada should be renewed on the basis of the agreement reached on August 28, 1992?' The majority of Canadians who voted on the referendum rejected the Charlottetown Accord. The failure of the Meech Lake Accord and rejection of the Charlottetown Accord by Canadians contributed to the defeat of the Progressive Conservative government in the 1993 federal election.

45 For a discussion of popular and partisan opposition to multiculturalism in the late 1980s and early 1990s, see Abu-Laban and Stasiulis, 'Ethnic Pluralism under Siege.'

46 See House of Commons, *Minutes of the Special Committee on Visible Minorities*, 16–39.

47 Ibid.

48 See Vered Amit-Talai, 'The Minority Circuit: Identity Politics and the Professionalization of Ethnic Activism,' in V. Amit-Talai and C. Knowles, eds, *Re-situating Identities: The Politics of Race, Ethnicity, Culture* (Peterborough, ON: Broadview Press, 1996), 89–114.

49 See Peter S. Li, *Ethnic Inequality in a Class Society* (Toronto: Wall and Thompson, 1988); P.S. Li, 'Race and Gender as Bases of Class Fractions and Their Effects on Earnings,' *Canadian Review of Sociology and Anthropology* 29 (1992): 488–510; and P.S. Li, 'Self-employment among Visible Minority Immigrants, White Immigrants, and Native-born Persons in Secondary and Tertiary Industries of Canada,' *Canadian Journal of Regional Science* 20 (1997): 103–17.

50 See Li, 'Race and Gender as Bases of Class Fractions,' 497.

51 See Li, 'Self-employment among Visible Minority Immigrants'; Li, 'The Market Value and Social Value of Race'; and Krishna Pendakur and Ravi Pendakur, *Earnings Differentials among Ethnic Groups in Canada* (Ottawa: Department of Canadian Heritage, Strategic Research and Analysis, 1996).

52 See Peter S. Li, 'Earnings Disparities between Immigrants and Native-born Canadians,' *Canadian Review of Sociology and Anthropology* 37.3 (2000): 284–311.
53 See, e.g., Rosalie S. Abella, *Report of the Royal Commission on Equality in Employment* (Ottawa: Minister of Supply and Services, 1984); Vic Satzewich and Peter S. Li, 'Immigrant Labour in Canada: The Cost and Benefit of Ethnic Origin in the Job Market,' *Canadian Journal of Sociology* 12 (1987): 229–41; and Jeffrey G. Reitz and Raymond Breton, *The Illusion of Difference: Realities of Ethnicity in Canada and the United States* (Toronto: C.D. Howe Institute, 1994).
54 See Gurcharn Basran and Li Zong, 'Devaluation of Foreign Credentials as Perceived by Non-White Professional Immigrants,' *Canadian Ethnic Studies* 30 (1998): 6–23; and Kathryn McDade, *Barriers to Recognition of the Credentials of Immigrants in Canada* (Ottawa: Institute for Research on Public Policy, 1988).
55 See Teresa Scassa, 'Language Standards, Ethnicity and Discrimination,' *Canadian Ethnic Studies* 26 (1994): 105–21; Frances Henry, *Who Gets the Work in 1989?* (Ottawa: Economic Council of Canada, 1989); and Frances Henry and Effie Ginsberg, *Who Gets the Work? A Test of Racial Discrimination in Employment* (Toronto: Social Planning Council of Metro Toronto and Urban Alliance on Race Relations, 1985).
56 See Scassa, 'Language Standards.'
57 See Baukje Miedema and Nancy Nason-Clark, 'Second-class Status: An Analysis of the Lived Experiences of Immigrant Women in Fredericton.' *Canadian Ethnic Studies* 21 (1989): 63–73.
58 See Angus Reid Group, *Multiculturalism and Canadians: Attitude Study 1991 National Survey Report*, report submitted to Multiculturalism and Citizenship Canada, 1991; and Rudolf Kalin and J.W. Berry, 'Interethnic Attitudes in Canada: Ethnocentrism, Consensual Hierarchy and Reciprocity,' *Canadian Journal of Behavioural Science* 28 (1996): 253–61.
59 See Peter S. Li, 'Unneighbourly Houses or Unwelcome Chinese: The Social Construction of Race in the Battle over "Monster Homes" in Vancouver, Canada,' *International Journal of Comparative Race & Ethnic Studies* 1 (1994): 14–33.
60 The Reform party campaigned during the 1993 election to eliminate the federal multiculturalism programs as a means to reduce the deficit. See, e.g., *Globe and Mail*, National edition, 14 Dec. 1993, A1 and A2. After the election, the Reform party continued its attack on multiculturalism on the grounds that it is divisive and unnecessarily costly. For example, Reform member Art Hanger, an MP representing Calgary Northeast, said in the

House of Commons in 1994: 'It appears to me to be somewhat contradictory to state that immigrants under the present system are being integrated into Canadian society. My understanding of what integration means is that an immigrant embraces the Canadian way of life and Canadian culture, while having the freedom to preserve his own culture, but if he chooses to do so he should have to do [it] at his own expense, on his own time without government assistance. Multiculturalism as it is now practiced, emphasizes differences and tends to separate the different ethnic communities, while being funded by the federal government' (House of Commons, *Debates*, 27 Jan. 1994, 455).

61 See Angus Reid Group, *Multiculturalism and Canadians*.

62 See ibid., and Kalin and Berry, 'Interethnic Attitudes in Canada.'

63 See Angus Reid Group, *Multiculturalism and Canadians*, 24.

64 Ibid., 35.

65 'Canadians Want Mosaic to Melt, Survey Finds,' *Globe and Mail*, 14 Dec. 1993, A1, A2.

66 'Canadians Showing Signs of Cultural Insecurity,' *Globe and Mail*, 11 Mar. 1994, A6.

67 See Howard-Hassmann, '"Canadian" as an Ethnic Category.'

68 Citizenship and Immigration Canada, *Into the 21st Century: A Strategy for Immigration and Citizenship* (Ottawa: Minister of Supply and Services Canada, 1994).

69 For example, in a government-initiated conference to develop a strategy for citizenship and immigration, the following question was posed to the participants: 'Does the current cultural mix prevent adequate integration of newcomers?' See Citizenship and Immigration Canada, *Canada 2005: A Strategy for Citizenship and Immigration* (Ottawa: Citizenship and Immigration Canada, 1994), 46.

70 See Li, 'The Market Value and Social Value of Race.'

71 Statistics Canada, *The Daily*, 17 Feb. 1998.

72 S.Y. Dai and M.V. George, *Projections of Visible Minority Population Groups, Canada, Provinces and Regions, 1991–2016*, Statistics Canada, Cat. 91-541-XPE (Ottawa: Ministry of Industry, 1996).

5. Aboriginal People, Public Policy, and Social Differentiation in Canada

Terry Wotherspoon

1. Introduction: Social Trends and Aboriginal Policy Issues

Aboriginal people generally occupy highly disadvantaged positions relative to the Canadian population. As documented in several sources, most notably the 1996 *Report of the Royal Commission on Aboriginal Peoples*, Aboriginal people as a whole rate well below national averages on key socio-economic indicators of well-being and success. Persons identifying themselves as being of Aboriginal ancestry earn less, have less education, have lower rates of labour force participation, and are under-represented in key occupations and organizational positions in comparison with the general population. Aboriginal people are also more likely than the average to experience conditions associated with social disadvantage and marginalization. Their chances of dropping out of school, being unemployed, living in poverty, being supported by social assistance, being homeless or living in substandard housing, contracting or dying from HIV/AIDS and other infectious diseases, being incarcerated or in conflict with the law, and being the victims of serious accidents and violent crimes are much higher than Canadian norms.

Counterposed against these indications of relative deprivation are the emergence of successful First Nations business, public, and community enterprises, a growing body of well-trained and articulate Aboriginal professionals and leaders, and a resurgence of interest in Aboriginal languages, traditional cultural practices, and spirituality. A diverse range of innovative programs and initiatives intended to ameliorate less than satisfactory socio-economic conditions and to foster the advancement of Aboriginal people is being introduced by federal, provincial, municipal, and First Nations governments, and by Aboriginal and non-Aboriginal organizations in the private and voluntary sectors.

Mixed public views with respect to Aboriginal affairs parallel these divergent conditions. While Canadians as a whole are perceived to enjoy one of the most favourable qualities of life in the world, the conditions and treatment experienced by the nation's Aboriginal people are a common source of national embarrassment in international eyes.[1] An increasing majority of Canadians feel that little progress has been made in recent years to address serious Aboriginal concerns such as land claims, unemployment, poverty, and racism. Paradoxically, substantial proportions of the population feel that governments are doing too much for Aboriginal people, that First Nations are responsible for their own problems and should not have special advantages relative to other Canadians, and that First Nations are not managing their own affairs well.[2]

Against this background, public policy occupies a central role as both a contributing factor to present circumstances and a foundation for future directions. In just over a century, Aboriginal policy has expanded from being one of the most unified policy fields, under the banner of 'Indian affairs,' to its present state as a highly complex, disparate, and sometimes indeterminate array of domains. Aboriginal issues such as land claims settlements and self-government arrangements in themselves constitute a unique and important policy field, but they also have significant consequences for more general policy realms. The purpose of this chapter is to outline some of the key trends identified in a growing body of academic and policy literature on Aboriginal people in Canada, highlighting characteristic dimensions of social differentiation. The discussion is oriented, more specifically, to questions of how policy developments have affected, and been framed with respect to, the relative standing of Aboriginal people in Canadian society, what implications they have for different segments of the Aboriginal population, and what policy issues are most pressing in the face of emergent trends.

2. Aboriginal People and Social Differentiation

Social differentiation is understood in this analysis as a process in which people are allocated into diverse social positions and circumstances characterized by unequal resources, opportunities, and life chances. This approach is distinguished from classical social scientific orientations that, following the traditions of Spencer and Durkheim, associate differentiation with an evolutionary growth of social complexity and divisions of labour that under normal circumstances, contribute positively to social cohesion. While some reference is made to social differentiation in this broader, more generic sense of difference, the analysis here is most concerned with how changes in policy and socio-economic conditions produce, reproduce, or transform fundamentally unequal life chances among social groups.

Aboriginal people and their relations with other Canadians are characterized by two interrelated levels of differences and inequalities – between groups and within groups. In other words, Aboriginal people collectively experience marked differences with the general population in terms of socio-economic circumstances, political participation, and cultural experiences, but they are also an internally differentiated population.

At the level of between-group comparisons, Aboriginal people occupy distinct social positions, and share cultural and historical backgrounds, that distinguish them from other groups in Canada. The indigenous heritage of the first peoples, unlike that of persons of European origin and of other immigrant groups, constitutes a particular relationship to the land and environment that is acknowledged in principles of Aboriginal rights and special status. Aboriginal traditions are rooted in common ways of knowing or orientations to spiritual, natural, and social worlds that differentiate them from other cultural groups.[3] Moreover, policies and practices, often of a discriminatory nature, targeted explicitly at indigenous people, have contributed to experiences, histories, and conditions that are unique to Aboriginal people. These distinctions are acknowledged legally and conceptually, for instance, in the designation of Aboriginal people as a category apart from other 'visible minorities' discussed in the previous chapter by Peter Li. Social analysis and policy formulation, in other words, must take into account the distinctive characteristics that shape the lives of Aboriginal people relative to other Canadians.

It is also necessary, however, to develop an understanding of within-group differentiation. Aboriginal people, like any other social group, do not all have the same experiences and social positions as one another. Distinct cultural traditions, legal designations, and personal and social histories are associated with diverse identities and circumstances. Gender, age, legal status, region and residence patterns, and differential access to social, economic, and political resources affect life opportunities and chances in different and changing ways. Processes of group identification, inclusion, and exclusion may both be imposed on and enacted by various Aboriginal communities. Analytical and policy approaches that view Aboriginal people as a homogeneous category may lead to inflexible and inappropriate strategies to address designated problem areas and development issues.[4] Consequently, social analysis and policy formulation must also examine the implications of emerging policies, practices, and structures for diverse segments of the Aboriginal population.

Differentiation is evident even in problems associated with efforts to define the term 'Aboriginal.' Many variants of the term have been employed in particular ways to signify different legal definitions, organizational memberships, and self- or group identity.[5] The term 'Aboriginal' is employed in this paper generally to refer to all indigenous groups, including First Nations, Métis, Inuit, or any other category of First Peoples in Canada, based on ancestry or identity.

3. Conceptual Framework

This chapter examines how policy has shaped and responded to social differentiation with respect to Aboriginal people in Canada. Policy is understood in terms of its contributions to social regulation and the accommodation of diverse social interests.

Public policy, following Pal, may be broadly conceptualized as 'a course of action or inaction chosen by public authorities to address a given problem or an interrelated set of problems.'[6] Policy involves making choices and adopting strategies that not only frame the action to be taken (or not taken), but also influence how problems come to be defined and posed in public terms.[7] Nation-states exercise authority and utilize policy, to varying degrees, subject to complex, shifting constellations of interests, in order to coordinate and regulate economic activity and to shape the life and character of their subjects and citizens. Consequently, policies and the issues they address are not always comprehensive or unified. They are grounded, nonetheless, in particular ideational frameworks or paradigms as well as in specific material circumstances that influence the problems that arise, how they are perceived, and how they are responded to.

Historically, colonial and Canadian policy interventions enabled the state and affiliated private interests to gain access to land and labour traditionally utilized by First Nations, to designate who is to be considered as Indian, and to regulate relations among Aboriginal people, the state, and other social sectors. Domestic events, such as the National Policy in the nineteenth century and northern development in the mid-twentieth century, have altered these relations over time. Increasingly, international events like resistance to colonial regimes, civil rights activism, and changing conceptions of development have also become important in reconfiguring relations between Aboriginal people and governments in Canada.[8] Brock locates contemporary Aboriginal issues and challenges in the context of competing tensions between global and domestic forces.[9] Pressures to promote globalization and political-economic integration across national boundaries have made it difficult for nation-states to make and implement autonomous policies about markets, cultures, and other decision-making realms. At the same time, pressures for decentralization and sectoral alliances or allegiances based on region, ethnicity, and other nationalist forces have posed internal challenges to national sovereignty. Given the complex interpenetration of internal and external forces, these tensions have varying and often contradictory impacts both for Aboriginal people and for Canadian public and private life more generally, potentially undermining the achievement of national social and economic cohesion.

In the review of literature and discussion that follows, social differentiation and policy are analysed in terms of questions related to regulation and accommodation. Regulation operates at several interrelated levels. Social regulation includes policies and mechanisms that define Aboriginal people and specify their relations with the state and other people. Political regulation operates through legal and institutional frameworks that specify rights, offer access to services, and facilitate decision-making for Aboriginal people. Economic regulation occurs through frameworks that control or specify access to and use of material resources by Aboriginal people. It is important to recognize, however, that regulation does not always operate unilaterally or in accordance with intended consequences. Processes of accommodation enter into responses by the state and associated institutions or agencies to diverse interests and needs, sometimes peacefully and other times through resistance and struggle. As much of the literature of the past two decades has highlighted, in contrast with earlier prevailing orientations, Aboriginal people have not simply been passive objects and victims of policies imposed on them by external governments and agencies. With mixed but increasingly impressive results over several generations, they have adopted diverse strategies to define and assert their interests in their communities and wider public venues.

Differentiation, in this analysis, is posed as a phenomenon that is continually being produced and reproduced rather than something that is natural and unchanging. Particular attention is paid to how state policies, interacting with economic and social developments, have contributed or responded to processes of social differentiation, affecting the life chances and circumstances of Aboriginal people in diverse and unequal ways. The chapter addresses key themes in the academic and policy literature, outlining explanations and processes associated with the production of differentiation. It then examines changing dimensions of social differentiation related to demographic trends, employment and income, education and occupation, and social conditions. It concludes by exploring contradictions associated with recent initiatives such as self-government, identifying several important policy and research directions that arise from the analysis.

4. Overview of the Public Policy and Social Science Literature

Extensive bodies of literature in several fields document Aboriginal people and their cultures, histories, and relations with other groups. Historical analysis has given us detailed descriptions of the nature of Aboriginal societies and their wider interactions, especially since – and from the perspective of – contact with Europeans. Ethnographic accounts of Aboriginal communities in various times and places have given us a richer understanding of the practices and experiences that characterize indigenous people's lives and conditions. Social scientific research and policy analysis have outlined several important bases of comparison between Aboriginal and non-Aboriginal populations, and examined major dimensions of participation in public and private life. More recently, the voices of Aboriginal people have extended this knowledge and added new orientations through the detailing of oral histories and indigenous perspectives on the world that have often been neglected, undermined, or misrepresented in the mainstream literature. Representative cases in the literature are drawn upon in the next section in order to understand how processes of regulation and accommodation, especially through state policy, have affected social differentiation for Aboriginal people.

5. Theoretical Perspectives on Aboriginal People and Social Differentiation

The social scientific and policy literature on differentiation as it applies to Aboriginal people characteristically tends to be descriptive or implicit in its adoption of analytical frameworks. However, underlying such analyses are dynamic and changing theoretical perspectives and assumptions. The literature has both reflected and shaped public and policy expectations about Aboriginal people's positions and relations in the Canadian context. Research conducted until the late 1960s, for instance, placed emphasis on differences between Indians and others, highlighting artefacts, disappearing cultures, or factors that facilitated or inhibited the potential assimilation of Indians into the dominant society. Tremblay and Lévesque, assessing Québec-based social scientific (primarily anthropological) research on indigenous people, observe a lack of critical reflection until recently, with greater theoretical emphasis in the French-language literature and a more applied focus in the English literature.[10] Contemporary research, in the context of diverse struggles for representation and self-determination by various Aboriginal groups, has been more sensitive to issues of power and Aboriginal voice, and has often adopted a somewhat eclectic approach that draws on several perspectives.[11] Several broad theoretical orientations have predominated in the literature of the past two decades. Each offers distinct research and policy directions shaped by different analytical assumptions and approaches.

Liberal and structural functionalist approaches focus on how various Aboriginal and non-Aboriginal groups enter into relations with one another as discrete cultures or entities. This analysis has commented on periodic conflicts and tensions between groups, but its characteristic concern is with historical evolutionary patterns, particularly towards eventual assimilation or incorporation into Canadian society as a whole. Emphasis is placed on the measurement of gaps between groups or on how conditions like badly formulated policies or racism impede Aboriginal people from integrating into the dominant society or achieving success on their own terms.[12] A representative theme within this approach is the cultural discontinuity thesis, which stresses how the orientations and expectations of mainstream institutions work against Aboriginal people insofar as they are based on standards that not only differ from, but ignore and undermine, indigenous people and their heritage.[13] Another prevalent theme, in both popular accounts and academic analysis, is the active role played by specific government policies and officials, missionaries, and other agents to regulate and shape Aboriginal people's lives or to subordinate Aboriginal people's interests.[14] This work, given its concern for how external forces can impede Aboriginal people's opportunities, often bears a strong kinship with conflict approaches. However, it is classified here as liberal in nature due to its focus on particular cultures or organizations and the relatively independent ability of each agent to define and act in its own specific interest.

Interpretative and micro-level approaches concentrate on the processes of interaction that occur in specific settings and the ways in which people construct meaning and identity. Particular emphasis is given to the ways in which specific forms of Aboriginal identity have been formed, as a consequence of racism, discrimination and frustration in wider social interactions, in resistance to colonization and marginalization, and through understanding and encompassing indigenous heritage. Much of this literature originates in oral histories and personal encounters in residential schools and other specific circumstances, but pays relatively little attention to broader issues of policy formation or social differentiation.[15] Nonetheless, interpretative analysis can offer critical insights into the processes that contribute to differential social identities and circumstances, as well as a means to broaden our knowledge base and to constitute a 'challenge to conventional ways of seeing.' The reclaiming of Aboriginal voices in literature and social science, for instance, has been particularly important for Aboriginal women's struggles to regain a sense of self-worth.[16] Insights are also provided into how state control and Aboriginal resistance change over time through the interaction of material conditions and policies with cultural practices and identities.[17]

Critical analysis, focusing more explicitly on social and institutional structures than on human agency, encompasses a broad range of distinct approaches. A prominent critical theoretical framework is the internal colonial model.[18] This approach views contemporary policies as the perpetuation of historical subordination of Aboriginal people and their lands by government and other dominant institutions. Aboriginal people have come to be marginalized as a result of economic and social development strategies that have destroyed indigenous societies and restricted people's rights and options. Recent analysis has attempted to advance the colonization thesis by acknowledging the struggles by First Nations and other indigenous people for decolonization, representation, and self-determination and to situate internal dependency in the changing context of world systems.[19] Class and other forms of structured inequality also contribute to the perpetuation of educational and economic gaps between Aboriginal and non-Aboriginal populations.[20]

Marxist analysis highlights these latter perspectives, stressing how indigenous people have suffered as a consequence of subordination by dominant class forces. This approach situates oppression directly within capitalist requirements for the preservation of stable markets and political conditions that allow for profitable investment, production, and trade, such as the fur trade, megaprojects associated with northern development, and state enforcement of discriminatory practices in education, welfare, justice, and other domains.[21] Conventional Marxist analysis has paid relatively little attention to Aboriginal–state relations in Canada,[22] reinforcing concerns by Aboriginal critics who feel that Marxism undermines their own interests by remaining one-dimensional and Eurocentric in nature.[23] However, Marxism has generated some interest within Aboriginal scholarship and activism for its potential to link historical processes of domination with struggles and prospects for self-determination.[24]

An alternative critical challenge to dominant forms of thinking emerges through feminism and gender studies. This analysis, in contrast to a gender-blind emphasis on Aboriginal people as a homogeneous cultural entity, articulates Aboriginal women's experiences and circumstances. Research highlights the perpetuation of discrimination, inequality, and the absence of women's representation in conventional and First Nations organizations, even after the Constitution Act in 1982 and Bill C-31 in 1985 mandated formal gender equality that had been absent in the earlier Indian Act.[25] Feminist perspectives have moved women's concerns and contributions to the centre of analysis of both traditional and contemporary societies by showing, for instance, how women's contributions have been socially constructed as marginal despite their critical importance to the maintenance of family and community ties and the preservation of vitality in Aboriginal cultures.[26]

Nonetheless, feminist analysis, typically more than Marxism, tends to experience a somewhat uneasy relationship with indigenous studies and perspectives. Much of the conventional work in both those approaches has subsumed the histories and positions of Aboriginal people within frameworks that do not fully address first people's specific realities and orientations. Consequently, many researchers who address issues of gender inequality among Aboriginal people have emphasized the need for analytical accounts and political strategies that acknowledge the unique nature of Aboriginal women's experiences,[27] or the combination of factors that disadvantage Aboriginal women through violence and other forms of 'multiple jeopardy.'[28]

In these latter respects, there is some affinity between the presentation of Aboriginal people's perspectives and emergent postmodernist approaches to social critique. Both reject any single, linear, historical and causal framework, highlighting instead the contingent and fragmented nature of identity and the importance of bringing the voices of oppressed people from the margins to the centre of struggles over meaning and vision in their lives.[29] A parallel focus lies with recognition that the analysis of Aboriginal people requires an understanding of indigenous ways of knowing that are constituted as distinct forms of thought integrally related to people's cultural heritage and everyday experiences.[30] The incorporation of Aboriginal perspectives points, as well, to the need to re-examine the concepts of social differentiation and inequality. Conventional measures, such as statistical analysis of different rates of income or labour force participation, are useful as general indicators of relative socio-economic standing, but they fail to address the complete range of material, social, and spiritual factors that affect people's lives. Monture-Angus contends that concepts like 'disadvantage' conceal racism by neglecting to consider the richness of personal and social relationships that constitute Aboriginal communities.[31]

Each of these approaches offers important, but often partial, accounts of how differentiation has been produced and experienced among Aboriginal people through policies and interactions with other institutions and groups. Recent conflict-oriented theories have attempted to provide more complete understandings of these relationships by examining processes of domination, resistance, and accommodation as complex, interrelated, and changing phenomena.

An approach loosely categorized as critical political economy is concerned to integrate analysis not only of how Aboriginal people have been marginalized and excluded from central social, political, and economic activities, but also of how they have attempted to redefine and negotiate a more meaningful place in mainstream and indigenous social settings. Historical patterns of development are framed within ongoing social action and wider political, social, and economic arrangements.[32] Class, race, gender, and other key social relations unfold through the complex interplay among various external agents, structures of regulation, and Aboriginal communities, which themselves are multidimensional.[33]

A focus on shifting relations of conflict, accommodation, and resistance provides a framework to investigate how social differentiation is produced and changes over time. State policy, along with other economic and institutional structures, sets parameters for the kinds of choices and opportunities that are available to Aboriginal people in Canada. But policy itself is produced and modified in real historical circumstances through negotiation and struggle by various social actors and interests. The discussion now turns to consideration of those policies and conditions that have been most strongly implicated in processes of social differentiation among Aboriginal people.

6. Differentiation among Aboriginal Societies

The designation 'First Nations' reflects diversity among indigenous cultures and social organization. Ethnographic and archaeological research has constructed detailed portrayals of day-to-day life and social organizations, dating back several centuries, that were highly varied from one setting to the next.[34] Even though many of these accounts are premised on curiosity about societies that were obsolete or presumed to be vanishing, and grounded in the observers' own biases and expectations, they point to the coexistence of diverse living circumstances and social, political, and cultural forms well before contact with outsiders arriving in North America, and government policies, began to alter those realities.[35]

7. Legislative Regulation and Social Differentiation

Government policy and legislation have contributed, directly and indirectly, to changing and contradictory forms of social differentiation and regulation that affect Aboriginal people. The lineage of control in its strongest and most persistent forms has shifted historically from missionaries and religious orders to residential schools and the child and social welfare systems, to the criminal justice system and current debates over band rights and membership.

Indian Affairs policy, since the late colonial period, has been based on explicit recognition of distinctions between those considered to be 'Indians' and other Canadians, for most of that time under the guise of assimilationist objectives.[36] Formal recognition and legal categorization (e.g., Indian status, Métis, Inuit, band membership, and Aboriginal rights) have both material and symbolic importance. Regardless of their origins, these categories are used by and against specific groups of people as potential bases of identity and interaction, as well as frameworks to determine inclusion in or exclusion from rights, privileges, and activities. The state, in these regards, regulates Aboriginal people as subjects – it defines who is an Indian, and specifies what kinds of persons Indians are expected to be and under what kinds of conditions a person can or cannot remain an Indian.

The first legal definitions of 'Indians,' contained in land protection legislation adopted in Upper and Lower Canada in 1850, were reinforced by subsequent introduction and maintenance of the Indian register, and incorporated in the Indian Act in 1876.[37] These legal categories and definitions have been subject to considerable change over time, reflecting diverse administrative, jurisdictional, and cultural concerns.[38] Under the Indian Act, BNA Act, and various other federal and provincial legislative acts, statutory recognition has been given to specific categories of people, including the Métis, Inuit, Inuk, and Indians who have come to be known as 'C-31s.' Since 1981, the broader designation of 'Aboriginal and treaty rights' has also been recognized formally, and several groups, including the Métis and non-status Indians, continue efforts to ensure recognition and delineation of their own status and entitlements.[39] Various First Nations are also granted particular forms of legal recognition under self-government and claims agreements that pertain to specific people or territories.

Moss and Opekokew detail the many forms of discriminatory legislation enacted from before the time of Confederation that provide for differential treatment between Indians and other Canadians and among particular categories of indigenous people.[40] Legislative regulation has been directed most powerfully towards status Indians living on reserves. The Royal Commission on Aboriginal Peoples observes, with reference to changes to the Indian Act and related regulations since the late nineteenth century, that '[m]any of these amendments eroded the protected status of reserve lands. Others enabled band governments to be brought under almost complete supervision and control. Yet others allowed almost every area of the daily life of Indians on reserves to be regulated or controlled in one way or another.'[41] The legacy of legal differentiation is reflected in contemporary gaps in living conditions and socio-economic circumstances for registered Indians living on reserves, in comparison with the general Canadian population and with other categories of Aboriginal people.[42]

Procedures for the enfranchisement of Indians, outlined in the Indian Act until amendments under Bill C-31 in the mid-1980s, illustrate the state's efforts to regulate subjects and identity. In principle, enfranchisement refers to a situation in which Indians were deemed fit for integration into the mainstream society, marked by the loss of their formal status as Indians. As originally outlined in pre-Confederation statutes later incorporated into the Indian Act, enfranchisement was open to Indians who were literate and relatively well educated, free of debt, and declared to be of good moral character. It was initially voluntary for men, although the wives and children of enfranchised men became automatically enfranchised themselves.[43] The most controversial aspect of enfranchisement was the provision, eliminated under Bill C-31, that removed Indian status from Indian women who married non-Indian men, along with their offspring, while Indian men who married non-Indian women not only retained status but had status endowed on their wives and children.[44]

Such measures had a mixed impact on people's lives and options. Loss of Indian status, especially for the few individuals who did opt for voluntary enfranchisement, could signify the achievement of education levels, employment opportunities, and voting rights that meant integration into urban, industrial society. At the same time, legal and cultural barriers were set up to differentiate Indians from those who were no longer defined and accepted as Indians. Individuals who pursued social and economic opportunities, regardless of whether or not they sought enfranchisement, frequently had to migrate off-reserve, meaning that reserves lost members who could provide valuable leadership and services essential for the advancement of their communities. Those who lost Indian status were no longer formally eligible to reside on reserves, and lost access to services provided to registered Indians by the federal government. This problem was most serious for women who lost their status through marriage, many of whom severed ties with community support groups and service networks upon migration to urban areas. One major consequence of this policy has been the sharp segmentation in experiences among urban Aboriginal women between the most highly disadvantaged and others who have been able to make considerable improvements in educational and occupational status in recent years.[45]

Some of the most blatant discriminatory provisions were removed under Bill C-31, following legal challenges by Aboriginal women and other groups. However, not all longstanding concerns were ameliorated, while new problems and inequalities have arisen. Several recurrent issues show how statutory definitions of social categories, regardless of how they are framed, can produce conflict and differentiation. These include questions about the rights of off-reserve band members, status Indians who are not granted band membership, and band members who do not have status; financial and administrative difficulties associated with the distribution of benefits and services to the increased population base created by new or reinstated registrants eligible under Bill C-31; social and political tensions between long-time band members and new 'C-31s'; and the creation of status eligibility criteria that produce familial and generational divisions.[46]

The issue of legal status takes on greater significance in relation to broader questions concerning Aboriginal rights and entitlements that have emerged since the 1970s. The general concept of Aboriginal rights is widely understood to refer to formal recognition that indigenous people have sovereignty as First Nations, derived from distinct forms of cultural, social, and political organization that constitutes their heritage as original occupants of the land. The concept emerged in a negative manner in the sense that it is rooted not in traditional Aboriginal cultures, but was a category imposed by the British crown in order to make legitimate the subsequent transfer of lands to the crown.[47]

Interest in Aboriginal rights issues peaked in the mid-1980s in the context of constitutional negotiations, the acknowledgment of those rights in the 1982 Constitution Act (sect. 35), and mounting frustration by segments of the Aboriginal population over the lack of progress towards substantiation of those rights in land claims and governance issues.[48] These issues are the subject of strong political and legal contention. First Nations have maintained that indigenous people, through continuous use of the land, have developed broad, sovereign forms of government, and social and legal organizations, that are associated with particular entitlements. Federal and provincial governments have been more inclined to limit the definition and scope of Aboriginal rights, emphasizing that rights and entitlements can only be negotiated to the extent that they lie within legitimate state domains. Although there are also political and academic stances that suggest Aboriginal rights should be extinguished or interpreted in the most restrictive ways, much more compelling legal and historical evidence points to a conception of Aboriginal people as 'citizens plus' whose Canadian citizenship is underlined by rights and status (however these come to be defined in specific terms) derived from their heritage as original occupants and stewards of the land.[49]

Recent policy and academic literature, in this light, has shifted attention from the broad notion of Aboriginal rights as entitlement to a preoccupation with the more particular concept of self-government and, especially, the details involved with a diverse range of negotiations and implementation of land claims settlements and self-government agreements. Self-government issues remain complex and diverse – the definition in the Constitution Act of Aboriginal people encompasses three groups (Indians, Métis, and Inuit); distinctive interests and approaches to self-government are represented by each of those groups as well as off-reserve Indians and urban Aboriginal people; and the Indian Act limits the definition and enactment of self-government, as well as the ability to keep pace with the many specific initiatives being negotiated and implemented in different locales and regions, including vast territories where no treaties were ever made.[50] Hogg and Turpel suggest a need to bridge two extreme positions in all of this: broad recognition of inherent Aboriginal rights without an overall framework would retain flexibility applicable to diverse circumstances and aspirations among Aboriginal people, while a more 'detailed blueprint' could apply to all self-governments.[51] Subsequent statements and actions by the federal government, both through its response to the Royal Commission on Aboriginal Peoples and the multifaceted self-government negotiations with various First Nations, have implied general concurrence with this position.

The diversity of First Nations and of the situations of Aboriginal people throughout different regions, and the varying involvement and approach adopted by different provincial and federal administrations, make difficult any comprehensive statements about these negotiations and agreements.[52] Jhappan, commenting on the legal dimensions of rights and claims, observes the remarkable success that Aboriginal people have had in advancing a natural law discourse of rights and justice in the face of the courts' reliance upon a legal positivist approach grounded in common law. Nonetheless, he observes that the continued hegemony of the legal positivist approach poses ongoing obstacles to that progress.[53] The success of claims and self-government resolutions are also affected by the complex interplay among political alignments (partisan and otherwise), economic forces, and social structural factors.

Land entitlements and self-determination initiatives have provided much-needed access to resources and services for members of specified communities, groups, bands, or tribal councils. Aboriginal business enterprises, government services, and other arrangements have created jobs and addressed important community needs. Nonetheless, formal recognition of Aboriginal rights and self-government negotiations, along with constitutional acknowledgment of plural forms of Aboriginal status, have increased possibilities that cultural and political allegiances will become fragmented and partial, and that distinctions between Aboriginal and non-Aboriginal populations will become further entrenched. Struggles over band membership around Bill C-31 exemplify the difficulties associated with reconciling formal status and distribution of controlled and limited resources.

In short, policies directly related to First Nations and other Aboriginal people have created legal distinctions and regulated the lives and rights of particular groups in different ways. These forms of differentiation have often been associated, as well, with differential entitlements and unequal distributions of resources, resulting in pronounced disparities not only between Aboriginal and non-Aboriginal people, but also among diverse segments of the Aboriginal population.

8. General Policy and Socio-economic Differentiation

The various policy initiatives outlined in the previous section exist in a context of wider policy decisions and social practices. Many of these have special importance for Aboriginal people and their relations with non-Aboriginal groups and organizations. At least eleven federal government departments, other than Indian and Northern Affairs, fund special programs or initiatives specific to First Nations or other Aboriginal groups, such as the National Native Alcohol and Drug Program (Health Canada), the Aboriginal Partnership for labour force development (Human Resources Development Canada), and the First Nations Policing Policy (Solicitor General).[54] Numerous provincial and territorial departments also offer a wide range of comparable or unique programs. It is important, as well, to acknowledge the impact of programs with general applicability on Aboriginal people and the opportunities available to them. As Hylton observes, 'Aboriginal people in Canada are disproportionately affected by the problems that social programs are intended to address.'[55] Given that specific Aboriginal policy concerns are related to Aboriginal people's interests with respect to more general social problems, attention needs to be paid to issues of Aboriginal representation on policy and program bodies and to structural factors that produce inequalities.

Pressure by various Aboriginal organizations for representation at constitutional negotiations, legal and political dimensions of land claims issues, and the spectre of violent confrontations by First Nations groups frustrated at the lack of resolution of long-standing claims and grievances have placed a sense of urgency on Aboriginal involvement in a wide range of issues. Sensitivity has been growing to the importance of consulting with and involving Aboriginal people on matters like the development of new social policies or the social and economic impact of major initiatives involving natural or human resources. Aboriginal people and members of Aboriginal organizations now sit as representatives or observers at a diverse array of tables across the country, unlike in previous eras when First Nations involvement was ignored or excluded even in discussions about the Indian Act.

However, long-standing contacts, patterns of interaction, regulations, and insensitivity to cultural and historical circumstances continue to marginalize Aboriginal people from substantial policy, economic, and institutional decision-making that affects them. Both an overt legacy of racism and more subtle discriminatory practices and structures contribute to the exclusion of Aboriginal people from central roles in many organizations. Regulations that many First Nations people cannot meet, such as requirements for property ownership or status as a municipal ratepayer that define eligibility to stand for election, prevent Aboriginal people from attaining full representation on school boards and other important public bodies.[56] As well as a need to incorporate Aboriginal personnel and perspectives in key sites, greater understanding is also required of how Aboriginal people are more likely than many other Canadians to live or be involved in circumstances where they may become stigmatized, criminalized, or victimized.[57] Numerous cases, most visible in areas like education, child welfare, and criminal justice, demonstrate how policies intended for general application combine with those specific to Aboriginal people, producing a particular burden when the cultures and circumstances of a minority population are not taken into account.[58] Demographic factors, employment and income, education and occupation, and social conditions each reflect distinct aspects of differentiation. While many of these dimensions are widely shared, it is important to emphasize, as well, that unique material and cultural circumstances among Aboriginal bands or communities generate considerable differentiation in the ways that pertinent concerns, and strategies to address them, are framed and experienced.

9. Demographic Factors

Several population and geographical dimensions signify differences between the Aboriginal and non-Aboriginal population as well as bases of differentiation within the Aboriginal population. Figures on the size of the Aboriginal population in Canada vary according to definitional and methodological factors. The 1996 census, for instance, collected data on Aboriginal people through two questions related to ethnic origin and identity. Just over 1.1 million people indicated that their ethnic origin, or ancestry, was Aboriginal, while on the question of identity, 799,010 people, or 2.8 per cent of the total Canadian population, identified themselves as North American Indian, Métis, or Inuit.[59] However, actual figures are somewhat higher, because enumeration was not conducted or completed on 77 reserves, and census forms did not reach many locations in which Aboriginal people are concentrated. Indian and Northern Affairs Canada identified a registered Indian population of 610,874 for 1996, which is about 57,000 more than the number of people who identified themselves as North American Indian on the census.[60] The Royal Commission on Aboriginal Peoples projected a total Aboriginal population of 811,400 for 1996, while Frideres, using a more inclusive definition of Aboriginal ancestry, estimated a total Aboriginal population of over one million; Indian and Northern Affairs Canada estimates place the total Aboriginal population by 2000 at just below 1.4 million.[61]

Three population-related factors are most significant for an understanding of social differentiation – the age structure, higher than average population growth, and the geographical distribution of the Aboriginal population. The first two issues are closely related to one another. The average age of the Aboriginal population in 1996 (25.5 years) was ten years younger than that of the Canadian population as a whole, with children under fifteen years constituting over one-third (35%) of the Aboriginal population compared with a comparable proportion of one-fifth for the general population.[62] The young age structure reflects higher birth rates in the Aboriginal population. Among registered Indians, birth rates are more than double the Canadian rate, and while infant mortality rates continue to be higher than comparable national rates, they declined by about one-third between the mid-1980s and mid-1990s.[63] By contrast, only 4 per cent of the Aboriginal population, compared with 12 per cent of the total Canadian population, were 65 years and over.[64] The current demographic structure indicates that the Aboriginal population will continue for at least another generation to grow at a faster rate than the Canadian average. Siggner and colleagues also point to 'ethnic mobility' as a contributing factor to this growth insofar as Aboriginal people may be more likely to self-identify within designated categories on the census and other documents in the context of the increasing profile of Aboriginal rights issues and entitlements.[65]

Several implications arise from the combined impact of a youth-concentrated age structure and high birth rates. As public debate over health care services and allocation of resources concentrate on the 'greying' of the population, the health care needs of Aboriginal communities are oriented more fully to prenatal care, childhood, and youth matters. Associated concerns such as accidents and injuries, parenting and child-care needs, sexually-transmitted diseases, substance abuse, and involvement in criminal and violent behaviour are prevalent. Nationally, for instance, public demands for tougher initiatives to counter perceived increases in criminal activity by young people coincide with the stabilization or reduction of Canadian crime and youth crime rates. In this context, a relative increase in the Aboriginal youth cohort, especially among those who live in conditions where they are likely to be at risk for engaging in or being victimized by criminal activity, may single them out as subjects of even further disproportionate public and legal scrutiny.[66] Younger people also tend to be more mobile than older people, especially when they are less established or are willing to move in search of education, employment, or social opportunities. Following Cheal's analysis, earlier in this volume, of the 'privileging of prime-age workers,' its high youth concentration places the Aboriginal population in particular jeopardy with respect to future economic prospects.

Continuing growth in Aboriginal populations is likely to intensify critical needs related to housing, social assistance, education, and access to jobs and community services.[67] This is a special concern in specific regions, notably the Prairies and northern Canada, which have the highest concentrations of Aboriginal populations. The share of the population identifying themselves on the 1996 census as Aboriginal was 61.9 per cent in the Northwest Territories, 20.1 per cent in the

Yukon, about 11.5 per cent in Manitoba and Saskatchewan, and between 0.7 and 2.6 per cent in every province east of Manitoba.[68] In the case of Saskatchewan, projections indicate that by 2006 nearly one-third of the school-age population will be of Aboriginal ancestry compared to current levels of about one-fifth.[69]

Moreover, in contrast to Canada's highly urbanized national and immigrant populations, about 70 per cent of Aboriginal people live outside of census metropolitan areas, including nearly one-third on rural reserves, one-quarter in smaller urban centres, and one-fifth in rural and isolated areas off-reserve. Among urban Aboriginal people, large numbers live in Toronto and Vancouver but constitute less than 2 per cent of the total populations of those cities, while they represent about 7 per cent of the populations in several prairie cities, including Winnipeg, Saskatoon, and Regina.[70]

Legal status is strongly associated with regional and residential patterns. By virtue of treaty provisions and entitlements, nearly three-fifths (58.5%) of registered Indians live on-reserve, although due to the combined impact of Bill C-31, greater recognition of the rights of band members living off-reserve, and pressures to leave reserves for personal reasons or to seek work and advanced education, the proportion of the registered Indian population living off-reserve will continue to increase in the coming decades.[71] The Métis population is concentrated in the prairie region, and the Inuit in the north. Among people living in urban centres, Aboriginal women outnumber men by a larger than average percentage, reflecting in part the impact of loss of status and band membership under the Indian Act both before and as a result of continuing problems with Bill C-31.[72] Complex migration patterns, both on- and off-reserve, and among rural and urban areas, suggest that there will be long-term skewed distributions among Aboriginal populations.[73]

Population distributions are especially significant for the administration and delivery of programs and services tailored to the needs of Aboriginal people. Problems arise when fiscal, political, and situational factors do not take into account sensitivity to the diversity of Canada's First Nations and Aboriginal communities. Governments and agencies in remote regions or areas where the Aboriginal population is small or highly dispersed may be disinclined or find it difficult to provide a full range of appropriate services. In urban areas, too, despite recent improvements, serious deficiencies continue relative to the funding and implementation of, and Aboriginal voice in, supportive programs and services.[74] A special challenge is posed by the need to ensure policies and programs that maintain responsiveness to specific, local needs at the same time that there is some equity and coordination of programs, services, and knowledge across jurisdictions. Southcott's analysis, in the next chapter, points to trends of gradual social and economic decline in many of the areas in which Aborignal people are most highly concentrated, even amidst general tendencies towards regional convergence.

10. Employment and Income

Employment and income data provide a crude but important indicator of the relative well-being and socio-economic standing of different groups of people. In terms of overall comparisons between populations, for those aged fifteen and over, Aboriginal people are less likely to participate in the labour force (by about 10%), are more likely to be unemployed (by about 2.5 times), are more likely to work on a part-time or seasonal basis (by about 20%), and have lower earnings (by 34% overall and by 21% for those working full-year full-time). In 1995, 57 per cent of Aboriginal people reported earnings, with an average employment income of $17,382, while 66 per cent of the national population reported earnings, with average employment income of $26,474.[75] Despite some indications that gaps between Aboriginal people and the general population are closing, long-term projections suggest that equity will not be achieved – or that margins may even widen – over the next several years.[76]

Why is this so, given evidence that improvements are occurring in employment, earnings and incomes, and education levels for Aboriginal people? Statistics Canada analysis indicates that about 60 per cent of the difference in average earnings can be accounted for by factors like age (given the younger age composition of the Aboriginal population), lower education, and work patterns.[77] Aboriginal workers are highly concentrated in industries like trade, food and beverage services, construction, natural resources, and government services, many of which are subject to low wages and instability. Bernier observes that variations in the distribution of age and education levels account for between 21 and 23 per cent of the difference in wage inequality between Aboriginal workers and the national average, while occupation accounts for 13 to 15 per cent.[78] According to Department of Indian and Northern Affairs analysis, community location, such as the high concentration of the on-reserve registered Indian population in rural areas with few development opportunities, can account for 41.7 per cent of the variation in average individual income and 23 per cent of the variation in labour force participation rate for men, and 37.6 per cent of the comparable rate for women.[79] However, as the relatively low percentages indicate, these factors cannot explain all of the inequalities between Aboriginal and non-Aboriginal people. More 'invisible' indicators (viewed from standard labour force analysis) such as racism, discrimination, and personal circumstances also affect the employment opportunities and choices for Aboriginal people. The Aboriginal People's Survey revealed that 18 per cent of all Aboriginal respondents, and 22 per cent of those living on-reserve, identified the consideration that 'they were Aboriginal' as a deterrent to finding stable employment.[80] As Li points out in the previous chapter, 'the politics of difference' have a disproportionate negative impact on Aboriginal people.

Variations also occur within the Aboriginal population. Registered Indians living on-reserve have labour force participation rates about ten percentage points below the average for all Aboriginal people, and average incomes 24 per cent below those of Aboriginal people living off-reserve.[81] Regional and gender variations are evident, as well, within the on-reserve population. The relative disadvantage in labour market and occupational experiences of urban Aboriginal people living in western Canada compared with their eastern counterparts may be due, in part, to earlier pressures for off-reserve migration and economic integration in the east.[82] In recent years, women living on-reserve in Saskatchewan and Manitoba have had labour force participation rates well below the average rates for registered Indian women living on-reserve, while those in the Yukon, Northwest Territories, British Columbia, and Ontario have had above-average participation; among men, similar patterns hold, although those living in Nova Scotia and Newfoundland have also had labour force participation rates consistently below the averages for all registered Indian men living on-reserve.[83] Bernier observes greater inequality in wage distribution among Aboriginal workers than among the Canadian workforce as a whole, with greater polarization in wage distribution among Aboriginal women than for Aboriginal men and a lower gender gap in wage distribution on-reserve. Segmentation among Aboriginal people has also accelerated given the higher than average rates of participation, particularly among women and youth, in the non-standard employment relations, including temporary work and entrepreneurship, discussed in Vosko's chapter earlier in this volume. These trends are increasingly evident as economic opportunities become widely dispersed for those living in urban areas.[84]

11. Education and Occupation

As with economic indicators, a distinct and only gradually diminishing 'education gap' exists between Aboriginal and non-Aboriginal people. Census data for 1996 reveal that 54 per cent of the Aboriginal population fifteen years of age and over had not completed high school and only 4.5 per cent had university degrees or diplomas, compared with levels of 35 and 16 per cent, respectively, for the non-Aboriginal population.[85] Increases in educational attainment among the younger population, and higher than average levels of post-secondary enrolment for Aboriginal people aged 25 and over, suggest that some improvements are occurring. Nonetheless, the increases in educational attainment among Aboriginal people are barely keeping pace with national educational advancement as greater emphasis is placed on the merits of lifelong learning and credential upgrading. Statistics Canada analysis of census data trends indicates that, even within the relatively well-educated cohort of persons aged 20 to 29, Aboriginal people 'remained only one-half as likely to have a postsecondary degree or diploma, one-fifth as likely to have graduated from university and over twice as likely not to have completed high school.'[86] Overall dropout rates for Aboriginal students are more than double the comparable rates for the Canadian population 18 to 20 years of age, and only one-quarter of Aboriginal students who leave school, compared to nearly half of all early school leavers, are reported as returning to school.[87]

As with employment indicators, there are considerable variations in educational status within the Aboriginal population. In Manitoba, Saskatchewan, and the Northwest Territories, for instance, the proportions of Aboriginal people aged fifteen and over with less than high school education are above the national average for Aboriginal people, while the converse is true for the Atlantic provinces, Ontario, British Columbia, and the Yukon.[88] Similarly, education levels tend to be higher in urban areas relative to rural and isolated areas, partly because employment opportunities requiring higher education and educational institutions, especially at advanced levels, are more likely to be concentrated in larger centres. Among adult members of the Musqueam band in Vancouver, for example, only 6 per cent have less than grade 9 and 31 per cent have a university degree, in stark contrast to the God's Lake reserve in northern Manitoba, in which only 2.5 per cent have a university degree and 35 per cent have less than grade 9.[89]

For Aboriginal people, parallel with broader trends in Canada and many other developed nations, women are now outpacing men in their educational enrolments and attainments. The Federation of Saskatchewan Indian Nations reports that, among Aboriginal people in that province, more women are now attaining higher post-secondary credentials in all fields except applied sciences.[90] Education levels, combined with labour markets and economic structures, are closely related to occupational stratification. While relatively similar overall occupational patterns are evident between Aboriginal people and the total Canadian labour force, Aboriginal people are about twice as likely as average to be employed in government services.[91] Disparities exist with respect to different categories of legal status or Aboriginal identity: registered Indians are twice as dependent on government service employment than the Aboriginal population as a whole; Métis and registered Indians are slightly more likely than other Aboriginal people and non-Aboriginal people to be engaged in primary industries; and registered Indians and Inuit are somewhat less likely than other groups to be employed in tertiary industries outside of the government, education, and health sectors. Ross calculates that it would cost about $400 million to upgrade the average levels of schooling among on-reserve Indians to the same level as for the Métis and non-status population, but that such investment would yield a return of $5 billion over ten years in increased earnings and decreased transfer payments.[92]

These labour market patterns are further differentiated across diverse regions and local settings. For instance, the Royal Commission on Aboriginal Peoples identifies three distinct types of Aboriginal economies characterized by specific labour market dynamics – First Nations reserves and rural Métis communities, urban Aboriginal economies, and northern economies.[93] Similarly, some analysis highlights differences between categories of Aboriginal people in urban areas – one consists of a transient population, generally younger, with limited formal education and skills and few stable social contacts, who face the most severe and marginal living conditions; another includes persons who are more highly educated and better equipped to take advantage of social, educational, and labour market opportunities. Further differentiation operates between regions (with marked differences between cities in the east and prairie regions) and within distinct sites.[94] There is also significant variation, even within regions, in the resource bases, employment experiences, and development strategies experienced by specific bands, reserves, and Aboriginal communities. These uneven conditions often reflect historical conditions and even chance (such as the location of reserves on lands where oil revenues could not be foreseen in the treaty-making process), but frequently they are the consequence of administrative and political decisions.

Less attention has been paid to gender differentiation in Aboriginal occupational patterns, but clear distinctions are apparent between men's and women's work in both Aboriginal and non-Aboriginal populations. As is characteristic of women's position in the labour force in general, Aboriginal women are concentrated most highly in clerical, service, and low-level professional occupations, with higher than average employment particularly in poorer-paying service positions and government-related professional activities.[95]

Some improvements in Aboriginal people's educational and occupational circumstances are reinforced by a variety of community support mechanisms and program initiatives in education, training, and labour market development. Growing representation by Aboriginal people in a wide range of occupations and education and training programs signifies the emergence of a labour force that may be equipped for participation in public- and private-sector positions operated by either Aboriginal or conventional agencies. Nonetheless, several administrative, fiscal, and jurisdictional barriers restrict the accomplishment of equitable and successful participation.[96] Despite increasing numbers of positions for Aboriginal people with advanced education and training, there will also be difficulties in finding sufficient numbers of qualified individuals as long as Aboriginal students remain marginalized or filtered out from the education system at early levels.[97]

Two more general factors are likely to affect the extent to which Aboriginal people can achieve full, meaningful participation in the labour force, even if they attain parity with the rest of the population in credentials and qualifications. The first is related to the heavy reliance on the government sector for work, while the second concerns the tendency towards an increasingly polarized employment structure. Government-sector employment of Aboriginal people has been enhanced by government's lead, at least relative to most private-sector employers, in implementing employment equity measures, the proliferation of positions associated with the negotiation and adoption of various self-government initiatives, the development at various government levels of diverse programs tailored specifically for Aboriginal people, and the strong presence of government services in areas such as social welfare, health care, criminal justice, and housing in communities with high proportions of Aboriginal residents. Although employment in the government sector is not likely to disappear, with projected growth in relevant areas given the complex profile of Aboriginal affairs, pressures for fiscal constraint, restructuring of state services, and privatization measures leave many state employees vulnerable in the face of shifting priorities and often with limited prospects for career advancement. The more general problem relates to the way in which economic and workplace changes are affecting employment, wages, and job security for all labour market participants, as the preceding analyses by Vosko, Cheal, and Li have emphasized in this book.[98] The population as a whole is becoming better educated and more highly trained. While this occurs in part in conjunction with increased skill demands of jobs, substantial proportions of the Canadian population are facing underemployment characterized by lack of jobs or opportunities to utilize the skills and training they have achieved.[99] There are mixed trends, suggesting further labour market and occupational polarization among the Aboriginal population. While prospects for Aboriginal people are improving through increased access to education, training, and jobs, labour market dynamics indicate that opportunities for those who have been marginalized from education and employment become more dismal; and not all those who do attain high credentials may benefit, either.[100]

12. Social Conditions

The prevalent image of social conditions experienced by Aboriginal people within many communities, as portrayed in a large body of readily accessible popular, academic, and policy literature, is one in which deprivation, despair, marginalization, and daily struggles for survival are widespread.[101] Over the past two decades, though, these depictions have been mitigated by stories of identity and hope recaptured, communities rebuilt, and promises for self-sufficiency replacing the damaging legacy of the past.

Several fundamental and distressing realities cannot be ignored – Aboriginal people face considerably higher than average chances of experiencing serious social and personal problems related to physical and mental health, safety, violence, justice, housing, substance abuse, family, and poverty, each of which compounds other risk factors. The

1996 census reveals, for instance, that 44 per cent of the Aboriginal population, more than double the national rate of 20 per cent, lived below the low-income cut-off rate defined by Statistics Canada.[102] Nearly half (47.6 per cent) of new HIV cases diagnosed in Saskatchewan in 1997, and over one-third of those in Edmonton, were Aboriginal people.[103] There are troubling signs that many difficulties will be perpetuated and reproduced through later generations. In terms of family structure, for instance, the 1996 census revealed that about 23 per cent of on-reserve families and 36 per cent of off-reserve registered Indian families were headed by a lone parent, compared to a rate of 13 per cent for the total Canadian population, while one-third of Aboriginal children under the age of fifteen, living in a census family, lived with a lone parent, a rate more than double that for the total population.[104] About 60 per cent of Aboriginal children under the age of six, compared to a national rate of about 25 per cent, lived in low-income families, and suicide rates among Aboriginal youth aged 15 to 24 were eight times higher than national rates for males and five times for females.[105]

Hidden behind the statistics are everyday experiences, relations, and orientations to the world that give unique shape to people's lives. Factors like the retention of traditional languages are important to the development of strong identities and communities. Aboriginal children are keenly aware of the strong impact, directly or indirectly, of issues like safety, racism, discrimination, family support, and caring relationships on their schooling experiences.[106] The feminization of poverty in urban areas, especially among Aboriginal women who are single parents, creates pressures that are both immediate and that affect individuals' prospects for future social and economic security.[107] In these regards, Aboriginal and non-Aboriginal people in many situations share common experiences when crucial factors are held constant. As other chapters in this volume make evident, phenomena like poverty or incarceration, for instance, reflect social-class disadvantage regardless of racial or ethnic background, while for those with greater opportunity, the labour market and income advantages of Aboriginal people with the highest levels of educational attainment are similar to those of non-Aboriginal people.[108] Most disturbing in these analyses is the continued existence of a substantial 'underclass,' comparable to that observed by Wilson in the United States, consisting of people whose futures are marked by little hope to rise above marginalization and deep disadvantage.[109]

Appropriate definitions of what constitutes 'problems' as well as the development of programs, policies, and effective solutions to address them require sensitivity to these various interconnected dimensions of social differentiation. The importance of cultural factors to how such problems are constructed and responded to must also be acknowledged. As increasing numbers of indigenous people become positioned to take advantage of emerging opportunities for social and economic participation, attention needs to be paid as well to how widely the more favourable prospects will become open to the Aboriginal population as a whole. The opportunities that are being created or becoming available for those with sufficient skills, knowledge, and social networks are not shared with sizeable numbers of Aboriginal people, particularly those whose basic concerns are more immediate. For many of these people, social and economic success, by conventional indicators, presupposes the cultivation of basic life skills, safe and healthy environments, and supportive family, community, and governance forms that previous institutional arrangements have not been able to provide.

13. Deregulation, Self-determination and New Regulatory Measures

Many commentators have pointed to the emergence over the past two decades of what Weaver has called a 'new paradigm' in Canada's Aboriginal policy.[110] Attention has shifted from a preoccupation with regulation and control over the lives and affairs of First Nations towards the development of parallel or cooperative measures oriented to self-determination and improvements in the quality of life for Aboriginal people. These initiatives have been accelerated as the state has sought strategies to accommodate or contain pressures arising from both litigation over land claims and Aboriginal rights and potentially violent confrontations arising from mounting frustration at the lack of action to address unresolved grievances or due to conflicting interpretations of rights and jurisdictional authority.[111]

The tremendous number of new initiatives, and the pace at which they are emerging, reflects the diversity of circumstances for Aboriginal people. Many of these are truly innovative, exciting, and successful, others are beset with serious challenges, and some have had mixed results or worse. The successful establishment of social programs run by Aboriginal people is seen by Hylton to depend on such factors as the ability to incorporate Aboriginal culture and effective community participation in programs, the creation of economic benefit for Aboriginal communities, the provision of a wide range of cost-effective services that meet community needs, and reduced dependency on the state; common problems arise through jurisdictional concerns, an absence of adequate or stable resources, and lack of infrastructure and long-range planning mechanisms.[112]

Community agencies and policy-makers are posed with a major but important task: to begin to chronicle and take stock of the various initiatives in several domains, in order to base future planning and action on a clear understanding of what works, what doesn't, and what kinds of visions and resources can be shared across jurisdictions. In the process, potential contradictions arise as Aboriginal people, on their own and in conjunction with non-Aboriginal governments and organizations, work to achieve meaningful social participation and control over their lives. The discussion below is guided by questions about the extent to which state regulation has diminished or merely changed in form, and what consequences these transformations have for social differentiation.

14. The Contradictory Nature of Regulation and Self-determination

Self-determination by First Nations and other Aboriginal people encompasses several realities and possibilities, ranging from the establishment of small-scale business ventures or community services agencies, to the devolution of control over particular programs from the federal government to band administration, to more comprehensive self-government jurisdiction over a defined territory. Each of these developments is grounded in particular conceptions and dimensions of Aboriginal control that presuppose a shift from regulation by non-Aboriginal authorities to control by Aboriginal agencies or organizations.

The current approach to self-determination involves primarily negotiation on a case-by-case basis or establishment of programs and services to meet specific needs or unique community initiatives. Although not conducive to policy development, this framework is often necessary, and can be somewhat successful, insofar as it addresses the particular circumstances that characterize each community, group, or region, given the diversity highlighted in the preceding analysis. Many First Nations and Aboriginal organizations regard the community, and internal decision-making autonomy, as the critical unit in successful self-government, allowing for some ability to merge contemporary concerns with cultural traditions.[113] Nonetheless, the absence of comprehensive guidelines and standards also produces fragmentation and divisiveness. Inequalities can emerge when information is not shared about what is possible, when resources and programs are diffuse, when Aboriginal organizations take on institutional characteristics that are antithetical to the achievement of their initial mandates, or when leaders at local and national levels compete for voice and legitimacy.[114] These circumstances contain several contradictory dimensions.

15. Finance and Administration

The thrust to Aboriginal self-determination has been motivated by a complex array of economic, social, and political factors. Despite increasing general consensus about the need for and value of self-determination, several analysts express concern that the devolution of government services to Aboriginal organizations and broader recognition of self-government is part of an overall state strategy to reduce expenditures and rationalize or privatize government services.[115] Government officials counter that spending on Aboriginal affairs has increased rather than declined in recent years, and has become more pronounced as a policy priority.[116]

Regardless of which perspective is taken, persistent fiscal and administrative limitations have visibly undercut the effectiveness of several self-government initiatives. Numerous policies and regulations, even though associated with the general principles of self-government or self-determination, limit the achievement of true autonomy. New difficulties arise, or existing ones may be reproduced, if self-government is simply a matter of having different administrators for old programs. Considerable attention has been paid to difficulties associated with the structure of funding agreements, such as Alternative Funding Agreements (AFAs), that devolve federal program administration to First Nations, and to the limitations of formulae developed to determine funding transfers to band or tribal councils. In the case of AFAs, for instance, set time frames limit First Nations' ability to develop long-term plans, while funding transfers from the Department of Indian and Northern Affairs to First Nations in areas like education, health, and social services are often calculated and distributed in a manner that produces considerable variation and uncertainty from one jurisdiction and budget year to another.[117]

Because not all Aboriginal people are eligible for or engage in self-government initiatives, attention must also be paid to the reality that multiple and parallel administrative and organizational forms are likely to persist in many jurisdictional areas. In education, which has a longer and more extensive history of Aboriginal control than other fields, over half (59.2%) of registered Indian children living on-reserve attended band schools in 1998–9, compared to less than one-third a decade earlier. Nonetheless, significant numbers of off-reserve Aboriginal, non-status Indian, and Métis children, along with over two out of five on-reserve children, attend provincial or private schools.[118]

The emergence of alternative legal and justice systems, child-welfare and family service agencies, and other organizations alongside mainstream systems points to continuing challenges related to sharing information, communication, and coordination among agencies. Many self-government-related issues are comparable to general matters of federal and provincial jurisdiction, including constitutional negotiations, cost-shared fiscal arrangements, and assurance of minimal program and service standards. The strongest successes emerge when self-government and devolution of services to local levels have sufficient resources, infrastructure, cooperation, and consultation among affected groups in place to ensure that program targets can be met effectively.[119] In these respects, dual concerns require continuing attention – responsiveness to specific community demands and requirements, and provisions to ensure equitable access to quality programs and services across jurisdictions.

16. Representation

The resolution to questions related to representation – and the extent to which those who negotiate and administer self-government and band-controlled initiatives have a clear mandate from the community – is critical to the achievement of effective self-determination. One of the strengths of many self-government agreements (portrayed as a hallmark of the Nunavut agreement, for instance) has been a resolve to incorporate and integrate community input, responsiveness to local concerns, and cultural traditions into contemporary structures. However, these efforts have also been accompanied by recurrent tensions over vision, mandates, and strategies.

Aboriginal women have been among the most vocal advocates for community representation. Their concerns emerge from their frequent absence from participation in leadership roles, although there is considerable debate over what effective representation would constitute and at what level it should be engaged.[120] While there is a strong gender component to these issues, they are also more general in nature. Voyageur, citing Fiske, highlights the growing potential for chiefs and band or tribal council members to serve as 'power brokers' who can control the allocation of resources within local governance, creating personal spheres of influence and inequities in the community.[121] Much attention has been focused on the ways in which these processes operate as forms of exclusion to limit the membership, input, and rights of particular segments of the population, notably around decisions about reinstating band membership to those affected by Bill C-31 and about the extension of voting rights, services, and other provisions to off-reserve band members. Highly marginalized people, such as those who are most transient, underqualified, or living in inner-city areas, remain especially vulnerable as long as they have limited political representation. Issues of taxation have variable impact on diverse segments of the Aboriginal population, as well. Decisions about residence and the operation of business establishments are affected by discrepancies in tax-exempt status between reserve lands and other locales.

Issues of representation and responsibility have gained profile through recent demands by some segments of the membership, as well as non-Aboriginal observers, for self-governing Aboriginal organizations to adopt higher standards of accountability than currently exist. Some critics argue forcefully that Aboriginal self-determination creates a new order of government that bypasses current constitutional and representative frameworks.[122] Current controversies in several prairie-region First Nations arising from the distribution of band funds acquired through land entitlements, gaming, and self-government arrangements have also brought to the forefront questions about accountability and equity. In many instances, the concerns of band members frustrated at their lack of input into local decision-making are echoed by outside critics suspicious of or hostile to Aboriginal self-determination. The development and changing nature of lobbying efforts, potential alliances or convergences among apparently discrete interests, and potential manipulation of media attention bear particular scrutiny in these regards.

Self-governing bodies counter that representation is affected by the retention of extensive regulatory powers by federal and external authorities through fiscal and monitoring requirements that limit the achievement of true Aboriginal control. Courchene and Powell suggest that uncertainty over jurisdictional powers and land tenure can only be overcome by strong measures like full provincial status for First

Nations.[123] Moreover, relatively little attention has been paid to initiatives that are oriented to greater inclusiveness within Aboriginal communities, such as the development of band constitutions in some Saskatchewan communities that are attempting to fuse traditional decision-making processes with contemporary legal and political frameworks.[124] Fleras views the emergence of Aboriginal nationhood as a problem of overlapping sovereignties, expressed in the form of tensions between rational bureaucratic control and 'indigenization.'[125] Several significant questions arise out of these considerations, including the relative importance of individual and collective rights within new political units and the extent to which traditional notions of consensus-based decision-making are desirable and possible in contemporary circumstances.

Issues relating to representation are problematic on a larger scale, as well, given the diversity of organizations that operate at national, regional, and provincial levels. The major organizations, like the Assembly of First Nations, the Congress of Aboriginal Peoples, the Inuit Tapirisat of Canada, and the Métis National Council, and corresponding provincial organizations, are constituted in accordance with legal status. Others, such as the Native Women's Association of Canada on the political front and the National Association of Friendship Centres on the social/cultural front, draw from across legal designations of Aboriginal people in accordance with identity or more specific concerns. The varied mandates and activities of each organization are understandable given their diverse political, legal, and social interests. At the same time, the large number of groups and voices often creates political and logistical complications for negotiating or planning new public or private-sector initiatives that involve or affect Aboriginal people. As a result, struggles over resources and negotiation of bases of identity are common.[126] As some jurisdictions are beginning to recognize, there are benefits to the establishment of a common forum or Aboriginal round table, both in Canada and internationally, to share information and priorities and coordinate new developments. At the very least, as signified by events such as the Cree assertion that their own sovereignty claims are central to debates over Québec sovereignty and periodic discussions over constitutional reform procedures, federal and provincial governments are beginning to recognize the risks of ignoring Aboriginal representation and interests.[127] Debates over the meaning and nature of Aboriginal sovereignty are in these senses critical to wider considerations about the nature of the Canadian state and problems of social cohesion.[128]

17. Economic and Social Development

The nature of economic development, and its relationship to social development priorities, represents another area in which frequent uncertainty and tension arise. The labour-market and employment statistics cited earlier point to the strong need for substantial enhancement of economic opportunities for Aboriginal people in both Aboriginal and non-Aboriginal sectors. Increased education and training opportunities, along with the creation or expansion of a land base through claims settlements and treaty land entitlements, contain considerable potential for Aboriginal economic development. Band-controlled schooling initiatives, for instance, provide employment for Aboriginal teachers at the same time as they affect school retention and educational attainment rates for many First Nations. Similarly, community health centres, addiction treatment programs, and daycare services oriented to Aboriginal clientele offer family support and provide previously denied access to skills training programs and employment. Evidence from Saskatchewan and Ontario suggests that the majority of First Nations are pursuing economic development objectives that involve community participation, collective ownership, and sensitivity to both economic self-sufficiency and improvements to socio-economic conditions.[129] Many observers point in particular to the promise of small business to renew economic activity among Aboriginal people; indeed, such an approach receives official support through substantial investment in new training and initiatives by the federal government. Advocates of these strategies cite a high degree of compatibility between entrepreneurship and traditional Aboriginal economic and cultural practices in the form of 'capitalism with an Aboriginal face.'[130] Enterprises that meet particular community needs or arise out of cultural and community resources are posed as especially encouraging, but alternative areas like tourism, gaming, and casino development have also gained considerable profile because of their lucrative potential.[131] Locally driven economic development coexists with increasing interest from non-Aboriginal investors and businesses attracted by prospects for readily available sources of land, labour, and regulatory advantages.[132] Provisions for tax-exempt status for First Nations enterprises and employees on-reserve, though changing and complex in nature, are useful incentives for the establishment of viable economic development on reserve lands.[133]

Analysis typically focuses attention on positive dimensions associated with the creation of economic opportunities, given the serious problems they are intended to overcome. However, scrutiny must also be given to the quality and distribution of jobs and related benefits and to longer-term prospects for current economic development initiatives. Investment on reserves by multinational corporations can carry dangers of exploitation, dependency, and fractionalization within communities. With respect, especially, to larger developments, First Nations' reliance on external capital and imposed planning mechanisms can undermine local autonomy and marginalize indigenous perspectives.[134] Band- and reserve-based businesses, as a consequence of government regulation and socio-economic conditions, encounter unique problems as well as advantages related to the procurement of capital, taxation issues, and access to necessary resources.[135] Resource bases, wealth, administrative procedures, and discretionary, statutory, and regulatory control by the federal government on-reserve are among the factors that produce considerable uncertainty and diversity among Aboriginal economic development initiatives.[136]

Despite the promise that Aboriginal enterprise holds to provide widespread benefit by encompassing community needs and cultural practices, there is a risk that the 'privatization' of Aboriginal people will reproduce or solidify class divisions by concentrating control over capital and resources among select groups of investors and managers, along with reliance on external businesses and investors.[137] In many instances, Aboriginal governments and enterprises need to reconcile their commitment to provide employment for community members with a shortage of individuals who possess the necessary training or qualifications for the positions, especially when there are competing demands for highly qualified Aboriginal people by a wide range of public- and private-sector organizations. At the same time, many communities contain a large pool of knowledgeable and qualified people whose skills and talents are under utilized because of an absence of meaningful opportunities or lack of recognition of their informal education. Increasing numbers of band enterprises and communities are also contending with unique issues, such as the reconciliation of workers' rights with notions that unionization is incompatible with Aboriginal sovereignty.

Social development priorities, while reliant upon the presence of economic resources and supportive government and community infrastructures, are closely related to, and sometimes in tension with, economic development. Despite general consensus that social and economic development must coexist as major priorities, pragmatic and ideological factors have often led to the diversion of resources and energies from one to the other. Some observers view market-based strategies, fostering investment in human resources and capital, as necessary for the creation of conditions that will overcome dependency and facilitate community development.[138] In many cases, however, especially where financial resources are highly limited in scope or where their allocation is marked by restrictive terms of reference, basic community needs may be subverted to higher-profile and sometime dubious or risky business ventures.

Whatever the long-term potential for such development, many Aboriginal communities require attentiveness to immediate social problems. The provision of education and training opportunities, for instance, presupposes that all members of particular communities have access to adequate housing, safe and nurturing physical and emotional environments, and mechanisms to ensure that their credentials will lead to meaningful jobs. This assumption, in many cases, is incorrect, insofar as substantial segments of the Aboriginal population require fundamental resources and social supports that most Canadians take for granted. Even when basic needs are met, the need for adequate child-care services, transportation, healthy living conditions, and other factors differentially affect people's abilities to take advantage of educational and employment options. Many of these needs are relatively invisible, or not given the same priority as higher-profile investments, especially when many community members lack sufficient voice and resources to advance their interests on the political agenda. These disparities in social needs and political power are significant at the band or community as well as the individual level. Material and geographical factors such as access to viable land, resources, and services affect a community's economic prospects, but they also influence social concerns in less tangible but nontheless critical ways, including even the prospects to envision and plan for a more secure future. Similarly, political and social decisions, reflecting diverse ideologies, cultural backgrounds, and developmental prospects, can vary widely and make a profound difference in the paths chosen by particular communities.

18. Summary and Discussion

Self-determination, mechanisms to facilitate widespread consultation and participation, and social and economic development strategies have shown promise for overcoming critical dimensions of relative disadvantage that are experienced widely among the Aboriginal population. Each of these developments, at the same time, is accompanied by limiting or contradictory factors that have the prospect of reproducing existing patterns of differentiation or producing new inequalities.

First Nations self-government and Aboriginal self-determination, along with a wide range of alternative governmental and community arrangements, constitute an ongoing process of state formation, the terms of which are highly complex and still being worked out. In some cases, dominant administrative and organizational structures are reproduced through the simple transferral of programs and services from the state to First Nations or Aboriginal bodies. In other cases, parallel or multiple arrangements exist within and across diverse jurisdictions. Several Aboriginal communities and governing bodies are struggling to develop unique forms of governance, administration, and program-delivery agencies that are tailored to their own specific histories, cultural traditions, and needs.

Given the diversity of circumstances across groups and communities, and the failure of many previous approaches to governance and service provision for Canada's Aboriginal people, the multiplicity of emerging approaches may yield successful, meaningful alternatives to address needs and issues that require flexibility and innovation. Contained within these developments, however, are diffuse forms of power, regulation, and accommodation that may undermine social cohesion and generate unnecessary confusion and competition at the same time as they obscure more enduring structural constraints and inequalities. As the focus on the impact of differentiation as a basis of exclusion and inequality has maintained, policy analysis must remain sensitive to questions about the distribution of opportunities, resources, and life chances among diverse segments of both the Aboriginal and general populations.

19. Policy Implications

This chapter has been concerned primarily with the nature and causes of social differentiation among Aboriginal people and between Aboriginal people and other Canadians. Social policy, both generally and in specific orientation to Aboriginal people, has been shown to be a major contributing factor to such differentiation. Policy also serves as a critical tool to address many of the ensuing social and economic problems, focused in recent years on factors that differentiate Aboriginal people from other Canadians. These considerations give rise to several major policy implications.

There is growing consensus, but not unanimity, among governments, Aboriginal people, and Canadian public opinion that Aboriginal people have distinct experiences and needs due to their historical circumstances and to ongoing processes of social exclusion and differentiation. Many Aboriginal people require a wide range of resources and services over and above those available to Canadians as a whole. Job creation, employment equity, mentorship arrangements, income support, and training programs oriented to youth and adults with prior levels of skills and qualifications are important, but basic programs to support healing, early childhood and family services, healthy communities, language and identity, and life skills are also essential. Moreover, policy development must take into account formal recognition of Aboriginal 'special status' and rights. These factors are critical in order to give substance to the four principles (recognition, respect, sharing, and responsibility) of a 'renewed relationship' outlined by the 1996 Royal Commission on Aboriginal Peoples. These realities suggest the need to maintain the coexistence of programs and service delivery arrangements tailored specifically to Aboriginal people even as Aboriginal people are encompassed wtihin more general federal and provincial programs.

Aboriginal people, as well, constitute a diverse population with differential needs, problems, and successes. Policy interventions must acknowledge this diversity with a range of objectives and programs oriented to particular locales and clientele. The current array of initiatives is positive insofar as it encourages flexibility, innovation, and responsiveness to the needs of specific communities or groups of people. However, common data bases and arrangements to share information, resources, and expertise are increasingly necessary to foster a strong understanding of initiatives, successes, and limitations of programs in different jurisdictions. Qualitative as well as quantitative indicators are required in order to assess how policy and programs operate as processes rather than as simple input/outcome mechanisms. Public policy development, and public- and private-sector organizations, must seek ways to engage and sustain meaningful participation by Aboriginal people in a manner that reflects the diversity of the Aboriginal population. Although responsiveness to these requirements points to potentially debilitating adminstrative and policy implementation frameworks, consideration should be given to alternative intergovernmental arrangements that could facilitate regular, open communication, representative decision-making, and viable, cost-effective service delivery procedures.

There is a critical need for both policy coordination and research that reaches across jurisdictions not only to assess needs and problems on an ongoing basis, but also to ensure that there is a sharing of initiatives that are truly innovative and effective. In all of these regards, sensitivity to structural and institutional factors that transcend localized circumstances must be maintained in order to ensure parity and equity, and to identify underlying problems that may not be readily apparent through conventional indicators. Strategies need to be developed to identify ways in which flexibility and accountability can be seen as compatible rather than competing demands in planning, service delivery, and the administration of social and economic programs.

Ultimately, program assessment and evaluation must not be led astray by isolated improvements that mask ongoing, fundamental problems and inequalities. Similarly, they must not be swayed by the narrowly defined dynamics of popular opinion or political agendas. Failure to attend to these issues is likely to produce further marginalization and undermine commitment and attachment to Canadian society among large segments of the Aboriginal population.

Notes

1 See Angus E. Reid and Margaret M. Burns, *Canada and the World: An International Perspective on Canada and Canadians* (Winnipeg: Angus Reid Group, 1992), 11–12; and United Nations Development Programme, *Human Development Report* (New York: Oxford University Press, 1997).

2 See Assembly of First Nations, *First Nations Issues Survey – Full Report* (Ottawa: Assembly of First Nations, 1998); and J. Rick Ponting, 'Racism and Stereotyping of First Nations,' in V. Satzewich, ed., *Racism and Social Inequality in Canada: Concepts, Controversies and Strategies of Resistance* (Toronto: Thompson Educational Publishing, 1998), 286ff.

3 See Marie Battiste, 'Enabling the Autumn Seed: Toward a Decolonized Approach to Aboriginal Knowledge, Language and Education,' *Canadian Journal of Native Education* 22.1 (1998): 16–27.

4 See James S. Frideres, 'Indian Economic Development: Innovations and Obstructions,' in J.W. Friesen, ed., *The Cultural Maze: Complex Questions on Native Destiny in Western Canada* (Calgary: Detselig, 1991), 77.

5 See Andrew J. Siggner, Eric Guimond, Gustave Goldmann, and Norbert Robitaille, 'Aboriginal Population Characteristics: Are We Informed by the Aggregate Picture?' presented at Canadian Population Society Annual

meetings (June 1998), 2–3; Louis-Edmond Hamelin, 'Thèmes de l'autoch-tonie canadienne,' *Recherches sociographiques* 35.3 (1994): 421–32.

6 See Leslie A. Pal, *Beyond Policy Analysis: Public Issue Management in Turbulent Times* (Scarborough, ON: ITP Nelson, 1997).

7 See Frank Fischer and John Forester, 'Editors' Introduction,' in F. Fischer and J. Forester, eds, *The Argumentative Turn in Public Policy Analysis and Planning* (Durham, NC: Duke University Press, 1993), 2.

8 See Katherine Graham, Carolyn Dittburner, and Frances Abele, *Public Policy and Aboriginal Peoples 1965–1992*, Volume 1, *Soliloquy and Dialogue: Overview of Major Trends in Public Policy Relating to Aboriginal Peoples* (Ottawa: Minister of Public Works and Government Services Canada, 1996), 18–21.

9 See Kathy Brock, 'Aboriginal People: First Nations,' in A.F. Johnson and A. Stritch, eds, *Canadian Public Policy: Globalization and Political Parties* (Toronto: Copp Clark, 1997), 191–3.

10 See Marc-Adélard Tremblay and Carole Lévesque, *Québec Social Science and Canadian Indigenous Peoples: An Overview of Research Trends, 1960–1990* (Ottawa: Canadian Polar Commission, 1997).

11 See J. Rick Ponting, 'Editor's Introduction,' in J.R. Ponting, ed., *First Nations in Canada: Perspectives on Opportunity, Empowerment, and Self-Determination* (Toronto: McGraw-Hill Ryerson, 1997), 3–4.

12 See Russell Lawrence Barsh, 'Canada's Aboriginal Peoples: Social Integration or Disintegration?' *Canadian Journal of Native Studies* 14.1 (1994): 1–46.

13 See Patrick Brady, 'Native Dropouts and Non-Native Dropouts in Canada: Two Solitudes or a Solitude Shared?' *Journal of American Indian Education* 35.2 (Winter 1996): 12.

14 See, e.g., Pauline Comeau and Aldo Santin, *The First Canadians: A Profile of Canada's Native People Today*, 2nd ed. (Toronto: James Lorimer and Co., 1995); Geoffrey York, *The Dispossessed: Life and Death in Native Canada* (Toronto: Little, Brown and Co., 1990); Helen Buckley, *From Wooden Ploughs to Welfare: Why Indian Policy Failed in the Prairie Provinces* (Montreal and Kingston: McGill-Queen's University Press, 1992); J.R. Miller, *Shingwauk's Vision: A History of Native Residential Schools* (Toronto: University of Toronto Press, 1996); and Sally Weaver, *Making Canadian Indian Policy: The Hidden Agenda, 1968–1970* (Toronto: University of Toronto Press, 1981).

15 See, e.g., Elizabeth Furniss, *Victims of Benevolence: Discipline and Death at the Williams Lake Indian Residential School, 1891–1920* (Williams Lake, BC: Cariboo Tribal Council, 1992).

16 See Freda Ahenakew and H.C. Wolfart, *kôhkominawak otâcimowiniwâwa: Our Grandmothers' Lives as Told in Their Own Words* (Regina: Canadian Plains Research Center, 1998); and Julia Emberley, 'Aboriginal Women's Writing

and the Cultural Politics of Representation,' in C. Miller and P. Chuchryk, eds, *Women of the First Nations: Power, Wisdom, and Strength* (Winnipeg: University of Manitoba Press, 1996), 97–112.

17 See, e.g., Linda Pertusati, *In Defense of Mohawk Land: Ethnopolitical Conflict in Native North America* (Albany: State University of New York Press, 1997); and Katherine Pettipas, *Severing the Ties That Bind: Government Repression of Indigenous Religious Ceremonies on the Prairies* (Winnipeg: University of Manitoba Press, 1994).

18 See, e.g., Rita M. Bienvenue, 'Colonial Status: The Case of Canada's Indians,' in R.M. Bienvenue and J.E. Goldstein, eds, *Ethnicity and Ethnic Relations in Canada: A Book of Readings* (Toronto: Butterworths, 1985), 199–214; and David G. Perley, 'Aboriginal Education in Canada as Internal Colonialism,' *Canadian Journal of Native Education* 20.1 (1993): 118–28.

19 See Menno Boldt, *Surviving as Indians: The Challenge of Self-Government* (Toronto: University of Toronto Press, 1993); Mylène Jaccoud, 'L'exclusion sociale et les Autochtones,' *Lien social et politiques – RIAC* 34 (1995): 93–100; Pierre Lepage, 'Un regard au-delà des chartes: Le racisme et la discrimination envers les peuples autochtones,' *Recherches amérindiennes au Québec* 25.3 (1995): 29–45; Marie-Anik Gagné, *A Nation within a Nation: Dependency and the Cree* (Montreal: Black Rose Books, 1994); and Tony Haddad and Michael Spivey, 'All or Nothing: Modernization, Dependency and Wage Labour on a Reserve in Canada,' *Canadian Journal of Native Studies* 12.2 (1992): 203–28.

20 See David P. Ross, *Education as an Investment for Indians on Reserves: The Causes of the Poor Education Levels and the Economic Benefits of Improving Them* (Ottawa: Canadian Council on Social Development, 1991); and Jeremy Hull, 'Socioeconomic Status and Native Education in Canada,' *Canadian Journal of Native Education* 17.1 (1990): 1–14.

21 See Ward Churchill, 'Marxism and the Native American,' in W. Churchill, ed., *Marxism and Native Americans* (Boston: South End Press, 1983), 183–203; and Stanley Ryerson, *The Founding of Canada* (Toronto: Progress Books, 1960).

22 See Frances Abele and Daiva Stasiulis, 'Canada as a "White Settler Colony": What about Natives and Immigrants?' in W. Clement and G. Williams, eds, *The New Canadian Political Economy* (Kingston, Montreal: McGill-Queen's University Press, 1989), 256.

23 See Frank Black Elk, 'Observations on Marxism and Lakota Tradition,' in Churchill, *Marxism and Native Americans*, 137–57; and Russell Means, 'The Same Old Song,' in ibid., 19–33.

24 See Howard Adams, *Prison of Grass*, 2nd ed. (Saskatoon: Fifth House Pub-

lishers, 1990); David Bedford, 'Marxism and the Aboriginal Question: The Tragedy of Progress,' *Canadian Journal of Native Studies* 14.1 (1994): 101–17; and Churchill, 'Marxism and the Native American.'

25 See Kathleen Jamieson, *Indian Women and the Law in Canada: Citizens Minus* (Ottawa: Minister of Supply and Services, 1978); Janet Silman, *Enough Is Enough: Aboriginal Women Speak Out* (Toronto: Women's Press, 1987); Margaret A. Jackson, 'Aboriginal Women and Self-Government,' in J.H. Hylton, ed., *Aboriginal Self-Government in Canada: Current Trends and Issues* (Saskatoon: Purich Publishing, 1994), 180–98; and Lilianne E. Krosenbrink-Gelissen, 'Caring Is Indian Women's Business, but Who Takes Care of Them? Canada's Indian Women, the Renewed Indian Act, and Its Implications for Women's Family Responsibilities, Roles and Rights,' in R. Kuppe and R. Potz, eds, *Law and Anthropology: International Yearbook for Legal Anthropology, Volume 7* (Dordrecht: Martinus Nijhoff Publishers, 1992), 107–30.

26 See Sarah Carter, 'Categories and Terrains of Exclusion: Constructing the "Indian Woman" in the Early Settlement Era in Western Canada,' in K.S. Coates and R. Fisher, eds, *Out of the Background: Readings on Canadian Native History* (Toronto: Copp Clark, 1996), 177–95; and Russell Smandych and Gloria Lee, 'Women, Colonization and Resistance: Elements of an Amerindian Autohistorical Approach to the Study of Law and Colonialism,' *Native Studies Review* 10.1 (1995): 21–46.

27 See Patricia A. Monture-Angus, *Thunder in My Soul: A Mohawk Woman Speaks* (Halifax: Fernwood Publishing, 1995), 229–35; and Mary Ellen Turpel/Aki Kwe, 'Patriarchy and Paternalism: The Legacy of the Canadian State for First Nations Women,' *Canadian Journal of Women and the Law* 6 (1993): 187–9.

28 See Linda Gerber, 'Multiple Jeopardy: A Socio-Economic Comparison of Men and Women among the Indian, Metis and Inuit Peoples of Canada,' *Canadian Ethnic Studies* 22.3 (1990): 69–84; and Cora J. Voyageur, 'Contemporary Indian Women,' in D.A. Long and O.P. Dickason, eds, *Visions of the Heart: Canadian Aboriginal Issues* (Toronto: Harcourt Brace and Co., 1996), 93–115.

29 See, e.g., Claude Denis, *We Are Not You: First Nations and Canadian Modernity* (Peterborough, ON: Broadview Press, 1997).

30 See Battiste, 'Enabling the Autumn Seed.'

31 See Monture-Angus, *Thunder in My Soul*, 13–14.

32 See Vic Satzewich and Terry Wotherspoon, *First Nations: Race, Class, and Gender Relations* (Toronto: Nelson, 1993); Ponting, 'Editor's Introduction,' 14; and James S. Frideres, *Aboriginal Peoples in Canada: Contemporary Conflicts*, 5th ed. (Scarborough, ON: Prentice Hall Allyn and Bacon Canada, 1998).

33 See Vic Satzewich, 'Indian Agents and the "Indian Problem" in Canada in 1946: Reconsidering the Theory of Coercive Tutelage,' *Canadian Journal of Native Studies* 17.2 (1997): 227–57; and Joe Sawchuk, *The Dynamics of Native Politics: The Alberta Métis Experience* (Saskatoon: Purich Publishing, 1998).

34 See, e.g., Margaret Conrad, Alvin Finkel, and Cornelius Jaenen, *History of the Canadian People*, Volume 1, *Beginnings to 1867* (Toronto: Copp Clark Pitman, 1993).

35 See Bruce G. Trigger, *Natives and Newcomers: Canada's 'Heroic Age' Reconsidered* (Toronto: University of Toronto Press, 1985); and Treaty 7 Elders and Tribal Council, *The True Spirit and Original Intent of Treaty 7* (Montreal and Kingston: McGill-Queen's University Press, 1996), 83–108.

36 See Christian Couvrette, 'La cité ethnique: l'institutionnalisation de la différence,' *Recherches sociographiques* 35.3 (1994): 455–76; Government of Canada, Royal Commission on Aboriginal Peoples (RCAP), *Report of the Royal Commission on Aboriginal Peoples*, Volume 1, *Looking Forward, Looking Back* (Ottawa: Minister of Supply and Services Canada, 1996), 263.

37 Canada, RCAP, *Report*, vol. 1, 269–70.

38 See Frideres, *Aboriginal Peoples in Canada*, 23–40.

39 See Harry W. Daniels, ed., *The Forgotten People: Métis and Non-status Indian Land Claims* (Ottawa: Native Council of Canada, 1979); and R.E. Gaffney, G.P. Gould, and A.J. Semple, *Broken Promises: The Aboriginal Constitutional Conferences* (Fredericton: New Brunswick Association of Métis and Non-Status Indians, 1984).

40 See Wendy Moss, *History of Discriminatory Laws Affecting Aboriginal People* (Ottawa: Library of Parliament Research Branch, 1987); and Delia Opekokew, *The Political and Legal Inequalities among Aboriginal Peoples in Canada* (Kingston, ON: Institute of Intergovernmental Relations, Background paper no. 14, 1987).

41 See Canada, RCAP, *Report*, vol. 1, 281.

42 See, e.g., Paula Mallea, *Aboriginal Law: Apartheid in Canada* (Brandon, MB: Bearpaw Publishing, 1994); and Government of Canada, Department of Indian Affairs and Northern Development, *Socio-Economic Indicators in Indian Reserves and Comparable Communities 1971–1991* (Ottawa: Minister of Public Works and Government Services Canada, 1997), 43.

43 See Canada, RCAP, *Report*, vol. 1, 271–5.

44 See ibid., 270, and Jamieson, *Indian Women and the Law*, 38, for conflicting interpretations of the government's intent.

45 See Gerber, 'Multyple Jeopardy'; and Allison M. Williams, 'Canadian Urban Aboriginals: A Focus on Aboriginal Women in Canada,' *Canadian Journal of Native Studies* 12.1 (1997): 75–101.

46 See Frideres, *Aboriginal Peoples in Canada*, 33–5; Canada, RCAP, *Report*, Volume 4, *Perspectives and Realities* (1996), 33ff.; Krosenbrink-Gelissen, 'Caring Is Indian Women's Business,' 118–22.

47 See Boldt, *Surviving as Indians*, 26.

48 See, e.g., David W. Elliott, 'Aboriginal Title,' in B.W. Morse, ed., *Aboriginal Peoples and the Law* (Ottawa: Carleton University Press, 1985), 48–121; David C. Hawkes, ed., *Aboriginal Peoples and Government Responsibility: Exploring Federal and Provincial Roles* (Ottawa: Carleton University Press, 1989); and Gaffney, Gould, and Semple, *Broken Promises*.

49 See Jane Allain and Elaine Gardner O'Toole, 'Aboriginal Rights,' *Current Issue Review* 89-11E (Ottawa: Library of Parliament Research Branch, Minister of Supply and Services Canada, 1995), 2; Tom Flanagan, *First Nations? Second Thoughts* (Montreal: McGill-Queen's University Press, 2000); and Alan C. Cairns, *Citizens Plus: Aboriginal Peoples and the Canadian State* (Vancouver: UBC Press, 2000).

50 See Jill Wherrett and Jane Allain, 'Aboriginal Self-Government,' *Current Issue Review* 89-5E (Ottawa: Library of Parliament Research Branch, Minister of Supply and Services Canada, 1995), 1; and Frideres, *Aboriginal Peoples in Canada*, 63.

51 See Peter W. Hogg and Mary Ellen Turpel, 'Implementing Aboriginal Self-Government: Constitutional and Jurisdictional Issues,' *Canadian Bar Review* 74.2 (June 1995): 192–5.

52 See Theresa M. Dust, *The Impact of Aboriginal Land Claims and Self-Government on Canadian Municipalities: The Local Government Perspective* (Toronto: ICURR Press, 1995); and Roslyn Kunin, ed., *Prospering Together: The Economic Impact of the Aboriginal Title Settlements in B.C.* (Vancouver: Laurier Institution, 1998).

53 See C. Radha Jhappan, 'Natural Rights vs. Legal Positivism: Indians, the Courts, and the New Discourse of Aboriginal Rights in Canada,' *British Journal of Canadian Studies* 6.1 (1991): 94–5.

54 See Indian and Northern Affairs Canada (INAC) and Canadian Polar Commission (CPC), *2000–2001 Estimates. Part III: Report on Plans and Priorities* (Ottawa: Minister of Public Works and Government Services Canada, 2000), 9.

55 See John H. Hylton, 'The Case for Self-Government: A Social Policy Perspective,' in Hylton, ed., *Aboriginal Self-Government in Canada*, 39; and Thomas J. Courchene and Lisa M. Powell, *A First Nations Province* (Kingston, ON: Institute of Intergovernmental Relations, Queen's University, 1992), 36.

56 See Ron Common, 'A Search for Equity: A Policy Analysis of First Nations

Representation on School Boards,' *Education Canada* 31.3 (Fall 1991): 4–5.

57 See Carol LaPrairie, *Seen but Not Heard: Native People in the Inner City* (Ottawa: Minister of Public Works and Government Services Canada, 1994).

58 See, e.g., Suzanne Fournier and Ernie Crey, *Stolen from Our Embrace: The Abduction of First Nations Children and the Restoration of Aboriginal Communities* (Vancouver: Douglas & McIntyre, 1997); Paula Mallea (for Government of Manitoba), *Report of the Aboriginal Justice Inquiry of Manitoba: The Justice System and Aboriginal People* (Winnipeg: Queen's Printer, 1991); and Assembly of First Nations, *National Overview of First Nations Child Care in Canada* (Ottawa: Assembly of First Nations, 1995), 36.

59 See Statistics Canada, '1996 Census: Aboriginal Data,' *The Daily*, 13 Jan. 1998, 1–2, and '1996 Census: Ethnic Origin, Visible Minorities,' *The Daily*, 17 Feb. 1998, 5.

60 See Indian and Northern Affairs Canada (INAC), *Basic Departmental Data 1997* (Ottawa: Minister of Public Works and Government Services Canada, 1998), 5.

61 See Canada, RCAP, *Report*, vol. 1, 15; Frideres, *Aboriginal Peoples in Canada*, 26–7; INAC and CPC, *2000-2001 Estimates*, 4.

62 See Statistics Canada, '1996 Census: Aboriginal Data,' 6.

63 See Alain Bélanger and Jean Dumas, *Report on the Current Demographic Situation in Canada 1997. Current Demographic Analysis* (Ottawa: Minister of Industry, Science and Technology, 1998), 15; and INAC, *Basic Departmental Data*, 24.

64 See Statistics Canada, '1996 Census: Aboriginal Data,' 7.

65 See Siggner et al., 'Aboriginal Population Characteristics,' 3; and François Nault, Jiajian Chen, M.V. George, and Mary Jane Norris, *Population Projections of Registered Indians, 1991–2015* (Ottawa: Statistics Canada, 1993).

66 See Patricia A. Monture-Angus, 'Lessons in Decolonization: Aboriginal Overrepresentation in Canadian Criminal Justice,' in Long and Dickason, *Visions of the Heart*, 341–2; and Peter Carrington, 'Trends in Youth Crime in Canada, 1977–1996,' *Canadian Journal of Criminology* 41.1 (January 1999): 25.

67 See Four Directions Consulting Group, *Implications of First Nations Demography: Final Report* (Winnipeg: Indian and Northern Affairs Canada, 1997).

68 See Statistics Canada, '1996 Census: Aboriginal Data,' 2.

69 See Saskatchewan Education, *Partners in Action: Action Plan of the Indian and Métis Education Advisory Committee* (Regina: Saskatchewan Education, 1991), 5.

70 Ibid., 5–6.

71 See INAC, *Basic Departmental Data*, 7.

72 See Mary Jane Norris, 'Contemporary Demography of Aboriginal Peoples

in Canada,' in Long and Dickason, *Visions of the Heart*, 192–4.

73 See Mary Jane Norris and Daniel Beavon, 'Registered Indian Mobility and Migration: An Analysis of 1996 Census Data,' paper presented to Canadian Population Society meetings, Lennoxville, Quebec, June 1999.

74 See Evelyn J. Peters, 'Self-Government for Aboriginal People in Urban Areas: A Literature Review and Suggestions for Research,' *Canadian Journal of Native Studies* 12.1 (1992): 51–74.

75 See Canada, RCAP, *Report*, Volume 2, *Restructuring the Relationship* (1996), 803; and Statistics Canada, '1996 Census: Education, Mobility and Migration,' *The Daily*, 14 Apr. 1998, 10–11.

76 See Canada, RCAP, *Report*, vol. 2, 802–3; Federation of Saskatchewan Indian Nations, *Saskatchewan and Aboriginal Peoples in the 21st Century: Social, Economic and Political Changes and Challenges* (Regina: PrintWest Publishing Services, 1997), 78–81; and Four Directions Consulting, *Implications of First Nations Demography*, 92–7.

77 See Statistics Canada, '1996 Census: Sources of Income, Earnings and Total Income, and Family Income,' *The Daily*, 12 May 1998, 11.

78 See Rachel Bernier, *The Dimensions of Wage Inequality among Aboriginal Peoples* (Ottawa: Statistics Canada, Analytical Studies Branch, Research Paper Series no. 109, December 1998), 10–11.

79 See Canada, Indian Affairs and Northern Development, *Socio-Economic Indicators in Indian Reserves*, 20–3, 32–3.

80 See Statistics Canada, *Schooling, Work and Related Activities, Income, Expenses and Mobility: 1991 Aboriginal Peoples Survey* (Ottawa: Minister of Industry, Science and Technology, 1996), 96–108.

81 See Statistics Canada, 'Sources of Income,' 11.

82 See LaPrairie, *Seen but Not Heard*.

83 See INAC, *Basic Departmental Data*, 59–60.

84 See Bernier, *The Dimensions of Wage Inequality*, 5, 13, 15.

85 See Statistics Canada, '1996 Census: Education,' 6.

86 Ibid., 7.

87 See Sid Gilbert, Lynn Barr, Warren Clark, Matthew Blue, and Deborah Sunter, *Leaving School: Results from a National Survey* (Ottawa: Minister of Supply and Services Canada, 1993), 23.

88 Calculated from Statistics Canada, '1996 Census: Aboriginal Data.'

89 See INAC, *First Nation Profiles* (Ottawa: Indian and Northern Affairs Canada, 1999).

90 See Federation of Saskatchewan Indian Nations, *Saskatchewan and Aboriginal Peoples in the 21st*, 89–90.

91 See Canada, RCAP, *Report*, vol. 2, 802.

92 See Ross, *Education as an Investment for Indians on Reserves.*

93 See Canada, RCAP, *Report,* vol. 4, 806ff.

94 See Larry Krotz, *Urban: The Strangers in Canada's Cities* (Edmonton: Hurtig Publishers Ltd, 1980), 156; LaPrairie, *Seen but Not Heard,* 77–9, 223–4.

95 See Gerber, 'Multiple Jeopardy'; Wotherspoon and Satzewich, *First Nations: Race, Class and Gender Relations,* 58–72.

96 See Hylton, 'The Case for Self-Government,' 37; Sub-Committee on Aboriginal Education, *Sharing the Knowledge: The Path to Success and Equal Opportunities in Education,* Report of the Standing Commitee on Aboriginal Affairs and Northern Development (Ottawa: Canada Communication Group, 1996), 48.

97 See Working Margins Consulting Group, *Indian Post-School Education in Saskatchewan,* discussion paper prepared for Office of the Treaty Commissioner, Saskatoon (Winnipeg: Working Margins Consulting Group, 1992), 50.

98 See OECD, *The OECD Job Study. Evidence and Explanations. Part I – Labour Market Trends and Underlying Forces of Change* (Paris: OECD, 1994); and Lars Osberg, Fred Wien, and Jan Grude, *Vanishing Jobs: Canada's Changing Workplaces* (Toronto: Lorimer, 1995).

99 See D.W. Livingstone, *The Education-Jobs Gap: Underemployment or Economic Democracy* (Boulder, CO: Westview Press, 1998), 52ff.

100 See Steven McBride and Patrick Smith, 'The Impact of Aboriginal Title Settlements on Education and Human Capital,' in R. Kunin, ed., *Prospering Together: The Economic Impact of the Aborigenal Title Settlements in B.C.* (Vancouver: Laurier Institution, 1998), 183, 198.

101 See, e.g., Frideres, 'Indian Economic Development'; Larry Krotz, *Indian Country: Inside Another Canada* (Toronto: McClelland and Stewart, 1990); Canada, RCAP, *Report,* vols. 1, 2, 4; ibid.,*Report,* Volume 3, *Gathering Strength* (1996); Geoffrey York, *The Dispossessed: Life and Death in Native Canada* (Toronto: Little, Brown and Co., 1990).

102 See Statistics Canada, 'Sources of Income,' 20.

103 See Saskatoon Star-Phoenix, 'HIV Infecting More Natives,' 18 Jan. 1999, A1–2.

104 See Statistics Canada, '1996 Census: Aboriginal Data,' 8; Four Directions Consulting, *Implications of First Nations Demography,* 38.

105 See Statistics Canada, 'Sources of Income,' 20; Government of Canada, RCAP, *Choosing Life: Special Report on Suicide among Aboriginal People* (Ottawa: Minister of Supply and Services Canada, 1995).

106 See Bernard Schissel and Terry Wotherspoon, *An Investigation into Indian and Métis Student Life Experience in Saskatchewan Schools* (Saskatoon:

Research report prepared for Saskatchewan Indian and Métis Education Research Project, 1998).

107 See Williams, 'Canadian Urban Aboriginals,' 82.

108 See R. Armstrong, J. Kennedy, and P.R. Oberle, *University Education and Economic Well-Being: Indian Achievement and Prospects* (Ottawa: INAC, 1990); and Marcia Santiago, *Post-Secondary Education and Labour Market Outcomes for Registered Indians* (Ottawa: Indian Affairs and Northern Development Canada, 1997).

109 See William J. Wilson, *When Work Disappears: The World of the New Urban Poor* (New York: Knopf, 1997).

110 See Sally Weaver, 'A New Paradigm in Canadian Indian Policy for the 1990s,' *Canadian Ethnic Studies* 22.3 (1990): 8–18.

111 See David Alan Long, 'Trials of the Spirit: The Native Social Movement in Canada,' in Long and Dickason, *Visions of the Heart*, 377–96; and J.R. Miller, 'Great White Father Knows Best: Oka and the Land Claims Process,' *Native Studies Review* 7.1 (1991): 23–52.

112 See Hylton, 'The Case for Self-Government,' 35–7.

113 See Awasis Agency of Northern Manitoba, *First Nations Family Justice: Mee-noo-stah-tan Mi-ni-si-win* (Thompson, MB: Awasis Agency of Northern Manitoba, 1997), xiii; Grand Council of the Crees (Eeyou Astchee), *Never without Consent: James Bay Crees' Stand against Forcible Inclusion into an Independent Quebec* (Toronto: ECW Press, 1998), 38–9; and Mary Ellen Turpel/Aki Kwe, 'Aboriginal Peoples and the Canadian Charter of Rights and Freedoms: Contradictions and Challenges,' *Canadian Woman Studies* 10.2–3 (1989): 154–5.

114 See Peter McFarlane, 'Aboriginal Leadership,' in Long and Dickason, *Visions of the Heart*, 141–2; Sawchuk, *The Dynamics of Native Politics*, 159.

115 See Murray Angus, *'And the Last Shall Be First': Native Policy in an Era of Cutbacks* (Toronto: NC Press Ltd, 1991); and Augie Fleras and Jean Leonard Elliott, *The Nations Within: Aboriginal–State Relations in Canada, the United States, and New Zealand* (Toronto: Oxford University Press, 1992), 49–50.

116 See INAC, *Backgrounder: Gathering Strength: Canada's Aboriginal Action Plan* (Ottawa: INAC, 1999).

117 See Sub-Committee on Aboriginal Education, *Sharing the Knowledge*, 48.

118 See INAC, *Basic Departmental Data*, 35.

119 See Dust, *The Impact of Aboriginal Land Claims*, 55–8; and Kunin, ed., *Prospering Together*.

120 See Jackson, 'Aboriginal Women and Self-Government,' 188–9.

121 See Voyageur, 'Contemporary Indian Women,' 109; and Joanne Fiske,

'Native Women in Reserve Politics: Strategies and Struggles,' *Journal of Legal Pluralism* 30 (1990): 123.

122 See Melvin H. Smith, *Our Home or Native Land? What Government's Aboriginal Policy Is Doing to Canada* (Victoria: Crown Western, 1995).

123 See Courchene and Powell, *A First Nations Province*, 50.

124 See Erland Atimoyoo, 'Representation and Political Decision-Making in a Cree Perspective,' unpublished M.A. non-thesis project, Dept. of Sociology, University of Saskatchewan, 1998.

125 See Augie Fleras, 'The Politics of Jurisdiction: Indigenizing Aboriginal–State Relations,' in Long and Dickason, *Visions of the Heart*, 147–77.

126 See Ontario Native Women's Association, 'Post Patriation: The Antithesis of Termination to Special Status of the Aboriginal Peoples,' *Fireweed: A Feminist Quarterly* 16 (1983): 100–6; and McFarlane, 'Aboriginal Leadership.'

127 See Grand Council of the Crees, *Never without Consent*; Recherches Amérindiennes au Québec, *Autochtones et Québécois: La rencontre des nationalismes* (Montreal: Recherches amérindiennes au Québec, 1995); and Renée Dupuis, *Tribus, peuples et nations: Les nouveaux enjeux des revendications autochtones au Canada* (Quebec: Les Éditions du Boréal, 1997).

128 See Thomas Isaac, 'The Concept of the Crown and Aboriginal Self-Government,' *Canadian Journal of Native Studies* 14.2 (1994): 221–50; and C. Radha Jhappan, 'Global Community? Supranational Strategies of Canada's Aboriginal Peoples,' *Journal of Indigenous Studies* 3.1 (1992): 59–91.

129 See Robert B. Anderson, 'The Business Economy of the First Nations in Saskatchewan: A Contingency Perspective,' *Canadian Journal of Native Studies* 15.2 (1995): 309–46; and Ian Chapman, Don McCaskill, and David Newhouse, 'Management in Contemporary Aboriginal Organizations,' *Canadian Journal of Native Studies* 11.2 (1991): 333–49.

130 See Katherine Beaty Chiste, 'The Aboriginal Small Business Community,' in K.B. Chiste, ed., *Aboriginal Small Business and Entrepreneurship in Canada* (North York, ON: Captus Press, 1996), 5–9; and David R. Newhouse, 'Modern Aboriginal Economies: Capitalism with an Aboriginal Face,' in RCAP, *Sharing the Harvest: The Road to Self-Reliance* (Ottawa: Minister of Supply and Services Canada, 1993), 95–6.

131 See Native Investment and Trade Association, *Gamex '93. Successful First Nations Gaming in Canada II*, Conference/Trade show program (Vancouver, May 1993).

132 See Calvin Helin, *Doing Business with Native People Makes Sense* (Victoria, BC: Praxis Publishing and Native Investment and Trade Association, 1991), 43.

133   See Richard H. Bartlett, *Indians and Taxation in Canada*, rev. 3rd ed. (Saskatoon: University of Saskatchewan Native Law Centre, 1992).

134   See Haddad and Spivey, 'All or Nothing.'

135   See John M. Parkinson, 'Sources of Capital for Native Businesses: Problems and Prospects,' *Canadian Journal of Native Studies* 8.1 (1988): 54–5.

136   See Steven Globerman, 'Investment and Capital Productivity,' in Kumin, *Prospering Together*, 163–4; and Ross D. Tunnicliffe, 'Barriers to Business Financing: The Legal Context,' in *Financing First Nations: Investing in Aboriginal Business and Governments*, conference manual (Vancouver, June 1993), 1–2.

137   See Doug Daniels, 'The Coming Crisis in the Aboriginal Rights Movement: From Colonialism to Neo-colonialism to Renaissance,' *Native Studies Review* 2.2 (1986): 97–115; Wotherspoon and Satzewich, *First Nations*, 260; and Terry Wotherspoon, 'Indian Control or Controlling Indians? Barriers to the Occupational and Educational Advancement of Canada's Indigenous Population,' in T. Wotherspoon, ed., *Hitting the Books: The Politics of Educational Retrenchment* (Toronto and Saskatoon: Garamond and Social Research Unit, 1991), 269.

138   See, e.g., Helman Drost, Brian Lee Crowley, and Richard Schwindt, *Market Solutions for Native Poverty* (Toronto: C.D. Howe Institute, 1995).

6. Spatially Based Social Differentiation in Canada's Future: Trends in Urban/Non-urban Differences in the Next Decade

Chris Southcott

1. Introduction

This chapter examines the current structure of urban/non-urban differences in Canada by focusing on trends in social differentiation. Historically, Canadian governments have had to develop policies to deal with inequalities among regions and rural decline. Most agree that globalization, technological change and the information revolution, and post-industrialism in general, will have an effect on how governments deal with spatially based social and economic problems. Some suggest that sub-trends such as the 'de-spacialization' of production, new communications technology, and the increased importance of recreational and leisure services will have a positive effect on these differences. Some in fact talk about, and provide empirical evidence of a 'rural renaissance.' Others talk about the increase in differentiation occurring because of these trends, the impact of technological change on employment and farm ownership in agricultural regions, the environmental and employment problems created by new technology in fishing regions, and the effect of technological rationalization, globalization and industrialization on resource-dependent industrial towns. This chapter argues that all sides are right to a certain extent. Their disagreement is in part related to problems with the spatial categories we use. Contemporary definitions of 'region' and 'rural/urban' have, to a certain extent, provoked such disagreements. In particular, the linking of the category 'region' with province and the categorization of all non-urban regions as homogeneous 'rural' areas has confused the notion of spatial differentiation. I argue that a more productive categorization of regions in Canada sees them as six region types: urban regions, urban fringe regions, resource-dependent industrial regions, agricultural regions, fishing regions, and northern Native regions.

With these new categorizations this paper reviews the empirical evidence of trends in spatial differentiation. This evidence shows a divergence of social, economic, demographic, and cultural factors between urban and urbanized rural regions, and the rest of Canada. Some of the changes the first two regions are experiencing include rapid economic and population growth, economic diversification, high rates of immigration, ethnic differentiation, and increased levels of education. Apart from the northern Native regions, which are experiencing a certain degree of population growth and relative increases in the levels of education, all other regions of Canada are experiencing, to a varying degree, stagnation in both economic and population growth, low rates of economic diversification and levels of education relative to the urban and urban fringe region types, low rates of immigration and, as a result, ethnic homogenization, and an ageing population. Research on social differentiation shows that structures of economic inequality, ethnic and racial relations, and gender differences vary from region to region.

In the chapter's concluding section the reasons for these continuing spatially based social differences in light of the potentially positive aspects of such trends as globalization, technological change, and new communications technology, and in light of the trend towards convergence of these differences in other Western countries, are discussed. The reasons are complex and can not be reduced to a simple formula. We show how staples theory continues to be a useful in explaining these differences when combined with elements of regulation theory. We also show that the importance of Canada's tertiary sector, the physical size and low population density of Canada, the relative absence of social problems in urban areas, and the climatic, aesthetic, and social disadvantages of Canada's non-urban areas can also be used to explain the continued lack of regional convergence.

The chapter will be based primarily on a review of literature which includes that of the disciplines of sociology, anthropology, economics, and geography. The initial review will be based on the principal journals of each discipline, with the addition of the *Canadian Journal of Regional Science*. This journal review will be supplemented by a review of other literature such as books and research reports.

Social differentiation is used in a very general sense here. I do not use it as an indicator of social complexity, as was done by Herbert Spencer and Emile Durkheim, but instead in a more modern sense as an indicator of unequal access to power and the resources of power. The differences between these two meanings of social differentiation was first noted by Peter Blau.[1] The first meaning he called social differentiation based on 'heterogeneity.' The second meaning refers to 'inequality.' According to Blau, social differentiation based on heterogeneity is beneficial to society. Social differentiation based on inequality is problematic as an obstacle to the social cohesion of that society.

2. Contemporary Social Theory and Projected Spatial Trends

The models and conceptual frameworks that we currently use to understand spatially based social differentiation are a product of industrialism. According to these frameworks the evolution of industrialism has necessitated the creation of large urban centres. The classical liberal economic theorists saw urbanization as a by-product of industrial progress. The rise of urban areas stimulated the first thoughts on the difference between urban and non-urban areas and the creation of an urban/rural distinction.[2] In these early formulations most non-urban areas were characterized by farming. As a result, rural society became identified with an agricultural lifestyle. For most theorists, ranging from Herbert Spencer to Karl Marx to Emile Durkheim, the rise of urban society and the decline of rural society were both inevitable and positive for society. Despite the fact that some defended the value of the rural way of life and of rural culture, this idea changed little during the twentieth century.

Concerning regions, the problem of differing patterns of development in separately defined 'regions' within 'industrialized' nations did seem to occupy the thoughts of social scientists until the 1930s. Unequal regional development between industrialized and non-industrialized countries was looked upon as a temporary phenomenon caused by the lack of exposure to capitalist/industrial forces. In Canada, however, as early as the 1920s some had started to suggest that nations/regions which depended on the production of 'staples' for their economic growth could experience problems. Harold Innis believed that Canada's colonial development, combined with the tendencies of staples production towards external 'leakages' would promote 'regional imbalances.'

The period immediately following the Second World War was characterized by a recognition among social scientists that not all regions of the world were developing as the West had. 'Dependency theory,' developed originally in Latin America, pointed out that the roots of regional underdevelopment lay in the relationship of one region to other regions. In particular, 'central' developed regions tended to control development in underdeveloped regions by making these regions dependent on them. In sociology in particular these theories had an immediate impact on explanations of regional inequality in Canada.[3] Such theories could be combined with staples theory and the 'hinterlander' tradition to provide a uniquely Canadian form of dependency theory.

2.1 Post-Industrialism?

The above theories of spatial differentiation have been characterized by the belief that we are now in an industrialized society. Industrialism, through the factory system and other associated factors, causes urbanization. Industrialism, through structures of centralized control, allows some regions to exploit other regions. Since the 1970s, social scientists have begun to talk about a fundamental transformation occurring in contemporary society. Industrialism is decreasing in importance. The forces of industrialism are being superseded by new post-industrial/ post-modern/post-Fordist forces.[4] Does this mean that the spatial patterns of industrialism will be affected? If industrialism led to urbanization, will post-industrialism lead to de-urbanization? Will the control of the industrial regions over peripheral regions be lessened? Will the spatially based patterns of social differentiation characterized by industrialism be replaced by new patterns? Will there be a convergence of the social characteristics of the rural and urban areas and the different regions of Canada?

In terms of more empirically oriented research there are those who believe we are moving into a period where spatial differences are of decreasing importance – that we are seeing a 'convergence' of spatial formations. In the United States, as early as the 1970s, geographers were pointing to a reversal of the twentieth-century urbanization trend. Non-metropolitan areas were growing faster than metropolitan areas. Berry referred to it as 'counterurbanisation,' while Weeks talked about a 'rural renaissance' in America.[5] In Canada, Parenteau, in a much more reserved fashion, talked about a 'slowdown in the rates of urbanisation.'[6]

As early as 1980 Gibbins was noting that many of the regional differences between eastern and western Canada were disappearing.[7] Research in the 1990s pointed to the end of the regionally based 'syndrome of polarities.'[8] Canadian regions were undergoing a process of 'convergence.' Declining differences in provincial rates of suicide and divorce were seen as a sign of this convergence.[9] Others pointed to the trend towards the equalization of provincial per capita GDP and earned income per capita.[10] These observations led many to conclude that regions are now undergoing a process of 'de-differentiation,' and that regions are no longer important sources of social differentiation.

Some point to these trends as a logical development in the shift from an industrial economy to a 'knowledge/information' economy. New telecommunications technologies mean that physical distance is no longer as important an issue in economic development. Knowledge-based services can be provided from anywhere via telephone, fax, and the internet. People no longer have to live in cities to work. They now have the freedom to choose where they want to live. Many would prefer to live in non-urban areas, as they have a 'higher quality of life.' The economic resuscitation of rural Ireland is seen as an example of what is possible through the knowledge economy.[11]

Recent empirical evidence points out that this change may be occurring in some parts of the country. Chambers and Deans talk about a 'rural renaissance' occurring in Alberta, where many rural communities grew at a faster rate than the major cities from 1991 to 1996.[12] This rebirth of the rural areas is due in large part to 'telecommuting.' Fully 86 per cent of the people they surveyed 'exported' their services to distant customers. Changes in telecommunications technology make life in these areas possible. People who normally would work and live in the city now choose to live in rural areas 'because of the quality of life.'

While these notions have not gained a great deal of legitimacy among some academics, in the practical affairs of community development they hold out hope for communities in non-urban areas. Most academics, while they may or may not believe in an 'urban/non-urban convergence,' and while they seem to acknowledge the 'potential' for development in non-urban regions,[13] do not see the technological changes of the knowledge/information economy as favouring the non-urban areas.

3. Convergence or Divergence? The Problems of the Existing Conceptual Frameworks

Are transformations in the past thirty years having an effect on spatially based social differentiation? Are regions becoming more alike?

Are rural areas experiencing a 'renaissance'? Are the 'have/have not' distinctions between central and peripheral regions and rural and urban areas disappearing? Before we look at the existing empirical evidence in greater detail we need to point out that part of the problem in answering this question comes from the existing spatial categories. These categories have been constructed in varying ways for varying reasons. An analysis of the construction of these categories will better enable us to understand the problems of using them as a means of understanding spatially based trends in social differentiation.

3.1 The Social Construction of Regions

The importance of the social construction of 'region' as a concept is best exemplified by comparing the differing definitions in anglo-Canadian sociology and franco-Québécois sociology. Each leads to differing interpretations of 'regional trends.'[14] In anglo-Canadian sociology the standard definition of a region is a province or group of provinces. The major division between regions is between Ontario, the West, the Atlantic provinces, and Quebec. According to certain sociologists, for the past few decades the provinces have been experiencing a process of convergence.[15] Recent studies of provincial differences show that these differences are now less significant. Since regional differences are becoming less and less important, interest in studying regional inequalities is declining.

In franco-Québécois sociology the region is usually an intra-provincial territory sharing a similar socio-economic livelihood and socio-historic past. The main divisions are between the central urban regions and peripheral regions. The inequalities between the central urban regions and the peripheral regions are either increasing or maintaining themselves at a high level. Regional differences continue to be seen as important, and, as a result, interest in regional disparities continues to be high.

3.2 The Social Construction of an Urban/Rural Distinction

The same conceptual problems can be seen with the spatial categories urban and rural. Problems with the definition of rural have made some what for the doing away of the concept of rural.[16] To use Bonner's terms, rural is always defined as the 'other' to urban.[17] Rural has come to mean the opposite of however the social scientist wanted to define urban. If for Max Weber the city was 'capitalist,' then the rural areas must be 'non-capitalist.' If for others the city was industrial, then rurality must mean non-industrial.

In fact, the industrial definition of urban seems to have been the most popular in the twentieth century. As John Bryden has noted, 'rural areas everywhere have been associated with agriculture.'[18] Agriculture, as a historical precursor to industrialism, becomes associated with the rural 'other.' Indeed, much of what constitutes rural sociology or rural geography is associated with agriculture. This clearly is problematic when one considers that rural areas, from an analytical perspective, are all those areas that are non-urban. If rural is defined in the more popular sense as an agricultural lifestyle, where does that leave non-agricultural, non-urban areas?

As others have suggested, a new categorization of rurality needs to be created.[19] This especially seems to be the case in Canada. Bollman and Biggs point out that Canada's rural areas are extremely heterogeneous.[20] They highlight the fact that different 'resource bases' have led to the development of 'different economic and social conditions associated with their exploitation.'[21] In their words, 'the heterogeneity of rural areas may make the distinctions between urban and rural areas more misleading than informative.' Whereas 'the norm' for other developed countries is to have much of the land base engaged in agriculture, this is less so in Canada. The vast northern tundra and the boreal forests of the Canadian Shield make up the majority of the Canadian land mass. Neither are characterized by an agricultural economy or lifestyle to any great extent. In Canada, therefore, we have an even more pressing need to come up with new spatial categories.

4. Towards a New Model of Spatial Forms

What is interesting about the problems Canadians have in coming up with adequate spatial categories to study social differentiation is that geographers have shown that Canada's spatial structure is actually quite simple. According to John Britton, 'Though the Canadian economy is sectorally diverse, its geographic patterns, from regions specialising in primary production to locations of metropolitan development, prove relatively simple to generalise.'[22] This simple spatial pattern, furthermore, has shown itself to be remarkably stable over the years. How can we then conceptualize this 'simple' spatial pattern?

In order to do so we must abandon the traditional regional categories and urban/rural distinctions. Instead I will isolate what Coffey and Polèse have called 'region types.'[23] These region types are not conventional contiguous geographical regions. They are areas that can be seen to share a similar socio-economic situation. The notion of region type is a convenient one in that we can use it in a manner similar to Max Weber's use of 'ideal types.' They may never exist in reality in the way that we describe them, but they are essential as an analytical tool.

With this in mind the question then becomes, 'How do I decide how to define a similar socio-economic situation.' I believe the best way to do so is by relying on the insights of Canadian political economy and, in particular, on staples theory, accompanied by the insights of urban sociology, urban geography, and regulation theory. The usefulness of staples theory in explaining Canadian regionalism is nothing new. It has long been used to explain why regional inequality exists in Canada.[24] Various versions of it have been criticized for overemphasizing either geographical determinism or economic determinism. Lately, new attempts have been made to create a more 'holistic' type of staples theory.[25]

In choosing staples as the basis for differentiating our 'region types' we do not mean to say that different regions are different solely because they produce a different staple. Following the lead of Max Weber and his observations on rurality, we mean to point out that many communities that produce a particular staple share more than the production of the staple or a similar geographical/environmental location. They also share similar socio-historic conditions. Most importantly, they share the fact that their 'foundations' were laid during a similar historical period, the period when that commodity was in demand on the international market. These foundations bear the imprint of the social relations and culture of that particular period. The similarity of these historical foundations is often just as important in defining these region types as the production relations associated with a particular type of commodity.

These ideas have already been pointed out by Trevor Barnes in his use of staples theory.[26] According to Barnes, much of Canada's geographic space is characterized by commodity specialization. These areas have developed 'affiliated political, social, and economic institutions' that bear the imprint of the particular commodity that is produced. Barnes points out, using regulation theory, that not only do these areas bear the imprint of that particular commodity, but they bear the imprint of the historical period when the demand for that commodity created development in that area. He believes that the 'Fordist' relations particular to the immediate postwar period played a major role in determining the conditions of staples-based communities.

In this chapter I take this idea a bit further. While all staples-producing regions were influenced by Fordism, the actual impact varied from commodity area to commodity area due to the presence of 'pre-existing' foundations. Communities based on the production of forest products and minerals were the 'most Fordist' because most came into being during the historical period characterized by these relations. Most resource-dependent communities of the Canadian Shield did not exist before the twentieth century. As a result, their foundations were based on these Fordist relations. Many of the agricultural communities of the Prairies and southern Ontario came into being in during the nineteenth century, when pre-Fordist relations of 'competitive capitalism' were predominant.[27] Fordist relations were 'built on' to the pre-existing foundations, usually producing a period of conflict. The mixing of these two types of relations created a unique socio-cultural environment. Fishing communities in Quebec and Atlantic Canada often had their foundations laid before the nineteenth century, and as such had 'pre-capitalist' or 'mercantilist capitalist' foundations upon which were placed competitive capitalist relations and Fordist relations.[28]

The most populous category of region types cannot be categorized according to a staple. For the purposes of understanding social differentiation, the large urban areas of Canada must represent a separate category. The social relations existing in large urban areas are similar no matter what the geographical location. Here social relations are affected somewhat by prior socio-historic periods, but the dominant relations are new ones, whether they be called post-industrial, post-Fordist, or post-modern.

The second most populous category cannot be linked to a staple either, but is linked to relations in urban areas. Geographers in Canada refer to this region type as the 'urban fringe.' These are areas that are often classified as rural, but whose social relations are more similar to those of the city. Individuals are 'suburbanites' or 'exurbanites' who chose to live in these areas for varying reasons, but who are still socially and economically 'linked' to the city. These areas are almost always adjacent to large urban centres, but their limits have been expanded through recent innovations in telecommunications.

The last category is characterized neither by a staple nor by urban relations. Much of the northern areas of Canada is dominated by social relations that pre-date European contact. These northern areas are characterized primarily by a Native society whose foundations are found in an era of hunting and gathering. European-influenced social relations have tried at various times and various ways to build on these foundations, usually producing conflict and social distress. Despite this influence, the earlier forms of social relations, altered somewhat by European contact, remain the dominant form of reference for these communities. These then are the six region types that I have chosen in order to analyse spatially based social differentiation in Canada:

1 Urban areas: the largest category and the most dynamic; characterized by the predominance of post-industrial social relations
2 The urban fringe: the second-largest category; characterized by the combination of urban post-industrial relations and a 'non-urban' setting
3 Agriculture-dependent areas: existing primarily in southern Ontario and Quebec and the southern areas of the prairie provinces; characterized by the combination of competitive capitalist and Fordist social relations
4 Resource-dependent areas: existing primarily on the Canadian Shield; characterized by the forest and mining industries, and primarily by Fordist social relations
5 Fishing-dependent areas: existing primarily in Atlantic Canada; characterized by the combination of mercantilist capitalist, competitive capitalist, and Fordist social relations
6 Northern Native areas: dominated by Native societies built around hunting and gathering traditions, but which have come into contact with more recent Euro-American forms of relations

As was mentioned earlier, this typology is created for the primary purpose of analysing spatially based social differentiation. It is interesting, however, that it is similar to one developed by Ray Bollman at Statistics Canada as a means of differentiating rural areas of Canada.[29] Using cluster analysis of socio-economic and demographic variables in all census divisions, Bollman found that the greatest regional differences are between two types of areas that he labelled 'primary settlements' (the seven largest urban areas) and the 'native north.' Upon further analysis of the remaining census divisions, he found marked similarities among five other types of areas, the urban frontier (the urban fringe), rural nirvana (outlying areas of the urban fringe), agro-rural (agriculture-dependent), rural enclave (fishing-dependent), and resourced areas (resource-dependent). It should be noted that there are problems in using census divisions as a basis for deciding on the 'geographical locations' of these areas, as these divisions often are too large and combine a variety of region types. Nonetheless, Bollman's analysis of the 'clustering' of similar socio-economic and demographic census variables is extremely helpful in supporting our typology and, indeed, the need for a more in-depth examination of spatially based social differentiation.

5. Spatially Based Social Differentiation in Canada: A Description of Trends

This typology allows us to show with greater clarity that different areas in Canada are being affected in different ways by recent socio-economic changes. It enables us to describe how the patterns of social differentiation vary from one region type to another. We do not try and offer here an exhaustive list of all the varying elements of social differentiation, but simply present brief descriptions of the latest research. Even with restricting ourselves to research published in the last ten years, problems arise in summarizing the material in the space of this paper. We will therefore tend to concentrate on a discussion of varying spatial patterns of social differentiation as they relate to socio-economic status, gender, and race/ethnicity.

6. General Spatial Trends

6.1 Regional/Provincial Convergence

As was mentioned earlier, geographers in Canada have noted the stability of 'the spatial concentration of the production and distribution systems of the Canadian economy,'[30] especially in light of the 'massive regional dislocation that has shaken the U.S. economy since the 1970s.'[31] Still Britton has shown that there have been some interesting changes recently. He notes that provincial per capita GDP has shown a 'fairly strong' move towards convergence since 1981. Provincial earned income per capita has also tended to show convergence, but to a lesser degree. Research by economists has also shown a tendency towards provincial convergence, although the interpretations of why this is happening differ. Coulombe and Lee believe that this provincial convergence is due to the combination of two factors: the increasing regional economic integration brought about by globalization and the increasing importance of 'knowledge-intensive and service sectors.'[32] This last point is explained by the fact that the mobility of these sectors in greater than in 'the traditional manufacturing sector.' According to Coulombe and Lee, this mobility will increase as 'improved communications and transportation technologies are likely to push economies further towards convergence.'[33]

Helliwell's research confirms the trend towards provincial economic convergence, at least in so far as provincial per capita incomes are concerned.[34] He believes the major reason for this convergence is migration. It is not that economies of the poorer provinces are catching up with those of the wealthier provinces by showing stronger growth. Rather, people are moving from the poorer provinces to the richer ones. Lee, in a later article, takes issue with the notion that convergence can be explained by migration.[35] He states that there is a convergence of productivity levels between provinces that seems to be linked to a convergence of 'human capital' measures. As an important indicator he notes that the percentage of workers with university degrees in poorer provinces is catching up with the rates in wealthier provinces.

Another explanation for this trend offered by some sociologists links provincial convergence to a convergence of rates of urbanization. McGahan has shown that, outside of the Atlantic provinces, there has been a convergence of provincial rates of urbanization since 1981.[36] Hay has shown that, going back to 1951, one can see a trend towards the convergence of provincial rates of urbanization that includes the Atlantic provinces.[37]

While there appears to be a general agreement on the convergence of provincial economic indicators, there is some disagreement as to why this is happening. What is important to highlight from this research is that this provincial convergence is not necessarily a convergence of region types. Most explanations offered – migration out of poorer areas and convergence of rates of provincial urbanization in particular – do not translate into an equalization of 'access to resources' among these region types. They demonstrate an increase in growth in central urban areas and hence a divergence of growth patterns between the urban region type and the others. The human capital explanation may in fact mean a convergence of region types if it shows a convergence of levels of education rates between individuals living in the different region types.

6.2 Rural/Urban Convergence

As was mentioned earlier, geographers in the United States discovered that in the 1970s rates of urbanization reversed themselves. They claimed that a 'population turnaround' was occurring. The same trend was observed in western European countries. According to Canadian geographers, this trend has not been occurring in Canada. In 1988 Alun, Keddie, and Smit showed that, apart from Quebec from 1976 to 1981, this 'turnaround' has not occurred in Canada,[38] a conclusion reconfirmed in a study by Keddie and Joseph published in 1991. They stated that any 'apparent' turnaround in Canada was in fact due to two interrelated factors: the reclassification of 'urban' and 'rural' categories in the census data[39] and 'urban spillover.'[40] The movement of people into the area surrounding urban areas, or suburbanization, looks like rural growth, when in fact this movement is directly related to urban growth. Coffey and Polèse came to the same conclusions. In a 1998 article they state that 'decongestion' is the best explanation for any apparent change. They point out that while manufacturing employment had an increasing propensity to leave the larger urban areas during this period, the new engine of economic growth, the service sector, showed less of a tendency towards decentralization.

Why has Canada not shown the tendency towards rural/urban convergence seen in most other developed nations? Coffey and Polèse point to three main reasons. The first is related to Canada's 'tertiary' economy. As their research has shown, the 'tertiary' or service sector of the economy is the most resistant to decentralization. Canada's economy is the most highly 'tertiarized' in the developed world. Thus, it is more resistant to this trend. The second reason is the fact that because of 'its areal extent and its low population density, Canada's peripheral regions are considerably more peripheral than those of other countries.'[41] The difficulty of access, due in large part to greater distances, to urban regions from these regions makes them less attractive than rural areas in other countries. As well, unlike other countries' peripheral regions, Canada's tend not to have attractive climates. The third reason relates to 'push' factors. According to Coffey and Polèse, 'Canada has not yet developed the urban diseconomies of scale (congestion, pollution, crime) that underlie the flight from urban areas in many other developed countries.'[42] The explanations offered by Keddie and Alun are similar to some of the reasons offered by Coffey and Polèse. It is the 'unique' environment of Canada's rural areas that makes a population turnaround less likely here than in other countries.[43]

As was the case for 'provincial/regional convergence,' the existing research on 'urban/rural convergence' does not indicate a convergence of our previously described region types, but an increase in the economic importance of urban and urban fringe region types for Canada. This research points out that the remaining four region types show little of the dynamism found in the first two. The reasons for this are factors unique to the Canadian 'spatial economy.' This description of the general spatial trends in Canada demonstrates the importance of using typologies such as ours to understand properly the differing trends of spatially based social differentiation.

7. The Urban Region Type

7.1 Conceptual Limitations

The great danger in using an ideal-type conceptual scheme is that the constructed 'type' is often mistaken for a real situation. In our discussion of the trends in the urban region type the reader may believe that we are describing a situation that is the same in all 'urban' areas in Canada, but this is not what we are trying to do. In constructing an ideal type we are selecting certain characteristics that best represent the phenomena we are trying to describe. In doing so, the author necessarily injects certain 'biases' into the description as to what are the 'best' characteristics to describe the 'essence' of the phenomena. It should be stated at the outset, then, that the 'urban region type' that I hope to describe is one that is closer to the conditions of Toronto than to those of Thunder Bay even though both are 'Census Metropolitan Areas (CMAs).' Before we construct our urban type we need to discuss the variations within the phenomena that limit the usefulness of our typology. Definitions of what is an urban area vary considerably, from any community with a population over 1000 to the twenty-five CMAs defined by Statistics Canada. Since we are only describing an 'ideal type,' we are not concerned with questions of 'which community' should be considered an urban area. For the purposes of this initial discussion we will use the more commonly accepted CMA definition. Within these CMAs there is a tremendous amount of diversity. Before we can discuss common characteristics we have to discuss the differences.

McGahan notes that these urban variations are of two types: demographic and functional.[44] In terms of demographic variations, size is perhaps one of the most obvious. As of 1991 only three of Canada's CMAs had a population of more than one million while eight had populations of less than 200,000. Rates of growth for these communities also varied. From 1986 to 1991 Vancouver's population grew 16.1 per cent and Toronto's grew by 13.4 per cent. In contrast, the CMAs of Chicoutimi-Jonquière and Thunder Bay grew by 1.6 and 1.8 per cent respectively.[45]

The functional variations relate to the economic specializations of the different CMAs. Although in principle urban areas have diversified economies, they do have what Rao has called 'functional areas of specialisation.'[46] According to Rao, Canada's CMAs can be divided into eight such areas: manufacturing, mining, finance, transport, community service, trade, construction, and public administration. While these areas are important, Rao's own research has indicated that rates of specialization decreased from 1971 to 1981, indicating an increasing economic diversification of all CMAs.

Noting recent changes in urban economic structures, Broadway has divided Canada's CMAs into two main types: national/regional service centres and others.[47] He believes that the seven urban areas he has categorized as service centres best demonstrate the changes that urban centres are experiencing, as these have the fastest growth and are characterized by the autonomous aspects of 'post-industrial' trends. Our region type leans towards these centres. While not specific to any one city, our regional type is closer to conditions in Toronto, Montreal, Vancouver, and Calgary than to those in any of the other twenty-one CMAs. Indeed, it may be that one should further divide this urban category in to a 'global cities' type and the rest of Canada's CMAs.

7.2 General Trends

The first characteristic of urban region types in Canada is high rates of growth. As was already discussed, unlike other developed countries Canada has not experienced a process of 'counter urbanization.' In fact metropolitan concentration has increased in the three largest CMAs – Toronto, Montreal, and Vancouver – increasing their percentage of the total Canadian population. Bourne points out that urban concentration has partially been offset by a decentralization of population and jobs, but this trend is best characterized as urban slipovers.[48] This urban spatial concentration is especially true for high-growth economic activities. Coffey has noted the urban concentration of 'high order ser-vices,'[49] while Britton notes the same concentration of 'high tech activities.'[50] Metropolitan concentration in Canada has been accompa-nied by a change in the economies of urban areas. Manufacturing has decreased in its relative importance, and has been replaced by the 'new-age economies'[51] of the service and knowledge sectors. Coffey and Polèse have suggested that this concentration is due to the 'agglomeration economies' of the larger urban areas and access to a large skilled labour pool.[52]

With this change in the economic base of urban areas came changes in the demographic structures of the population. To meet the demands of the new economy the populations of these urban areas have become increasingly educated.[53] As well, the ethnic composition of the cities has changed as the bulk of new immigrants to Canada moves to the largest urban areas. This trend, combined with the increasing number of immigrants from non-European sources, means that the populations of these communities are becoming more and more ethnically diverse. These changes have had an effect on the culture of these communities as they increasingly exhibit aspects of what has been called 'post-industrial culture.'[54]

7.3 Trends in Social Differentiation

What does all this mean as far as social differentiation is concerned? In terms of socio-economic status, urban areas represent the wealthiest areas of Canada. Average incomes and levels of education are highest in the largest cities.[55] Yet despite this wealth there exists a high degree of economic inequality. The highest rates of poverty are found in Canada's largest urban areas.[56] According to Hajnal Canada has proportionally more people in concentrated urban poverty than does the United States,[57] and trends indicate that urban poverty is increasing.[58] Research by MacLachlan and Sawada shows that economic inequality, measured in terms of the distribution of household income, is on the increase in these urban centres.[59] The middle class in these centres is in decline.

Broadway states that this poverty is primarily in the 'inner city' areas, which 'contain disproportionate concentrations of less educated, low income, and unemployed persons.'[60] Unemployment decreases as one moves from core to suburbs,[61] and median household income increases with distance from the urban core. According to Broadway, these trends are increasing with shifts 'in manufacturing and employment to the suburbs and beyond.'[62] Yet this same research shows variations in these patterns among urban areas; 'national/regional service centres' have 'either stable or declining levels of deprivation' when compared to other urban centres.[63]

Explanations of this increasing concentration of urban poverty are offered by Hajnal. Race/ethnicity is seen as an influencing factor in that 'Aboriginal peoples, Blacks, and French are much more likely to be located in concentrated urban poverty than are British.'[64] Still, 'most people in concentrated urban poverty are in fact white.'[65] The clearest explanations of urban poverty according to Hajnal are the structural dislocations caused by the decline of manufacturing in these centres. In Hajnal's words, '[M]anufacturing employment losses do appear to be related to concentrated urban poverty.'[66]

Another trend of social differentiation is the changing racial and ethnic composition of Canada's largest urban centres caused by recent patterns of immigration. While Canada as a country has been experiencing a relatively high rate of immigration lately, the effects of this trend are not equally dispersed across the country. Most recent immigrants to Canada are attracted to the large 'gateway' urban centres such as Toronto, Montreal, and Vancouver.[67] This 'urbanization' of immigration is a trend that has been increasing steadily since the Second World War.[68]

While the importance of recently arrived immigrants in large urban centres is, in itself, serving to differentiate the urban region type from the other types, this differentiation is further enhanced by the fact that most recent immigrants are from non-European sources and are visible minorities.[69] Fully 94 per cent of Canada's visible minorities lived in CMAs in 1996; 70 per cent lived in Vancouver, Toronto, and Montreal.[70] Visible minorities represent 32% of the population in Toronto, 31% in Vancouver, and 12% in Montreal. By contrast, in smaller, more peripheral industrial urban areas such as Thunder Bay the visible minority population represents only 2.3 per cent of the population; in Chicoutimi, they represent only 0.6 per cent. Although discussion of the actual implication of this trend is surprisingly absent from academic journals, this is being rectified by the work of the four Centres of Excellence established under the 'Metropolis' project to study the effects of international immigration on Canada's cities.[71]

Research on gender relations specific to Canada's large urban centres is also surprisingly absent from academic journals, perhaps because of indications that the important aspects of gender relations are not specific to these areas; that they are shared by all women no matter where they live. Still, the fact that labour markets in these urban areas have undergone the greatest amount of restructuring and exhibit 'post-Fordist' or post-industrial relations to the greatest extent means that the new gender relationships that are produced are worthy of discussion. Olfert and Stabler have pointed out that women in urban areas participate in this restructuring to a greater extent than do non-urban females.[72] Several researchers have mentioned the importance of gender in relation to the situation of recent immigrants and visible minorities to Canada.[73] Juteau has pointed out that there exist important differences between immigrant women and immigrant men, and between immigrant women and non-immigrant women, in such things as labour force participation, educational attainment, social isolation and dependency.[74]

8. The Urban Fringe Region Type

8.1 Conceptual Limitations

The notion of urban-rural fringe has been used for some time by geographers in Canada. According to Troughton, it is an area where Canadian rural geographers have become recognized 'as experts.'[75] Surprisingly few other disciplines have seemed interested in the phenomenon. This is perhaps related to the fact that it can be seen as an 'intermediary' phenomenon – a mixture of urban and rural forces. As such, its characteristics could be perceived as not being important in their own right. This chapter argues that the forms of social differentiation found in urban fringe areas are unique. The combination of rural and urban relations found in these areas produce a particular type of society – not properly rural and not properly urban. As well, as many 'exurbanites' move to these areas to get away from the city, the type of people living in these areas are often quite different. Urban fringes vary according to the type of area they are founded in. Most have been extended into land that has an agricultural social foundation. A minority of urban fringes have been extended into land that has a resource-dependent or a fishing-based social foundation. There are also variations within an urban fringe. Since there are no objectively defined boundaries for this region type, areas within the fringe can be generally portrayed by a continuum, with areas closest to urban areas exhibiting more urban tendencies and areas furthest away from the urban areas exhibiting more non-urban tendencies.

The term urban fringe is used here in a more open and general manner than in some academic work. Parenteau and Earl, for example, define urban fringe as an 'urban area within a CMA, but outside of the urbanised core.'[76] They refer as well to the 'rural fringe,' which they define as 'all territory within a CMA lying outside of the urban areas.' Our definition of urban fringe includes their concept of rural fringe. Indeed, it goes beyond that concept in that it is not necessarily limited to the constructed boundaries of a Census Metropolitan Area. Here the term urban fringe has been chosen instead of rural fringe because of the belief that the dynamic forces at work in these areas are a result of proximity to urban areas. It is a region where the dynamic forces of suburban and exurban migration mix with restructuring non-urban forces.

8.2 General Trends

Similar to the urban region type, the urban fringe region type typically exhibits high rates of population growth.[77] This growth is primarily in the rural non-farm category, as these areas are 'predominantly zones of residential commuting to urban employment.'[78] In those areas closest to the urban areas, new residents are primarily daily commuters. As one becomes more and more distant from the urban cores new growth is still linked to urban economic activity, but individuals are increasingly 'telecommuters,' people who visit the urban core occasionally but do much of their work using the new technologies of telecommunications.[79] In fact, if one were to single out any region type where changing information and communications technology was having an important effect, it would have to be the urban fringe. Since growth in the fringe is primarily linked to proximity to the urban region type, the growth area of the urban fringe is being extended by these technological changes. In his research on the suburbanization of Toronto offices, Matthew has pointed out that improvements in the cost and efficiency of telecommunications have meant that access needs between production plants and technical services can be satisfied within one and a half hours driving time.[80] Just as new transportation technologies facilitated the development of suburbs in the postwar era, so the new telecommunications technology is serving to extend the influences of urban forces into the countryside.

The reasons for the migration of individuals into the urban fringe vary. Research by Davies and Yeats has indicated that there tend to be two groups of people.[81] The exurban village group is similar to the suburbanites of the fifties, sixties, and seventies. They move into the urban fringe to find better and more affordable housing as well as safer environments to raise their children. These migrants are not searching to escape the city so much as looking for a more liveable urban lifestyle. The second group of migrants is referred to by Davies and Yeats as the 'exurban-rural group. These individuals are more openly anti-urban. They move to the urban fringe in order to escape the urban lifestyle. Another trend identified by both Dahms and Halseth is the movement of retirees into the urban fringe.[82] Areas of the urban fringe with certain recreational and aesthetic amenities are benefiting from the movement of seniors out of urban areas.

It is important to point out that growth in the urban fringe is not entirely related to residential patterns. Coffey and Polèse have noted the shift in manufacturing to the urban fringe that occurred during the 1970s.[83] The reasons for these shifts varied, but include the search for more space, lower costs, and cheaper labour. This trend may have continued in the 1990s but presumably at a lower level, as manufacturing activities as a whole are on the decline. Matthew's research has pointed to the suburbanization of service-sector activities in the Toronto area.[84] Coffey and Drolet note a similar trend in Montreal, but unlike trends in some American cities, this shift of some services towards the periphery of the metropolitan regions has not threatened the viability of the urban core.[85] As well, research by Bryant and Johnston has indicated that the extension of urban forces into the fringe may have a positive impact on pre-existing economic activities such as agriculture.[86]

8.3 Trends in Social Differentiation

The types of social differentiation in urban fringe regions combine urban relations and those found in the non-urban region into which the urban fringe has been extended. As mentioned earlier, in most cases this is the agricultural region type. The exurban migrants tend to be families that can afford to move out of the city. As a result, they tend to be better off and have a higher social status than both the residents of urban cores and other residents of the urban fringe.[87] Thus, class differences exist between these migrants and the 'original' inhabitants of the area, as was shown in Halseth's study of cottage conversion in the 'rural-recreational countryside.'[88] Barrett's anthropological research in Dufferin County, Ontario, is another example of research done on these new class relations. His work shows that, unlike the situation in similar areas of the United States, where socio-economic inequalities were hidden or denied, class inequalities in Dufferin County were taken as natural and accepted, at least by the new exurban elite.[89]

Barrett's work has also shown the newly emerging ethnic relations in these areas. Whereas the pre-existing population tended to be primarily British, the exurban migrants are more diverse ethnically. While Barrett found that prejudice was widespread, it was focused primarily in the newcomer community. Those who had fled the multiracial society of Toronto were upset that it had followed them to the urban fringe.

While Barrett's research also deals with changing gender relations, other research has attempted to concentrate primarily on this issue. Preston and McLafferty's work has looked at the social construction of gender relations in the suburbs.[90] While the situation of women in urban areas varies by location, there are noticeable commonalties in the situation of women in the suburbs. Women here are more likely to be married than are women in the central urban areas. Domestic responsibilities may force suburban women to find work closer to home. This aspect of life in the suburbs is aggravated further by a lack of child care and other services in the suburbs. These aspects mean that the 'gender differential' is more pronounced in suburban locations than in central urban areas.[91]

9. The Resource-dependent Region Type

9.1 Conceptual Limitations

The notion of a resource-dependent region type refers to 'resource-dependent communities' or 'single-industry towns.' These are the forestry and mining towns that dominate large areas of the Canadian Shield. These communities are generally defined as new (founded during the twentieth century), small (fewer than 30,000), isolated, planned, and dominated by one resource-based industry. The dominance of one main industry means that there exists a high degree of 'dependency' in these communities and, because of the cyclical nature of commodity production, they have a high degree of instability. The specific economic characteristics are as follows: there is one dominant employer, usually a large industrial corporation based outside the region; the industry is capital-intensive and technologically intensive; jobs are primarily unskilled or semi-skilled 'blue-collar' occupations; wages are relatively high; there are few employment opportunities for women; and there is a small retail sector, and a small service sector.

Demographically these communities are characterized by a highly mobile population, a high degree of youth out-migration, a young population with fewer older people, more males than females, larger families, and greater ethnic diversity. The culture of these towns tends to be dominated by a high degree of dependency; it is a 'wage-earner' (as opposed to a 'stake-holder') culture, male-dominated and blue-collar, with lower levels of formal education and a negative environment for women.

Sociologists such as Lucas and Himelfarb have shown these towns to be different than agricultural-based and fishing-based communities. According to Lucas, fishing, agricultural, and tourist towns, while they may be resource-dependent, are not single-industry communities. Such communities are made up of 'small capitalists (and) entrepreneurs' who have a lifestyle that 'differentiates them from the population of a community with a single industry base.'[92] While resource-dependent communities do show a certain degree of homogeneity in some aspects of community life, they do differ according to their age[93] and resource base.[94]

9.2 General Trends

Generally speaking, these communities are not experiencing the growth seen in the urban regional types. Since the 1970s they have been experiencing a slow decline in population.[95] This varies according to province, however. The resource sectors of Quebec and Ontario were the first to experience the 'Fordist' boom of the postwar era. Since then there has been a shift west and north as companies looked for new sources of supply. The last 'resource-dependent community' in Ontario was established in 1956, while in British Columbia it was in the 1980s. As well, northern Alberta's forest sector has greatly expanded in the 1980s and 1990s.

Research conducted in the 1990s has started to question the Lucas/Himelfarb model. Heather Clemenson examined census data from 1976, 1981, and 1986 in an attempt to see if single-industry towns had diversified their economies during this period.[96] She found that the stability of these communities was affected by the resource base. Fishing communities were the most stable and mining communities the least stable. She also found that in the mining and forest communities labour force dependency had decreased. This decrease, she believes, was not due to 'industrial diversification' as we normally perceive it. Instead, what seems to be happening is a resource base diversification. Mining towns diversify into forestry and forestry towns diversify into mining. Ehrensaft and Beeman have indicated that change is occurring in the occupational and industrial structures of resource-dependent communities.[97] They note the declining importance of jobs in the primary sectors and the increasing importance of employment in the public sector and administrative services.

The most serious recent re-examination of the work of Lucas, Himelfarb, and other 'seminal' researchers was done by Randall and Ironside.[98] Using census data from 1971 and 1986, they retested some of the hypotheses arising from this earlier research. Their research indicated that these communities are not uniform entities; communities varied according to the resource base they were dependent upon. They also found that the non-resource economic sectors of these towns were now more significant than had been indicated in the earlier work and that women were benefiting from increased employment opportunities in these sectors.

Others have pointed out the impact of economic restructuring in these communities. Britton has described resource industries as being at a decision point.[99] Hayter depicts the restructuring going on in the forest communities as the effect of 'post-Fordism,' characterized by corporate restructuring, downsizing, new 'flexible' labour relations, and technological changes.[100] Wallace has shown the same trends occurring in mining communities,[101] as has Maclaren in the energy sector.[102] Nontheless, it is often difficult to generalize about the nature of the restructuring, since studies have shown that it varies from place to place.[103]

In addition to this restructuring, other changes are occurring that affect life in the resource-dependent region type. More and more resource exploitation is being challenged by the notion of sustainability.[104] Decisions about future development no longer depend solely on market assumptions of profitability. Governments have been increasingly forced to regulate these activities based on long-term environmental and social sustainability. As well, these communities have experienced an increase in cultural differences with the large urban centres. As Wallace and Shields note, the large urban centres of Canada have been increasingly characterized by a 'post-industrial' culture.[105] The 'dominant social class' in these areas is made up of 'knowledge workers,' professionals no longer engaged in the production of material goods. These individuals 'engage with nature' as part of their lifestyle and not as part of their livelihood. The culture in resource-dependent communities is still very much conditioned by the industrial relations upon which the town is based and its 'exploitive' relationship to nature. Increasingly there exist 'contested terrains' regarding such issues as land use that usually translate into restructuring brought on by the 'cultural hegemony' of post-industrial urban values.

Other research indicates that the age structure of these towns no longer shows a younger population overall. The percentage of people over sixty-five in many of these communities now tends to be higher than national and provincial averages, but this varies according to the age of the town.[106] As well, sex ratios have tended to converge with that of other communities.

9.3 Trends in Social Differentiation

These communities are still characterized by standard industrial relations. The dominant culture is still male-oriented and working class.[107] In terms of employment structure, the 'central work world' is still predominant, although industrial jobs in the primary and manufacturing sectors have declined steadily since the 1970s. Fordist relations are therefore much more the norm than in the urban region types.[108] This is not to say that these communities have not escaped post-Fordist influences, as Barnes and Hayter have pointed out .[109] Ehrensaft and Beeman and Randall and Ironside have both noted the increase in public service and administrative service jobs in these communities.[110] The percentage of jobs in the service sector is comparable to national norms, but public sector service jobs and 'hospitality' service jobs are over-represented. Still, in terms of social differentiation according to class/socio-economic status, when compared to changes in the urban regional type, changes have been minimal.

The seminal research on single-industry towns indicated that the general levels of education in these communities were lower than the national averages, a fact explained by the omnipresence of low-skilled industrial employment. While there has been a general increase in the levels of education in these communities, this increase has been less than the national and provincial increases.[111] In other words, the differences in levels of education between this region type and the rest of the country are increasing.

Many of the studies conducted during the 1950s and 1960s noted that these communities were characterized by a high degree of ethnic diversity. This diversity was a result of large numbers of immigrants being attracted to these towns during the first half of the twentieth century. As employment growth declined during the late 1960s, fewer immigrants were drawn to these communities. As a result, these towns have little experience with immigrants from non-European sources. While the number of foreign-born residents may still be relatively large, most are European. The number of visible minorities living in these communities is most often less than 2 per cent.[112] The absence of new immigrants, and in fact of migrants of any kind other than those leaving the community, has meant that the existing ethnic groups have undergone a process of 'ethnic homogenization.' In English Canada this means that these communities are made up of a fairly homogeneous, white, anglophone, Christian population. The new global diversities that characterize the populations of Canada's largest urban regions are absent in resource-dependent communities.

Research done on these communities in the 1970s indicated that the job market was characterized by a rigid sexual division of labour.[113] The inability of women to get jobs in the resource industries and the underdevelopment of secondary industry and services meant there were few job opportunities for women. In addition, little attention was paid to the needs of women in these communities. As the title of an NFB film in 1979 indicated, these towns were 'No Place for a Woman.' Recent studies have indicated some change in these conditions. Gill's research on Tumbler Ridge, BC, supports the notion that the situation of women in single-industry towns may not be as problematic as indicated in the Lucas/Himelfarb model.[114] Randall and Ironside found that the non-resource economic sectors of these towns were now more significant than had been indicated in the earlier work and that women were benefiting from increased employment opportunities in these sectors.[115] Indeed, according to the 1996 census, women in these communities now occupy 44.5 per cent of jobs.[116] The job market is still gender-segmented, however, in that women are still absent from the standard industrial jobs but over-represented in public sector employment and in the hospitality services. In comparison with national female employment structures, women in resource-dependent communities are under-represented in professional and blue-collar industrial jobs and over-represented in sales and service jobs. As research by Vosko and Beuckert has indicated, women still are excluded from important decisions affecting these communities such as land planning.[117]

10. The Agricultural Region Type

10.1 Conceptual Limitations

The description of an agricultural region type is problematic in that these regions vary by the historical period of their initial development and by their structures. Troughton has pointed out that the development of agricultural areas in eastern and western Canada is separated by varying 'temporal sequences.'[118] Agriculture in eastern Canada peaked by 1880 and enjoyed a fifty to seventy-year period of relative stability. Agriculture in western Canada grew rapidly starting in 1880. This growth was terminated just as rapidly by the depression of the 1930s. Because of these historical differences the agricultural communities of eastern Canada have been characterized as ethnically homogeneous – either British or French. The Prairies were developed during the 'open door' period of immigration and as such their agricultural communities were somewhat more ethnically diverse. As well, the socio-economic foundations of agricultural communities in eastern Canada were laid primarily during periods of mercantilist and competitive capitalism, whereas the agricultural communities of western Canada were exposed to the initial instances of Fordist/monopoly capitalism. In addition to these historical variations, Troughton notes that agricultural areas as a whole can be divided up into three separate structurally distinct 'zones': core agricultural, marginal peripheral, and fringe.[119] The core agricultural zones are those areas of the prairie provinces, southern Ontario, and southern Quebec where agricultural activities remain the primary economic activity. The marginal peripheral zones are areas of marginal farmland on the outer fringes of the agricultural core. The fringe zones are areas within the urban fringe where agriculture is still an activity but where it is no longer the primary activity. Despite these variations there is value in constructing an agricultural region type based primarily on core agricultural areas with a competitive capitalist socio-historic foundation as its 'essence.'

10.2 General Trends

It should be pointed out that it is surprisingly difficult to provide a general description of the trends found in agricultural region types. There are many empirical studies of trends in 'rural' areas, but here, as pointed out earlier, rural means all non-urban areas. While agricultural areas are an important part of non-urban areas and while rural and agricultural are often terms used interchangeably by researchers, there are clear problems with using 'rural' empirical evidence to describe trends in agricultural areas.

Despite these problems, some empirical research does limit itself to trends in agricultural areas. These studies highlight the general decline in population occurring in agricultural region type areas.[120] This decline in the population is occurring despite the fact that farm production levels have remained relatively stable. The total number of farms is decreasing as remaining farms are getting bigger. According to Troughton the rate of decline varies by zone.[121] Farming in the marginal peripheral zone has decreased the most, as populations there have shifted into forestry and mining or migrated. This finding has also been seen in numerous studies of these areas in Quebec.[122] Core agricultural zones are losing population but to a lesser degree than marginal peripheral zones. Fringe zones are not losing population. They are losing agricultural population despite the fact that agriculture in this zone can remain profitable. The loss comes from the pressures of urban encroachment on prime agricultural lands in these areas. While farming is still profitable, residential and other types of development are even more profitable.[123]

Troughton has noted that most of these changes occurring in agricultural areas are related to the 'industrialization' of agriculture. Industrialization is the term used to describe the processes whereby 'agriculture has shifted from low levels of productivity, based on large numbers of small to medium-sized mixed farms, to production dominated by much smaller numbers of larger sized and/or more highly capitalised, specialist enterprises.'[124] The impact of industrialization varies between eastern and western Canada. In the Prairies, it has meant that larger farms have become specialized, with higher levels of productivity, in wheat and a few grains and oilseeds. In eastern Canada core areas have shifted from mixed agriculture to 'the raising of individual types of livestock, utilising intensive housing and feeding methods.'[125] This trend has also meant the rise of larger, more capital-intensive farming operations. Such operations can exist in a more managed system of supply and demand through the use of such mechanisms as marketing boards and transportation subsidies. Problems develop when market instability disrupts the process of industrial agricultural rationalization.

Research on the effects of industrialization on agricultural communities has produced varying conclusions. Research dealing primarily with prairie agricultural communities points fairly conclusively to the decline of these communities as populations decrease and service employment shifts to more metropolitan areas.[126] Other studies indicate that the industrialization of agriculture has not affected the 'social cohesion' of these communities.[127] Agricultural communities are managing to survive, in large part thanks to non-utilitarian community cultural attributes.[128] Other research noting the cultural attributes of these communities points to the continuing neo-conservative values that dominate them.[129]

In addition to the above trends, other changes mentioned in recent research include the ageing of agricultural families, increases in levels of education that do not keep up with national or provincial increases, an increase in off-farm work, declining rates of farm family incomes, and an increase in the number of female farm operators.[130]

10.3 Trends in Social Differentiation

In terms of trends in socio-economic differentiation on an inter-regional level, the declining incomes of farm families has already been mentioned. Despite the findings on the urban core, certain sectors of farming have among the highest levels of poverty in Canada. Reimer, Ricard, and Shaver have shown that average incomes are lower in rural areas then in urban areas.[131] Nonetheless, this a lower portion of rural households live below the low income cut-off (LICO) than families in other areas. This is related to the fact that the LICO for rural areas is 26 per cent lower than for metropolitan levels.

There is surprisingly little recent research on changes in socio-economic differentiation within farming populations despite the increasing industrialization of agriculture. Research by Winson in central Canada does indicate that such changes are structurally complex and are not characterized by a polarization between a small number of 'bourgeois' corporate farmers and a large agricultural proletariat.[132] Winson's research indicates that structures are different according to the commodity produced and that it is not easy to distinguish an underlying trend.

There has been little or no analysis of intra- or inter-regional ethnic/racial differentiation for farming communities. Simard has pointed out the problems in Quebec with getting new immigrants to settle in farming areas.[133] An analysis of census data shows that there are very few visible minorities and very few new immigrants who settle in these communities.[134] The populations of these communities appear to be similar in terms of their ethnic homogeneity. While the ethnic diversity of some agricultural communities in western Canada may have been important at one point in time, the absence of new immigrants has meant the decline of such diversity.

There does appear to be quite a bit of recent empirical research on gender relations in the agricultural region type. Research by Dion and Welsh indicates that by 1986 farm women had higher rates of participation in the labour force than women in the total population.[135] This is a drastic change from the situation in the 1950s, when farm women had considerably lower rates of labour force participation than the general female population. While the statistics for 1986 show the higher rates of participation across all age and education levels, Dion and Welsh note that the difference is even more extreme among the least educated. Income levels seem to affect the differences between the participation levels of farm women and the general female population in that, while at all levels farm women's participation is higher, the difference diminishes as the income increases.

Smith has used the changes in women's contribution to agriculture up to 1986 to develop a new typology of the position of women in this area.[136] Her research also shows the increasing participation of farm women in the labour force, a contribution that varies according to five types: on-farm work, household work, off-farm work, decision-making, and volunteer work. Smith indicates that male-female differences in all these types of activities are decreasing, but that there are still important differences in almost all the categories. These differences have been noted by Leckie in her research on obstacles to the participation of women in the agricultural system.[137] According to Leckie, the major source of these obstacles is 'tradition.'

Shaver has also tried to analyse the changing role of women in farming.[138] She finds that the reasons for these changes are complex. They cannot be characterized as either the masculinization or feminization of farming, nor can they be seen as the result of the 'modernization' of farming technologies or the increasing importance of capitalistic relations in farming. Rather, they are a result of a complex interaction between these two trends.

11. The Fishing Region Type

11.1 Conceptual Limitations

The fishing region type is arguably the oldest and smallest of the region types dealt with in this chapter.[139] The first difficulty one faces in trying to argue for a fishing region type is the fact that there are three distinct 'fishing regions': the West Coast, inland freshwater fishing areas, and the East Coast. A study directed by Patricia Marchak in the 1980s pointed to the unique conditions of fishing on the West Coast.[140] It highlighted the relatively recent development of the industry and its communities and the absence of a prior history of domestic production. The predominance of capitalist relations are pointed out as well as the ethnic divisions that have existed in the industry. The research done by Marchak's team stresses the similarity between the fishing industry and its communities and the other resource-dependent communities of British Columbia. Little attention has been focused on the freshwater fishing industry lately. One can presume that this is due to the fact that, apart from its importance for some Native communities, it is a relatively marginal activity with few communities depending upon it for their survival.

While studies of West Coast fishing highlight the similarities with other resource-dependent activities, studies of East Coast fishing appear to emphasize the unique characteristics of their communities. Although industrial capitalism has substantially affected the fishing industry since the Second World War, these changes have been laid down on a previously established traditional fishing society characterized by 'domestic commodity production.'[141] The importance of these historical differences between the East and West Coast fishing communities are seen in research done on East Coast fishing communities. While West Coast fishing communities were formed in a manner similar to resource-dependent communities, the historical foundations of East Coast fishing communities make these settlements unique. It is thus primarily East Coast fishing communities that justify the creation of a particular fishing region type. In our discussion of the fishing region type we are referring to the coastal fishing communities of eastern Quebec, New Brunswick, Prince Edward Island, Nova Scotia, and Newfoundland and Labrador.

11.2 General Trends

Kennedy has indicated that the populations of these communities are on the decline, a decline accelerated by the Northern Cod Moratorium of 1992.[142] Emigration out of these communities has increased as the inability to fish cod removed the primary economic activity of many of them. While the Atlantic Groundfish Strategy contained programs aimed at developing alternative economic activities, these programs have not very been successful at diversifying the economies of these communities. This decline is not limited to fishing communities dependent on groundfish, however, Maurice Beaudin points to the continuing 'marginalisation' of fishing communities in the Gulf of St Lawrence.[143]

The future of such communities can no longer be assured through fishing alone. What is interesting about these communities is that despite the devastating effects of the depletion of the fish, life satisfaction in these communities remains high. In research conducted before the moratorium, Felt and Sinclair found no difference between life in these poverty-ridden, high-employment communities and in Canada as a whole.[144] The reason, they argue, is the realization among these populations that although things are bad in their community, things would probably be worse for them in a large urban centre. Felt and Sinclair point out that the members of these communities recognize that there are advantages to living there – they can 'own their own residence without mortgage claims, avail themselves of a significant informal labour exchange among friends and kin, be close to family and friends as well as have access to a wide range of outdoor recreational pursuits.'[145] Without this recognition of life satisfaction, related to the historical development of these communities, their decline would be even greater than is now occurring.

11.3 Trends in Social Differentiation

Trends in social differentiation have undoubtedly been altered by the Northern Cod Moratorium. Unfortunately, there has been little research on this topic published in academic works since then. Sinclair has noted the shifts in class relations occurring in these communities before 1992. He saw the steady decline of traditional 'domestic commodity producers ... a form of production in which household members who own the means of production supply the labour to produce fish for sale ... Goods are sold in order to acquire means of subsistence ... Accumulation of capital ... is not the driving force of this economic activity.'[146] Domestic commodity producers have been replaced by the more capitalistic classes of 'petty capitalists' and 'wage workers.' Sinclair points out that competitive forces led to the increasing use of new technology in fishing, and this led to higher levels of productivity. These higher levels of productivity, combined by inadequate government management policies, led to the present collapse of the groundfish fishery. The industrialization of fishing from the 1940s to the 1980s did provide some benefits to these communities in the form of higher incomes and new jobs in fish-processing factories. As is now seen, however, these benefits were short-lived.

There has been little or no work done recently on race/ethnic differentiation in these communities. This is perhaps due to the high degree of ethnic homogeneity in Atlantic fishing communities. It is somewhat surprising that no one has looked at the changing relations between francophones and anglophones in these communities, especially in the Gaspé region and northern New Brunswick. As well, recent conflicts between Natives and non-Natives over fishing in these areas do seem to indicate that this topic may be worthy of some investigation.

Social differentiation based on gender has been the subject of considerable research. In the 1980s a debate developed between Donna Davis, whose research indicated that gender differentiation in these communities was changing, and Marilyn Porter, whose research indicated that it had not changed substantively.[147] Research published in 1992 by Sinclair and Felt supported Porter's findings. There were persistent sexual divisions of labour in the communities they studied. These sexual divisions maintained themselves despite the increasing importance of women's wage labour in fish-processing plants. According to Sinclair and Felt, the main reasons for the persistence of this phenomenon was the traditional 'fishing culture' in these communities. Research by Barbara Neis tempers these analyses somewhat in noting a shift in gender relations in these communities.[148] She sees aspects of 'familial patriarchy' as being on the decline and being altered by the 'social patriarchy' found in social welfare institutions.

12. The Northern Native Region Type

12.1 Conceptual Limitations

While the majority of the population in the more northern areas of Canada live in communities of the resource-dependent type, these areas are also characterized by communities of a very different sort: Native communities. In constructing the northern Native region type we have to be aware that there is often a close geographical and social proximity to resource-dependent communities. Despite this proximity, the obvious differences between the two necessitate the construction of this specific region type.

A problem develops over whether to differentiate between 'northern' Native communities and 'southern' Native communities. Robert

Bone has pointed out that, according to his definition of 'northern' – which includes the boreal subarctic – only about one-quarter of the Native population of Canada live in this region.[149] There is a danger in excluding other Native communities from this region type. Is there a fundamental difference between northern and southern Native communities? If so, in which category of region type should the southern Native communities be placed?

In response to these questions I hope to take a wider definition of the north than that presented by Bone. As a result, this region type will hopefully be useful in understanding the situation and the trends faced by most Native communities in Canada. It should be understood that whatever definition we choose, there are going to be internal differences among Native communities; we can never develop an 'all-inclusive' description of characteristics. As well, we have to try and highlight those characteristics that differentiate these communities from other 'region types.' In doing this we may put forward characteristics that are shared by a minority of Native communities. Still, if these characteristics are important in isolating differing trends of 'spatially based social differentiation,' they need to be highlighted.

12.2 General Trends

Many researchers have pointed out the differences between Native and non-Native communities. While there may be social and economic differences among the other region types of Canada, the differences between the northern Native region type and the others are much more profound. These differences include, in addition to the important cultural issues, a whole list of economic and social inequalities and social problems.[150] There is little academic research indicating that things have improved much over the past few years. As the Royal Commission on Aboriginal Peoples and Terry Wotherspoon's chapter in this volume both point out, serious problems continue to exist. The impact of 'mega-projects' on these Native communities has been an important issue in recent research.[151] They are typically industrial in nature and affect the communities in varying ways. While he doesn't use the term 'Fordist,' Niezen's research has indicated that the rapid introduction of Fordist-style relations has conflicted with the traditional hunting and gathering economy and traditions. This conflict has led to serious situations of social instability and the myriad social problems that and instability brings.[152]

One response to these issues is the movement for an increase in Native control of development, as seen in recent treaty negotiations and best exemplified in the Inuvialuit agreements[153] and the Nunavut accords. Such control becomes increasingly important in light of the likelihood of more developments in the future and, in particular, oil and gas developments in the more northern areas.[154]

In terms of general demographic changes, Maslove and Hawkes have pointed out that these communities have actually been growing due to high birth rates.[155] Related to these high birth rates, the populations of these communities tend to be younger than average. Educational differences between these communities and national norms tend to be large. Still, there is some evidence that the trend is towards a decrease in the rates of difference.[156]

12.3 Trends in Social Differentiation

As noted earlier, there is little research indicating that the relative socio-economic status of Native communities has improved much recently. According to Wotherspoon and Satzewich, 'In relation to non-aboriginals, aboriginal peoples have lower average incomes, lower rates of labour force participation, higher rates of unemployment, and tend to be over represented in unskilled manual-labour positions.'[157] Peter Usher and others have noted that most northern Native communities can be characterized as having a 'mixed' economy.[158] In this mixed economy 'income-in-kind' from the land through traditional economic activities and cash income from wages and social transfers are shared between community members.

Abele makes the case that this mixed economy can only be maintained through state policy measures to regulate land use and provide social transfers. In the current 'post-Fordist' climate the ability of the state to provide such measures is increasingly questioned, and thus the mixed economies of these communities are threatened. Stabler and Howe have pointed to the 'impending crisis' arising in the Northwest Territories due to the 'fiscal austerity' of governments and the reduction of social transfers.[159]

Race and ethnic relations within these communities are characterized by a high degree of homogeneity. By their nature these communities are almost always based on a common band and/or First Nation membership. Race relations become extremely important with regard to their relationships to non-Native communities. In the resource-dependent communities that tend to neighbour the northern Native communities, whether one is an Aboriginal or not is the primary source of social differentiation.[160] Conflicts over treaty rights and land use regulations almost always produce a high degree of tension between Natives and non-Natives in areas where there is a significant non-Native population.[161] Dunk's research has gone a long way towards explaining the nature of this tension from the point of view of non-Natives, indicating that it is related to both regional and class relations. Natives are perceived as the favoured group of urban-based, elite political and social interests.[162]

Research by Prattis and Chartrand has pointed to the importance of a 'cultural division of labour' in the northern Native region type. This division is a system of socio-economic 'segregation' between Natives and non-Natives whereby Natives occupy 'the bottom of the segregation system.'[163] While being negative for these communities, this cultural division of labour does at times serve to encourage the maintenance of Native culture and identity.

Gender relations have been of an increasing concern in these communities. Many of the social problems experienced there are borne especially hard by women.[164] Increasingly, Native women are forming their own organizations in order to fight not only the system of inequality characterizing Native–non-Native relations, but also the gender inequalities inherent therein.[165]

13. Conclusion

13.1 Continuing Differences

The above literature review of recent academic research shows a divergence of social, economic, demographic, and cultural trends in Canada among these six region types. The urban and urban fringe region types are experiencing high rates of both demographic and economic growth, related primarily to the 'post-industrial' sectors of the economy. The agricultural and resource-dependent region types are both experiencing slow rates of demographic and economic decline. The fishing region type was experiencing a slow decline, the rate of which seems to have increased since 1992. The northern Native region type is experiencing some demographic growth due to high rates of birth, but this growth is not mirrored in economic growth, although the movement towards greater self-government may produce this result.

Accompanying these differing regional patterns of growth are differing trends in social differentiation. The urban region type is most affected by the rise of 'post-industrialism.' It is also experiencing increasing degrees of economic inequality. Accompanying the growth of economic wealth is the growth of urban poverty, a condition linked to the social and economic dislocations caused by the decline of manufacturing. Economic growth has combined with changes in immigration laws to cause a considerable change in the ethnic and racial composition of Canada's cities. This increased diversity is causing an increase in the cultural differences between the urban region type and the others. Within the urban region type, problems related to racial and ethnic inequalities are becoming more and more visible. On the surface, gender-related social differentiation is on the decrease as 'post-industrial' tendencies seem to increase employment opportunities for women. As well, in the dynamic, constantly changing atmosphere of the urban region type, the forces of tradition are constantly being challenged.

The urban fringe region type exhibits some of the same trends in social differentiation, but is also experiencing very different ones. The socio-economic differentiation is characterized by a well-to-do exurban population and a less well-off 'native' population. The differences between these two groups is not only economic; it is also cultural as the urbane culture of the newcomers comes into conflict with the 'traditional' culture of the 'natives.' Part of this conflict is due to the spread of the new urban ethnic patterns into a previously homogeneous native population. The gender-related social differentiation is unique in that while gender relations among the native population may be more influenced by tradition than in the newcomer population, the 'suburban' nature of the newcomer population means that the 'gender differential' of this population may be closer to that of the native population than to the urban population's.

The resource-dependent region type was formed by the forces of industrialism and it remains a society dominated by these Fordist forces. While their numbers are declining, well-paid unionized blue-collar male workers remain the predominant socio-economic category in these communities. While things are changing, workers still have to deal with the control of their community by an outside multinational corporation. Increasingly, however, they also have to defend resource industrialism and do battle with the new post-industrial enemies of urban environmentalism. Lack of new immigrants to these communities has meant that their former ethnic diversity is being transformed into homogeneity. Gender relations in these communities, traditionally characterized by a strict sexual division of labour, are changing. An increase in the service sector has meant that more jobs are available for women. Still, women are not being given jobs in the resource industries, and the male-oriented blue-collar culture of these communities seem little affected by the post-industrial cultural changes found in the urban region type.

The agricultural region type is still trying to adjust itself from a competitive capitalist foundation to a Fordist restructuring. Post-industrialism seems to be absent from the economic base of this region type, although globalization is having an effect. While discussion of the effects of recent changes on the class structure within these communities is difficult due to the diversity of the situation of farmers and their employees, in general the socio-economic situation of these workers has declined when compared to that of urban and urban fringe region workers. As is the case in resource-dependent regions, because of a lack of new immigrants agricultural areas are experiencing increasing ethnic homogenization. Although farming traditions continue to place obstacles in the way of women's participation, the economic difficulties of farming have meant a fairly important increase in their involvement in farming. Within the activities exercised on the farm, however, there still exists a sexual division of labour.

Fishing communities are still having to integrate the forces, not only of Fordist industrialism, but also of competitive capitalism, with their foundation base of 'traditional' or subsistence/mercantilist capitalism. While certain post-industrial forces such as tourism may play a role in these communities, the socio-economic differentiations are based on the combination of these three previous historical periods. Fishers shift from traditional subsistence fishing to being petty capitalists to performing wage labour in fish processing plant. Perhaps because these communities have traditionally been ethnically homogeneous, social differentiation based on ethnicity is not discussed in recent research. This is not the case for social differentiation based on gender, however. Sexual divisions of labour are maintaining themselves despite the fact that the wage labour of women is of increasing importance. The traditions of the fishing culture run too deep for this change to have a significant effect on gender relations.

Northern Native communities are attempting to mix a subsistence hunting and fishing foundation with the forces of Fordist industrial resource development. All struggle to survive by combining traditional economic activities with occasional wage labour and social transfers.

The decline of these social transfers now threatens this 'mixed economy.' They continue to exist in difficult social and economic conditions, with lower rates of labour force participation and an over-representation in unskilled manual-labour positions. Tension often exists between these communities and neighbouring non-Native resource-dependent communities. Socio-economic segregation often exists between Natives and non-Natives, with Natives occupying the bottom of the segregation system. Most of the social problems existing in these communities are borne especially hard by women.

13.2 Their Explanation

While the empirical research indicates continuing spatially based social differentiation, few of the studies mentioned attempt to develop in-depth explanations of why this trend exists in Canada when it appears to be decreasing in other Western countries. The reasons appear to be complex and can not be reduced to a simple formula. Canadian political economy, and in particular staples theory, continues to provide a partial explanation.[166] As discussed earlier in the chapter much of Canada's geographic space is characterized by commodity specialization. These areas have developed political, social, and economic institutions that bear the imprint of the particular commodity that is produced. They bear not only that commodity's imprint, but also the imprint of the historical period when the demand for that commodity created development in that area.

Although all staples-producing regions were influenced by Fordism, the actual impact varied from commodity area to commodity area due to the presence of 'pre-existing' foundations. Communities based on the production of forest products and minerals were the 'most Fordist' because most came into being during the historical period characterized by these relations. Most resource-dependent communities of the Canadian Shield did not exist before the twentieth century. As a result, their foundations were based on these Fordist relations. The above discussion of recent trends in social differentiation shows that the 'particularly pure form' of relations of industrial capitalism found by Luxton in these communities in the 1970s continues to exercise a specific influence here.

In the agricultural communities of the Prairies, southern Ontario, and southern Quebec the traditional 'competitive capitalist' pre-Fordist social relations dominant in the nineteenth century continue to serve as a base for these communities in their response to the pressures of both industrialism and post-industrialism. Social differentiation continues to be influenced by 'tradition' and 'farming culture.' Similarly, the unique aspects of social differentiation found in fishing communities in Quebec and Atlantic Canada are shown to be influenced by even earlier social relations, which are still having to adjust to the pressures of competitive capitalism, Fordist industrialism, and post-industrialism.

The unique aspects of social differentiation in the northern Native region type are not as adequately explained by staples theory. Northern Native communities continue to be influenced by their traditions of subsistence hunting and gathering. While the other non-urban region types have had difficulty adapting to subsequent types of social relations, the problems for Native communities are understandably intensified because of their unique cultural conditions.

The most populous category of region types cannot be categorized according to a staple. For the purposes of understanding social differentiation, the large urban areas of Canada must represent a separate category. The social relations existing there are similar no matter what the geographical location. They are affected somewhat by prior sociohistoric periods, but the dominance of the new post-industrial relations are the most unique aspect of social differentiation. Urban fringe relations are characterized as being a combination of a unique kind of post-industrial urban and 'native' non-urban relations.

While the unique aspects of Canada's spatial trends in social differentiation can be partially explained by staples theory, other explanations have been offered in the literature that supplement this view and allow a more adequate understanding of the phenomena. As discussed earlier, Coffey and Polèse point to three main reasons why Canada has not followed the pattern of other developed countries towards urban-rural convergence.[167] The first is related to Canada's 'tertiary' economy. Their research has shown that the 'tertiary' or service sector of the economy is the most resistant to decentralization. Canada's economy is the most highly 'tertiarized' in the developed world, and as such is more resistant to this trend. The second reason involves to the physical size of Canada and its low population density. In other countries rural areas benefit from the fact that distance to a major urban area is not that great. Canada's rural areas tend to be more distant from urban areas, and as a result are less likely to benefit from decentralized urban activities that still require relations with the city. The difficulty of access, due in large part to greater distances, to more urban regions from these regions makes them less attractive than rural areas in other countries. The third reason relates to 'push' factors. According to Coffey and Polèse, life in Canada's urban centres has not degraded to the point that people want to move out of the city to escape its social problems. Keddie and Alun offer similar explanations of the absence of urban-rural convergence in Canada, but highlight the fact that Canada's rural areas do not exercise much 'pull' on urban populations.[168] The climatic, aesthetic, and social attributes of Canada's peripheral regions are such that they are not that attractive to urbanites.

Notes

1 See Peter Blau, 'Parameters of Social Structure,' in P. Blau, ed., *Approaches to the Study of Social Structure* (New York: Free Press, 1976).
2 See Kieran Bonner, 'Reflexivity, Sociology and the Rural-Urban Distinction in Marx, Tonnies and Weber,' *Canadian Review of Sociology and Anthropology* 35.2 (1998): 165–89.
3 See Robert Brym and Bonnie Fox, *From Culture to Power: The Sociology of English Canada* (Toronto: Oxford University Press, 1989).
4 For a summary of these 'transformation theories' see David Harvey, *The Condition of Postmodernity* (Cambridge: Blackwell, 1989).
5 See Berry and Weeks as quoted in Joseph Alun, Philip Keddie, and Barry Smit, 'Unravelling the Population Turnaround in Rural Canada,' *Canadian Geographer* 32.1 (1988): 17–30.
6 Ibid.
7 See Roger Gibbins, *Prairie Politics and Society: Regionalism in Decline* (Scarborough, ON: Butterworths, 1980).
8 See L.W. Kennedy, R.A. Silverman, and D.R. Forde, 'Homicide in Urban Canada: Testing the Impact of Economic Inequality and Social Disorganization,' *Canadian Journal of Sociology* 16.3 (1991): 397–410.
9 See John Goyder, 'The Canadian Syndrome of Polarities: An Obituary,' *Canadian Review of Sociology and Anthropology* 30.1 (1993): 1–12.
10 See John Britton, ed., *Canada and the Global Economy: The Geography of Structural and Technological Change* (Montreal and Kingston: McGill-Queen's University Press, 1996).
11 See J. David House, 'Knowledge-based Development in the North: New Approaches to Sustainable Development,' in J. Käkönen, ed., *Politics and Sustainable Growth in the Arctic* (Aldershot, UK: Dartmouth, 1993), 88.

12 See Ted Chambers and Mae Deans, *The Rural Renaissance in Alberta: Some Empirical Evidence* (Edmonton: University of Alberta, 1998).
13 See Benjamin Higgins, 'Foreword,' in R. Lamarche, ed., *Capitalizing on the Information Economy: A New Approach in Regional Development* (Moncton: Canadian Institute for Research on Regional Development, 1990).
14 For a more in-depth elaboration see Chris Southcott, 'The Study of Regional Inequality in Quebec and English Canada: A Comparative Analysis,' *Canadian Journal of Sociology* 24.4 (1999).
15 See Gibbins, *Prairie Politics and Society*; and Kennedy, Silverman, and Forde, 'Homicide in Urban Canada.'
16 See Robert Pahl, 'The Urban-Rural Continuum,' *Sociologia Ruralis* 6 (1966); and Keith Hoggart, 'Let's Do Away with Rural,' *Journal of Rural Studies* 6.3 (1990): 245–57.
17 See Kieran Bonner, *A Great Place to Raise Kids: Interpretation, Science, and the Urban-Rural Debate* (Montreal and Kingston: McGill-Queen's University Press, 1997).
18 See John Bryden, 'Some Preliminary Perspectives on Sustainable Rural Communities,' in John Bryden, ed., *Towards Sustainable Rural Communities* (Guelph: University School of Rural Planning and Development, 1994), 46.
19 Ibid.
20 See Ray Bollman and Brian Biggs, 'Rural and Small Town Canada: An Overview,' in R. Bollman, ed., *Rural and Small Town Canada* (Toronto: Thompson Educational Publishing, 1992).
21 Ibid., 4.
22 See Britton, *Canada and the Global Economy*, 15.
23 See William Coffey and Mario Polèse, 'Locational Shifts in Canadian Employment, 1971–1981: Decentralization v. Decongestion,' *Canadian Geographer* 32.3 (1988): 248–56.
24 See Wallace Clement and Glen Williams, eds, *The New Canadian Political Economy* (Montreal and Kingston: McGill-Queen's University Press, 1989).
25 See Wallace Clement, ed., *Understanding Canada: Building of the New Canadian Political Economy* (Montreal and Kingston: McGill-Queen's University Press, 1997).
26 See Trevor Barnes, 'External Shocks: Regional Implications of an Open Staple Economy,' in Britton, *Canada and the Global Economy*.
27 There is of course considerable variance between southern Ontario and the Prairies. Some agricultural communities of southern Ontario were established during 'pre-capitalist' times, while some prairie communities were established in conditions that could be termed 'Fordist.'
28 It should be noted that in some parts of Quebec and the Maritimes the agri-

cultural foundations were laid in a 'feudal period,' upon which were built mercantilist capitalist, competitive capitalist, and Fordist relations.

29 See Bollman, 'A Preliminary Typology of Rural Canada,' in Bryden, *Towards Sustainable Rural Communities*.
30 See Britton, *Canada and the Global Economy*, 10.
31 Ibid., 4.
32 See Serge Coulombe and Frank Lee, 'Convergence across Canadian Provinces, 1961–1991,' *Canadian Journal of Economics* 28.4a (1995): 886–98.
33 Ibid., 897.
34 See John Helliwell, 'Convergence and Migration among Provinces,' *Canadian Journal of Economics* 29 (1996): 324–30.
35 See Frank Lee, 'Convergence in Canada?' *Canadian Journal of Economics* 29 (1996): 331–36.
36 See Peter McGahan, *Urban Sociology in Canada* (Toronto: Harcourt, Brace and Co., 1995), 5.
37 See David Hay, 'Rural Canada in Transition: Trends and Developments,' in D. Hay and G. Basran, eds, *Rural Canada in Transition* (Toronto: Oxford University Press, 1992).
38 See Joseph Alun, Philip Keddie, and Barry Smit, 'Unravelling the Population Turnaround in Rural Canada,' *Canadian Geographer* 32.1 (1988): 17–30.
39 See Philip Keddie and Joseph Alun, 'Reclassification and Rural vs Urban Population Change in Canada, 1976–1981: A Tale of Two Definitions,' *Canadian Geographer* 35.4 (1991): 412–20.
40 See Philip Keddie and Joseph Alun, 'The Turnaround of the Turnaround? Rural Population Change in Canada, 1976–1986,' *Canadian Geographer* 35.4 (1991): 378.
41 See Coffey and Polèse, 'Locational Shifts in Canadian Employment,' 255.
42 Ibid.
43 See Keddie and Alun, 'Reclassification,' 419.
44 See McGahan, *Urban Sociology in Canada*.
45 It is interesting to point out, however, that all CMAs in Canada showed an increase in population during this period.
46 See McGahan, *Urban Sociology in Canada*.
47 See Michael Broadway, 'Differences in Inner City Deprivation: An Analysis of Seven Canadian Cities,' *Canadian Geographer* 36.2 (1992): 189–96.
48 See Larry Bourne, 'Normative Urban Geographies: Recent Trends, Competing Visions, and New Cultures of Regulation,' *Canadian Geographer* 40.1 (1996): 7.
49 See William Coffey, 'The Role and Location of Service Activities in the Canadian Space Economy,' in Britton, *Canada and the Global Economy*.

50 See John Britton, 'High-Tech Canada,' in Britton, *Canada and the Global Economy.*

51 See Bourne, 'Normative Urban Geographies.'

52 See Coffey and Polèse, 'Locational Shifts in Canadian Employment.'

53 See McGahan, *Urban Sociology in Canada.*

54 See Iain Wallace and Rob Shields, 'Contested Terrains: Social Space and the Canadian Environment,' in Clement, *Understanding Canada.*

55 See McGahan, *Urban Sociology in Canada.*

56 See Michael Hatfield, *Concentrations of Poverty and Distressed Neighbourhoods in Canada* (Ottawa: Human Resources Development Canada, Applied Research Branch, Working Papers Series, 1997).

57 See Zoltan Hajnal, 'The Nature of Concentrated Urban Poverty in Canada and the United States,' *Canadian Journal of Sociology* 20.4 (1995): 497–528. It should be noted that Hatfield's research indicates that 'absolute living standards in extremely poor and distressed neighbourhoods in Canada are probably above those in similarly situated neighbourhoods in USA inner cities.' Hatfield, 'Concentrations of Poverty,' 22.

58 See Hatfield, 'Concentrations of Poverty.'

59 See Ian MacLachlan and Sawada Ryo, 'Measures of Income Inequality and Social Polarization in Canadian Metropolitan Areas,' *Canadian Geographer* 41.1 (1997): 377–97.

60 See Broadway, 'Differences in Inner City Deprivation,' 189.

61 See Bourne, 319.

62 Ibid.

63 Ibid.

64 See Hajnal, 'The Nature of Concentrated Urban Poverty,' 513.

65 Ibid., 514.

66 Ibid., 518.

67 See Jane Badets, 'Canada's Immigrants: Recent Trends,' in *Canadian Social Trends,* vol. 2 (Toronto: Thompson Educational Publishing, 1994); and Ronald Logan, 'Immigration during the 1980s,' in *Canadian Social Trends,* vol. 2.

68 See Brian Ray, 'Immigrant Settlement and Housing in Metropolitan Toronto,' *Canadian Geographer* 38.3 (1994): 262–6.

69 See Joanne Moreau, 'Changing Faces: Visible Minorities in Toronto,' in *Canadian Social Trends,* vol. 2.

70 See Statistics Canada, '1996 Census: Education, Mobility and Migration,' *The Daily,* 14 April 1998.

71 See Baha Abu-Laban and Tracy Derwing, eds, *Responding to Diversity in the Metropolis: Building an Inclusive Research Agenda* (Edmonton: Prairie Centre of Excellence, 1997).

72 See Rose Olfert and Jack Stabler, 'Industrial Restructuring of the Prairie Labour Force: Spatial and Gender Impacts,' *Canadian Journal of Regional Science* 17.2 (1994): 133–52.

73 See Nahla Abdo, 'Gender Is Not a "Dummy": Research Methods in Immigration and Refugee Studies,' in Abu-Laban and Derwing, *Responding to Diversity in the Metropolis*; and Danielle Juteau, 'Gendering Immigration/ Integration Policy Research: Research Gaps,' in ibid.

74 See Juteau, 'Gendering Immigration Research.'

75 See Michael J. Troughton, 'Rural Canada and Canadian Rural Geography – An Appraisal,' *Canadian Geographer* 39.4 (1995): 296.

76 See Robert Parenteau and Louise Earl, 'Workers in the Urban Shadow,' in Bollman, *Rural and Small Town Canada*.

77 See Troughton, 'Rural Canada.'

78 Ibid., 296.

79 See Chambers and Deans, *The Rural Renaissance in Alberta*.

80 See R. Malcolm Matthew, 'The Suburbanization of Toronto Offices,' *Canadian Geographer* 37.4 (1993): 293–306.

81 See Suzanne Davies and Maurice Yeats, 'Exurbanization as a Component of Migration: A Case Study in Oxford County, Ontario,' *Canadian Geographer* 35.2 (1991): 177–86.

82 See Fred Dahms, 'The Greying of South Georgian Bay,' *Canadian Geographer* 40.2 (1996): 148–63.

83 See Coffey and Polèse, 'Locational Shifts in Canadian Employment.'

84 See Matthew, 'The Suburbanisation of Toronto Offices.'

85 See William Coffey and Rejean Drolet, 'La décentralisation des services supérieurs dans la région métropolitaine de Montréal, 1981–1989,' *Canadian Geographer* 38.3 (1994): 215–29.

86 See Christopher R. Bryant and Thomas Johnston, *Agriculture in the City's Countryside* (Toronto: University of Toronto Press, 1992).

87 See Bourne, 'Normative Urban Geographies.'

88 See Greg Halseth, *Cottage Country in Transition* (Montreal and Kingston: McGill-Queen's University Press, 1998).

89 See Stanley Barrett, *Paradise: Class, Commuters, and Ethnicity in Rural Ontario* (Toronto: University of Toronto Press, 1994).

90 See Valerie Preston and Sara McLafferty, 'Gender Differences in Commuting at Suburban and Central Locations,' *Canadian Journal of Regional Science* 26.2 (1993): 237–59.

91 Ibid., 242.

92 Rex Lucas, *Minetown, Milltown, Railtown: Life in Canada's Communities of Single Industry* (Toronto: University of Toronto Press, 1971), 14.

93 Alison Gill, 'Women in Isolated Resource Towns: An Examination of Gender Differences in Cognitive Structures,' *Geoforum* 21.3 (1990): 347–58.

94 James Randall and R.G. Ironside, 'Communities on the Edge: An Economic Geography of Resource-Dependent Communities in Canada,' *Canadian Geographer* 40.10 (1996): 17–35.

95 Keddie and Alun have pointed out the difficulty in examining population trends in these types of communities due to 'resource exploitation cycles.' See Keddie and Alun, 'Reclassification.'

96 Heather Clemenson, 'Are Single Industry Towns Diversifying?: An Examination of Fishing, Forestry and Mining Towns,' in Bollman, *Rural and Small Town Canada.*

97 Philip Ehrensaft and Jennifer Beeman, 'Distance and Diversity in Nonmetropolitan Economies,' in Bollman, *Rural and Small Town Canada.*

98 Randall and Ironside, 'Communities on the Edge.'

99 See Britton, *Canada and the Global Economy.*

100 See Roger Hayter, 'Technological Imperatives in Resource Sectors: Forest Products,' in Britton, *Canada and the Global Economy.*

101 See Iain Wallace, 'Restructuring in the Canadian Mining and Mineral-Processing Industries,' in Britton, *Canada and the Global Economy.*

102 See Virginia Maclaren, 'Redrawing the Canadian Energy Map,' in Britton, *Canada and the Global Economy.*

103 See Suzanne Mackenzie and Glenn Norcliffe, 'Restructuring in the Canadian Newsprint Industry,' *Canadian Geographer* 41.1 (1997): 2–6.

104 See House, 'Knowledge-based Development in the North.'

105 See Wallace and Shields, 'Contested Terrains.'

106 See Chris Southcott, *Resource Dependent Communities in a Post-Industrial Era* (Thunder Bay: Lakehead Centre for Northern Studies, 1999).

107 See Thomas Dunk, *It's a Working Man's Town: Male Working-Class Culture in Northwestern Ontario* (Montreal and Kingston: McGill-Queen's University Press, 1991).

108 See Southcott, *Resource Dependent Communities.*

109 See Trevor Barnes and Roger Hayter, 'The Little Town That Did,' *Regional Studies* 26 (1992): 647–63.

110 See Randall and Ironside, 'Communities on the Edge'; and Ehrensaft and Beeman, 'Distance and Diversity.'

111 See Southcott, *Resource Dependent Communities.*

112 See '1996 Census: Education, Mobility and Migration.'

113 See Meg Luxton, *More than a Labour of Love* (Toronto: Women's Press, 1980).

114 See Gill, 'Women in Isolated Resource Towns.'

115 See Randall and Ironside, 'Communities on the Edge.'

116 See Southcott, *Resource Dependent Communities*.

117 As cited in Maureen Reed, 'Seeing Trees: Engendering Environmental and Land Use Planning,' *Canadian Geographer* 41.4 (1997): 398–414.

118 See Troughton, 'Rural Canada,' 292.

119 Ibid.

120 See Olfert and Stabler, 'Industrial Restructuring of the Prairie Labour Force,' 133–52; Hay, 'Rural Canada in Transition'; and Judie McSkimmings, 'The Farm Community,' in *Canadian Social Trends*, vol. 2.

121 See Troughton, 'Rural Canada.'

122 See Charles Côté, *Désintégration des régions: Le sous-développement durable au Québec* (Chicoutimi: Édition JCL, 1991); and H. Dionne and J. Larrivée, eds, *Les villages ruraux menacés: Le pari du développement* (Rimouski: GRIDEQ, 1989).

123 See M.F. Fox, 'Canada's Agricultural and Forest Lands: Issues and Policy,' *Canadian Public Policy* 14.3 (1988): 266–81; and Mary Anne Burke, 'Loss of Prime Agricultural Land,' in C. McKie and K. Thompson, eds, *Canadian Social Trends* (Toronto: Thompson Educational Publishing, 1990).

124 See Troughton, 'Rural Canada,' 296.

125 Ibid., 297.

126 See Olfert and Stabler, 'Industrial Restructuring.'

127 See Gloria Leckie, 'Continuity and Change in the Farm Community: Brooke Township, Ontario 1965–1986,' *Canadian Geographer* 33.1 (1989): 31–45.

128 See Philip Hansen and Alicja Muszynski, 'Crisis in Rural Life and Crisis in Thinking: Directions for Critical Research,' *Canadian Review of Sociology and Anthropology* 27.1 (1990): 1–22.

129 See Lorna Erwin, 'Neo-conservatism and the Pro-family Movement,' *Canadian Review of Sociology and Anthropology* 30.3 (1993): 401–20; and Trevor Harrison and Harvey Krahn, 'Populism and the Rise of the Reform Party in Alberta,' *Canadian Review of Sociology and Anthropology* 32.2 (1995): 127–50.

130 See McSkimmings, 'The Farm Community,' 265–8.

131 See Bill Reimer, Isabelle Ricard, and Frances Shaver, 'Rural Deprivation: A Preliminary Analysis of Census and Tax Family Data,' in Bollman, *Rural and Small Town Canada*.

132 See Anthony Winson, 'In Search of the Part-Time Capitalist Farmer: Labour Use and Farm Structure in Central Canada,' *Canadian Review of Sociology and Anthropology* 33.1 (1996): 89–110.

133 See Miriam Simard, 'La régionalisation de l'immigration,' *Recherches sociographiques* 37.3 (1996): 439–69.
134 See '1996 Census: Education, Mobility and Migration.'
135 See Marcelle Dion and Steve Welsh, 'Participation of Women in the Labour Force,' in Bollman, *Rural and Small Town Canada*.
136 See Pamela Smith, *From Traps to Draggers: Domestic Commodity Production in Northeast Newfoundland, 1850–1982* (St John's: ISER, Memorial University, 1985)
137 See Gloria Leckie, 'Female Farmers in Canada and the Gender Relations of a Restructuring Agricultural System,' *Canadian Geographer* 37.3 (1993): 212–30.
138 See Frances M. Shaver, 'Women, Work and Transformations in Agricultural Production,' *Canadian Review of Sociology and Anthropology* 27.3 (1990): 341–56.
139 Here one also has to point out the existence of agricultural communities in Quebec and Acadia as early as the 16th century.
140 See Patricia Marchak, Neil Guppy, and John McMullan, eds, *Uncommon Property: The Fishing and Fish-Processing Industry in British Columbia* (Toronto: 1988); and Alicya Muszynski, *Cheap Wage Labour: Race and Gender in the Fisheries of British Columbia* (Montreal and Kingston: 1996).
141 See John C. Kennedy, 'At the Crossroads: Newfoundland and Labrador Communities in a Changing International Context,' *Canadian Review of Sociology and Anthropology* 34.3 (1997): 297–317; and Peter Sinclair, 'Atlantic Canada's Fishing Communities: The Impact of Change,' in D. Hay and G. Basran, eds, *Rural Sociology in Canada* (Toronto: Oxford University Press, 1992), 84–98.
142 See Kennedy, 'At the Crossroads.'
143 See Maurice Beaudin, 'Contrer la marginalisation des zones littorales: Les communautés de pêche du golfe du Saint-Laurent,' *Canadian Journal of Regional Science* 19.2 (1996): 161–74.
144 See Lawrence Felt and Peter Sinclair, 'Home Sweet Home: Dimensions and Determinants of Life Satisfaction in an Underdeveloped Region,' *Canadian Jounal of Sociology* 16.1 (1991): 1–21.
145 Ibid., 18.
146 See Sinclair, 'Atlantic Canada's Fishing Communities.'
147 See Peter Sinclair and Lawrence Felt, 'Separate Worlds: Gender and Domestic Labour in an Isolated Fishing Region,' *Canadian Review of Sociology and Anthropology* 29.1 (1992): 55–71; see also Martha MacDonald and P. Connelly, 'Class and Gender in Fishing Communities in Nova Scotia,' *Studies in Political Economy* 30 (1989): 61–86.

148 See Barbara Neis, 'From "Shipped Girls" to "Brides of the State": The Transition from Familial to Social Patriarchy in the Newfoundland Fishing Industry,' *Canadian Journal of Regional Science* 26.2 (1993): 185–211.

149 See Robert Bone, *The Geography of the Canadian North: Issues and Challenges* (Toronto: Oxford University Press, 1992).

150 See James S. Frideres, *Native Peoples in Canada: Contemporary Conflicts* (Scarborough: Prentice-Hall, 1988); and Terry Wotherspoon and Vic Satzewich, *First Nations: Race, Class and Gender Relations* (Scarborough: Nelson, 1993).

151 See Bone, *The Geography of the Canadian North.*

152 See Ronald Niezen, 'Power and Dignity: The Social Consequences of Hydro-electric Development for the James Bay Cree,' *Canadian Review of Sociology and Anthropology* 30.4 (1993): 510–29.

153 See Bone, *The Geography of the Canadian North.*

154 See Maclaren, 'Redrawing the Canadian Energy Map.'

155 See Allan Maslove and David Hawkes, 'The Northern Population,' in *Canadian Social Trends*, vol. 2.

156 See Wotherspoon and Satzewich, *First Nations.*

157 Ibid., 42.

158 See Frances Abele, 'Understanding What Happened Here,' in W. Clement, *Understanding Canada.*

159 See Jack Stabler and Eric Howe, 'Native Participation in Northern Development: The Impending Crisis in the NWT,' *Canadian Public Policy* 16.3 (1990): 262–83.

160 See David Stymeist, *Ethnics and Indians: Social Relations in a Northwestern Ontario Town* (Toronto: Peter Martin Associates, 1975); and Dunk, *It's a Working Man's Town.*

161 See Paul Driben, 'Fishing in Uncharted Waters: A Perspective on the Indian Fishing Agreements Dispute in Northern Ontario,' in Chris Southcott, ed., *Provincial Hinterland.*

162 See Dunk, *It's a Working Man's Town.*

163 See J. Prattis and J.P. Chartrand, 'The Cultural Division of Labour in the Canadian North: A Statistical Study of the Inuit,' *Canadian Review of Sociology and Anthropology* 27.1 (1990): 53.

164 See Wotherspoon and Satzewich, *First Nations.*

165 See Abele, 'Understanding What Happened Here.'

166 It should be pointed out that it is not surprising to find out that a theory used to define a phenomenon is found to be an explanation of that phenomenon. The tautological implications are recognized by the author.

167 See Coffey and Polèse, 'Locational Shifts in Canadian Employment.'

168 See Keddie and Alun, 'Reclassification.'

7. Differentiation, Social Policy, and Citizenship Rights

Danielle Juteau

Through the analyses and explanations provided, this book fills the gap observed by Jane Jenson in her influential article on social cohesion,[1] in which she notes that recent Canadian literature on inclusion and exclusion does not account for patterns of distribution of resources and power based on social relations such as sex/gender, race, and language. We have identified the dynamics fuelling new patterns of racialized, gendered, spatial, and age-related social differentiation in Canada. We have linked social differentiation to economic, political, and normatively determined processes that affect the life chances of individuals, produce social boundaries, and structure social categories that are attributed lower social worth. We have explored how social differentiation operates between and within groups. I will now turn to the implications that proceed from this analysis of social differentiation, outlining its broad consequences for policy analysis and policy orientations. I will indicate how the perspective favoured here ties in with the democracy tradition of social change, which in turn raises the question of citizenship rights in a pluralist setting.

1. Analysing Social Policies: The Need for a Broad Outlook

The first set of suggestions concerns policy analysis. First, the pertinence and effectiveness of a historical perspective for apprehending evolving patterns of racialized, gendered, spatial, and age-related social differentiation clearly emerges. This is why a broad outlook on the impact of social programs and policies on social differentiation and inequalities is preferred to a narrower focus on input/outcome measures.

Second, the fact that social categories are constructed and subject to change is stressed. It follows, therefore, that their very definition constitutes an object of inquiry, and that the role of policy interests in determining their boundaries should not be overlooked. That adequate answers to policy-oriented questions require that social categories be redefined is clearly indicated by Southcott's analysis of rurality and region types and Cheal's discussion of the upper boundary of 'youth.'

Third, it is strongly felt that 'general policies,' as well as those targeting specific groups, must be taken into account. While the examination of the Indian Act by Wotherspoon and of the Multiculturalism Policy by Li draws out the explicit interconnections between policy and social differentiation, Vosko's and Cheal's analyses shed light on the mechanisms through which policies deemed neutral also produce and/or reinforce various strands of differentiation. Furthermore, a detailed analysis of both types of policies indicates that while public policies alleviate social inequalities, they also engender new forms of social differentiation.

Fourth, the need to examine the public sector as a whole, and not only policies, is underlined. Government actions such as cutbacks, withholding employment opportunities, and denying income transfers (e.g., employment insurance and social assistance) have had negative consequences for the young. The effect of employment practices in the federal public service on shaping the relationship between the SER/NSER distinction and gender differentiation in the Canadian labour market also illustrate the public sector's impact.

Fifth, in view of the triadic relationship linking economic conditions, the normative order, and social policies, the analysis of social policies cannot be dissociated from conceptions of what is desirable: these conceptions provide a framework for the definition of issues, they delineate priorities and legitimize choices. The construction of the SER as a white male norm, the changing relationship between this norm and the practice of full-time, full-year work, the assimilationist component of the Indian Act, and the definition of cultural difference as fragmentation attest to this interconnection.

Sixth, a narrow approach to social policy and social change is rejected. Southcott's work on the embeddedness of rural-urban differentiations in broad historical developments and interlocking economic systems underlies this choice. Similarly, Cheal's study of age-related differentiation reveals that a limited focus on more training as well as on the relationship between education and job mismatch is inadequate. This is why he dismisses adopting a short-term bad-job labour market strategy in the expectation of life course equity, and argues for a review of the Employment Equity Act, suggesting that youth be included as a designated group.

I will now turn to policy orientations, which are, as we will see, closely connected to specific conceptions of the social order and social cohesion.

2. The Democracy Tradition of Social Cohesion and Group Monopoly

Social cohesion can be elucidated in terms of three competing theoretical traditions, each of which upholds a distinct conception of the social order.[2] The first, social cohesion theories, is rooted in a Durkheimian approach that examines the social order in terms of interdependence, shared loyalties, and solidarities. For its part, classical liberalism, which is tied to Tocquevillian liberalism, construes social order and cohesion in terms of private behaviour occurring in private institutions and networks. In the democracy tradition – the third paradigm – unequal life chances are viewed as constituting a source of conflict and, consequently, as being a major threat to social cohesion. These theoretical traditions correspond quite closely to the three paradigms, solidarity, specialization, and group monopoly, outlined in the introduction.

The perspective developed in this volume is closely related to the democracy tradition of social cohesion and to the group monopoly paradigm. Exclusion is not disassociated from socio-economic inequality, as it tends to be in the solidarity paradigm, which separates economic factors from cultural ones. Nor are actors seen as divorced from institutionalized economic and power structures, as they are in the second paradigm, which treats them as autonomous.

Here, social categories are viewed as constructed through unequal life chances and processes of differentiation and hierarchization that operate at concrete and normative levels. The individuals allocated to these categories are assigned differential worth, and this is used to justify their respective statuses as majorities and minorities.

Adopting the group monopoly paradigm and opting for the democracy tradition of social cohesion has many implications, theoretical and practical. A broader economic, political, and normatively informed analysis of diversity, which relates lack of cohesion to unequal life chances, is favoured. The sequence 'difference–fragmentation–weakened social cohesion–conflict' is discarded and replaced by a different one, 'unequal life chances–negative evaluation of salient differences–weakened social cohesion–conflict,' where conflict is ultimately linked to inequality. Differences per se are no longer the focus of attention; of import is why and when they become salient and significant. The desirability of an active, democratic government committed to policy orientations – and other measures – that will diminish social inequalities, better life chances, and produce new social identities, is stressed.

I will now turn to the concrete implications of the group monopoly paradigm and the democracy model of social cohesion in the Canadian context. Their implementation can be viewed as a process that corresponds to the extension of citizenship.

3. Mitigating Social Inequality in Canada: The Implementation of Citizenship Rights

Citizenship essentially refers to members of the community who are equal in terms of the rights and obligations associated with this status.[3] It comprises political actions and social practices[4] leading to the acquisition and exercise of citizenship rights, and to the achievement of full equality. These processes can be understood in terms of two related movements, involving the horizontal and vertical extension of citizenship rights.

Horizontal extension refers to the incorporation of formerly excluded social categories, such as women and Aboriginals. It also entails the redefinition of the boundaries of the community and, more precisely, of the criteria underlying belongingness. In the Canadian context, this means considering as 'Canadian' those who are not white, who are not Christians, and whose maternal language is neither French nor English; it requires the inclusion of visible and audible minorities as well as religious ones. This process entails a broader definition of *Canadianness*, where diversity is no longer equated with fragmentation and 'divisiveness.' The former solution of erasing differences through assimilationist policies should be completely discarded, as should all approaches that reduce the management of diversity to cultural differentiae. Essential in this context are the debates on the pluralist challenges to the universalizing concept of citizenship.

While Canada has been the site of innovative conceptions of multicultural citizenship, it must remain at the forefront in defending and implementing a pluralist view of contemporary societies. Not only must the Multiculturalism Act of 1988 be defended against right-wing opposition, it must focus on diversity rather than on static and essentialized differences. As Peter Li argues, such a response requires nothing less than a complete transformation of the normative order, in which equal worth is attributed to socially differentiated categories. The transformation of the normative order is closely related to the extension of the vertical dimension of citizenship rights. This necessitates the institutionalization of the legal, political, and social rights of citizenship.

The *legal* component of citizenship concerns fundamental rights such as freedom of speech and religion and equality before the law, which are reinforced through legislative and legal processes. It is important to note that efforts have been made in Canada to understand and implement these rights in terms of a pluralist vision that recognizes the legitimacy of diversity. From the British North America Act – and even before – to the Constitution Act and Charter of Rights and Freedoms adopted in 1982, provisions have guaranteed religious and linguistic diversity in Canada. The BNAA recognizes, for example, the educational rights of some religious minorities, namely, of Catholics and Protestants. Since 1982, article 23 of the Charter recognizes the right to instruction in a minority language. The *political* component of citizenship fosters the actualization of legal rights, namely, the right to participate in the political process, which includes the right to vote and the right to influence decision making. The importance of the political processes that foster protest and challenge the established social order is not to be underestimated. The means of influencing the political process differ according to types of groups. In the case of Aboriginals, for example, control over collective actions is important. In the new framework of Aboriginal rights, and the formal acknowledgment of these rights in the Constitution Act (section 35), land entitlements and self-determination initiatives are defined as the best means for redistributing resources and reducing inequalities between Aboriginals and non-Aboriginals. Equality requires, in this case, the recognition of rights to self-government. The extension of the political process itself, involving the participation of social actors beyond elite accommodation, as in the case of the Charlottetown accords, is also noteworthy.

While they constitute necessary conditions for equality, legal and political rights have no meaning unless all social categories possess the capacity, and thus the means, to accomplish their role in a credible manner. This is where the *social* component of citizenship comes in. Its institutionalization makes possible, as suggested by Marshall, the reduction of inequalities related to class and, I will add, to other forms of social differentiation such as those examined in this volume. Achieving de facto equality requires equal access to societal resources such as free schooling, health services, pensions, and fringe benefits. Past efforts in Canada towards equality of opportunity include the development of programs such as unemployment insurance, family allowances, pensions plans, health care, maternity leaves, transfer payments, and so on. Such measures have been recognized as insufficient, and the emphasis now rests on equality of results. This effort entails the recognition of past and present forms of discrimination, and the establishment of measures to combat them. Articles 15 and 28 of the Canadian Charter recognize that procedural equality may be insufficient to guarantee real equality and constitutionalize the legitimacy and need for affirmative action.[5]

All of the preceding indicates that Canada has adopted measures to implement differentiated legal, political, and social rights, as indicated for instance by articles 15, 28, 25, and 35 of the Charter. Nonetheless, the studies in this volume have shown that the economic circumstances of youth have deteriorated, that gender differentiation persists in the labour market, that visible minorities have lower market value, that the economic and social position of Aboriginals remains highly disadvantaged, and that fishing-, agriculture-, and resource-dependent areas experience economic decline. So where is the problem? The persistance of social inequalities lies, I submit, in the incomplete realization of social rights in Canada.

Among the many variables explored in this book, the spread of NSERs (non-standard employment relationships), which affects women, young adults, Aboriginals, and 'visible' minorities, stands out like a sore thumb. It is due in large part to factors such as the deterioration of collective bargaining and employment norms, the erosion of minimum standards legislation, and employment practices in the federal service. In retrospect, this retrogression does not come as a surprise. While Canada did develop a strategy oriented to providing a security net, it has not gone as far as some nordic countries in developing the welfare state. Consequently, it has not protected its citizens against some deleterious effects of capitalism.[6] Furthermore, since the seventies, the former synergy between economic and social policies has weakened considerably.[7] As pointed out by Maxwell,[8] the old economic and social model was stripped away as markets were permitted to make decisions. In order to achieve an inclusive and egalitarian citizenship, social rights must be emphasized and restored. This entails the expansion of SERs and real access for all to markets, public services, and income supports. State action is required to generate a greater equality of social condition, to lessen the impact of industrial restructuration, to facilitate social transfers, and to imagine new compensation systems.

In addition to having an active government intent on implementing social rights, Canada must strongly advocate a rhetoric of rights, which is now supported as the means best suited to promoting material redistribution and countering inequalities, social differentiation, and social fragmentation.[9]

In the end, social cohesion involves social justice and social equality, which entails the reduction of wealth and income disparities and the achievement of equality of opportunity and results across sex/gender, ethnic, and racialized, age-, and spatially related forms of hierarchization.[10]

Notes

1 Jane Jenson, 'Mapping Social Cohesion: The State of Canadian Research,' *Canadian Policy Research Networks* (CPRN study no. F/03), 1998: 12.
2 Ibid.
3 T.H. Marshall, 'Citizenship and Social Class,' in *Class, Citizenship, and Social Development* (New York: Doubleday, 1965 [1949]), 71–134.
4 See Danielle Juteau, 'Les enjeux de la citoyenneté: Un bilan sociologique,' in J. Black et al., eds, *Les enjeux de la citoyenneté: Un bilan interdisciplinaire* (Montréal: Immigrations et Métropoles, 1998), 47–72; Caroline Andrew, 'Ethnicities, Citizenship and Feminisms: Theorizing the Political Practices of Intersectionality,' in J. Laponce and W. Safran, eds, *Ethnicity and Citizenship – The Canadian Case* (London: Frank Cass, 1996), 64–81; Veit Bader, 'The Institutional and Cultural Conditions of Post National Citizenship,' paper presented at Social and Political Citizenship in a World of Migration congress (Institut européen de Florence, 1996); Susan James, 'The Goodenough Citizen: Female Citizenship and Independence,' in G. Bock and S. James, eds, *Beyond Equality and Difference* (London and New York: Rout-

ledge, 1992), 48–65; Yasemin N. Soysal, *Limits of Citizenship* (Chicago: University of Chicago Press, 1994); and Iris Marion Young, 'Together in Difference: Transforming the Logic of Group Political Conflict,' in W. Kymlicka, ed., *The Rights of Minority Cultures* (London: Oxford University Press, 1995), 155–76.

5 See Jenson, 'Mapping Social Cohesion,' 12.

6 See Jane Jenson and Martin Papillon, 'Le 'modèle canadien de diversité': Un répertoire en constante définition,' *Réseaux canadiens de recherche en politiques publiques*, 2001.

7 See Judith Maxwell, 'Toward a Common Citizenship: Canada's Social and Economic Choices,' *Reflexion*, no. 4, *Canadian Policy Research Networks* (CPRN) 40 (2001): 1–2.

8 Ibid., 6.

9 See Hilary Silver, 'Social Exclusion and Social Solidarity: Three Paradigms,' *International Labour Review* 133. 5–6 (1994): 27. The shift from a solidarity discourse to a rhetoric emphasizing social rights, is observed by Silver in the 1992 and 1994 European Commission reports.

10 See Judith Maxwell, 'Social Dimension of Economic Growth,' in *Eric John Hanson Memorial Lecture Series*, vol. 8 (University of Alberta, 1996): 13.

References

Abdo, Nahla. 'Gender Is Not a "Dummy": Research Methods in Immigration and Refugee Studies.' In Baha Abu-Laban and Tracy Derwing, eds, *Responding to Diversity in the Metropolis: Building an Inclusive Research Agenda*, 95–9. Edmonton: Prairie Centre of Excellence for Research on Immigration and Integration, 1997.

Abele, Frances. 'Understanding What Happened Here: The Political Economy of Indigenous Peoples.' In Clement Wallace, ed., *Understanding Canada: Building of the New Canadian Political Economy*, 118–40. Montreal and Kingston: McGill-Queen's University Press, 1997.

Abele, Frances, and Daiva Stasiulis. 'Canada as a "White Settler Colony": What about Natives and Immigrants?' In Wallace Clement and Glen Williams, eds, *The New Canadian Political Economy*, 240–77. Kingston and Montreal: McGill-Queen's University Press, 1989.

Abella, Rosalie S. *Report of the Royal Commission on Equality in Employment.* Ottawa: Minister of Supply and Services, 1984.

Abu-Laban, Baha, and Tracy Derwing, eds. *Responding to Diversity in the Metropolis: Building an Inclusive Research Agenda*. Edmonton: Prairie Centre of Excellence for Research on Immigration and Integration, 1997.

Abu-Laban, Yasmeen, and Daiva Stasiulis. 'Ethnic Pluralism under Siege: Popular and Partisan Opposition to Multiculturalism.' *Canadian Public Policy* 18.4 (1992): 365–86.

Acker, Joan. 'Class, Gender and the Relations of Distribution.' *Signs* 13.3 (1988): 473–97.

– 'Hierarchies, Jobs, Bodies: A Theory of Gendered Organizations.' *Gender and Society* 4.2 (1990): 139–58.

Adams, Howard. *Prison of Grass*. 2nd ed. Saskatoon: Fifth House Publishers, 1990.

Advisory Committee on the Changing Workplace. *Collective Reflection on the Changing Workplace*. Ottawa: Human Resources Development Canada, 1997.

Advisory Group on Working Time and the Distribution of Work. *Report of the Advisory Group on Working Time and the Distribution of Work*. Ottawa: Human Resources Development Canada, 1994.

Ahenakew, Freda, and H.C. Wolfart. *kôhkominawak otâcimowiniwâwa: Our Grandmothers' Lives as Told in Their Own Words*. Regina: Canadian Plains Research Center, 1998.

Akyeampong, E.B. 'A Statistical Portrait of the Trade Union Movement.' *Perspectives on Labour and Income*, Winter 1997.

Albo, Greg. 'The "New Realism" and Canadian Workers.' In *Canadian Politics: An Introduction*, 471-504. Toronto: Broadview Press: 1990.

Alexander, Jeffrey C., and Paul Colomy, eds. *Differentiation Theory and Social Change: Comparative and Historical Perspectives*. New York: Columbia University Press, 1990.

Alexander, T.J. 'Human Capital Investment: Building the "Knowledge Economy."' *Policy Options* 18.6 (1997): 5–8.

Allain, Jane, and Elaine Gardner O'Toole. 'Aboriginal Rights.' *Current Issue Review* 89-11E. Ottawa: Library of Parliament Research Branch, Minister of Supply and Services Canada, 1995.

Alun, Joseph, Philip Keddie, and Barry Smit. 'Unravelling the Population Turnaround in Rural Canada.' *Canadian Geographer* 32.1 (1988): 17–30.

Amit-Talai, Vered. 'The Minority Circuit: Identity Politics and the Professionalization of Ethnic Activism.' In Vered Amit-Talai and Caroline Knowles, eds, *Re-situating Identities: The Politics of Race, Ethnicity, Culture*, 89–114. Peterborough, ON: Broadview Press, 1996.

Anderson, Robert B. 'The Business Economy of the First Nations in Saskatchewan: A Contingency Perspective.' *Canadian Journal of Native Studies* 15.2 (1995): 309–46.

Andrew, Caroline. 'Ethnicities, Citizenship and Feminisms: Theorizing the Political Practices of Intersectionality.' In J. Laponce and W. Safran, eds, *Ethnicity and Citizenship – The Canadian Case*. London: Frank Cass, 1996.

Angus, Murray. *'And the Last Shall Be First': Native Policy in an Era of Cutbacks*. Toronto: NC Press Ltd., 1991.

Angus Reid Group. *Multiculturalism and Canadians: Attitude Study 1991 National Survey Report*. Report submitted to Multiculturalism and Citizenship Canada, 1991.

Anker, Richard. *Gender and Jobs*. Geneva: ILO, 1998.

Anthias, Floya, and Nira Yuval-Davis. *Racialised Boundaries: Gender, Race, Nation, Colour and Class and the Anti-racist Struggle.* London: Routledge, 1992.

Arat-Koc, Sedef. '"Importing Housewives": Non-Citizen Domestic Workers and the Crisis of the Domestic Sphere in Canada.' In Meg Luxton, Harriet Rosenberg, and Sedef Arat-Koc, eds, *Through the Kitchen Window*, 81–103. Toronto: Garamond, 1990.

Archambault, Richard, and Louis Grignon. *Decline in the Youth Participation since 1990: Structural or Cyclical?* Ottawa: Human Resources Development Canada, 1999.

Archibald, Kathleen. *Sex and the Public Service.* Ottawa: Ministry of Supply and Services, 1970.

Armstrong, Patricia. 'The Feminization of the Labour Force: Harmonizing Down in a Global Economy.' In I. Bakker, ed., *Rethinking Restructuring: Gender and Change in Canada*, 29–54. Toronto: University of Toronto Press, 1996.

Armstrong, Patricia, and Hugh Armstrong. 'The Segregated Participation of Women in the Canadian Labour Force, 1941–1971.' *Canadian Review of Sociology and Anthropology* 12.4 (1975): 369–84.

– *The Double Ghetto.* 3rd ed. Toronto: McClelland and Stewart, 1994.

Armstrong, R., J. Kennedy, and P.R. Oberle. *University Education and Economic Well-Being: Indian Achievement and Prospects.* Ottawa: Indian and Northern Affairs Canada, 1990.

Arthurs, H. 'Developing Industrial Citizenship: A Challenge for Canada's Second Century.' *Canadian Bar Review* 45 (1967): 786–830.

Assembly of First Nations. *Breaking the Chains: First Nations Literacy and Self-Determination.* Ottawa: Assembly of First Nations, 1994.

– *First Nations Issues Survey – Full Report.* Ottawa: Assembly of First Nations, 1998.

– *National Overview of First Nations Child Care in Canada.* Ottawa: Assembly of First Nations, 1995.

Association of Universities and Colleges of Canada. 'Making the Transition: No Two Paths Alike.' *Research File* 2.4 (1998): 1–11.

Atimoyoo, Erland. 'Representation and Political Decision-Making in a Cree Perspective.' Unpublished MA non-thesis project, Department of Sociology, University of Saskatchewan, 1998.

Avery, Donald. *Reluctant Host: Canada's Response to Immigrant Workers, 1896–1994.* Toronto: McClelland and Stewart, 1995.

Awasis Agency of Northern Manitoba. *First Nations Family Justice: Mee-noo-stahtan Mi-ni-si-win.* Thompson: Awasis Agency of Northern Manitoba, 1997.

Backhouse, Constance. *Petticoats and Prejudice: Women and the Law in Nineteenth-Century Canada.* Toronto: Women's Press, 1991.

Bader, Veit. 'The Institutional and Cultural Conditions of Post National Citizenship.' Paper presented at Social and Political Citizenship in a World of Migration congress, Institut européen de Florence, 1996.

Badets, Jane. 'Canada's Immigrants: Recent Trends.' In *Canadian Social Trends*, vol. 2 Toronto: Thompson Educational Publishing, 1994.

Baer, Douglas, Edward Grabb, and William Johnston. 'National Character, Regional Culture, and the Values of Canadians and Americans.' *Canadian Review of Sociology and Anthropology* 30.1 (1993): 13–36.

Baigent, Jim, et al. *A Report to the Honourable Moe Shihota Minister of Labour: Recommendations for Labour Law Reform.* British Columbia, 1992.

Banting, Keith, Charles Beach, and Gordon Betcherman. 'Polarization and Social Policy Reform.' In Keith Banting and Charles Beach, eds, *Labour Market Polarization and Social Policy Reform*, 1–19. Kingston: Queen's University School of Policy Studies, 1995.

Banton, Michael. 'Analytical and Folk Concepts of Race and Ethnicity.' *Ethnic and Racial Studies* 2.2 (1979): 127–38.

Barnes, Trevor. 'External Shocks: Regional Implications of an Open Staple Economy.' In John Britton, ed., *Canada and the Global Economy: The Geography of Structural and Technological Change*, 48–68. Montreal and Kingston: McGill-Queen's University Press, 1996.

Barnes, Trevor, and Roger Hayter. 'The Little Town That Did.' *Regional Studies* 26 (1992): 647–63.

Barr-Telford, Lynn, Geoff Bowlby, and Warren Clark. *The Class of 86 Revisited.* Ottawa: Statistics Canada, 1996.

Barrett, Stanley. *Paradise: Class, Commuters, and Ethnicity in Rural Ontario.* Toronto: University of Toronto Press, 1994.

Barsh, Russell Lawrence. 'Canada's Aboriginal Peoples: Social Integration or Disintegration?' *Canadian Journal of Native Studies* 14.1 (1994): 1–46.

Bartlett, Richard H. *Indians and Taxation in Canada.* Revised 3rd ed. Saskatoon: University of Saskatchewan Native Law Centre, 1992.

Basran, Gurcharn, and Li Zong. 'Devaluation of Foreign Credentials as Perceived by Non-White Professional Immigrants.' *Canadian Ethnic Studies* 30 (1998): 6–23.

Battiste, Marie. 'Enabling the Autumn Seed: Toward a Decolonized Approach to Aboriginal Knowledge, Language and Education.' *Canadian Journal of Native Education* 22.1 (1998): 16–27.

Beaudin, Maurice. 'Contrer la marginalisation des zones littorales: Les communautés de pêche du golfe du Saint-Laurent.' *Canadian Journal of Regional Science* 19.2 (1996): 161–74.

Beaudry, Paul, and David Green. *Cohort Patterns in Canadian Earnings: Assessing the Role of Skill Premia in Inequality Trends.* Toronto: Canadian Institute for Advanced Research, Working paper no. 96, 1997.

Bedford, David. 'Marxism and the Aboriginal Question: The Tragedy of Progress,' *Canadian Journal of Native Studies* 14.1 (1994): 101–17.

Bélanger, Alain, and Jean Dumas. *Report on the Current Demographic Situation in Canada 1997. Current Demographic Analysis.* Ottawa: Minister of Industry, Science and Technology, 1998.

Belous, Richard. 'How Human Resource Systems Adjust to the Shift toward Contingent Workers.' *Monthly Labour Review,* March 1989: 7.

Bernier, Rachel. *The Dimensions of Wage Inequality among Aboriginal Peoples.* Ottawa: Statistics Canada, Analytical Studies Branch, Research Paper Series no. 109, December 1998.

Betcherman, Gordon, and Norman Leckie. *Age Structure of Employment in Industries and Occupations.* Ottawa: Human Resources Development Canada, Applied Research Branch, Research Paper Series R-96-7E, 1995.

Betcherman, Gordon, and Graham Lowe. *The Future of Work in Canada.* Ottawa: Canadian Policy Research Networks and Renouf, 1997.

Betcherman, Gordon, and René Morissette. *Recent Youth Labour Market Experiences in Canada.* Ottawa: Statistics Canada, Analytical Studies Branch, Research Paper Series no. 63, 1994.

Bienvenue, Rita M. 'Colonial Status: The Case of Canada's Indians.' In Rita M. Bienvenue and J.E. Goldstein, eds, *Ethnicity and Ethnic Relations in Canada: A Book of Readings,* 199–214. Toronto: Butterworths, 1985.

Biggs, Brian, and Ray Bollman. 'Urbanization in Canada's Population.' In *Canadian Social Trends,* vol. 2 (Toronto: Thompson Educational Publishing, 1994), 67–72.

Bird, F., et al. *Report of the Royal Commission on the Status of Women.* Ottawa: Ministry of Supply and Services, 1970.

Black Elk, Frank. 'Observations on Marxism and Lakota Tradition.' In W. Churchill, ed., *Marxism and Native Americans,* 137–57. Boston: South End Press, 1983.

Blanchflower, David, and Richard Freeman. 'Why Youth Unemployment Will Be Hard to Reduce.' *Policy Options* 19.3 (1998): 3–7.

Blau, Peter. 'Parameters of Social Structure.' In Peter Blau, ed., *Approaches to the Study of Social Structure,* 220–53. New York: Free Press, 1975.

Blishen, Bernard, and Tom Atkinson. *Regional and Status Differences in Canadian Values.* Toronto: Institute of Behavioural Research, York University, 1981.

Blomström, Magnus, and Björn Hettne. *Development Theory in Transition.* London: Zed Books, 1984.

Blossfeld, Helen, and Catherine Hakim, eds. *Between Equalization and Marginal-*

ization: Women Working Part-Time in Europe and the USA. Oxford: Oxford University Press, 1997.

Boldt, Menno. *Surviving as Indians: The Challenge of Self-Government.* Toronto: University of Toronto Press, 1993.

Bollman, Ray. 'A Preliminary Typology of Rural Canada.' In John Bryden, ed., *Towards Sustainable Rural Communities,* 1–44. Guelph, ON: University School of Rural Planning and Development, 1994.

Bollman, Ray, and Brian Biggs. 'Rural and Small Town Canada: An Overview.' In Roy Bollman, ed., *Rural and Small Town Canada.* Toronto: Thompson Educational Publishing, 1992.

Bone, Robert. *The Geography of the Canadian North: Issues and Challenges.* Toronto: Oxford University Press, 1992.

Bonner, Kieran. *A Great Place to Raise Kids: Interpretation, Science, and the Urban-Rural Debate.* Montreal and Kingston: McGill-Queen's University Press, 1997.

– 'Reflexivity, Sociology and the Rural-Urban Distinction in Marx, Tonnies and Weber.' *Canadian Review of Sociology and Anthropology* 35.2 (1998): 165–89.

Bourne, Larry. 'Are New Urban Forms Emerging?' *Canadian Geographer* 33.4 (1989): 312–28.

– 'Normative Urban Geographies: Recent Trends, Competing Visions, and New Cultures of Regulation.' *Canadian Geographer* 40.1 (1996): 2–16.

Bowlby, Geoff. 'Relationship between Postsecondary Graduates' Education and Employment.' *Education Quarterly Review* 3.2 (1996): 35–44.

Boyd, Monica, and Edward Pryor. 'Young Adults Living in Their Parents' Homes.' *Canadian Social Trends* 13 (1989): 17–20.

Brady, Patrick. 'Native Dropouts and Non-Native Dropouts in Canada: Two Solitudes or a Solitude Shared?' *Journal of American Indian Education* 35.2 (Winter 1996): 10–20.

Breton, Raymond. 'Intergroup Competition in the Symbolic Construction of Canadian Society.' In Peter S. Li, ed., *Race and Ethnic Relations in Canada,* 2nd ed., 291–310. Toronto: Oxford University Press, 1999.

– 'The Production and Allocation of Symbolic Resources: An Analysis of the Linguistic and Ethnocultural Fields in Canada.' *Canadian Review of Sociology and Anthropology* 21.2 (1984): 123–44.

Brittan, Arthur, and Mary Maynard. *Sexism, Racism and Oppression.* New York: Basil Blackwell, 1985.

Britton, John. 'High-Tech Canada.' In Britton, ed., *Canada and the Global Economy,* 255–72.

Britton, John, ed. *Canada and the Global Economy: The Geography of Structural and Technological Change.* Montreal and Kingston: McGill-Queen's University Press, 1996.

Broad, David. 'The Casualization of Labour Force.' In A. Duff, D. Glenday, and

N. Pupo, eds, *Good Jobs, Bad Jobs, No Jobs: The Transformation of Work in the 21st Century.* Toronto: Harcourt Brace, 1997.

Broad, David, and Della McNeill. 'A Matter of Control: Saskatchewan Labour Standards and Part-Time Work.' Occasional paper, Social Administration Research Unit, University of Regina, 1995.

Broadway, Michael. 'Differences in Inner City Deprivation: An Analysis of Seven Canadian Cities.' *Canadian Geographer* 36.2 (1992): 189–96.

Brock, Kathy. 'Aboriginal People: First Nations.' In A.F. Johnson and A. Stritch, eds, *Canadian Public Policy: Globalization and Political Parties*, 189–211. Toronto: Copp Clark, 1997.

Brooks, A. 'Myth and Muddle – An Examination of Contracts for the Performance of Work.' *University of New South Wales Law Journal* 11.2 (1988).

Bryant, Christopher R., and Thomas Johnston. *Agriculture in the City's Countryside.* Toronto: University of Toronto Press, 1992.

Bryden, John, ed. *Towards Sustainable Rural Communities.* Guelph, ON: University School of Rural Planning and Development, 1994.

Brym, Robert, and Bonnie Fox. *From Culture to Power: The Sociology of English Canada.* Toronto: Oxford University Press, 1989.

Buckley, Helen. *From Wooden Ploughs to Welfare: Why Indian Policy Failed in the Prairie Provinces.* Montreal and Kingston: McGill-Queen's University Press, 1992.

Burke, Mary Anne. 'Loss of Prime Agricultural Land.' In Craig McKie and Keith Thompson, eds, *Canadian Social Trends*, 50–1. Toronto: Thompson Educational Publishing, 1990.

Cairns, Alan, C. *Citizens Plus: Aboriginal Peoples and the Canadian State*, Vancouver: UBC Press, 2000.

Calliste, Agnes. 'Race, Gender and Canadian Immigration Policy: Blacks from the Caribbean 1900–1932.' *Journal of Canadian Studies* 28.4 (1993): 131–50.

Cameron, Barbara. 'From Segmentation to Solidarity: A New Framework for Labour Market Regulation.' In D. Drache and A. Ranikin, eds, *Warm Heart, Cold Country: Fiscal and Social Policy Reform in Canada*, 193–212. Ottawa: Caledon Institute of Social Policy / Robarts Centre for Canadian Studies, 1995.

Campbell, Robert M. *The Full-Employment Objective in Canada, 1945–85: Historical, Conceptual, and Comparative Perspectives.* Ottawa: Economic Council of Canada, 1991.

Canadian Council on Social Development. 'Executive Summary: CCSD Response to Bill C-12, An Act Respecting Employment Insurance in Canada.' Submitted to the Standing Committee on Human Resource Development, 1996.

Canadian Labour Congress. 'Federal Budget 1995: Canadian Labour Congress Analysis.' Unpublished brief. 27 February 1995.

Canadian Youth Foundation. *Youth Unemployment: Canada's Hidden Deficit.* Ottawa: Canadian Youth Foundation, 1995.

'Canadians Showing Signs of Cultural Insecurity.' *Globe and Mail,* 11 March 1994, A6.

'Canadians Want Mosaic to Melt, Survey Finds.' *Globe and Mail,* 14 December 1993, A1, A2.

Carby, Hazel. 'White Woman Listen! Black Feminism and the Boundaries of Sisterhood.' In *The Empire Strikes Back: Race and Racism in 70's Britain,* 212–35. Edited by the Centre for Contemporary Cultural Studies, University of Birmingham. London: Hutchinson, 1982.

Card, David, and Thomas Lemieux. *Adapting to Circumstances: The Evolution of Work, School, and Living Arrangements among North American Youth.* Cambridge, MA: National Bureau of Economic Research, 1997.

Cardinal, Harold. *The Rebirth of Canada's Indians.* Edmonton: Hurtig Publishers, 1977.

Carrington, Peter. 'Trends in Youth Crime in Canada, 1977–1996.' *Canadian Journal of Criminology* 41.1 (January 1999): 1–32.

Carter, Sarah. 'Categories and Terrains of Exclusion: Constructing the "Indian Woman" in the Early Settlement Era in Western Canada.' In K.S. Coates and R. Fisher, eds, *Out of the Background: Readings on Canadian Native History,* 177–95. Toronto: Copp Clark, 1995.

Centre for Contemporary Cultural Studies (University of Birmingham). *The Empire Strikes Back: Race and Racism in 70's Britain.* London: Hutchinson, 1982.

Chambers, Ted, and Deans Mae. *The Rural Renaissance in Alberta: Some Empirical Evidence.* Edmonton: University of Alberta Western Centre for Economic Research, 1998.

Chamie, Nicholas. *Why the Jobless Recovery: Youth Abandon Labour Market.* Ottawa: Conference Board of Canada, 1995.

Chapman, Ian, Don McCaskill, and David Newhouse. 'Management in Contemporary Aboriginal Organizations.' *Canadian Journal of Native Studies* 11.2 (1991): 333–49.

Cheal, David. 'Repenser les transferts intergénérationnels.' In Claudine Attias-Donfut, ed., *Les solidarités entre générations,* 259–68. Paris: Nathan, 1995.

– *New Poverty.* Westport, CT: Greenwood, 1996.

Cheal, David, and Karen Kampen. 'Poor and Dependent Seniors in Canada.' *Ageing and Society* 18.2 (1998): 147–66.

Chiste, Katherine Beaty. 'The Aboriginal Small Business Community.' In K.B. Chiste, ed., *Aboriginal Small Business and Entrepreneurship in Canada,* 4–31. North York, ON: Captus Press, 1996.

Churchill, Ward. 'Marxism and the Native American.' In W. Churchill, ed., *Marxism and Native Americans*, 183–203. Boston: South End Press, 1983.

Clemenson, Heather. 'Are Single Industry Towns Diversifying? An Examination of Fishing, Forestry and Mining Towns.' In Ray Bollman, ed., *Rural and Small Town Canada*, 151–65. Toronto: Thompson Educational Publishing, 1992.

Clement, Wallace, ed. *Understanding Canada: Building of the New Canadian Political Economy*. Montreal and Kingston: McGill-Queen's University Press, 1997.

Clement, Wallace, and Glen Williams, eds. *The New Canadian Political Economy*. Montreal and Kingston: McGill-Queen's University Press, 1989.

Cockburn, Cynthia. *In the Way of Women: Men's Resistance to Sex Equality in Organizations*. Ithaca, NY: ILR Press, 1991.

Coffey, William. 'The Role and Location of Service Activities in the Canadian Space Economy.' In John Britton, ed., *Canada and the Global Economy: The Geography of Structural and Technological Change*, 335–51. Montreal and Kingston: McGill-Queen's University Press, 1996.

Coffey, William, and Rejean Drolet. 'La décentralisation des services supérieurs dans la région métropolitaine de Montréal, 1981–1989.' *Canadian Geographer* 38.3 (1994): 215–29.

Coffey, William, and Mario Polèse. 'Locational Shifts in Canadian Employment, 1971–1981: Decentralization v. Decongestion.' *Canadian Geographer* 32.3 (1988): 248–56.

Coish, David. 'The Wage Gap between Men and Women: An Update.' Catalogue 750002MPE95014. Ottawa: Statistics Canada, Income Research Paper Series, 1995.

Colin, Lindsay, Mary Sue Deveraux, and Micheal Bergob. *Youth in Canada*. Ottawa: Statistics Canada, 1994.

Comeau, Pauline, and Aldo Santin. *The First Canadians: A Profile of Canada's Native People Today*. 2nd ed. Toronto: James Lorimer and Co., 1995.

Common, Ron. 'A Search for Equity: A Policy Analysis of First Nations Representation on School Boards.' *Education Canada* 31.3 (Fall 1991): 4–7.

Compara Ministerial Task Force on Youth. *Take on the Future*. Ottawa: Government of Canada, 1996.

Conrad, Margaret, Alvin Finkel, and Cornelius Jaenen. *History of the Canadian Peoples*. Volume 1. *Beginnings to 1867*. Toronto: Copp Clark Pitman, 1993.

Conseil des affaires sociales. *Deux Québecs dans un: Rapport sur le développement social et démographique*. Boucherville: Gaëtan Morin, 1989.

Conseil permanent de la jeunesse (dir.) *Actes du colloque 'Jeunes adultes et précarité: Contraintes et alternatives.'* 62nd convention of l'Association canadienne-française pour l'avancement des sciences, Montreal, May 1994. Quebec: Gouvernement du Québec, 1995.

Corak, Miles. 'Introduction.' In Miles Corak, ed., *Labour Markets, Social Institutions, and the Future of Canada's Children*, 1–9. Ottawa: Statistics Canada, 1998.

– 'Unemployment Comes of Age: The Demographics of Labour Sector Adjustment in Canada.' In Surendra Gera, ed., *Canadian Unemployment: Lessons from the 80s and Challenges for the 90s*, 89–97. Ottawa: Supply and Services Canada, 1991.

Côté, Charles. *Désintégration des régions: Le sous-développement durable au Québec*. Chicoutimi: Édition JCL, 1991.

Côté, Lise, Christine Ross, Jocelyne Pronovost, and Richard Boyer. *Les comportements suicidaires chez les jeunes québécois de 15 à 24 ans*. Montreal: Santé Québec, 1992.

Coulombe, Serge, and Frank Lee. 'Convergence across Canadian Provinces, 1961–1991.' *Canadian Journal of Economics* 28.4a (1995): 886–98.

Courchene, Thomas J., and Lisa M. Powell. *A First Nations Province*. Kingston, ON: Institute of Intergovernmental Relations, Queen's University, 1992.

Couvrette, Christian. 'La cité ethnique: l'institutionnalisation de la différence.' *Recherches sociographiques* 35.3 (1994): 455–76.

Creese, Gillian. 'Gender Equity or Masculine Privilege? Union Strategies and Economic Restructuring in a White Collar Union.' *Canadian Journal of Sociology* 20.2 (1995): 143–66.

– 'Gendering Collective Bargaining: From Men's Rights to Women's Issues.' *Canadian Review of Sociology and Anthropology* 33.4 (1996): 437–56.

– 'Power and Pay: The Union and Equal Pay at B.C. Electric/Hydro.' *Labour / Le Travail* 32 (1993): 225–45.

– 'Sexual Equality and the Minimum Wage in B.C.' *Journal of Canadian Studies* 26 (1991): 120–40.

Crompton, Suzan. 'The Renaissance of Self-employment.' *Perspectives on Labour and Income*, Summer 1993: 22–32.

Crompton, Suzan and Michael Vickers. 'One Hundred Years of Labour Force.' *Canadian Social Trends* 57 (2000): 2–13.

Dagenais, Lucie. 'La jeunesse: Une construction du discours sociopolitique canadien de 1965 à 1989.' *Sociologie et sociétés* 28.1 (1996): 89–105.

Dahms, Fred. 'The Greying of South Georgian Bay.' *Canadian Geographer* 40.2 (1996): 148–63.

Dai, S.Y., and M.V. George. *Projections of Visible Minority Population Groups, Canada, Provinces and Regions, 1991–2016*. Statistics Canada, Catalogue 91-541-XPE. Ottawa: Ministry of Industry, 1996.

Daniels, Doug. 'The Coming Crisis in the Aboriginal Rights Movement: From

Colonialism to Neo-colonialism to Renaissance.' *Native Studies Review* 2.2 (1986): 97–115.

Daniels, Harry W., ed. *The Forgotten People: Métis and Non-status Indian Land Claims.* Ottawa: Native Council of Canada, 1979.

Davies, Scott, Clayton Mosher, and Bill O'Grady. 'Trends in Labour Market Outcomes of Canadian Post-Secondary Graduates, 1978–1988.' In Lorna Erwin and David MacLennan, eds, *Sociology of Education in Canada*, 352–69. Toronto: Copp Clark Longman, 1994.

Davies, Suzanne, and Maurice Yeats. 'Exurbanization as a Component of Migration: A Case Study in Oxford County, Ontario.' *Canadian Geographer* 35.2 (1991): 177–86.

Deniger, Marc-André. 'Crise de la jeunesse et transformations des politiques sociales en contexte de mutation structurale.' *Sociologie et sociétés* 28.1 (1996): 73–88.

– 'Une jeunesse paupérisée.' *Apprentissage et socialisation* 14.1 (1991): 11–17.

Denis, Claude. *We Are Not You: First Nations and Canadian Modernity.* Peterborough, ON: Broadview Press, 1997.

Denton, Frank, Peter Pineo, and Byron Spencer. *The Demographics of Employment.* Ottawa: Institute for Research on Public Policy, 1991.

Dion, Marcelle, and Steve Welsh. 'Participation of Women in the Labour Force: A Comparison of Farm Women and All Women in Canada.' In Roy Bollman, ed., *Rural and Small Town Canada*, 225–44. Toronto: Thompson Educational Publishing, 1992.

Dionne, H., and J. Larrivée, eds. *Les villages ruraux menacés: Le pari du développement.* Rimouski: GRIDEQ, 1989.

Driben, Paul. 'Fishing in Uncharted Waters: A Perspective on the Indian Fishing Agreements Dispute in Northern Ontario.' In Chris Southcott, ed., *Provincial Hinterland: Social Inequality in Northwestern Ontario*, 89–102. Halifax: Fernwood, 1993.

Drolet, Marie. 'The Persistant Gap: New Evidence on the Canadian Gender Wage Gap.' Catalogue 75F0002MIE99008. Ottawa: Statistics Canada, Income Research Paper Series, 1999.

Drolet, Marie, and René Morissette. *The Upward Mobility of Low Paid Canadians: 1993–1995.* Ottawa: Statistics Canada, Income and Labour Dynamics, Working Paper Series no. 75F0002MIE, 1998.

– *Working More? Working Less? What Do Canadian Workers Prefer?* Ottawa: Statistics Canada, Analytical Studies Branch, Research Paper Series no.104, 1997.

Drost, Helman, Brian Lee Crowley, and Richard Schwindt. *Market Solutions for Native Poverty.* Toronto: C.D. Howe Institute, 1995.

Duchesne, Doreen. 'Working Overtime in Today's Labour Market.' *Perspectives on Labour and Income*, Winter 1997: 9–15.

Duffy, Anne, and Norene Pupo. *The Part-time Paradox*. Toronto: McClelland and Stewart, 1992.

Dulude, Louise. *Seniority and Employment Equity for Women*. Kingston: Industrial Relations Centre, Queen's University, 1995.

Dunk, Thomas. *It's a Working Man's Town: Male Working-Class Culture in Northwestern Ontario*. Montreal: McGill-Queen's University Press, 1991.

Dunk, Thomas, Stephen McBride, and Randle Nelsen. *The Training Trap*. Halifax: Fernwood, 1996.

Dupuis, Renée. *Tribus, peuples et nations: Les nouveaux enjeux des revendications autochtones au Canada*. Quebec: Les Éditions du Boréal, 1997.

Dust, Theresa M. *The Impact of Aboriginal Land Claims and Self-Government on Canadian Municipalities: The Local Government Perspective*. Toronto: ICURR Press, 1995.

Economic Council of Canada. *Good Jobs, Bad Jobs: Employment in the Service Economy*. Ottawa: Ministry of Supply and Services, 1990.

Ehrensaft, Philip, and Jennifer Beeman. 'Distance and Diversity in Non-metropolitain Economies.' In Ray Bollman, ed., *Rural and Small Town Canada*, 193–224. Toronto: Thompson Educational Publishing, 1992.

Elliott, David W. 'Aboriginal Title.' In B.W. Morse, ed., *Aboriginal Peoples and the Law*, 48–121. Ottawa: Carleton University Press, 1985.

Emberley, Julia. 'Aboriginal Women's Writing and the Cultural Politics of Representation.' In C. Miller and P. Chuchryk, eds, *Women of the First Nations: Power, Wisdom, and Strength*, 97–112. Winnipeg: University of Manitoba Press, 1996.

Empson-Warner, Susan, and Harvey Krahn. 'Unemployment and Occupational Aspirations: A Panel Study of High School Graduates.' *Canadian Review of Sociology and Anthropology* 29.1 (1992): 38–54.

Erwin, Lorna. 'Neo-conservatism and the Pro-family Movement.' *Canadian Review of Sociology and Anthropology* 30.3 (1993): 401–20.

Esping-Andersen, Gøsta. 'After the Golden Age? Welfare State Dilemmas in a Global Economy.' In G. Esping-Andersen, ed., *Welfare States in Transition*, 1–31. London: Sage, 1996.

Federation of Saskatchewan Indian Nations. 'Positive-Sum Solutions in a World of Trade-Offs?' In Gøsta Esping-Andersen, ed., *Welfare States in Transition*, 256–67. London: Sage, 1996.

– *Saskatchewan and Aboriginal Peoples in the 21st Century: Social, Economic and Political Changes and Challenges*. Regina: PrintWest Publishing Services, 1997.

Felt, Lawrence, and Peter Sinclair. 'Home Sweet Home: Dimensions and Determinants of Life Satisfaction in an Underdeveloped Region.' *Canadian Journal of Sociology* 16.1 (1991): 1–21.

Finkel, Alvin. *Business and Social Reform in the Thirties*. Toronto: Lorimer, 1979.

– 'Trade Unions and the Welfare State in Canada, 1945–1990.' In C. Gonick, P. Phillips, and J. Vorst, eds, *Labour Gains, Labour Pains: 50 Years of PC 1003*, 59–73. Winnipeg: Society for Socialist Studies / Fernwood Publishing, 1996.

Finnie, Ross. *Earnings Dynamics in Canada: The Earnings Mobility of Canadians 1982–1992*. Ottawa: Human Resources Development Canada, Applied Research Branch, Working Paper Series W-97-3E.a, 1997.

– *Earnings Dynamics in Canada: The Distribution of Earnings in a Dynamic Context, 1982–1992*. Ottawa: Human Resources Development Canada, Applied Research Branch, Working Paper Series W-97-3E.b, 1997.

– *Earnings Dynamics in Canada: Earnings Patterns by Age and Sex in Canada, 1982–1992*. Ottawa: Human Resources Development Canada, Applied Research Branch, Research Paper Series R-97-11E, 1997.

Finnie, Ross, and Gaétan Garneau.'An Analysis of Student Borrowing for Postsecondary Education.' *Canadian Business Economics* 4.2 (1996): 51–64.

– 'Student Borrowing for Postsecondary Education.' *Education Quarterly Review* 3.2 (1996): 10–34.

Finnie, Ross, and Saul Schwartz. *Student Loans in Canada*. Toronto: C.D. Howe Institute, 1996.

Fischer, Frank, and John Forester. 'Editors' Introduction.' In F. Fischer and J. Forester, eds, *The Argumentative Turn in Public Policy Analysis and Planning*, 1–17. Durham, NC: Duke University Press, 1993.

Fiske, Joanne. 'Native Women in Reserve Politics: Strategies and Struggles.' *Journal of Legal Pluralism* 30 (1990): 121–37.

Flanagan, Tom. *First Nations? Second Thoughts*. Montreal: McGill-Queen's University Press, 2000.

Fleras, Augie. 'The Politics of Jurisdiction: Indigenizing Aboriginal–State Relations.' In D.A. Long and O.P. Dickason, eds, *Visions of the Heart: Canadian Aboriginal Issues*, 147–77. Toronto: Harcourt Brace, 1996.

Fleras, Augie, and Jean Leonard Elliott. *The Nations Within: Aboriginal–State Relations in Canada, the United States, and New Zealand*. Toronto: Oxford University Press, 1992.

Foot, David, and Rosemary Venne. *Labour Law's Little Sister: The Employment Standard Act and the Feminization of Labour*. Ottawa: Canadian Centre for Policy Alternatives, 1991.

– 'The Time Is Right: Voluntary Reduced Worktime and Workforce Demographics.' *Canadian Studies in Population* 25.2 (1998): 91–114.

Forrest, Ann. 'Bargaining Units and Bargaining Power.' *Relations Industrielles /
Industrial Relations* 41.4 (1986): 840–50.
– 'Securing the Male Breadwinner: A Feminist Interpretation of PC 1003.' In C.
Gonick, P. Phillips, and J. Vorst, eds, *Labour Gains, Labour Pains: 50 Years of PC
1003*, 139–55. Winnipeg: Society for Socialist Studies / Fernwood Publishing,
1995.
Four Directions Consulting Group. *Implications of First Nations Demography:
Final Report*. Winnipeg: Indian and Northern Affairs Canada, 1997.
Fournier, Suzanne, and Ernie Crey. *Stolen from Our Embrace: The Abduction of
First Nations Children and the Restoration of Aboriginal Communities*. Vancou-
ver: Douglas & McIntyre, 1997.
Fox, M.F. 'Canada's Agricultural and Forest Lands: Issues and Policy.' *Canadian
Public Policy* 14.3 (1988): 266–81.
Freeman, Richard, and Karen Needels. 'Skill Differentials in Canada in an Era
of Rising Labor Market Inequality.' In David Card and Richard Freeman,
eds, *Small Differences That Matter*, 45–67. Chicago: University of Chicago
Press, 1993.
Frideres, James S. *Aboriginal Peoples in Canada: Contemporary Conflicts*, 5th ed.
Scarborough, ON: Prentice-Hall Allyn and Bacon Canada, 1998.
– 'Indian Economic Development: Innovations and Obstructions.' In J.W. Frie-
sen, ed., *The Cultural Maze: Complex Questions on Native Destiny in Western
Canada*, 77–95. Calgary: Detselig, 1991.
Fudge, Judy. 'Exclusion, Discrimination, Equality and Privatization: Law, the
Canadian State, and Women Public Servants, 1908–1998.' Prepared for
SSHRC-funded project on Privatization, Feminization and the Law con-
ducted by scholars under auspices of the Feminist Legal Institute of
Osgoode Hall Law, Toronto, 1998.
– 'The Gendered Dimension of Labour Law: Why Women Need Inclusive
Unionism and Broader-Based Bargaining.' In L. Briskin and P. McDermott,
eds, *Women Challenging Unions: Feminism, Militancy, and Democracy*, 231–48.
Toronto: University of Toronto Press, 1993.
– *Labour Law's Little Sister: The Employment Standard Act and the Feminization of
Labour*. Ottawa: Canadian Centre for Policy Alternatives, 1991.
– 'Little Victories and Big Defeats: The Rise and Fall of Collective Bargaining
Rights for Domestic Workers in Ontario.' In A. Bakan and D. Stasiulus, eds,
Not One of the Family, 119–45. Toronto: University of Toronto Press, 1997.
Fudge, Judy, and Leah Vosko. 'Gender, Segmentation and the Standard
Employment Relationship in Canadian Labour Law and Policy.' *Economic
and Industrial Democracy* 22.2 (2001): 302.
Furniss, Elizabeth. *Victims of Benevolence: Discipline and Death at the Williams*

Lake Indian Residential School, 1891–1920. Williams Lake, BC: Cariboo Tribal Council, 1992.

Gaffney, R.E., G.P. Gould, and A.J. Semple. *Broken Promises: The Aboriginal Constitutional Conferences.* Fredericton: New Brunswick Association of Métis and Non-Status Indians, 1984.

Gagné, Marie-Anik. *A Nation within a Nation: Dependency and the Cree.* Montreal: Black Rose Books, 1994.

Gannage, Charlene. *Double Day, Double Bind.* Toronto: Women's Press, 1986.

Gardner, A. 'Their Own Boss.' *Canadian Social Trends,* Summer 1995: 26–36.

Gauthier, Madeleine. 'Les jeunes sans emploi sont-ils pauvres?' In M. Gauthier, ed., *Les nouveaux visages de la pauvreté,* 45–65. Quebec: Institut québécois de recherche sur la culture, 1987.

– 'La jeunesse au carrefour de la pauvreté.' *Apprentissage et Socialisation* 14.1 (1991): 51–61.

Gauthier, Madeleine, and Lucie Mercier. *La pauvreté chez les jeunes.* Quebec: Institut québécois de recherche sur la culture, 1994.

Gera, Surendra, and Philippe Massé. *Employment Performance in the Knowledge-based Economy.* Ottawa: Industry Canada Working Paper no.14 and Human Resources Development Canada Research Paper W-97-9E/F, 1996.

Gerber, Linda. 'Multiple Jeopardy: A Socio-Economic Comparison of Men and Women among the Indian, Métis and Inuit Peoples of Canada.' *Canadian Ethnic Studies* 22.3 (1990): 69–84.

Gibbins Roger. *Prairie Politics and Society: Regionalism in Decline.* Scarborough, ON: Butterworths, 1980.

Gilbert, Sid, Lynn Barr, Warren Clark, Matthew Blue, and Deborah Sunter. *Leaving School: Results from a National Survey.* Ottawa: Minister of Supply and Services Canada, 1993.

Gill, Alison. 'Women in Isolated Resource Towns: An Examination of Gender Differences in Cognitive Structures.' *Geoforum* 21.3 (1990): 347–58.

Globerman, Steven. 'Investment and Capital Productivity.' In R. Kunin, ed., *Prospering Together: The Economic Impact of the Aboriginal Title Settlements in B.C.,* 139–68. Vancouver: Laurier Institution, 1998.

Government of Canada. *Beneath the Veneer. The Report of the Task Force on Barriers to Women in the Public Service.* Ottawa: Ministry of Supply and Services, 1990.

– *Collective Reflection on the Changing Workplace: Report of the Advisory Committee on the Changing Workplace.* Ottawa: Public Works and Government Services Canada, 1997.

– *Employment Equity Act.* 1995. http://canada.justice.gc. ca/FTP/EN/Laws/Chap/E/E-5.4.txt.

- 'Youth Employment and Learning Strategy to Lay Groundwork for Modernizing School to Work Measures.' *News Release*. Ottawa: Government of Canada, 1994.
- Citizenship and Immigration Canada. *Into the 21st Century: A Strategy for Immigration and Citizenship*. Ottawa: Minister of Supply and Services Canada, 1994.
- Citizenship and Immigration Canada. *Canada 2005: A Strategy for Citizenship and Immigration*. Ottawa: 1994.
- Department of Indian Affairs and Northern Development. *Socio-Economic Indicators in Indian Reserves and Comparable Communities 1971–1991*. Ottawa: Minister of Public Works and Government Services Canada, 1997.
- Department of Manpower and Immigration. *The Immigration Program*. Ottawa: Information Canada, 1974.
- House of Commons. *Debates*, 1 May 1947, 2644–6.
- House of Commons. *Debates*, 27 January 1994.
- House of Commons. *Equality Now*. Report of the Special Committee on Visible Minorities in Canadian Society, 1984.
- House of Commons. *Minutes of Proceedings and Evidence of the Special Committee on Participation of Visible Minorities in Canadian Society.* 1983.
- House of Commons. *Multiculturalism: Building the Canadian Mosaic*. Report of the Standing Committee on Multiculturalism, 1987.
- Ministerial Task Force on Youth. *Take on the Future: Canadian Youth in the World of Work*. Ottawa: Government of Canada, 1996.
- Royal Commission on Aboriginal Peoples. *Choosing Life: Special Report on Suicide among Aboriginal People*. Ottawa: Minister of Supply and Services Canada, 1995.
- Royal Commission on Aboriginal Peoples. *Report of the Royal Commission on Aboriginal Peoples*. Volume 1. *Looking Forward, Looking Back*. Ottawa: Minister of Supply and Services Canada, 1996.
- Royal Commission on Aboriginal Peoples. *Report of the Royal Commission on Aboriginal Peoples*. Volume 2. *Restructuring the Relationship*. Ottawa: Minister of Supply and Services Canada, 1996.
- Royal Commission on Aboriginal Peoples. *Report of the Royal Commission on Aboriginal Peoples*, Volume 3. *Gathering Strength*. Ottawa: Minister of Supply and Services Canada, 1996.
- Royal Commission on Aboriginal Peoples. *Report of the Royal Commission on Aboriginal Peoples*, Volume 4. *Perspectives and Realities*. Ottawa: Minister of Supply and Services Canada, 1996.
- Royal Commission on Bilingualism and Biculturalism. *A Preliminary Report of the Royal Commission on Bilingualism and Biculturalism*. Ottawa, 1965.

– Royal Commission on Bilingualism and Biculturalism. *Report of the Royal Commission on Bilingualism and Biculturalism*. Volume 1. *Official Languages*. Ottawa, 1967.
– Royal Commission on Bilingualism and Biculturalism. *Report of the Royal Commission on Bilingualism and Biculturalism*. Volume 2. *Education*. Ottawa, 1968.
– Royal Commission on Bilingualism and Biculturalism. *Report of the Royal Commission on Bilingualism and Biculturalism*. Volume 3. *The Work World*. Ottawa, 1969.
– Royal Commission on Bilingualism and Biculturalism. *Report of the Royal Commission on Bilingualism and Biculturalism*. Volume 4. *The Cultural Contribution of Other Ethnic Groups*. Ottawa, 1969.
– Royal Commission on Bilingualism and Biculturalism. *Report of the Royal Commission on Bilingualism and Biculturalism*. Volume 5. *Federal Capital*; Volume 6: *Voluntary Associations*. Ottawa, 1970.
– Royal Commission on the Economic Union and Development Prospects for Canada. *Report*. Ottawa: Ministry of Supply and Services, 1985.
– Royal Commission on Equality in Employment. *Report of the Commission on Equality in Employment*. Ottawa: Minister of Supply and Services Canada, 1984.
– Royal Commission on the Status of Women. *Report*. Ottawa: Ministry of Supply and Services, 1970.
Goyder, John. 'The Canadian Syndrome of Polarities: An Obituary.' *Canadian Review of Sociology and Anthropology* 30.1 (1993): 1–12.
Graham, Katherine, Carolyn Dittburner, and Frances Abele. *Public Policy and Aboriginal Peoples 1965–1992*. Volume 1. *Soliloquy and Dialogue: Overview of Major Trends in Public Policy Relating to Aboriginal Peoples*. Ottawa: Minister of Public Works and Government Services Canada, 1996.
Grand Council of the Crees (Eeyou Astchee). *Never without Consent: James Bay Crees' Stand against Forcible Inclusion into an Independent Quebec*. Toronto: ECW Press, 1998.
Green, Paul, and Craig Riddell. 'The Economic Effects of Unemployment Insurance in Canada: An Empirical Analysis of UI Disentitlement.' *Journal of Labour Economics* 11.1–2 (1993): 596–620.
Grenon, Lee. 'Juggling Work and School.' In *Work Arrangements in the 1990s*, 85–102. Ottawa: Statistics Canada, 1998.
Guard, Julie. 'Womanly Innocence and Manly Self-Respect: Gendered Challenges to Labour's Postwar Compromise.' In C. Gonick et al., *Labour Gains, Labour Pains: 50 Years of PC 1003*, 119–38. Winnipeg: Society for Socialist Studies / Fernwood Publishing, 1995.

Guillaumin, Colette. *L'idéologie raciste: Genèse et langage actuel*. Paris: Mouton, 1972.

Guppy, Neil, and Scott Davies. *Education in Canada: Recent Trends and Future Challenges*. Ottawa: Statistics Canada, 1998.

Haddad, Tony, and Michael Spivey. 'All or Nothing: Modernization, Dependency and Wage Labour on a Reserve in Canada.' *Canadian Journal of Native Studies* 12.2 (1992): 203–28.

Hajnal, Zoltan. 'The Nature of Concentrated Urban Poverty in Canada and the United States.' *Canadian Journal of Sociology* 20.4 (1995): 497–528.

Hall, Stuart. 'Gramsci's Relevance for the Study of Race and Ethnicity.' *Journal of Communication Inquiry* 10.2 (1986): 5–27.

– 'Race, Articulation and Societies Structured in Dominance.' In *Sociological Theories: Race and Colonialism*, 305–45. Paris: UNESCO, 1980.

Halseth, Greg. *Cottage Country in Transition*. Montreal and Kingston: McGill-Queen's University Press, 1998.

Hamdani, Daood. 'The Temporary Help Service Industry: Its Role, Structure and Growth.' In *Service Indicators, 2nd Quarter*. Ottawa, Statistics Canada, Catalogue 63-016XPB, 1996.

Hamel, Jacques. 'Brèves notes sur une opposition entre générations.' *Sociologie et sociétés* 26.2 (1994): 165–76.

Hamelin, Louis-Edward. 'Thèmes de l'autochtonie canadienne.' *Recherches sociographiques* 35.3 (1994): 421–32.

Hansen, Philip, and Alicja Muszynski. 'Crisis in Rural Life and Crisis in Thinking: Directions for Critical Research.' *Canadian Review of Sociology and Anthropology* 27.1 (1990): 1–22.

Harrison, Trevor, and Harvey Krahn. 'Populism and the Rise of the Reform Party in Alberta.' *Canadian Review of Sociology and Anthropology* 32.2 (1995): 127–50.

Harvey, David. *The Condition of Postmodernity*. Cambridge: Blackwell, 1989.

Hatfield, Michael. *Concentrations of Poverty and Distressed Neighbourhoods in Canada*. Ottawa: Human Resources Development Canada, Applied Research Branch, Working Papers Series, 1997.

Hay, David. 'Rural Canada in Transition: Trends and Developments.' In David Hay and Gurcharn Basran, eds, *Rural Sociology in Canada*, 16–32. Toronto: Oxford University Press, 1992.

Hayter, Roger. 'Technological Imperatives in Resource Sectors: Forest Products.' In John Britton, ed., *Canada and the Global Economy: The Geography of Structural and Technological Change*, 101–22. Montreal and Kingston: McGill-Queen's University Press, 1996.

Hawkes, David C., ed. *Aboriginal Peoples and Government Responsibility: Exploring Federal and Provincial Roles*. Ottawa: Carleton University Press, 1989.

Hawkins, Freda. *Canada and Immigration: Public Policy and Public Concern*. Montreal: McGill-Queen's University Press, 1988.

Hébert, Yvonne. 'Methodological Issues in Gendering Immigration Research: Generation(s) and Regeneration.' In Baha Abu-Laban and Tracy Derwing, eds, *Responding to Diversity in the Metropolis: Building an Inclusive Research Agenda*, 103–8. Edmonton: Prairie Centre of Excellence for Research on Immigration and Integration, 1997.

Helin, Calvin. *Doing Business with Native People Makes Sense*. Victoria, BC: Praxis Publishing and Native Investment and Trade Association, 1991.

Helliwell, John. 'Convergence and Migration among Provinces.' *Canadian Journal of Economics* 29 (1996): 324–30.

Henry, Frances. *Who Gets the Work in 1989?* Ottawa: Economic Council of Canada, 1989.

Henry, Frances, and Effie Ginsberg. *Who Gets the Work? A Test of Racial Discrimination in Employment*. Toronto: Social Planning Council of Metro Toronto and the Urban Alliance on Race Relations, 1985.

Henry, Frances, Carol Tator, Winston Mattis, and Tim Rees. *The Colour of Democracy: Racism in Canadian Society*. Toronto: Harcourt Brace Canada, 1995.

Heron, Craig, and Robert Storey. 'Work and Struggle in the Canadian Steel Industry, 1900–1950.' In Craig Heron and R. Storey, eds, *On the Job: Confronting the Labour Process in Canada*. Kingston and Montreal: McGill-Queen's University Press, 1986.

Hickling, M. 'Flexibilization of the Workplace: Observations on Aspects of the Canadian Position.' *XVth International Congress on Comparative Labour*. Bristol, UK, 1998.

Hicks, Chantal. 'The Age Distribution of the Tax/Transfer System in Canada.' In Miles Corak, ed., *Government Finances and Generational Equity*, 39–56. Ottawa: Statistics Canada, 1998.

Himelfarb, Alex. 'The Social Characteristics of One-Industry Towns in Canada.' In Roy Bowles, ed., *Little Communities and Big Industries*, 16–43. Toronto: Butterworths, 1982.

'HIV Infecting More Natives.' *Saskatoon Star-Phoenix*, 18 January 1999, A1–2.

Hodgetts, J.E., W. McClosky, R. Whitaker, and V.S. Wilson. *The Biography of an Institution: The Civil Service Commission of Canada, 1908–1967*. Montreal and Kingston: McGill-Queen's University Press, 1972.

Hogg, Peter W., and Mary Ellen Turpel. 'Implementing Aboriginal Self-Government: Constitutional and Jurisdictional Issues.' *Canadian Bar Review* 74.2 (June 1995): 187–224.

Hoggart, Keith. 'Let's Do Away with Rural.' *Journal of Rural Studies* 6.3 (1990): 245–57.

Hostland, Doug. *Structural Unemployment in Canada: Some Stylized Facts*.

Ottawa: Human Resources Development Canada, Applied Research Branch, Research Paper Series R-96-1E, 1995.

– *What Factors Determine Structural Unemployment in Canada?* Ottawa: Human Resources Development Canada, Applied Research Branch, Research Paper Series R-96-2E, 1995.

House, J. David. 'Knowledge-based Development in the North: New Approaches to Sustainable Development.' In Jyrki Käkönen, ed., *Politics and Sustainable Growth in the Arctic*. Aldershot, UK: Dartmouth, 1993.

Howard-Hassmann, Rhoda E. '"Canadian" as an Ethnic Category: Implications for Multiculturalism and National Unity.' *Canadian Public Policy* 25.4 (1999): 523–37.

Hull, Jeremy. 'Socioeconomic Status and Native Education in Canada.' *Canadian Journal of Native Education* 17.1 (1990): 1–14.

Human Resources Development Canada. *Improving Social Security in Canada: A Discussion Paper*. Ottawa: Ministry of Supply and Services, 1994.

– 'Unemployment among Young People: A Comparison between Canada and the United States.' *Applied Research Bulletin* 4.1 (1998): http://www.hrdc-drhc.gc.ca/hrdc/corp/stra...publish/bulletin/mydocument/V4N1C10E.html.

Hunter, R. 'The Regulation of Independent Contractors: A Feminist Perspective.' *Corporate Business Law Journal* 5 (1992).

Hylton, John H. 'The Case for Aboriginal Self-Government: A Social Policy Perspective.' In J.H. Hylton, ed., *Aboriginal Self-Government in Canada: Current Trends and Issues*, 34–48. Saskatoon: Purich Publishing, 1994.

Iacovetta, Franca. '"Primitive Villagers and Uneducated Girls": Canada Recruits Domestics for Italy, 1951–52.' *Canadian Women's Studies* 7.4 (1986): 14–18.

– *Such Hardworking People: Italian Immigrants in Postwar Toronto*. Montreal: McGill-Queen's University Press, 1992.

Indian and Northern Affairs Canada. *Backgrounder: Gathering Strength: Canada's Aboriginal Action Plan*. Ottawa: Indian and Northern Affairs Canada, 1999.

– *Basic Departmental Data 1997*. Ottawa: Minister of Public Works and Government Services Canada, 1998.

– *First Nation Profiles*. Ottawa: Indian and Northern Affairs Canada, 1999.

Indian and Northern Affairs Canada and Canadian Polar Commission. *1998–99 Estimates. Part III: Report on Plans and Priorities*. Ottawa: Minister of Public Works and Government Services Canada, 1998.

– *2000–2001 Estimates. Part III: Report on Plans and Priorities*. Ottawa: Minister of Public Works and Government Services Canada, 2000.

International Labour Organization. *The Role of Private Employment Agencies in the Functioning of Labour Markets (Report VI)*. Geneva: International Labour Office, 1994.

- *World Employment Report, 1996/97.* Geneva: International Labour Office, 1997.

Isaac, Thomas. 'The Concept of the Crown and Aboriginal Self-Government.' *Canadian Journal of Native Studies* 14.2 (1992): 221–50.

Iyer, Nitya. 'Some Mothers Are Better than Others: A Re-examination of Maternity Benefits.' In Susan Boyd, ed., *Challenging the Public/Private Divide: Feminism, Law, and Public Policy,* 168–94. Toronto: University of Toronto Press, 1997.

Jaccoud, Mylène. 'L'exclusion sociale et les Autochtones,' *Lien social et politiques – RIAC* 34 (1995): 93–100.

Jackson, Margaret A. 'Aboriginal Women and Self-Government.' In J.H. Hylton, ed., *Aboriginal Self-Government in Canada: Current Trends and Issues,* 180–98. Saskatoon: Purich Publishing, 1994.

James, Susan. 'The Good-enough Citizen: Female Citizenship and Independence.' In G. Bock and S. James, eds, *Beyond Equality and Difference.* London and New York: Routledge, 1992.

Jamieson, Kathleen. *Indian Women and the Law in Canada: Citizens Minus.* Ottawa: Minister of Supply and Services, 1978.

Jennings, Philip. *School Enrolment and the Declining Youth Participation Rate.* Ottawa: Human Resources Development Canada, Applied Research Branch, Research Paper Series R-98-4E, 1998.

Jenson, Jane. '"Different" but Not "Exceptional": Canada's Permeable Fordism.' *Canadian Review of Sociology and Anthropology* 26.1 (1989): 69–94.

- 'Part-time Employment and Women: A Range of Strategies.' In I. Bakker, ed., *Rethinking Restructuring: Gender and Change in Canada,* 92–108. Toronto: University of Toronto Press, 1996.

- 'The Talents of Women, the Skills of Men.' In S. Wood, ed., *The Transformation of Work?* 141–55. London: Unwin Hyman, 1989.

Jenson, Jane, and Martin Papillon. 'Le "modèle canadien de diversité": Un répertoire en constante définition.' *Réseaux canadiens de recherche en politiques publiques,* 2001.

Jhappan, C. Radha. 'Natural Rights vs. Legal Positivism: Indians, the Courts, and the New Discourse of Aboriginal Rights in Canada.' *British Journal of Canadian Studies* 6.1 (1991): 60–100.

- 'Global Community? Supranational Strategies of Canada's Aboriginal Peoples.' *Journal of Indigenous Studies* 3.1 (1992): 59–91.

Juteau, Danielle. 'Les enjeux de la citoyenneté: Un bilan sociologique.' In Jerome Black et al., eds, *Les enjeux de la citoyenneté: Un bilan interdisciplinaire,* 47–72. Montreal: Immigrations et Métropoles, 1998.

- *L'ethnicité et ses frontières.* Montreal: Presses de l'Université de Montréal, 1999.

- 'Gendering Immigration/Integration Policy Research: Research Gaps.' In Baha Abu-Laban and Tracy Derwing, eds, *Responding to Diversity in the Metropolis: Building an Inclusive Research Agenda*, 99–103. Edmonton: Prairie Centre of Excellence for Research on Immigration and Integration, 1997.

Kalbach, Madeline A., and Warren E. Kalbach. 'Demographic Overview of Ethnic Origin Groups in Canada.' In Peter S. Li, ed., *Race and Ethnic Relations in Canada*, 2nd ed., 21–51. Toronto: Oxford University Press, 1999.

Kalin, Rudolf, and J.W. Berry. 'Interethnic Attitudes in Canada: Ethnocentrism, Consensual Hierarchy and Reciprocity.' *Canadian Journal of Behavioural Science* 28 (1996): 253–261.

Kapsalis, Constantine. *An Explanation of the Increasing Age Premium*. Ottawa: Statistics Canada, Analytical Studies Branch, Research Paper Series no. 112, 1998.

Kapsalis, Constantine, René Morissette, and Garnett Picot. *The Returns to Education, and the Increasing Wage Gap between Younger and Older Workers*. Ottawa: Statistics Canada, Analytical Studies Branch, Research Paper Series no. 131, 1999.

Kealy, Linda. 'Women and Labour during World War II: Women Workers and the Minimum Wage in Manitoba.' In M. Kinnear, ed., *First Days, Fightings Days: Women in Manitoba History*. Regina: Canadian Plains Research Center, 1987.

Keddie, Philip, and Joseph Alun. 'The Turnaround of the Turnaround? Rural Population Change in Canada, 1976–1986.' *Canadian Geographer* 35.4 (1991): 367–79.

- 'Reclassification and Rural vs Urban Population Change in Canada, 1976–1981: A Tale of Two Definitions.' *Canadian Geographer* 35.4 (1991): 412–20.

Kelly, Karen, Linda Howatson-Leo, and Warren Clark. 'I Feel Overqualified for My Job.' *Canadian Social Trends* 47 (1997): 11–16.

Kennedy, John C. 'At the Crossroads: Newfoundland and Labrador Communities in a Changing International Context.' *Canadian Review of Sociology and Anthropology* 34.3 (1997): 297–317.

Kennedy, L.W., R.A. Silverman, and D.R. Forde. 'Homicide in Urban Canada: Testing the Impact of Economic Inequality and Social Disorganization.' *Canadian Journal of Sociology* 16.3 (1991): 397–410.

Kerr, Don, Daniel Larrivée, and Patricia Greenhalgh. *Children and Youth: An Overview*. Ottawa: Statistics Canada, 1994.

Kerr, Don, and Bali Ram. *Population Dynamics in Canada*. Ottawa: Statistics Canada and Prentice-Hall Canada, 1994.

Klare, Karl. 'Judicial Deradicalization of the Wagner Act and the Origins of

Modern Legal Consciousness, 1937–1941.' *Minnesota Law Review* 62 (1978):
65–76.
– 'The Public/Private Distinction in Labor Law.' *University of Pennsylvania Law Review* 130 (1982): 1358–64.
Krahn, Harvey. 'Non-standard Work on the Rise.' *Perspectives on Labour and Income*, Winter 1995: 35–42.
– 'The School to Work Transition in Canada: New Risks and Uncertainties.' In Walter Heinz, ed., *The Life Course and Social Change*, 43–69. Weinheim: Deutscher Studien Verlag, 1991.
Krosenbrink-Gelissen, Lilianne E. 'Caring Is Indian Women's Business, but Who Takes Care of Them? Canada's Indian Women, the Renewed Indian Act, and Its Implications for Women's Family Responsibilities, Roles and Rights.' In R. Kuppe and R. Potz, eds, *Law and Anthropology: International Yearbook for Legal Anthropology, Volume 7*, 107–30. Dordrecht: Martinus Nijhoff Publishers, 1992.
Krotz, Larry. *Indian Country: Inside Another Canada*. Toronto: McClelland and Stewart, 1990.
– *Urban Indians: The Strangers in Canada's Cities*. Edmonton: Hurtig Publishers Ltd., 1980.
Kunin, Roslyn, ed., *Prospering Together: The Economic Impact of the Aboriginal Title Settlements in B.C.* Vancouver: Laurier Institution, 1998.
Kunz, Jean, and Grant Schellenberg. *Youth at Work in Canada*. Ottawa: Canadian Council on Social Development, 1999.
Lamarche, Rudolphe. *Capitalizing on the Information Economy: A New Approach in Regional Development*. Moncton: Canadian Institute for Research on Regional Development, 1990.
Langlois, Simon. 'Les rigidités sociales et l'insertion des jeunes dans la société québécoise.' In Fernand Dumont, ed., *Une société des jeunes?* 301–23. Québec: Institut québécois de recherche sur la culture, 1986.
LaPrairie, Carol. *Seen but Not Heard: Native People in the Inner City*. Ottawa: Minister of Public Works and Government Services Canada, 1996.
Lavoie, Claude. 'Youth Employment, Some Explanations and Future Prospects.' *Applied Research Bulletin* 2.2 (1996): 3–5.
Lavoie, Claude, and Ali Béjaoui. *La situation de l'emploi des jeunes au Canada: Quelques explications et perspectives d'avenir*. Ottawa: Human Resources Development Canada, Applied Research Branch, Research Paper Series R-98-10F, 1998.
Leckie, Gloria. 'Continuity and Change in the Farm Community: Brooke Township, Ontario 1965–1986.' *Canadian Geographer* 33.1 (1989): 31–45.

- 'Female Farmers in Canada and the Gender Relations of a Restructuring Agricultural System.' *Canadian Geographer* 37.3 (1993): 212–30.
Lee, Eddy. 'The Declaration of Philadelphia: Retrospect and Prospect.' *International Labour Review* 33.4 (1997): 467–84.
Lee, Frank. 'Convergence in Canada?' *Canadian Journal of Economics* 29 (1996): 331–6.
Leenaars, Antoon, and David Lester. 'The Changing Suicide Pattern in Canadian Adolescents and Youth, Compared to Their American Counterparts.' *Adolescence* 30 (1995): 539–47.
Lepage, Pierre. 'Un regard au-delà des chartes: Le racisme et la discrimination envers les peuples autochtones.' *Recherches amérindiennes au Québec* 25.3 (1995): 29–45.
Li, Peter S. *The Chinese in Canada.* 2nd edition. Toronto: Oxford University Press, 1998.
- 'Earning Disparities between Immigrants and Native-born Canadians.' *Canadian Journal of Sociology and Anthropology* 37.3 (2000): 289–311.
- 'The Economics of Brain Drain: Recruitment of Skilled Labour to Canada, 1954–86.' In Victor Satzewich, ed., *Deconstructing a Nation: Immigration, Multiculturalism and Racism in '90s Canada*, 145–62. Halifax, NS: Fernwood Publishing, 1992.
- *Ethnic Inequality in a Class Society.* Toronto: Wall and Thompson, 1988.
- 'The Market Value and Social Value of Race.' In Victor Satzewich, ed., *Racism and Social Inequality in Canada*, 113–30. Toronto: Thompson, 1998.
- 'The Multiculturalism Debate.' In Peter S. Li, ed., *Race and Ethnic Relations in Canada*, 2nd ed., 147–76. Toronto: Oxford University Press, 1999.
- 'Race and Gender as Bases of Class Fractions and Their Effects on Earnings.' *Canadian Review of Sociology and Anthropology* 29 (1992): 488–510.
- 'Self-employment among Visible Minority Immigrants, White Immigrants, and Native-born Persons in Secondary and Tertiary Industries of Canada.' *Canadian Journal of Regional Science* 20 (1997): 103–17.
- 'Unneighbourly Houses or Unwelcome Chinese: The Social Construction of Race in the Battle over "Monster Homes" in Vancouver, Canada.' *International Journal of Comparative Race & Ethnic Studies* 1 (1994): 14–33.
Li, Peter S., and B. Singh Bolaria. 'Canadian Immigration Policy and Assimilation Theories.' In John A. Fry, ed., *Economy, Class and Social Reality*, 411–22. Toronto: Butterworths, 1979.
Linder, Marc. *Farewell to the Self-employed: Deconstructing a Socioeconomic and Legal Solipsism.* New York: Greenwood Press, 1992.
Lindsay, Colin, Mary Sue Devereaux, and Michael Bergob. *Youth in Canada.* 2nd ed. Ottawa: Statistics Canada, 1994.

Lindstrom-Best, Varpu. '"I Won't Be a Slave": Finnish Domestics in Canada, 1911–1930.' In *Looking into My Sister's Eyes: An Exploration in Women's History,* 32–54. Toronto: Multicultural History Society of Ontario, 1986.

Lipsett, Brenda, and Marc Reesor. *Flexible Work Arrangements: Evidence from the 1991 and 1995 Survey of Work Arrangements.* Ottawa: Human Resources and Development Canada, 1997.

Little, Don. 'Earnings and Labour Force Status of 1990 Graduates.' *Education Quarterly Review* 2.3 (1995): 10–20.

– 'Financing Universities: Why Are Students Paying More?' *Education Quarterly Review* 4.2 (1997): 10–26.

Little, Don, and Louise Lapierre. *The Class of 90.* Ottawa: Statistics Canada, 1996.

Livingstone, D.W. *The Education-Jobs Gap: Underemployment or Economic Democracy.* Boulder, CO: Westview Press, 1998.

Logan, Ronald. 'Immigration during the 1980s.' *Canadian Social Trends*, vol. 2, 31–4. Toronto: Thompson Educational Publishing, 1994.

Long, David Alan. 'Trials of the Spirit: The Native Social Movement in Canada.' In D.A. Long and O.P. Dickason, eds, *Visions of the Heart: Canadian Aboriginal Issues*, 377–96. Toronto: Harcourt Brace Canada, 1996.

Lowe, Graham. *Women in the Administrative Revolution: The Feminization of Clerical Work.* Toronto: University of Toronto Press, 1987.

Lucas, Rex. *Minetown, Milltown, Railtown: Life in Canada's Communities of Single Industy.* Toronto: University of Toronto Press, 1971.

Luhmann, Niklas. 'The Paradox of System Diffentiation and the Evolution of Society.' In J.C. Alexander and P. Colomy, eds, *Differentiation Theory and Social Change: Comparative and Historical Perspectives*, 409–40. New York: Columbia University Press, 1990.

Luxton, Meg. *More than a Labour of Love.* Toronto: Women's Press, 1980.

MacDonald, Diane. 'Sectoral Certification: A Case Study of British Columbia.' *Canadian Labour and Employment Law Journal* 5 (1998): 243–67.

MacDonald, Martha. 'Gender and Recent Social Security Reform in Canada.' Paper prepared for Radcliffe Public Policy Institute, Boston, 1997.

MacDonald, Martha, and P. Connelly. 'Class and Gender in Fishing Communities in Nova Scotia.' *Studies in Political Economy* 30 (1989): 61–86.

Mackenzie, Suzanne, and Glenn Norcliffe. 'Restructuring in the Canadian Newsprint Industry.' *Canadian Geographer* 41.1 (1997): 2–6.

Maclaren, Virginia. 'Redrawing the Canadian Energy Map.' In John Britton, ed., *Canada and the Global Economy: The Geography of Structural and Technological Change*, 137–54. Montreal and Kingston: McGill-Queen's University Press, 1996.

MacLachlan, Ian, and Sawada Ryo. 'Measures of Income Inequality and Social Polarization in Canadian Metropolitan Areas.' *Canadian Geographer* 41.1 (1997): 377–97.

MacLeod, Kathryn. *The Seniority Principle: Is It Discriminatory?* Kingston: Industrial Relations Centre, Queen's University, 1987.

Mallea, Paula. *Aboriginal Law: Apartheid in Canada.* Brandon, MB: Bearpaw Publishing, 1994.

– *Report of the Aboriginal Justice Inquiry of Manitoba: The Justice System and Aboriginal People.* Winnipeg: Queen's Printer, 1991.

Malles, Paul. *Canadian Labour Standards in Law, Agreement and Practice.* Ottawa: Economic Council of Canada, 1976.

Marchak, Patricia, Neil Guppy, and John McMullan, eds. *Uncommon Property: The Fishing and Fish-Processing Industry in British Columbia.* Toronto: Methuen, 1987.

Marquardt, Richard. 'Labour Market Participation, Employment and Unemployment.' In *High School May Not Be Enough*, 29–42. Ottawa: Human Resources Development Canada, 1998.

– 'Quality of Youth Employment.' In *High School May Not Be Enough*, 43–50.

– *Enter at Your Own Risk: Canadian Youth and the Labour Market.* Toronto: Between the Lines, 1998.

Marshall, T.H. 'Citizenship and Social Class.' In *Class, Citizenship, and Social Development.* New York: Doubleday, 1965 [1949].

Maslove, Allan, and David Hawkes. 'The Northern Population.' *Canadian Social Trends*, vol. 2, 45–50. Toronto: Thompson Educational Publishing, 1994.

Matthew, R. Malcolm. 'The Suburbanization of Toronto Offices.' *Canadian Geographer* 37.4 (1993): 293–306.

Maxwell, Judith. 'Social Dimension of Economic Growth.' In *Eric John Hanson Memorial Lecture Series*, vol. 8: 13. University of Alberta, 1996.

– 'Toward a Common Citizenship: Canada's Social and Economic Choices.' *Reflexion*, no. 4, *Canadian Policy Research Networks* (CPRN) 40 (2001): 1–2.

McBride, Steven, and Patrick Smith. 'The Impact of Aboriginal Title Settlements on Education and Human Capital.' In R. Kunin, ed., *Prospering Together: The Economic Impact of the Aboriginal Title Settlements in B.C.*, 169–206. Vancouver: Laurier Institution, 1998.

McCallum, Margaret. 'Keeping Women in Their Place: The Minimum Wage in Canada.' *Labour / Le Travail* 17 (1986): 29–56.

McCay, B.J. 'Fish Guts, Hair Nets, and Unemployment Stamps: Women and Working Cooperative Fish Plants.' In P.R. Sinclair, ed., *A Question of Survival: The Fisheries and Newfoundland Society.* St John's, NF: Institute of Social and Economic Research, 1988.

McDade, Kathryn. *Barriers to Recognition of the Credentials of Immigrants in Canada.* Ottawa: Institute for Research on Public Policy, 1988.

McDermott, P. 'The Pay Equity Challenge to Collective Bargaining in Ontario.' In J. Fudge and P. McDermott, ed., *Just Wages: A Feminist Assessment of Pay Equity.* Toronto: University of Toronto Press, 1991.

McFarlane, Peter. 'Aboriginal Leadership.' In D.A. Long and O.P. Dickason, eds, *Visions of the Heart: Canadian Aboriginal Issues,* 117–45. Toronto: Harcourt Brace Canada, 1996.

McGahan, Peter. *Urban Sociology in Canada.* Toronto: Harcourt Brace and Co., 1995.

McSkimmings, Judie. 'The Farm Community.' *Canadian Social Trends,* vol. 2, 265–8. Toronto: Thompson Educational Publishing, 1994.

Means, Russell. 'The Same Old Song.' In W. Churchill, ed., *Marxism and Native Americans,* 19–33. Boston: South End Press, 1983.

Meunier, Dominique, Paul Bernard, and Johanne Boisjoly. 'Eternal Youth? Changes in the Living Arrangements of Young People.' In Miles Corak, ed., *Labour Markets, Social Institutions, and the Future of Canada's Children,* 157–69. Ottawa: Statistics Canada, 1998.

Meyerwitz, R. 'Organizing the United Automobile Workers: Women Workers at the Ternstedt General Motors Parts Plant.' In P.R. Milkman, ed., *Women, Work and Protest.* London: Routledge and Kegan Paul, 1985.

Miedema, Baukje, and Nancy Nason-Clark. 'Second-class Status: An Analysis of the Lived Experiences of Immigrant Women in Fredericton.' *Canadian Ethnic Studies* 21 (1989): 63–73.

Miles, Robert. *Racism.* New York: Routledge, 1989.

Miller, J.R. 'Great White Father Knows Best: Oka and the Land Claims Process.' *Native Studies Review* 7.1 (1991): 23–52.

– *Shingwauk's Vision: A History of Native Residential Schools.* Toronto: University of Toronto Press, 1996.

Monture-Angus, Patricia A. 'Lessons in Decolonization: Aboriginal Overrepresentation in Canadian Criminal Justice.' In D.A. Long and O.P. Dickason, eds, *Visions of the Heart: Canadian Aboriginal Issues,* 335–54. Toronto: Harcourt Brace Canada, 1996.

– *Thunder in My Soul: A Mohawk Woman Speaks.* Halifax: Fernwood Publishing, 1995.

Moreau, Joanne. 'Changing Faces: Visible Minorities in Toronto.' *Canadian Social Trends,* vol. 2, 81–4. Toronto: Thompson Educational Publishing, 1994.

Morgan, Nicole. *The Equality Game: Women in the Federal Public Service, 1908–1987.* Ottawa: Canadian Advisory Council on the Status of Women, 1988.

Morissette, René. 'Canadian Jobs and Firm Size: Small Firms Pay Less?' *Canadian Journal of Economics* 26.1 (1993): 159–66.
– 'Declining Earnings of Young Men.' *Canadian Social Trends* 46 (Autumn 1997): 8–15.
– 'The Declining Labour Market Status of Young Men.' In Miles Corak, ed., *Labour Markets, Social Institutions, and the Future of Canada's Children*, 31–50. Ottawa: Statistics Canada, 1998.
Morissette, René, and Charles Bérubé. *Longitudinal Aspects of Earnings Inequality in Canada*. Ottawa: Statistics Canada, Analytical Studies Branch, Research Paper Series no. 94, 1996.
Morissette, René, and Marie Drolet. *The Evolution of Pension Coverage of Young and Prime-Aged Workers in Canada*. Ottawa: Statistics Canada, Analytical Studies Branch, Research Paper Series no. 138, 1999.
Morissette, René, John Myles, and Garnett Picot. 'Earnings Polarization in Canada, 1969–1991.' In Keith Banting and Charles Beach, eds, *Labour Market Polarization and Social Policy Reform*, 23–50. Kingston, ON: Queen's University School of Policy Studies, 1995.
Morrison, Kelly. *Canada's Older Workers: A Discussion of Labour Market Issues*. Ottawa: Human Resources Development Canada, Applied Research Branch, 1996.
– *Job Loss and Adjustment Experiences of Older Workers 1988–1990*. Ottawa: Human Resources Development Canada, 1995.
Moss, Wendy. *History of Discriminatory Laws Affecting Aboriginal People*. Ottawa: Library of Parliament Research Branch, 1987.
Mückenberger, Ulrich. 'Non-standard Forms of Employment in the Federal Republic of Germany: The Role and Effectiveness of the State.' In Gerry Rogers and Janine Rogers, eds, *Precarious Employment in Labour Market Regulation: The Growth of Atypical Employment in Western Europe*, 267–85. Belgium: International Institute for Labour Studies, 1989.
Murphy, Raymond. 'A Weberian Approach to Credentials: Credentials as a Code of Exclusionary Closure.' In Lorna Erwin and David MacLennan, eds, *Sociology of Education in Canada*, 102–19. Toronto: Copp Clark Longman, 1994.
Muszynski, Alicya. *Cheap Wage Labour: Race and Gender in the Fisheries of British Columbia*. Montreal and Kingston: McGill-Queen's University Press, 1996.
Myles, John, Garnett Picot, and Ted Wannell. 'Does Post-industrialism Matter? The Canadian Experience.' In Gøsta Esping-Andersen, ed., *Changing Classes*, 171–94. London: Sage, 1993.
– *Wages and Jobs in the 1980s: Changing Youth Wages and the Declining Middle*. Ottawa: Statistics Canada, Analytical Studies Branch, Research Paper Series no. 17, 1988.

Native Investment and Trade Association. *Gamex '93: Successful First Nations Gaming in Canada II.* Conference / Trade show program, Vancouver, May 1993.

Nault, François, Jiajian Chen, M.V. George, and Mary Jane Norris. *Population Projections of Registered Indians, 1991–2015.* Ottawa: Statistics Canada, 1993.

Neis, Barbara. 'From "Shipped Girls" to "Brides of the State": The Transition from Familial to Science Patriarchy in the Newfoundland Fishery Industry.' *Canada Journal of Regional Science* 17.2 (Summer 1993): 185–211.

Newhouse, David R. 'Modern Aboriginal Economies: Capitalism with an Aboriginal Face.' In Royal Commission on Aboriginal Peoples, *Sharing the Harvest: The Road to Self-Reliance*, 90–100. Ottawa: Minister of Supply and Services Canada, 1993.

Ng, Roxana. 'Gendering Policy Research on Immigration.' In Baha Abu-Laban and Tracy Derwing, eds, *Responding to Diversity in the Metropolis: Building an Inclusive Research Agenda*, 108–12. Edmonton: Prairie Centre of Excellence for Research on Immigration and Integration, 1997.

Niezen, Ronald. 'Power and Dignity: The Social Consequences of Hydroelectric Development for the James Bay Cree.' *Canadian Review of Sociology and Anthropology* 30.4 (1993): 510–29.

Norris, Mary Jane. 'Contemporary Demography of Aboriginal Peoples in Canada.' In D.A. Long and O.P. Dickason, eds, *Visions of the Heart: Canadian Aboriginal Issues*, 179–237. Toronto: Harcourt Brace Canada, 1996.

Norris, Mary Jane, and Daniel Beavon. 'Registered Indian Mobility and Migration: An Analysis of 1996 Census Data.' Paper presented at the Canadian Population Society meetings, Lennoxville, Quebec, June 1999.

OECD. *The OECD Job Study.* Paris: OECD, 1994.

– *The OECD Job Study. Evidence and Explanations. Part I – Labour Market Trends and Underlying Forces of Change.* Paris: OECD, 1994.

O'Grady, J. 'Beyond the Wagner Act, What Then?' In D. Drache, ed., *Getting on Track*, 153–70. Montreal and Kingston: McGill-Queen's University Press, 1991.

Olfert, Rose, and Jack Stabler. 'Industrial Restructuring of the Prairie Labour Force: Spatial and Gender Impacts.' *Canadian Journal of Regional Science* 17.2 (1994): 133–52.

Omi, Michael, and Howard Winant. *Racial Formation in the United States from the 1960s to the 1980s.* New York: Routledge and Kegan Paul, 1986.

Ontario Native Women's Association. 'Post Patriation: The Antithesis of Termination to Special Status of the Aboriginal Peoples.' *Fireweed: A Feminist Quarterly* 16 (1983): 100–6.

Opekokew, Delia. *The Political and Legal Inequalities among Aboriginal Peoples in Canada*. Kingston, ON: Institute of Intergovernmental Relations, Background paper no. 14, 1987.

Ornstein, Michael. *A Profile of Social Assistance Recipients in Ontario*. North York, ON: Institute for Social Research, York University, 1995.

Osberg, Lars, Fred Wien, and Jan Grude. *Vanishing Jobs: Canada's Changing Workplaces*. Toronto: Lorimer, 1995.

Pahl, R. 'The Urban-Rural Continuum.' *Sociologia Ruralis* 6 (1966).

Paju, Michael. *The Class of '90 Revisited*. Ottawa: Human Resources Development Canada, 1997.

Pal, Leslie A. *Beyond Policy Analysis: Public Issue Management in Turbulent Times*. Scarborough, ON: ITP Nelson, 1997.

Pampel, Fred, and H. Elizabeth Peters. 'The Easterlin Effect.' In John Hagan and Karen Cook, eds, *Annual Review of Sociology* 21: 163–94. Palo Alto, CA: Annual Reviews Inc., 1995.

Panitch, Leo, and Donald Swartz. *The Assault on Trade Union Freedoms: From Consent to Coercion*. Toronto: Garamond Press, 1993.

Paquette, Jerry. 'Scolarité et revenu.' *Policy Options* 18.6 (1997): 57–61.

Parai, L. *Immigration and Emigration of Professional and Skilled Manpower during the Post-war Period*. Ottawa: Economic Council of Canada, 1965.

Parenteau, Robert, and Louise Earl. 'Workers in the Urban Shadow.' In Ray D. Bollman, ed., *Rural and Small Town Canada*, 129–50. Toronto: Thompson Educational Publishing, 1992.

Parkinson, John M. 'Sources of Capital for Native Businesses: Problems and Prospects.' *Canadian Journal of Native Studies* 8.1 (1988): 27–58.

Parmar, Pratibha. 'Gender, Race and Class: Asian Women in Resistance.' In Centre for Contemporary Cultural Studies at the University of Birmingham, ed., *The Empire Strikes Back: Race and Racism in 70's Britain*, 236–75. London: Hutchinson, 1982.

Parsons, Talcott. *The System of Modern Society*. Englewood Cliffs, NJ: Prentice-Hall, 1971.

Peck, J. *Work Place: The Social Regulation of Labor Markets*. New York: Guilford Press, 1996.

Pendakur, Krishna, and Ravi Pendakur. *Earnings Differentials among Ethnic Groups in Canada*. Ottawa: Department of Canadian Heritage, Strategic Research and Analysis, 1996.

Perley, David G. 'Aboriginal Education in Canada as Internal Colonialism.' *Canadian Journal of Native Education* 20.1 (1993): 118–28.

Persons, Stow. *Ethnic Studies at Chicago, 1905–45*. Chicago, University of Illinois Press, 1990.

Pertusati, Linda. *In Defense of Mohawk Land: Ethnopolitical Conflict in Native North America*. Albany: State University of New York Press, 1997.

Pes, Johanne, and Anne-Marie Blanchet. 'La rémunération à double ou à multiples paliers dans les conventions collectives en vigueur au Québec.' *Le Marché du Travail* 9.3 (1988): 79–89.

Peters, Evelyn J. 'Self-Government for Aboriginal People in Urban Areas: A Literature Review and Suggestions for Research.' *Canadian Journal of Native Studies* 12.1 (1992): 51–74.

Peters, Joseph. *An Era of Change: Government Employment Trends in the 1980s and 1990s*. Ottawa: Canadian Policy Research Networks and Renouf, 1999.

Pettipas, Katherine. *Severing the Ties That Bind: Government Repression of Indigenous Religious Ceremonies on the Prairies*. Winnipeg: University of Manitoba Press, 1994.

Phillips, Erin, and Paul Phillips. *Women and Work: Inequality in the Labour Market*. Toronto: Lorimer, 1993.

Phipps, Shelley. 'Poverty and Labour Market Change: Canada in Comparative Perspective.' In Keith Banting and Charles Beach, eds, *Labour Market Polarization and Social Policy Reform*, 59–88. Kingston, ON: Queen's University School of Policy Studies, 1995.

Picchio, Antonella. *Social Reproduction: The Political Economy of the Labour Market*. Cambridge: Cambridge University Press, 1992.

Picot, Garnett. *What Is Happening to Earnings Inequality and Youth Wages in the 1990s?* Ottawa: Statistics Canada, Analytical Studies Branch, Research Paper Series no. 116, 1998.

Picot, Garnett, and Andrew Heisz. *The Performance of the 1990s Canadian Labour Market*. Ottawa: Statistics Canada, Analytical Studies Branch, Research Paper Series no. 148, 2000.

Picot, Garnett, and John Myles. 'Social Transfers, Changing Family Structure and Low Income among Children.' *Canadian Public Policy* 22.3 (1996): 244–59.

Picot, Garnett, Ted Wannell, and Doug Lynd. *The Changing Labour Market for Postsecondary Graduates*. Ottawa: Statistics Canada, 1987.

Picot, Garnett, and Zhengxi Lin. *Are Canadians More Likely to Lose Their Jobs in the 1990s?* Ottawa: Statistics Canada, Analytical Studies Branch, Research Paper Series no. 96, 1997.

Pierson, Ruth. 'Gender and the Unemployment Insurance Debates in Canada, 1934–1940.' *Labour / Le Travail* 25 (Spring 1990): 77–105.

Pierson, Ruth, and Beth Light. *No Easy Road: Women in Canada, 1920s to 1960s*. Toronto: New Hogtown Press, 1990.

Polivka, Anne, and Thomas Nardone. 'On the Definition of "Contingent Work."' *Monthly Labour Review*, December 1989: 9–14.

Ponting, J. Rick. 'Editor's Introduction.' In J.R. Ponting, ed., *First Nations in Canada: Perspectives on Opportunity, Empowerment, and Self-Determination,* 3–18. Toronto: McGraw-Hill Ryerson, 1997.

– 'Racism and Stereotyping of First Nations.' In V. Satzewich, ed., *Racism and Social Inequality in Canada: Concepts, Controversies and Strategies of Resistance,* 269–98. Toronto: Thompson Educational Publishing, 1998.

Porter, Ann. 'Women and Income Security in the Post-War Period: The Case of Unemployment Insurance, 1945–1962.' *Labour / Le Travail* 31 (Spring 1993): 111–44.

Prattis, J. Ian, and Jean-Philippe Chartrand. 'The Cultural Division of Labour in the Canadian North: A Statistical Study of the Inuit.' *Canadian Review of Sociology and Anthropology* 27.1 (1990): 49–73.

Preston, Valerie, and Sara McLafferty. 'Gender Differences in Commuting at Suburban and Central Locations.' *Canadian Journal of Regional Science* 26.2 (1993): 237–59.

Privy Council P.C. 1956-785. *Canada Gazette,* part II, vol. 90, no. 11, 545–8, 24 May 1956.

– 1962-86. *Canada Gazette,* part II, vol. 96, no. 3, 126–44, 18 January 1962.

– 1967-1616. *Canada Gazette,* part II, vol. 101, no. 17, 1350–62, 16 August 1967.

– 1978-486. *Canada Gazette,* part II, vol. 112, no. 5, 757–88, 23 February 1978.

– 1983-3386. *Canada Gazette,* part II, vol. 119, no. 23, 4582–6, 31 October 1985.

– 1985-3246. *Canada Gazette,* part II, vol. 119, no. 23, 4582–6, 31 October 1985.

– 1990-2317. *Canada Gazette,* part II, vol. 124, no. 23, 4888–93, 25 October 1990.

Prügl, Elizabeth. 'Biases in Labor Law: A Critique from the Standpoint of Home-Based Workers.' In E. Boris and E. Prügl, eds, *Homeworkers in Perspective: Invisible No More,* 203–17. New York: Routledge, 1996.

Pulkingham, Jane. 'Remaking the Social Divisions of Welfare: Gender, Dependency and UI Reform.' *Studies in Political Economy* 7 (Summer 1998): 7–48.

Pupo, Norene. 'Always Working, Never Done: The Expansion of the Double Day.' In Anne Duffy, Daniel Glenday, and Norene Pupo, eds, *Good Jobs, Bad Jobs, No Jobs,* 144–87. Toronto: Harcourt Brace Canada, 1997.

Québec. Ministère du Travail. *Vers une équité intergénérationelle.* Quebec: Gouvernement du Québec, 1998.

– Secrétariat à la Jeunesse. *Indicateurs jeunesse: La jeunesse québécoise en chiffres (15–29 ans).* Quebec: Gouvernement du Québec, 1996.

Rahman, Syed Sajjadur, and Surendra Gera. 'Long-Term Unemployment in Canada: Its Causes and Policy Implications.' In Surendra Gera, ed., *Canadian Unemployment: Lessons from the 80s and Challenges for the 90s,* 99–115. Ottawa: Supply and Services Canada, 1991.

Randall, James, and R.G. Ironside. 'Communities on the Edge: An Economic

Geography of Resource-Dependent Communities in Canada.' *Canadian Geographer* 40.10 (1996): 17–35.

Rashid, Abdul. 'Seven Decades of Wage Changes.' *Perspectives on Labour and Income*, Summer 1993: 9–21.

Ray, Brian. 'Immigrant Settlement and Housing in Metropolitan Toronto.' *Canadian Geographer* 38.3 (1994): 262–5.

Recherches Amérindiennes au Québec. *Autochtones et Québécois: La rencontre des nationalismes*. Montreal: Recherches amérindiennes au Québec, 1995.

Redpath, Lindsay. 'Education-Job Mismatch among Canadian University Graduates: Implications for Employers and Educators.' *Canadian Journal of Higher Education* 24.2 (1994): 89–114.

Reed, Maureen. 'Seeing Trees: Engendering Environmental and Land Use Planning.' *Canadian Geographer* 41.4 (1997): 398–414.

Rehnby, Nadene, and Stephen McBride. *Help Wanted: Economic Security for Youth*. Ottawa: Canadian Centre for Policy Alternatives, 1997.

Reid, Angus E., and Margaret M. Burns. *Canada and the World: An International Perspective on Canada and Canadians*. Winnipeg: Angus Reid Group, 1992.

Reimer, Bill, Isabelle Ricard, and Frances Shaver. 'Rural Deprivation: A Preliminary Analysis of Census and Tax Family Data.' In Roy Bollman, ed., *Rural and Small Town Canada*, 319–36. Toronto: Thompson Educational Publishing, 1992.

Reitz, Jeffrey G., and Raymond Breton. *The Illusion of Difference: Realities of Ethnicity in Canada and the United States*. Toronto: C.D. Howe Institute, 1994.

Rex, John. *Race Relations in Sociological Theory*. London: Routledge, 1983.

Riddell, W. Craig. 'Human Capital Formation in Canada: Recent Developments and Policy Responses.' In Keith Banting and Charles Beach, eds, *Labour Market Polarization and Social Policy Reform*, 125–72. Kingston, ON: Queen's University School of Policy Studies, 1995.

Roberts, Barbara, and Danielle Juteau. 'Ethnicity and femininity: (d') après nos expériences.' *Canadian Ethnic Studies / Études ethniques au Canada* 13.1 (1981): 1–23.

Rogers, Gerry, and Janine Rogers, eds. *Precarious Jobs in Labour Market Regulation: The Growth of Atypical Employment in Western Europe*. Belgium: International Institute for Labour Studies, 1989.

Rosenberg, S. 'From Segmentation to Flexibility.' *Labour and Society* 14.4 (1989): 363–80.

Ross, David P. *Education as an Investment for Indians on Reserves: The Causes of the Poor Education Levels and the Economic Benefits of Improving Them*. Ottawa: Canadian Council on Social Development, 1991.

Ross, David, and Clarence Lochhead. 'Changes in Family Incomes and Labour Market Participation in Post-War Canada.' *Transition* 23.1 (1993): 5–7.

Rubery, J. 'Women in the Labour Market: A Gender Equality Perspective.' Working paper prepared for the OECD, October 1998.

Rubery, J., and F Wilkinson. *Employer Strategy and the Labour Market.* Oxford: Oxford University Press, 1994.

Russell, Bob. *Back to Work? Labour, State, and Industrial Relations in Canada.* Scarborough, ON: Nelson, 1990.

– 'A Fair or Minimum Wage? Women Workers, the State, and the Origins of Wage Regulation in western Canada.' *Labour / Le Travail* 28 (1991): 59–88.

Ryerson, Stanley. *The Founding of Canada.* Toronto: Progress Books, 1960.

Santiago, Marcia. *Post-Secondary Education and Labour Market Outcomes for Registered Indians.* Ottawa: Indian Affairs and Northern Development Canada, 1997.

Saskatchewan Education. *Partners in Action: Action Plan of the Indian and Métis Education Advisory Committee.* Regina: Saskatchewan Education, 1991.

Satzewich, Victor. 'Indian Agents and the "Indian Problem" in Canada in 1946: Reconsidering the Theory of Coercive Tutelage.' *Canadian Journal of Native Studies* 17.2 (1998): 227–57.

– 'Race, Racism and Racialization: Contested Concepts.' In Victor Satzewich, ed., *Racism and Social Inequality in Canada,* 113–30. Toronto: Thompson, 1998.

– *Racism and the Incorporation of Foreign Labour: Farm Labour Migration to Canada since 1945,* 227–57. London: Routledge 1997.

Satzewich, Victor, and Peter S. Li. 'Immigrant Labour in Canada: The Cost and Benefit of Ethnic Origin in the Job Market.' *Canadian Journal of Sociology* 12 (1987): 229–41.

Satzewich, Victor, and Terry Wotherspoon. *First Nations: Race, Class, and Gender Relations.* Toronto: Nelson, 1993.

Sawchuk, Joe. *The Dynamics of Native Politics: The Alberta Métis Experience.* Saskatoon: Purich Publishing, 1998.

Scassa, Teresa. 'Language Standards, Ethnicity and Discrimination.' *Canadian Ethnic Studies* 26 (1994): 105–21.

Schellenberg, Grant, and Christopher Clark. *Temporary Employment in Canada: Profiles, Patterns and Policy Considerations.* Ottawa: Canadian Council on Social Development, 1996.

Schenk, Chris. 'Fifty Years after PC 1003: The Need for New Directions.' In C. Gonick, P. Phillips, and J. Vorst, eds, *Labour Gains, Labour Pains: 50 Years of PC 1003,* 193–211. Winnipeg: Society for Socialist Studies / Fernwood Publishing, 1995.

Schermerhorn, R.A. *Comparative Ethnic Relations: A Framework for Theory and Research*. New York: Random House, 1970.

Schissel, Bernard, and Terry Wotherspoon. *An Investigation into Indian and Métis Student Life Experience in Saskatchewan Schools*. Saskatoon: Research report prepared for Saskatchewan Indian and Métis Education Research Project, 1998.

Schmidt, Gregory. 'Enhancing Gender Equality by Transitional Labour Markets.' Paris: OECD, 1998.

Schnapper, Dominique. *La France de l'intégration*. Paris: Gallimard,1991.

Scott, Joan. *Gender and the Politics of History*. New York: Columbia University Press, 1988.

Scott, Katherine, and Clarence Lochhead. 'Are Women Catching up in the Earning Race?' Ottawa: Canadian Council on Social Development, Paper no. 3, 1997.

Sharif, Najma, and Shelley Phipps. 'The Challenge of Child Poverty: Which Policies Might Help?' *Canadian Business Economics* 2.3 (1994): 17–30.

Shaver, Frances M. 'Women, Work and Transformations in Agricultural Production.' *Canadian Review of Sociology and Anthropology* 27.3 (1990): 341–56.

Siggner, Andrew J., Eric Guimond, Gustave Goldmann, and Norbert Robitaille. 'Aboriginal Population Characteristics: Are We Informed by the Aggregate Picture?' Paper presented at the Canadian Population Society meetings, Ottawa, June 1998.

Silman, Janet. *Enough Is Enough: Aboriginal Women Speak Out*. Toronto: Women's Press, 1987.

Silver, Hilary. 'Social Exclusion and Social Solidarity: Three Paradigms.' *International Labour Review* 133.5–6 (1994): 531–78.

Silvera, Makeda. *Silenced*. Toronto: Sister Vision Press, 1983.

Simard, Miriam. 'La régionalisation de l'immigration.' *Recherches sociographiques* 37.3 (1996): 439–469.

Sinclair, Peter. 'Atlantic Canada's Fishing Communities: The Impact of Change.' In David Hay and Gurcharn Basran, eds, *Rural Sociology in Canada*, 84–98. Toronto: Oxford University Press, 1992.

Sinclair, Peter, and Lawrence Felt. 'Separate Worlds: Gender and Domestic Labour in an Isolated Fishing Region.' *Canadian Review of Sociology and Anthropology* 29.1 (1992): 55–71.

Smandych, Russell, and Gloria Lee. 'Women, Colonization and Resistance: Elements of an Amerindian Autohistorical Approach to the Study of Law and Colonialism.' *Native Studies Review* 10.1 (1995): 21–46.

Smith, Melvin H. *Our Home or Native Land? What Government's Aboriginal Policy Is Doing to Canada*. Victoria: Crown Western, 1995.

Smith, Pamela. 'Beyond "Add Women and Stir" in Canadian Rural Society.' In David Hay and Gurcharn Basran, eds, *Rural Sociology in Canada*, 155–70. Toronto: Oxford University Press, 1992.

– *From Traps to Draggers: Domestic Commodity Production in Northeast Newfoundland, 1850–1982*. St John's: ISER, Memorial University, No. 31, 1985.

Southcott, C. *Resource Dependent Communities in a Post-Industrial Era*. Thunder Bay, ON: Lakehead Centre for Northern Studies, 1999.

– 'The Study of Regional Inequality in Quebec and English Canada: A Comparative Analysis.' *Canadian Journal of Sociology* 24.4 (1999).

Soysal, Yasemin N. *Limits of Citizenship*. Chicago: University of Chicago Press, 1994.

Stabler, Jack, and Eric Howe. 'Native Participation in Northern Development: The Impending Crisis in the NWT.' *Canadian Public Policy* 16.3 (1990): 262–83.

Standing, Guy. 'Global Feminization through Flexible Labour.' *World Development* 17.7 (1989): 1077.

Stasiulis, Daiva. 'Theorizing Connections: Gender, Race, Ethnicity, and Class.' In Peter S. Li, ed., *Race and Ethnic Relations in Canada*. Toronto: Oxford University Press, 1990.

Statistics Canada. *Adult Literacy in Canada*. Ottawa: Statistics Canada, 1991.

– *Catalogue 71-005-XPB*. Ottawa: Statistics Canada, 1997.

– *Catalogue 75-507E*. Ottawa: Statistics Canada, 1994.

– 'Earnings of Men and Women, 1997.' Catalogue 13-217-XIB. Ottawa: Statistics Canada, Income Statistics Division, 1998.

– *General Social Survey 1989*. Ottawa: Statistics Canada, 1991.

– *Historical Statistics of Canada*. Toronto: Macmillan of Canada, 1996.

– *Historical Statistics of Canada*. 2nd ed. Ottawa: Minister of Supply and Services Canada, 1983.

– 'Labour Force Survey, December 1998.' *Statistics Canada Daily*, http://www.statcan.ca/Daily/English/990108/d9, 1999.

– 'Labour Force Survey, July 1999.' *Statistics Canada Daily*, http://www.statcan.ca:80/Daily/English/990806/d990806a.htm, 1999.

– 'Labour Force Survey, July 2000.' *Statistics Canada Daily*, August 2000.

– *Labour Force Update: An Overview of the 1997 Labour Market*. Ottawa: Statistics Canada, 1998.

– *Labour Force Update: An Overview of the 1998 Labour Market*. Ottawa: Statistics Canada, 1999.

– *Labour Force Update: Youths and the Labour Market*. Ottawa: Statistics Canada, 1997.

– 1981 Census of Canada. *Population: Ethnic Origin*. Volume 1. Catalogue 92-911. Ottawa: Minister of Supply and Services Canada, 1984.

– *1986 Census Public Use Microdata File on Individuals: Documentation and User's Guide.* 1990.
– 1991 Census of Canada. *Age, Sex and Marital Status: The Nation.* Catalogue 93-310. Ottawa: Minister of Industry, Science and Technology, 1992.
– 1991 Census of Canada. *Ethnic Origin: The Nation.* Catalogue 93-315. Ottawa: Minister of Industry, Science and Technology, 1993.
– '1996 Census: Aboriginal Data,' *The Daily,* 13 January 1998.
– '1996 Census: Aboriginal Data.' *Statistics Canada Daily,* http://www.statcan.ca/Daily/English/980113/d980113.htm, 1998.
– '1996 Census: Education, Mobility and Migration.' *The Daily,* 14 April 1998.
– '1996 Census: Ethnic Origin, Visible Minorities.' *The Daily,* 17 February 1998.
– *1996 Census Public Use Microdata File on Individuals,* Documentation, 1996.
– *1996 Census Questions,* 1997.
– '1996 Census: Sources of Income, Earnings and Total Income, and Family Income.' *The Daily,* 12 May 1998.
– 'Paying Off Student Loans.' *Statistics Canada Daily,* http://www.statcan.ca/Daily/English/981208/d981208.pdf, 1998.
– *Schooling, Work and Related Activities, Income, Expenses and Mobility. 1991 Aboriginal Peoples Survey.* Ottawa: Minister of Industry, Science and Technology, 1996.
– 'Student Debt.' *Statistics Canada Daily,* http://www.statcan.ca:80/Daily/English/990730/d990730b.htm, 1999.
– *Survey of Work Arrangements, 1995.* Ottawa: Statistics Canada. Catalogue 7100MGPE, 1996.
– 'Working Teens.' *Canadian Social Trends* 35 (1994): 18–22.
Statutes of Canada. Employment Equity Act, c. 31, 1986.
Strong-Boag, Veronica. 'The Girl of the New Day: Canadian Working Women in the 1920s.' *Labour / Le Travail* 4 (1979): 31–64.
Stymeist, David. *Ethnics and Indians: Social Relations in a Northwestern Ontario Town.* Toronto: Peter Martin Associates, 1975.
Sub-Committee on Aboriginal Education. *Sharing the Knowledge: The Path to Success and Equal Opportunities in Education.* Report of the Standing Committee on Aboriginal Affairs and Northern Development. Ottawa: Canada Communications Group, 1996.
Sufrin, E. *The Eaton's Drive: The Campaign to Organize Canada's Largest Department Store, 1948–1952.* Toronto: Fitzhenry and Whiteside, 1982.
Sunter, Deborah. 'Youths – Waiting It Out.' *Perspectives on Labour and Income* 6.1 (1994): 31–6.
Sussman, Deborah. 'Moonlighting: A Growing Way of Life.' *Perspectives on Labour and Income,* Summer 1998: 24–31.

Swimmer, Gene. 'Collective Bargaining in the Federal Public Service of Canada: The Last Twenty Years.' In Gene Swimmer and M. Thompson, eds, *Public Sector Collective Bargaining in Canada*, 369–407. Kingston, ON: Industrial Relations Centre, Queen's University, 1995.

Swimmer, Gene, and M. Thompson. *Public Sector Collective Bargaining in Canada*. Kingston, ON: Industrial Relations Centre, Queen's University, 1995.

Tanner, Julian, Harvey Krahn, and Timothy Hartnagel. *Fractured Transitions from School to Work*. Toronto: Oxford University Press, 1995.

Tapin, J. 'Agences de placement temporaire.' Quebec: Bureau du Travail, 1993.

'Tomorrow's Second Sex.' *The Economist*, November 1998, A23.

Townson, Monica. *Non-Standard Work: The Implications for Pension Policy and Retirement Readiness*. Ottawa: Women's Bureau, Human Resources Development Canada, July 1997.

Treaty 7 Elders and Tribal Council. *The True Spirit and Original Intent of Treaty 7*. Montreal and Kingston: McGill-Queen's University Press, 1996.

Tremblay, Marc-Adélard, and Carole Lévesque. *Québec Social Science and Canadian Indigenous Peoples: An Overview of Research Trends, 1960–1990*. Ottawa: Canadian Polar Commission, 1997.

Trigger, Bruce G. *Natives and Newcomers: Canada's 'Heroic Age' Reconsidered*. Toronto: University of Toronto Press, 1985.

Troughton, Michael J. 'Rural Canada and Canadian Rural Geography: An Appraisal.' *Canadian Geographer* 39.4 (1995): 290–305.

Trudeau, Gilles. 'Temporary Employees Hired through a Personnel Agency: Who Is the Real Employer?' *Canadian Labour and Employment Law Journal* 5 (1998): 359–80.

Tunnicliffe, Ross D. 'Barriers to Business Financing: The Legal Context.' *In Financing First Nations: Investing in Aboriginal Business and Governments*. Conference manual. Vancouver, June 1993.

Turcot, Yves. 'La rémunération à double palier dans les conventions collectives au Québec: Evolution de la situation entre 1985 et 1990.' *Le Marché du travail* 13.11 (1992): 9–10, 78–94.

Turnbull, Barbara. 'Young Males Losing Ground in Wage Stakes.' *Toronto Star*, 28 July 1998, A2.

Turpel, Mary Ellen/Aki Kwe. 'Aboriginal Peoples and the Canadian Charter of Rights and Freedoms: Contradictions and Challenges.' *Canadian Woman Studies* 10.2–3 (1989): 149–57.

– 'Patriarchy and Paternalism: The Legacy of the Canadian State for First Nations Women.' *Canadian Journal of Women and the Law* 6 (1993): 174–92.

UNESCO. *Sociological Theories: Race and Colonialism*. Paris: UNESCO, 1980.

United Nations Development Program. *Human Development Report, 1997.* New York: Oxford University Press, 1997.

Ursel, Jane. *Private Lives, Public Policy: 100 Years of State Intervention in the Family.* Toronto: Women's Press, 1992.

Vosko, Leah F. '*Irregular* Workers, *New* Involuntary Social Exiles: Women and UI Reform.' In J. Pulkingham and G. Ternowetsky, eds, *Remaking Canadian Social Policy: Social Security in the Late 1990s,* 265–72. Toronto: Fernwood Press, 1996.

– 'Legitimizing the Triangular Employment Relationship: Emerging International Labour Standards in Comparative Perspective.' *Comparative Labour Law and Policy Journal,* Fall 1997: 43–77.

– 'No Jobs, Lots of Work: The Gendered Rise of the Temporary Employment Relationship in Canada, 1897–1997.' PhD dissertation, York University, 1998.

– 'Recreating Dependency: Women and UI Reform.' In D. Drache and A. Ranikin, eds, *Warm Heart, Cold Country,* 213–32. Toronto: Caledon Press, 1995.

– 'Regulating Precariousness?: The Temporary Employment Relationship under the NAFTA and the EC Treaty.' *Relations Industrielles / Industrial Relations* 53.1 (March 1998): 123–53.

– 'The Rise of the Temporary Help Industry in Canada and Its Relationship to the Decline of the Standard Employment Relationship as a Normative Model of Employment.' Background paper prepared for Collective Reflection on a Changing Workplace, *The Labour Program.* Ottawa: Health Resources Development Canada, 1997.

– *Temporary Work: The Gendered Rise of a Precarious Employment Relationship.* Toronto: University of Toronto Press, 2000.

Voyageur, Cora J. 'Contemporary Indian Women.' In D.A. Long and O.P. Dickason, eds, *Visions of the Heart: Canadian Aboriginal Issues,* 93–115. Toronto: Harcourt Brace 1996.

Walby, Sylvia. *Gender Transformations.* London: Routledge, 1997.

Walker, Julian. *Two-Tier Wage Systems.* Kingston: Industrial Relations Centre, Queen's University, 1987.

Wallace, Iain. 'Restructuring in the Canadian Mining and Mineral-Processing Industries.' In John Britton, ed., *Canada and the Global Economy: The Geography of Structural and Technological Change.* Montreal and Kingston: McGill-Queen's University Press, 1996.

Wallace, Iain, and Rob Shields. 'Contested Terrains: Social Space and the Canadian Environment.' In Wallace Clement, ed., *Understanding Canada: Building of the New Canadian Political Economy,* 386–408. Montreal and Kingston: McGill-Queen's University Press, 1997.

Wallace, Joan. *Part-Time Work in Canada: Report of the Commission of Inquiry into Part-Time Work.* Ottawa: Labour Canada, 1983.

Wannell, Ted. 'Losing Ground: Wages of Young People, 1981–1986.' In Craig McKie and Keith Thompson, eds, *Canadian Social Trends*, 221–3. Toronto: Thompson Educational Publishing, 1990.

Warskett, Rosemary. 'Bankworker Unionization and the Law.' *Studies in Political Economy* 25 (Spring 1988): 41–70.

– 'Can a Disappearing Pie Be Shared Equally? Unions, Women, and Wage "Fairness."' In L. Briskin and P. McDermott, eds, *Women Challenging Unions: Feminism, Democracy, and Militancy.* Toronto: University of Toronto Press, 1993.

– 'Political Power, Technical Disputes and Unequal Pay: A Federal Case.' In Judy Fudge and Patricia McDermott, eds, *Just Wages: A Feminist Assessment of Pay Equity*, 172–90. Toronto: University of Toronto Press, 1991.

– 'The Politics of Difference and Inclusiveness within the Canadian Labour Market.' *Economic and Industrial Democracy* 17 (1996): 587–625.

Weaver, Sally. *Making Canadian Indian Policy: The Hidden Agenda 1968–1970.* Toronto: University of Toronto Press, 1981.

– 'A New Paradigm in Canadian Indian Policy for the 1990s.' *Canadian Ethnic Studies* 22.3 (1990): 8–18.

Weber, Max. *Economy and Society.* Berkeley and Los Angeles: University of California Press, 1968 [1921–2].

Westwood, Sally, and Parminder Bhachu, eds. *Enterprising Women: Ethnicity, Economy and Gender Relations.* New York: Routledge, 1988.

– 'Where Have All the Smart Men Gone?' *Globe and Mail*, 28 December 1998, A18.

Wherrett, Jill, and Jane Allain. 'Aboriginal Self-Government.' *Current Issue Review* 89-5E. Ottawa: Library of Parliament Research Branch, Minister of Supply and Services Canada, 1995.

White, Julie. *Sisters and Solidarity: Women and Unions in Canada.* Toronto: Thompson Educational Publishing, 1993.

– *Women and Unions.* Ottawa: Canadian Advisory Council on the Status of Women, 1980.

Wieviorka, Michel. *La démocratie à l'épreuve: Nationalisme, populisme, ethnicité.* Paris: La Découverte, 1993.

Williams, Allison M. 'Canadian Urban Aboriginals: A Focus on Aboriginal Women in Canada.' *Canadian Journal of Native Studies* 12.1 (1997): 75–101.

Willms, J. Douglas. *International Adult Literacy Survey.* Ottawa: Statistics Canada, 1997.

– 'A New Paradigm in Canadian Indian Policy for the 1990s.' *Canadian Ethnic Studies* 22.3 (1990): 8–18.

Wilson, William J. *When Work Disappears: The World of the New Urban Poor*. New York: Knopf, 1997.

Winson, Anthony. 'In Search of the Part-Time Capitalist Farmer: Labour Use and Farm Structure in Central Canada.' *Canadian Review of Sociology and Anthropology* 33.1 (1996): 89–110.

Working Margins Consulting Group. *Indian Post-School Education in Saskatchewan*. Discussion paper prepared for the Office of the Treaty Commissioner, Saskatoon. Winnipeg: Working Margins Consulting Group, 1992.

Wotherspoon, Terry. 'Indian Control or Controlling Indians? Barriers to the Occupational and Educational Advancement of Canada's Indigenous Population.' In Terry Wotherspoon, ed., *Hitting the Books: The Politics of Educational Retrenchment*, 249–73. Toronto and Saskatoon: Garamond and the Social Research Unit, 1991.

Wotherspoon, Terry, and Victor Satzewich. *First Nations: Race, Class, and Gender Relations*. Scarborough, ON: Nelson, 1993.

Yalnizyan, Armine. *The Growing Gap*. Toronto: Centre for Social Justice, 1998.

York, Geoffrey. *The Dispossessed: Life and Death in Native Canada*. Toronto: Little, Brown and Co., 1990.

Young, Iris Marion. 'Together in Difference: Transforming the Logic of Group Political Conflict.' In Will Kymlicka, ed., *The Rights of Minority Cultures*. London: Oxford University Press, 1995.

Yuval-Davis, Nira, and Floya Anthias. *Woman–Nation–State*. New York: St Martin's Press, 1989.

Zong, Li, and Basran Gurcharn. 'Devaluation of Foreign Credentials as Perceived by Visible Minority Professional Immigrants.' *Canadian Ethnic Studies* 30 (1998): 6–23.